POLAR BEARS
A LIFE UNDER THREAT

MICHEL RAWICKI

POLAR BEARS
A LIFE UNDER THREAT

ACC ART BOOKS

CONTENTS

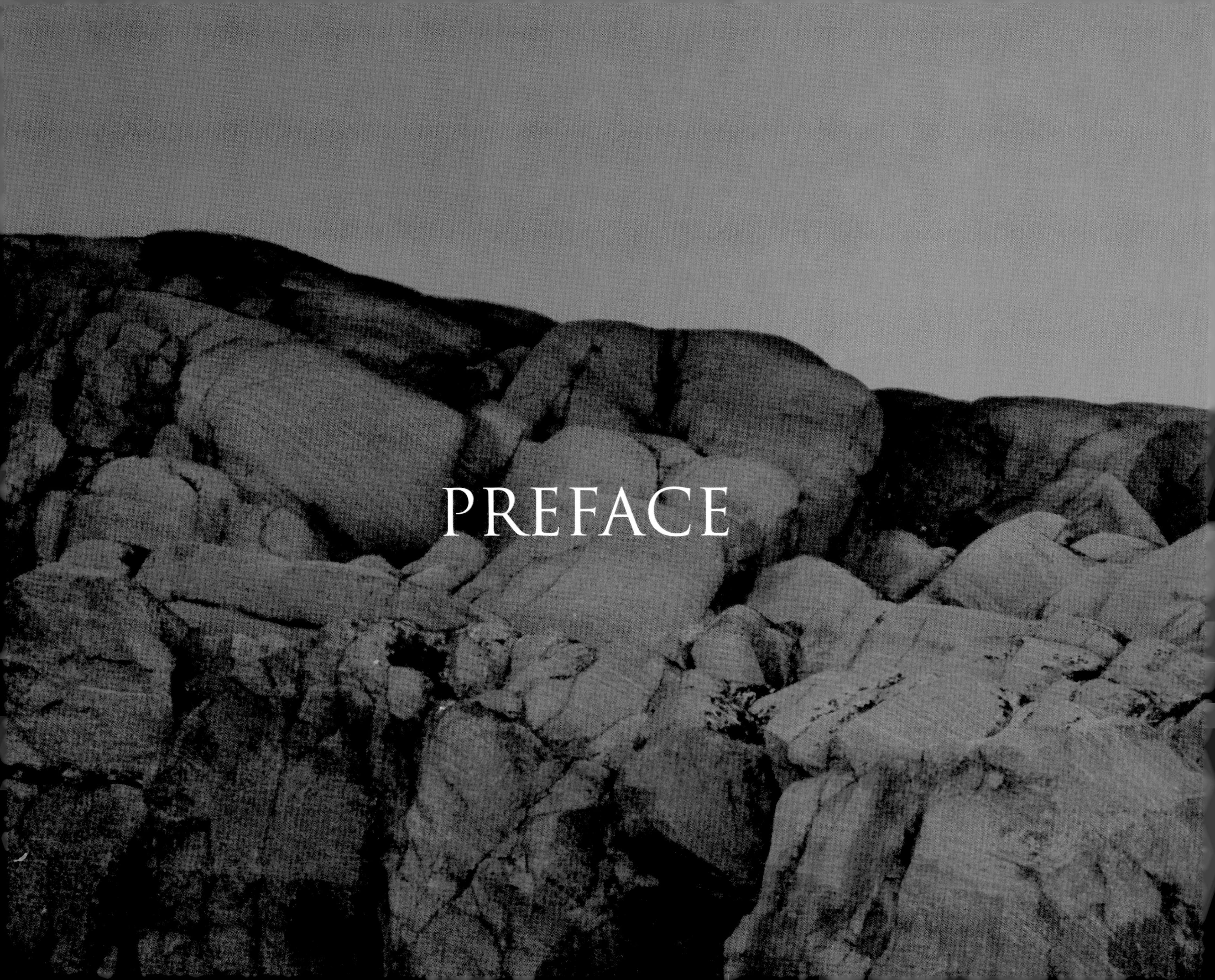

PREFACE

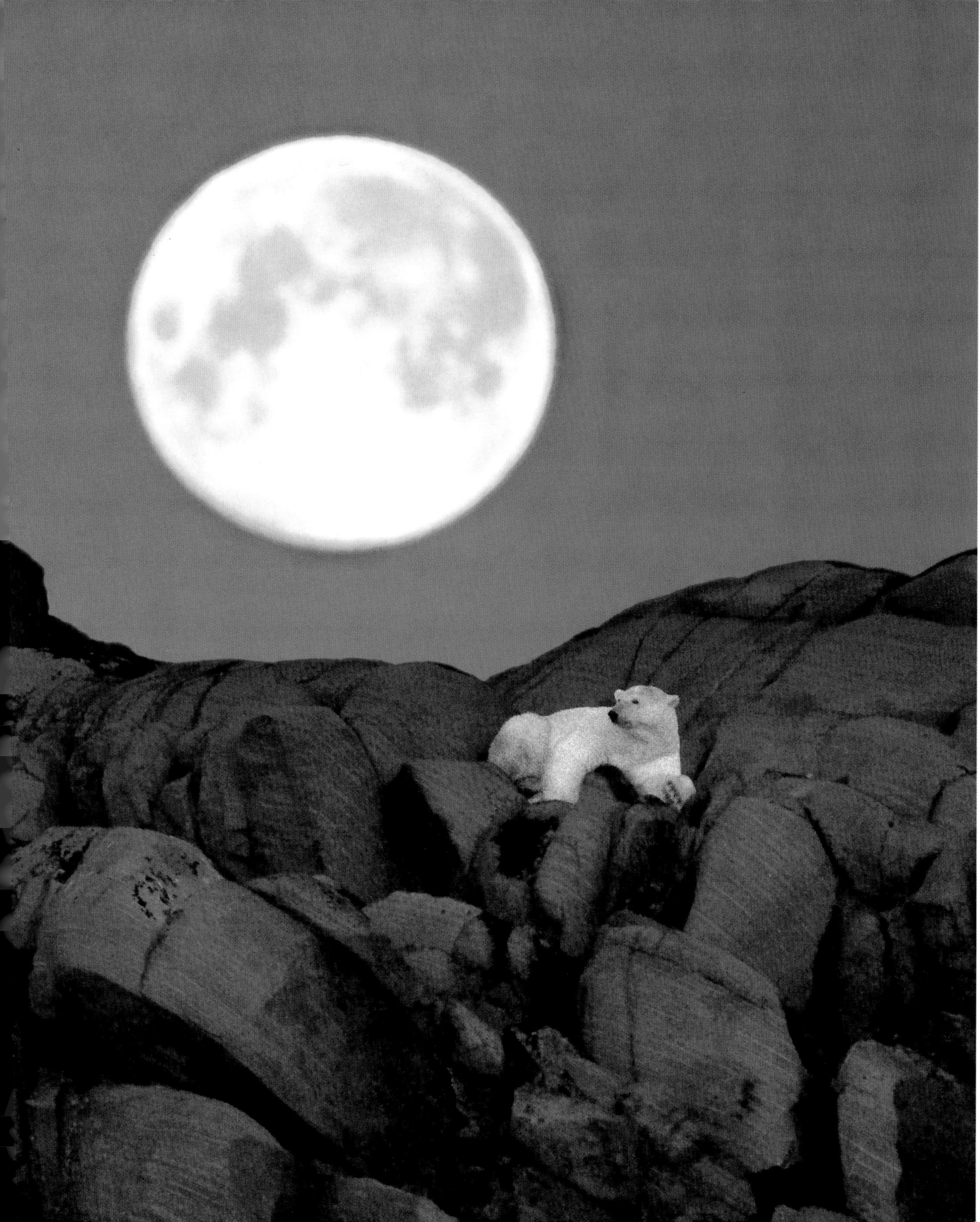

NANUQ AND THE COSMOS

A large area of the star-studded night sky visible in the
northern hemisphere is occupied by Ursa Major and Ursa
Minor, the Great and the Little Bear. The word 'Arctic' actually
originates from the Ancient Greek àrktos (bear): a reference
to these constellations, which are located near the celestial
North Pole. These names provide a link between the myths
surrounding this animal and the celestial boreal regions.

This may explain why the polar bear touches the human heart
all over the world. 'Nanuq' draws attention, subconsciously, to
our human status on a small, fragile planet at the heart of the
universe, and thus to our need to preserve it.

This is the message conveyed by Michel Rawicki through
the magnificent photographs gathered together in this book:
the fruit of more than twenty years' passionate travel in the
Arctic... The Land of the Polar Bear.

Hubert Reeves
Astrophysicist
Honorary President of the Association Humanité et
Biodiversité and of the Agence Française pour la Biodiversité

WHEN NATURE WHISPERS IN YOUR EAR

BY MICHEL RAWICKI

ONE DAY (I WAS ABOUT 15
BY THEN) I DECIDED TO GO
THROUGH THE SHOP DOOR.
THAT WAS THE BEGINNING
OF A LONG FRIENDSHIP
WITH THE OLD MAN INSIDE,
WHO SAT SURROUNDED
BY CAMERAS, ENLARGERS
AND BLACK AND WHITE
PHOTOGRAPHS.

My first memory of being cold dates from 1960. I was ten years old and went to Chamonix with my parents to take the cable car to the Aiguille du Midi. I remember experiencing my first 'thermal shock' when, in the middle of summer, I hugged the ice and held it in my arms. I did not understand what was happening; I simply realised that it was 'good'.

At the time, I was already taking photos with my Kodak Brownie Starflash, the model with the flash bulb fixed to the top. I was more interested in the shop window of the 'old-fashioned photographer' in the rue des Archives, Paris, than in going home to do my homework. One day (I was about 15 by then) I decided to go through the shop door. That was the beginning of a long friendship with the old man inside, who sat surrounded by cameras, enlargers and black and white photographs. The new scents, touching the sensitive surface of the photographic paper – it was all redolent of the past to my unconscious mind. Suddenly, that past was reality, with visual evidence…

At this time, when I was at secondary school, I used to help my parents at weekends on their market stall. This gave me a chance to earn some pocket money and also to discover that not only did I enjoy communicating with others, I also enjoyed the nomadic quality of my parents' working life (they set up their stall in a different place each day). They gave me a taste for meeting people and for travel.

One day at school I heard talk of a plan to set up a photographic laboratory in an empty room. I leapt at this opportunity, obviously, and with a small budget and some friends the adventure began – with our hands plunged into developer and fixative, lit by the darkroom's red bulb. At the same time, at the beginning of my second year, I encountered spirituality and philosophy thanks to a French teacher with a mystic streak. A new shock, but this time an internal one.

During a course on Plato we discussed the allegory of the cave and the shadows of reality that are projected on the wall, as seen by the chained men inside: a symbol of the problem human beings experience in achieving and sharing true wisdom. Later, this teacher taught us about Socrates and maieutics, or the art of 'giving birth' to thoughts. This activated a trigger in me. It was at this moment that I became aware of the fragility of the human race and its place in the universe. My first metaphysical anxieties, in a kind of way. "And if there was something else?" whispered Plato and Socrates in my ear. "And if there was somewhere else too, only visible and reachable inside of oneself? And if eyes were nothing more than windows?" This is the view of reality that I later struggled to convey through my telephoto lens, with as much sincerity as possible.

Months passed, and photography began to take up more and more of my time. I decided to abandon my studies when a friend offered me the opportunity to take his place as photography assistant to Claude Lelouch at Les Films 13. I was just nineteen and had managed to land a job in the arts. My confidence began to grow and I decided that this could mean something for my future. I moved from job to job as an assistant until 1973, the year I met the photographer JCD. This experience was to last fifteen years and varied between still-life shoots and producing characters in a play.

To feed my longing to get away and to discover new lands, I travelled every summer all over the world. First India and then Japan, where I discovered the ancestral art of bonsai, which mixed aesthetics with Nature, reducing trees in size and taming them in a plant pot.

On my return from this latest trip, I devoted a year to photographing these dwarf trees in a studio every weekend,

IN 1992, I RECEIVED A SECOND
'THERMAL SHOCK': STANDING
ON THE GREENLAND ICE
CAP AND OBSERVING THE
CALVING ICEBERGS IN DISKO
BAY – THE LARGEST ICEBERG-
PRODUCING GLACIER IN THE
NORTHERN HEMISPHERE.
THIS WAS MY FIRST
ENCOUNTER WITH
THE ARCTIC.

allowing Nature to penetrate to my core by 'whispering in my ear'. At last I had the sense that I was communicating with the 'being' of things, with the life that flowed inside me. Thanks to this intimate relationship with dwarf trees, my view of photography began to change, shifting from the aesthetic to the ethical, and to contemplation. Photography became a way of revealing and transmitting emotions, a therapeutic tool which calmed the pain caused to my soul by the spectacle of Nature. Finally, I left the studio and my mentor and set up StockImage, a photographic agency specialising in travel and nature.

In 1992, I received a second 'thermal shock': standing on the Greenland ice cap and observing the calving icebergs in Disko Bay – the largest iceberg-producing glacier in the northern hemisphere. This was my first encounter with the Arctic. I was blown away, completely engulfed by the monumental size and grandeur of the elements as they moved. A revelation. I went back several times. I think it was during one of these trips to Greenland, when I returned to the Ilulissat icefjord, that I really came to understand climate upheaval, and the danger it represented for the planet and the survival of the species.

In April 1995 we were astride the ice floe. The dogs were barking and we were intoxicated by the cold and the empty space. Ten years later, returning to the same place at the same time of the year, the ice floe had disappeared, having receded a few hundred kilometres northwards. This contributed to some deep reflection on my part and may have led me, twenty years after founding and managing the StockImage agency, to listen to the little voice of Nature whispering in my ear: "Why? Why continue? What are you trying to prove?"

At a time when 'climatic upheaval' was beginning to rhyme with 'digital upheaval', I decided to sell my company in order to return to hugging the ice once again.

2012 was a crucial year in my search. In April I decided to make a 250-kilometre journey between two villages around the Melville Bay, on the north-west coast of Greenland, with two Inuit hunters and a dog sleigh. During our two-week journey over the ice cap, away from the coast, I danced on the sleigh with my camera, inspired by the unspoiled purity of the frozen landscape. I realised again the extent to which Nature had become nourishment for my soul; I was 'becoming' Nature itself. The cracking of the glaciers when the sun warmed the ice mingled with the caress of the wind, murmuring the 'correct note' in my ear as if Nature was whispering to me privately. I felt I was in the right place for me, and the closer I got to the Pole, the more I discovered my 'interior pole', as if the notion of cold was inscribed in my DNA.

I lay spread-eagled on the ice floe, above 2,136 metres of water, training my lens on two adult bears as they fled in the distance, alarmed by the barking of our dogs. As I focused on the animal I was photographing, I became an integral part of the scene: small and large at the same time, under a frozen sky on a frozen sea, full of confidence, lying on this white desert, the symbol of impermanence and regeneration too... I remember comparing the way my lens allowed the light to penetrate it, to the way I allowed myself to be penetrated by the song of the wild.

2012 was a terrible year for me, in fact, because of the loss of someone I held very dear. This was a blow from which I would never recover. "When water freezes, it becomes ice, then when it melts it flows again. Everything that dies has to be reborn, everything that is born returns to its source, ice and water are not incompatible," says Hanshan, the Chinese poet.

Later, as if drawn by a magnet, I returned to the icy regions in search of comfort from contact with ice, with the animals and men and wild nature, the source of contemplation and inspiration. As time passed, I stopped looking for a solution to my problems to the exclusion of all else. I let my tears (sometimes mingled with the snow flakes of the Canadian winter) flow freely as I watched the flight of a snowy owl, or the appearance of an Arctic fox between two ridges of ice beside Hudson Bay.

Over three years I made nearly twenty trips, from Alaska to Siberia, watching a polar bear coming out of its lair for the first time with its young in a Canadian blizzard; or hearing the cry of red-crowned Japanese cranes at sunrise on a frozen river north of Hokkaido. This was nature so beautiful that it had to be protected for future generations; wildlife so intelligent and so amazingly adaptable, using the art of mimicry and camouflage for which it is so well-konwn.

We have so much to learn from the observation of nature. When it speaks to us privately, it is a source of wonder and gives us a strong feeling of belonging to the universe. Of course, you have to be bold and leave your comfort zone, your 'cave'; you have to find tools, a road, and the inspiration to use your skills, to go where you feel accepted. In this way, you can instil into your life the happiness of being able to contemplate the spectacle of nature, and respect for ancient peoples like the seal hunters of Greenland, the guardians of an age-old tradition, whose daily life has already been radically altered by climate change. Or the Nenets, reindeer herders of the Siberian Urals, with whom I love to spend time during the migration season of their herds, trying to put into practise as much as possible the admirable

thoughts of Thích Nhất Hanh: "Walk as if you are kissing the Earth with your feet".

Later, because anything that is not shared is lost, I published my first book, *L'Appel du Froid*. After its publication I travelled around France for two years, talking to bookshops and to the general public about 'cold' and its benefits. '*L'Appel du Froid*' was a general testament to the parts of the world that fascinate me. This second book is about the red thread which has unconsciously guided the majority of my trips. A mythical and fascinating figure, on to which since time immemorial our many fantasies have been projected: the polar bear, or 'Nanuq' in the Inuit language. I realised that in fact I had continually been crossing its path for the past twenty-five years, accumulating more photographs of polar bears than of any other species, at all stages of its development and in all situations. The thought that this animal has today become the emblem of global warming came as a revelation. It was the moment to publish a book which throws light on the reality of the situation of the polar bear today, but is first and foremost a homage to the polar bear's beauty and its poetry. I hope that the 200 photographs – which I have chosen from thousands, taken throughout my life – will touch you, and will be able to 'whisper in your ear' as they have whispered to me.

"Beauty will save the world", as Dostoevsky tells us in *The Idiot*.

WHAT IS YOUR IQ-PB?

(INTELLIGENCE QUOTIENT 'POLAR BEAR')

1

What colour is the skin of the polar bear?

A. White

B. Brown

C. Black

D. Grey

2

How fast can the polar bear run?

A. 24 km/h

B. 32 km/h

C. 40 km/h

D. 48 km/h

3

How thick is the fat beneath the polar bear's skin?

A. Up to 7.5 cm

B. Up to 8.75 cm

C. Up to 11.25 cm

D. Up to 12.25 cm

4

When do polar bears mate?

A. Summer

B. Autumn

C. Winter

D. Spring

5

When do the female bears give birth?

A. Summer

B. Autumn

C. Winter

D. Spring

6

What do baby bears eat?

A. Mother's milk

B. Seals

C. Beluga whales

D. Anything and everything

7

What percentage of fat does the mother's milk contain?

A. 0 to 10 %

B. 10 to 20 %

C. 20 to 30 %

D. 30 to 40 %

8

How much does the polar bear weigh at birth?

A. From 250 to 500 g

B. From 900g to 1kg

C. From 1.3 to 1.5kg

D. From 1.7 to 1.8 kg

9

How long does the polar bear live?

A. 9 to 12 years

B. 12 to 15 years

C. 15 to 18 years

D. 18 to 21 years

10

How much does an adult male polar bear weigh?

A. 340 kg

B. 450 kg

C. 550 kg

D. 680 kg

11

How much food – as a percentage of his body weight – can a polar bear eat in a single sitting?

A. 5 to 10 %

B. 10 to 15 %

C. 15 to 20 %

D. 20 to 25 %

12

What is the characteristic behaviour of a 'dominant male' polar bear?

A. It moves with its back to the wind

B. It moves with its face to the wind

C. It exhibits its stomach

D. It stands on its hind paws

13

What percentage of the total population of polar bears lives in Canada?

A. About 30 %

B. About 40 %

C. About 50 %

D. About 60 %

(see answers in the appendices at the back of the book)

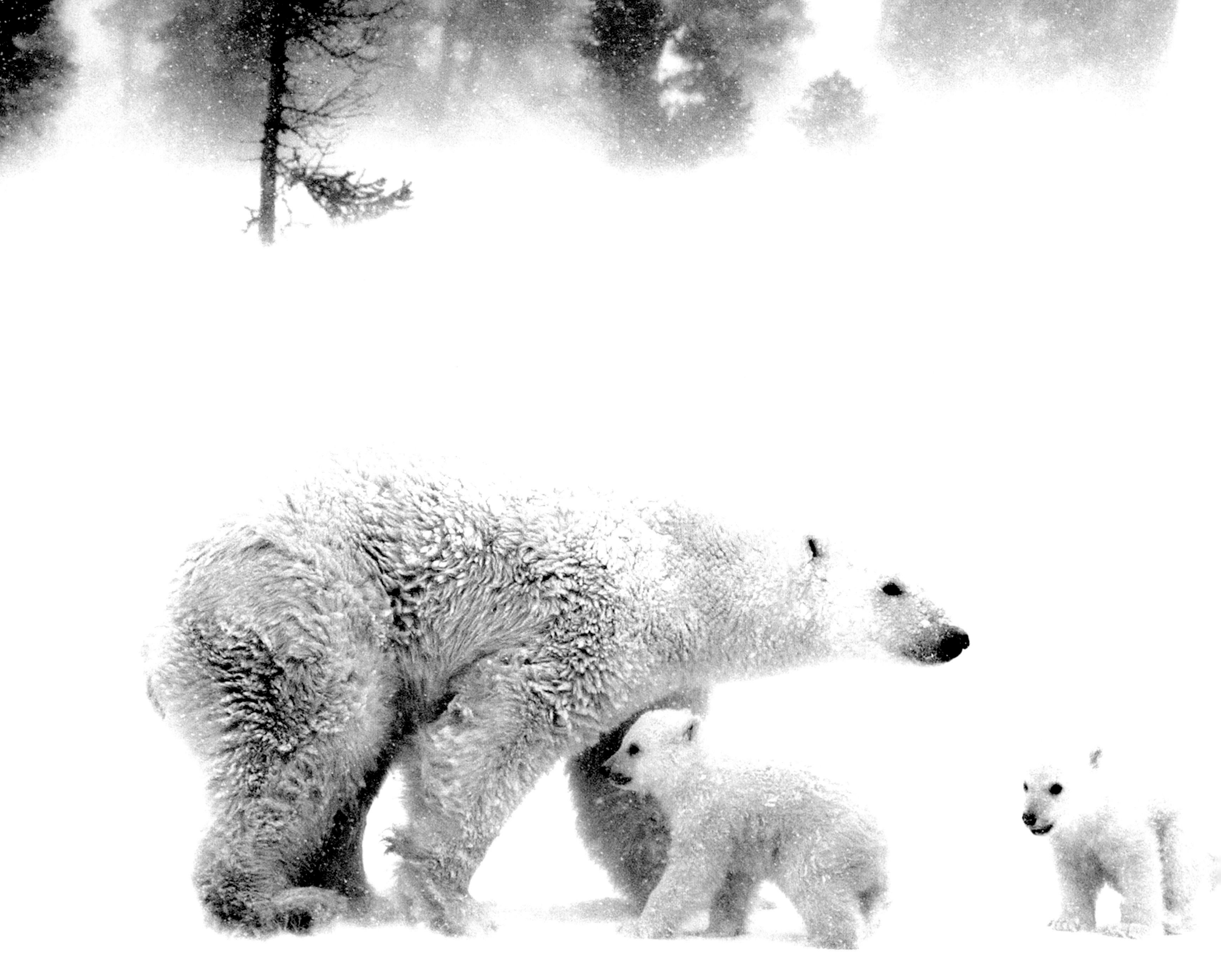

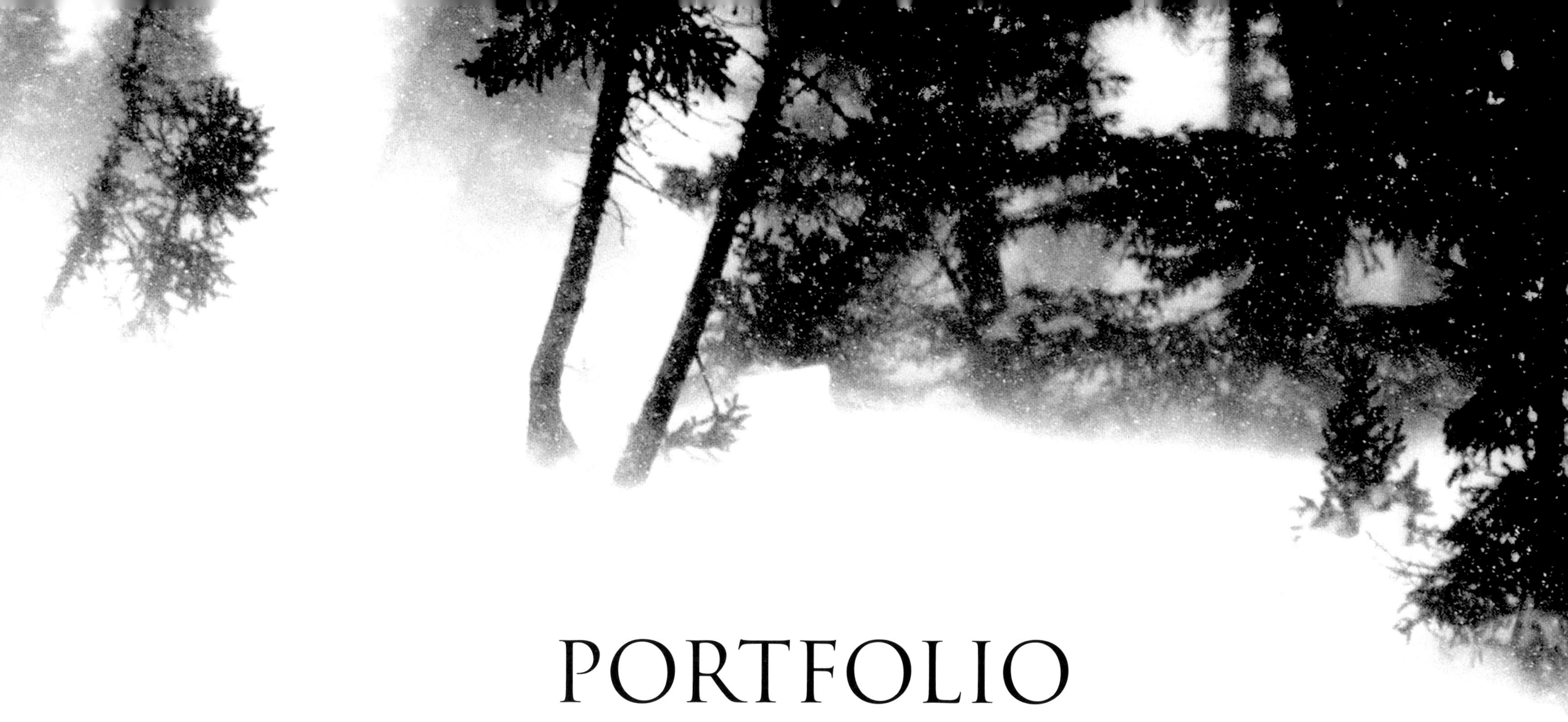

PORTFOLIO

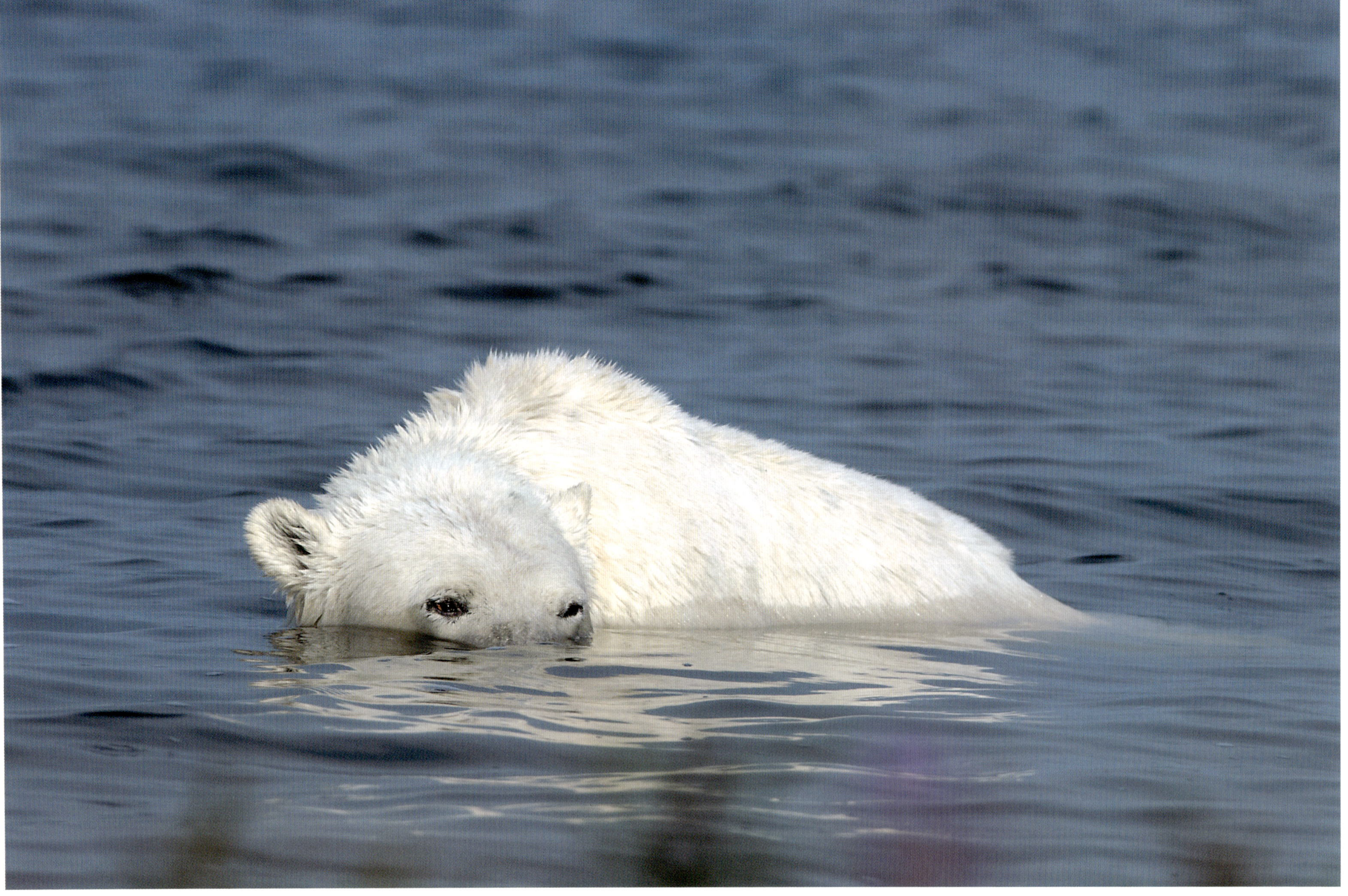

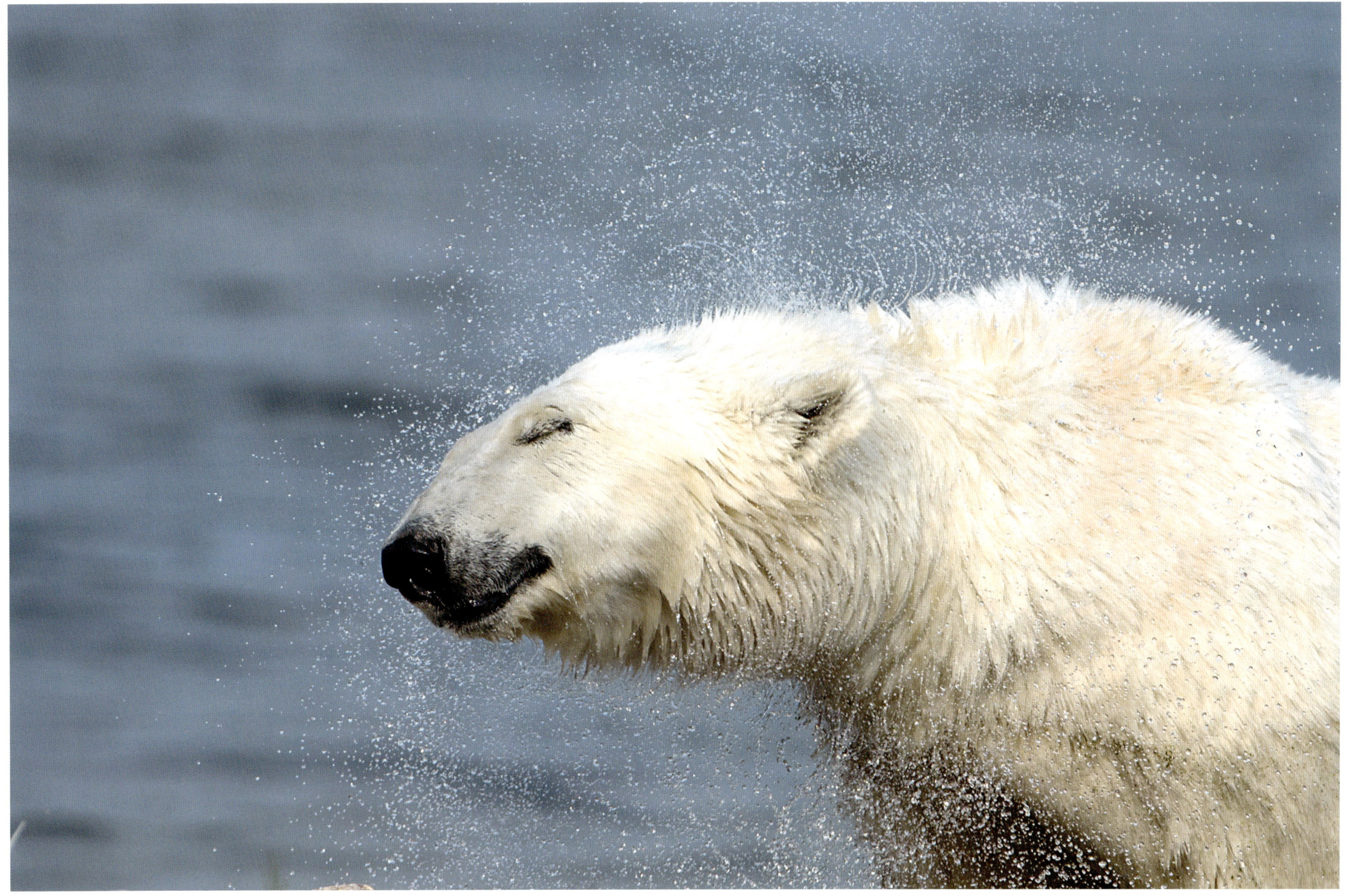

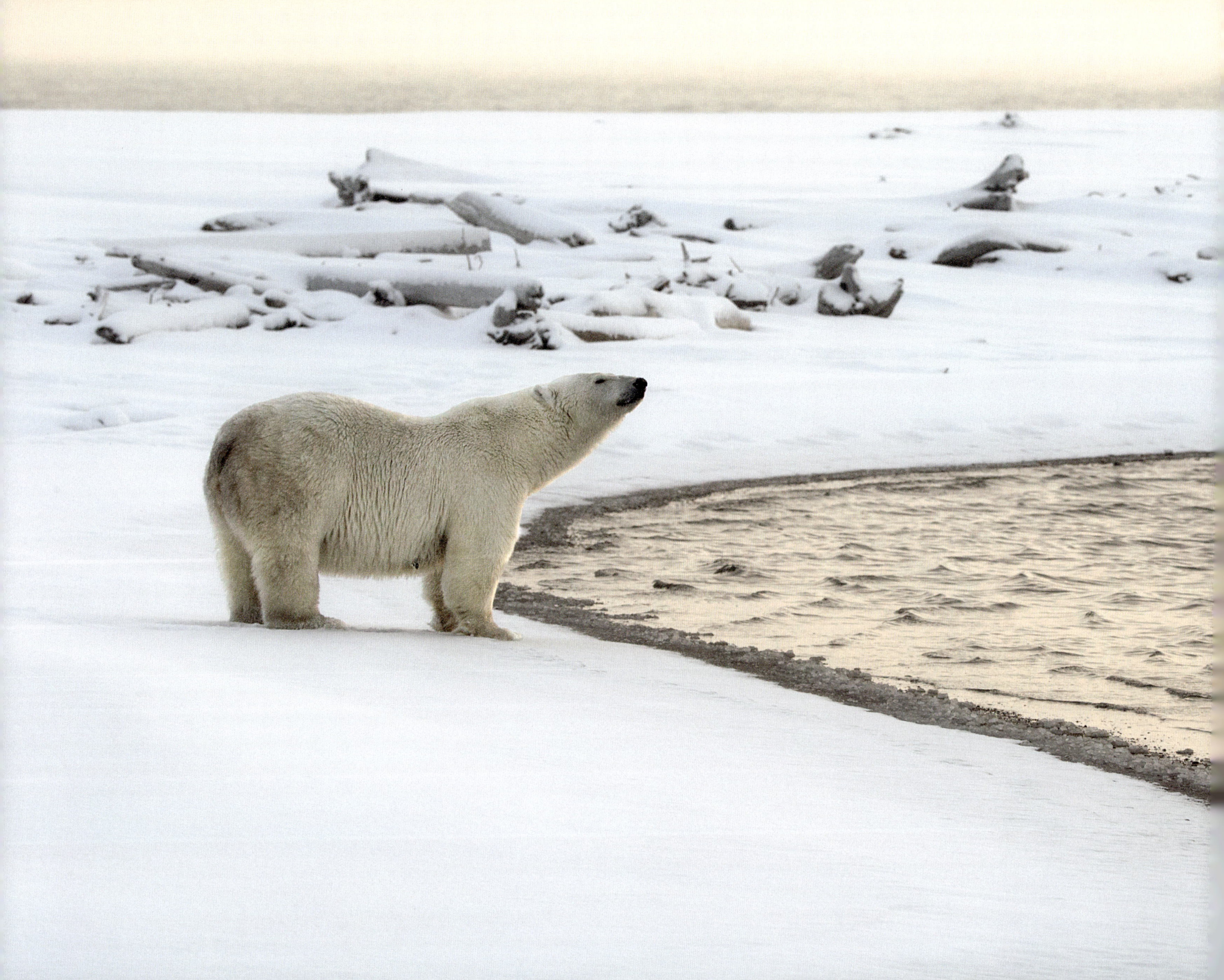

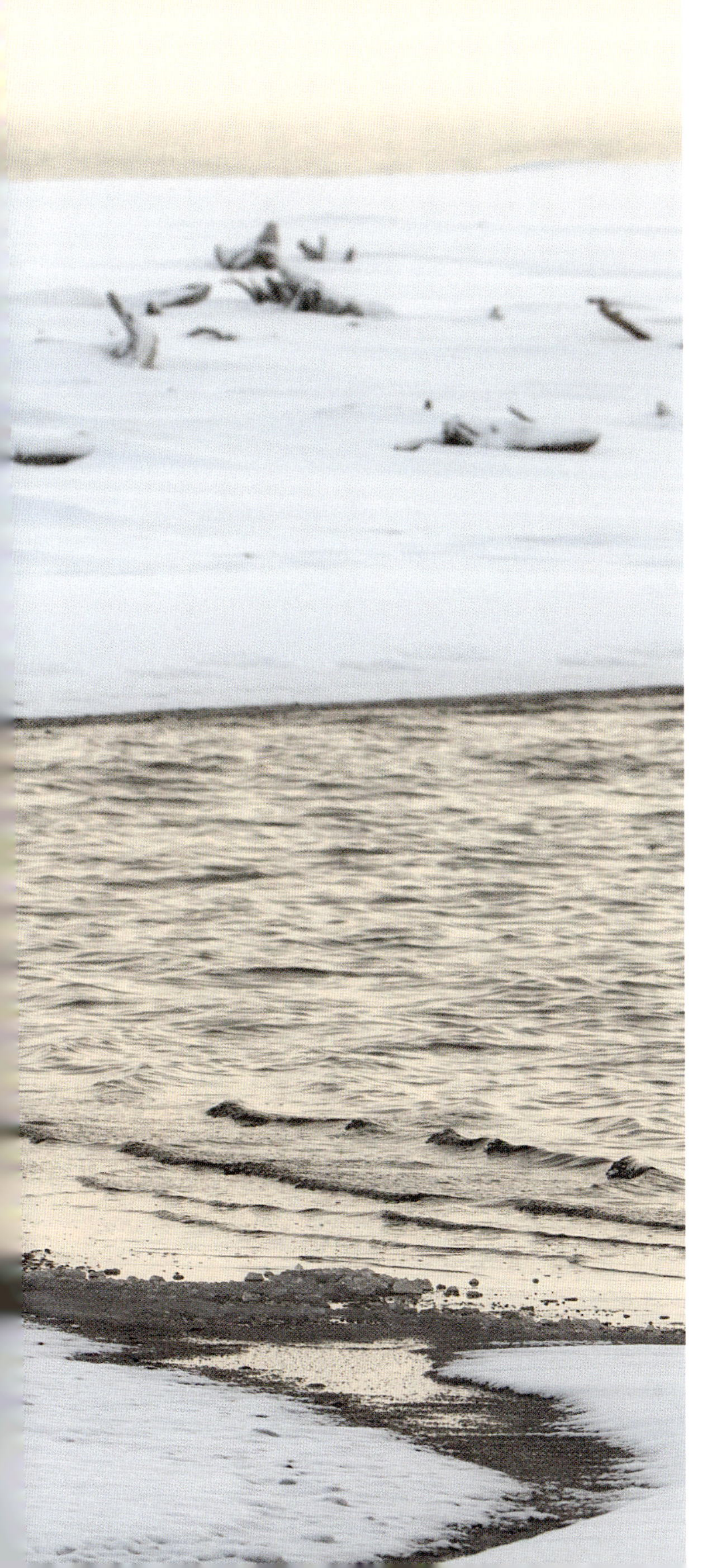

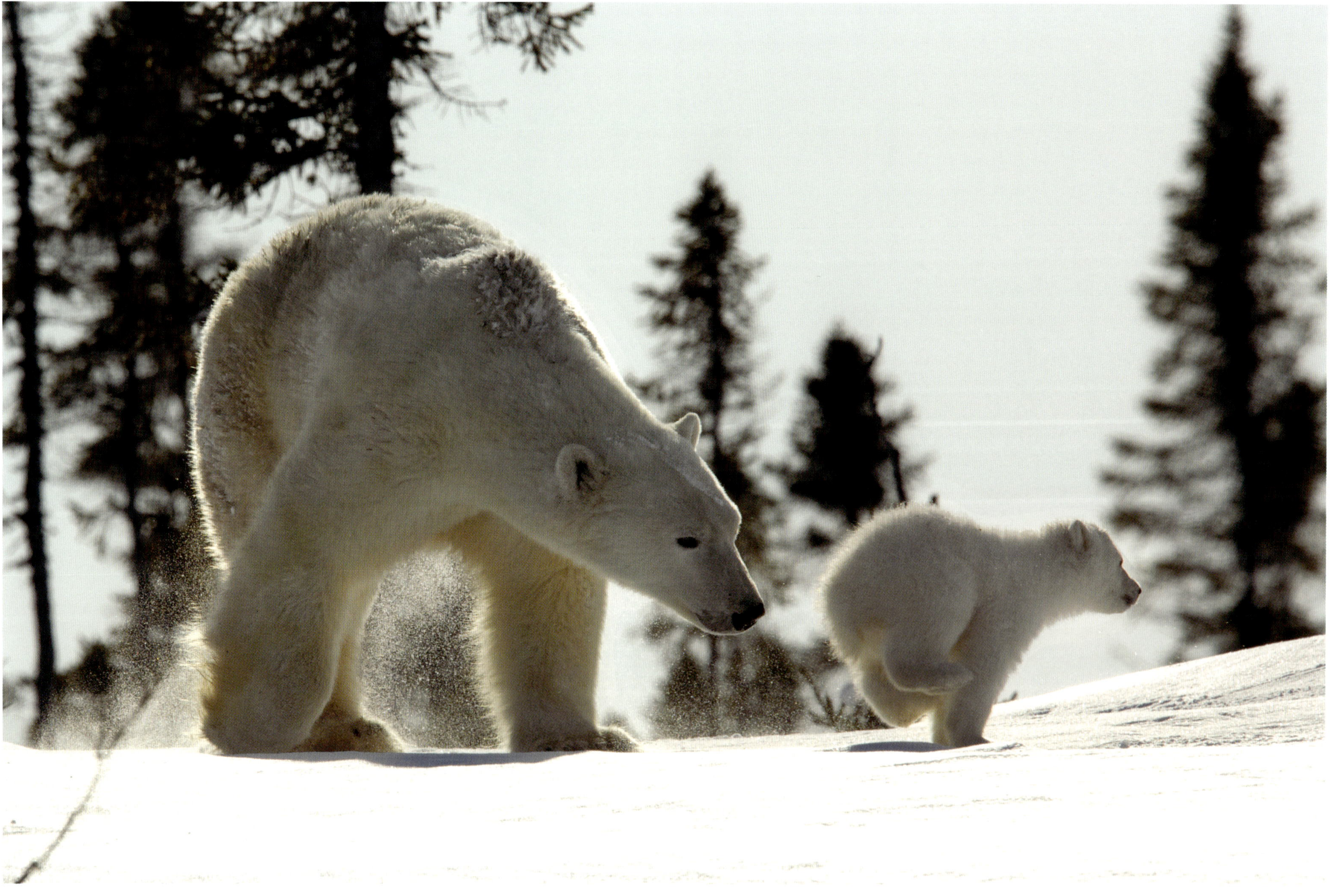

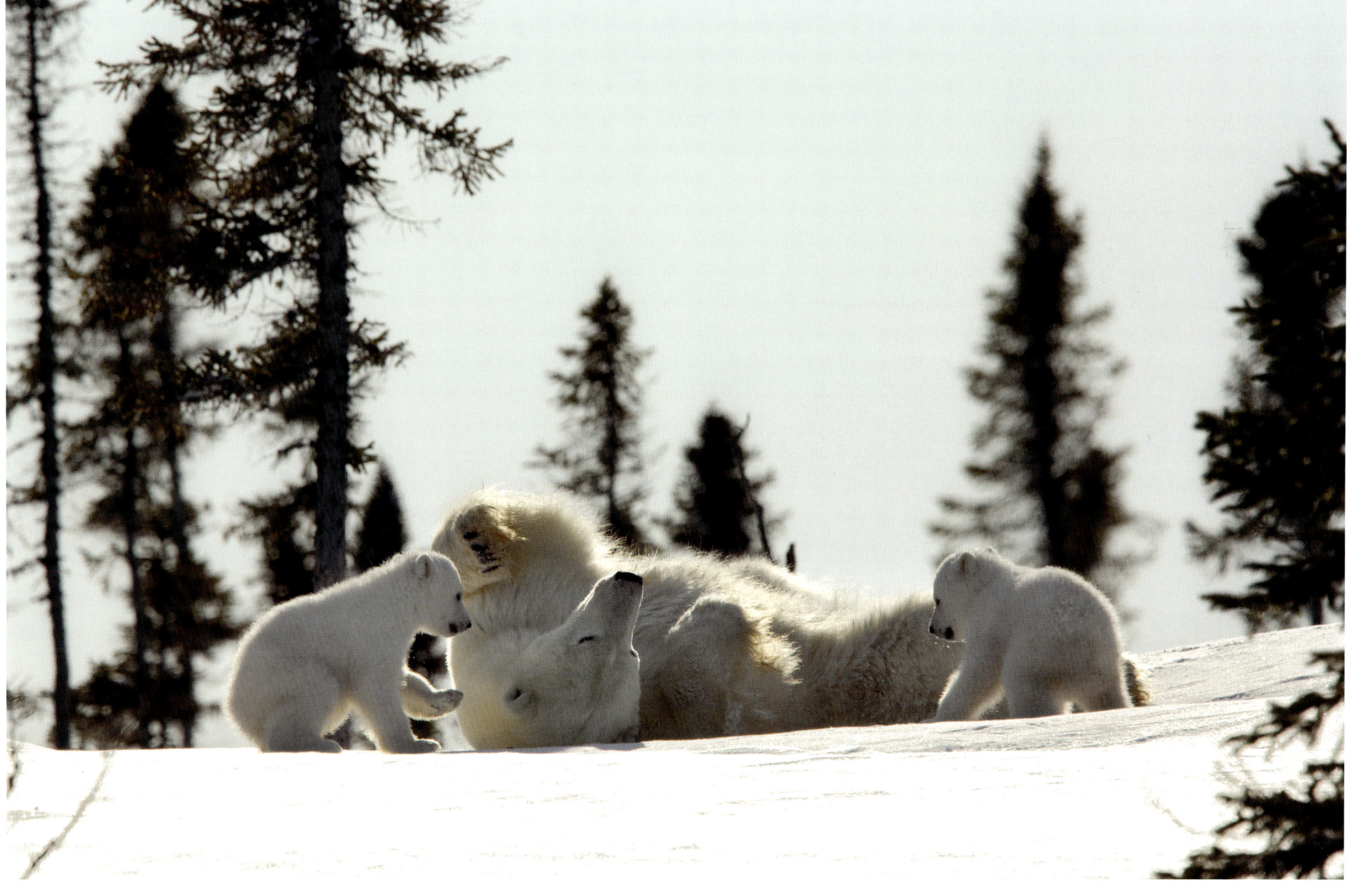

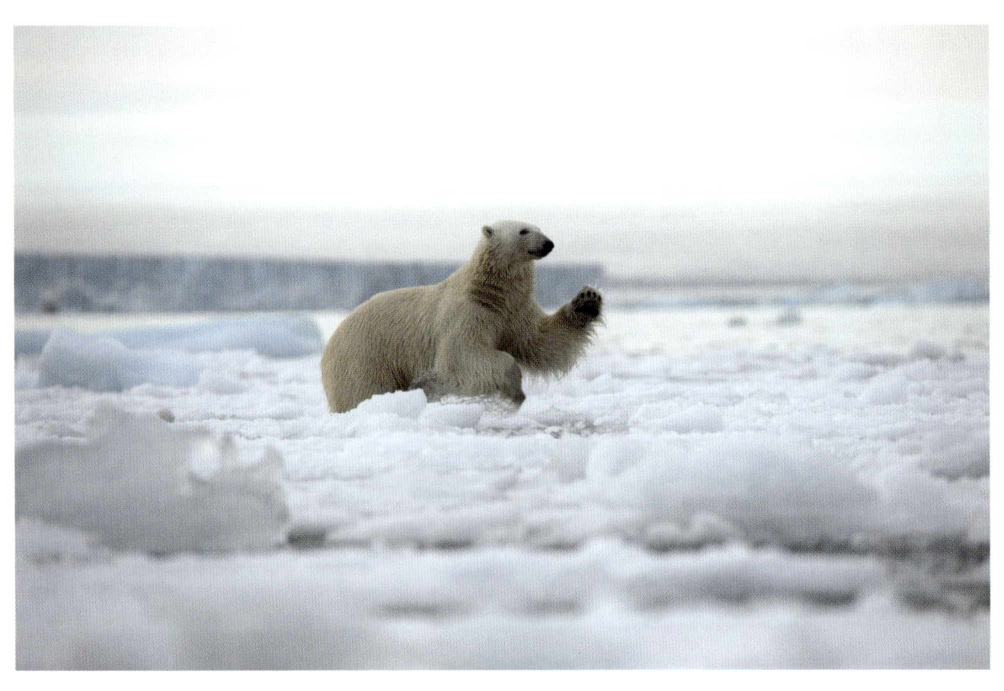
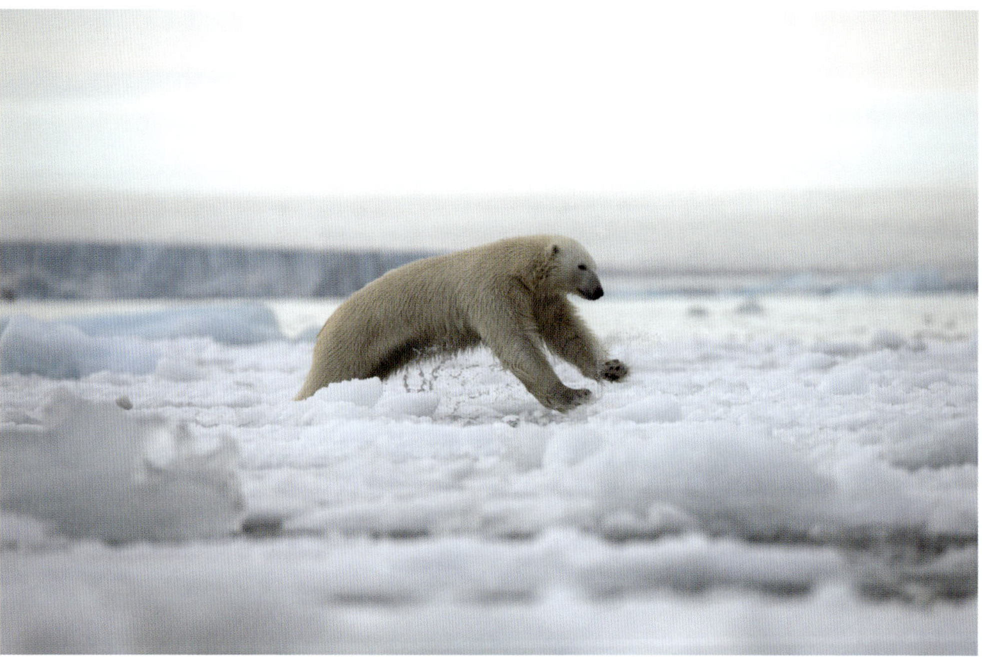
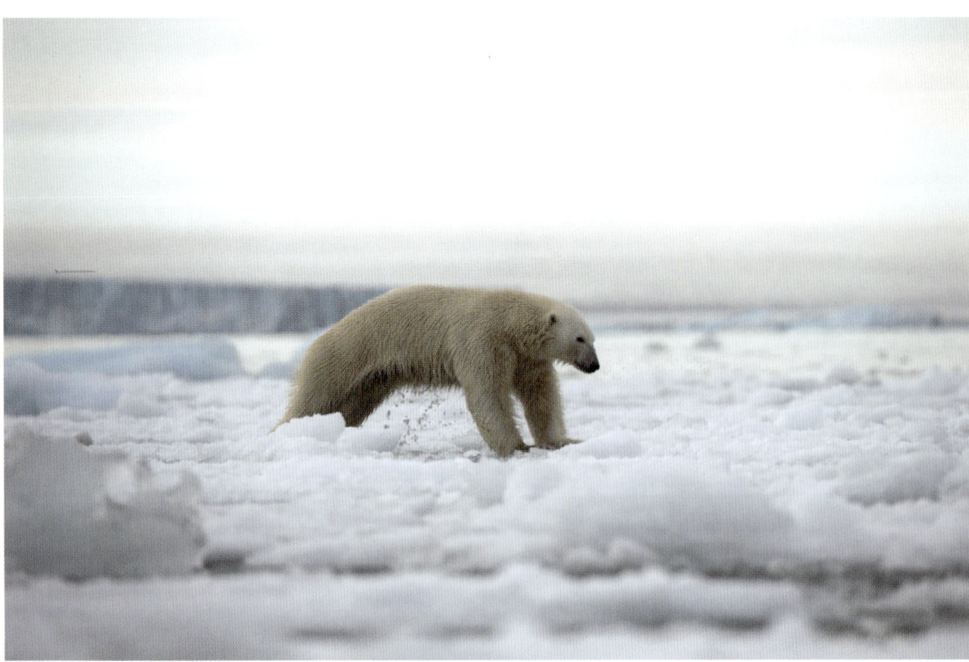
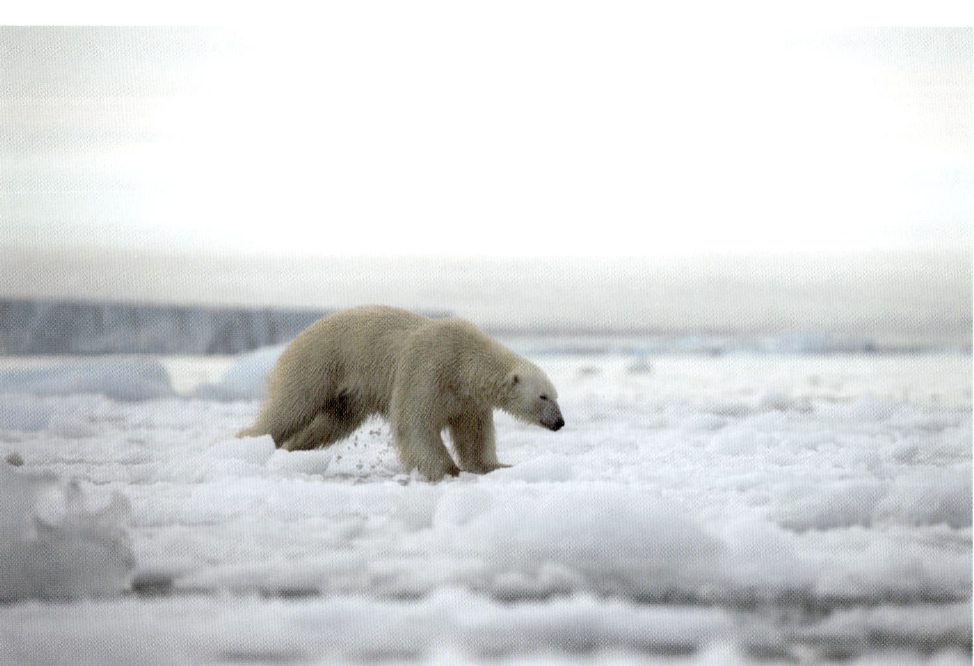

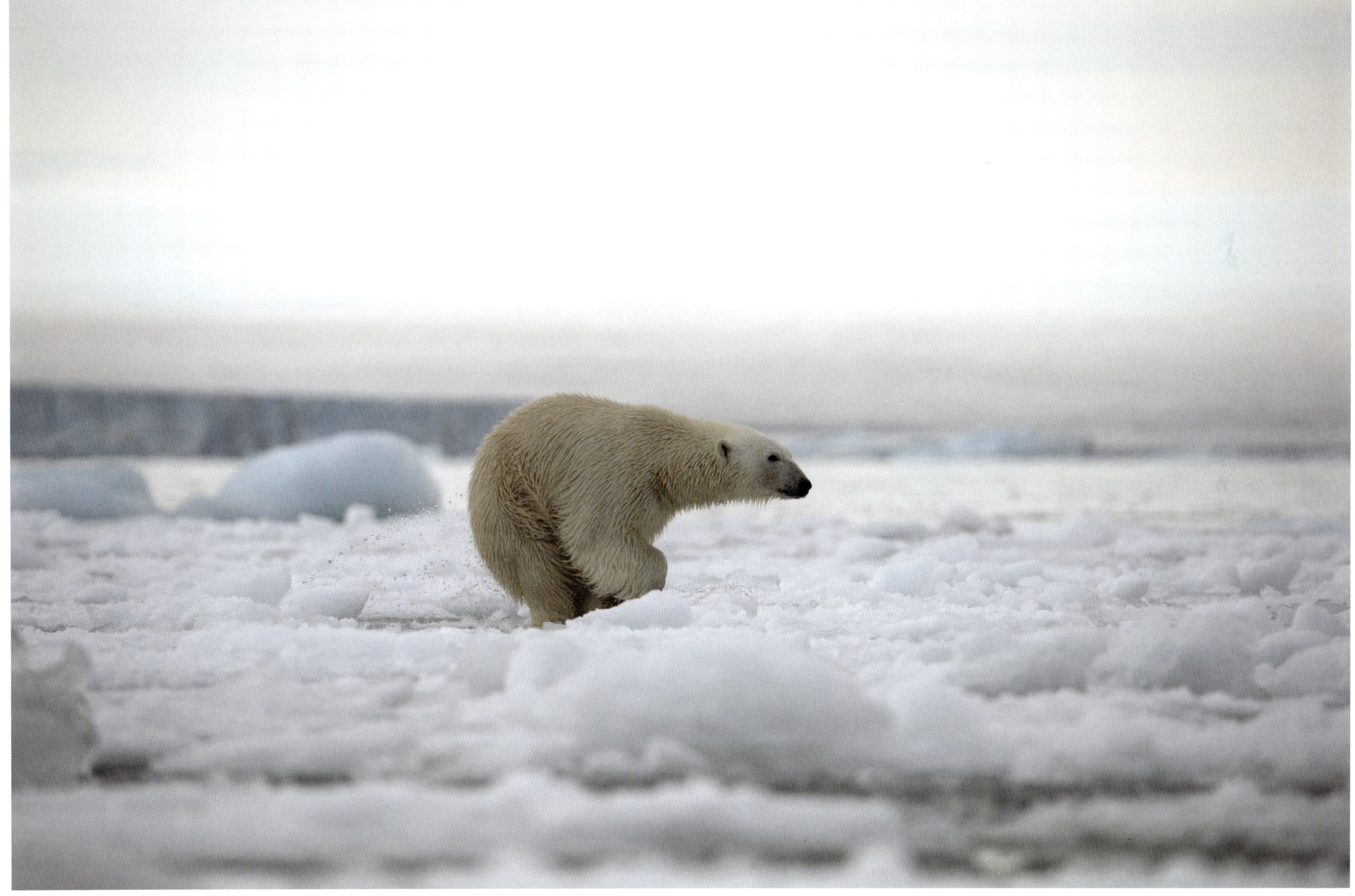

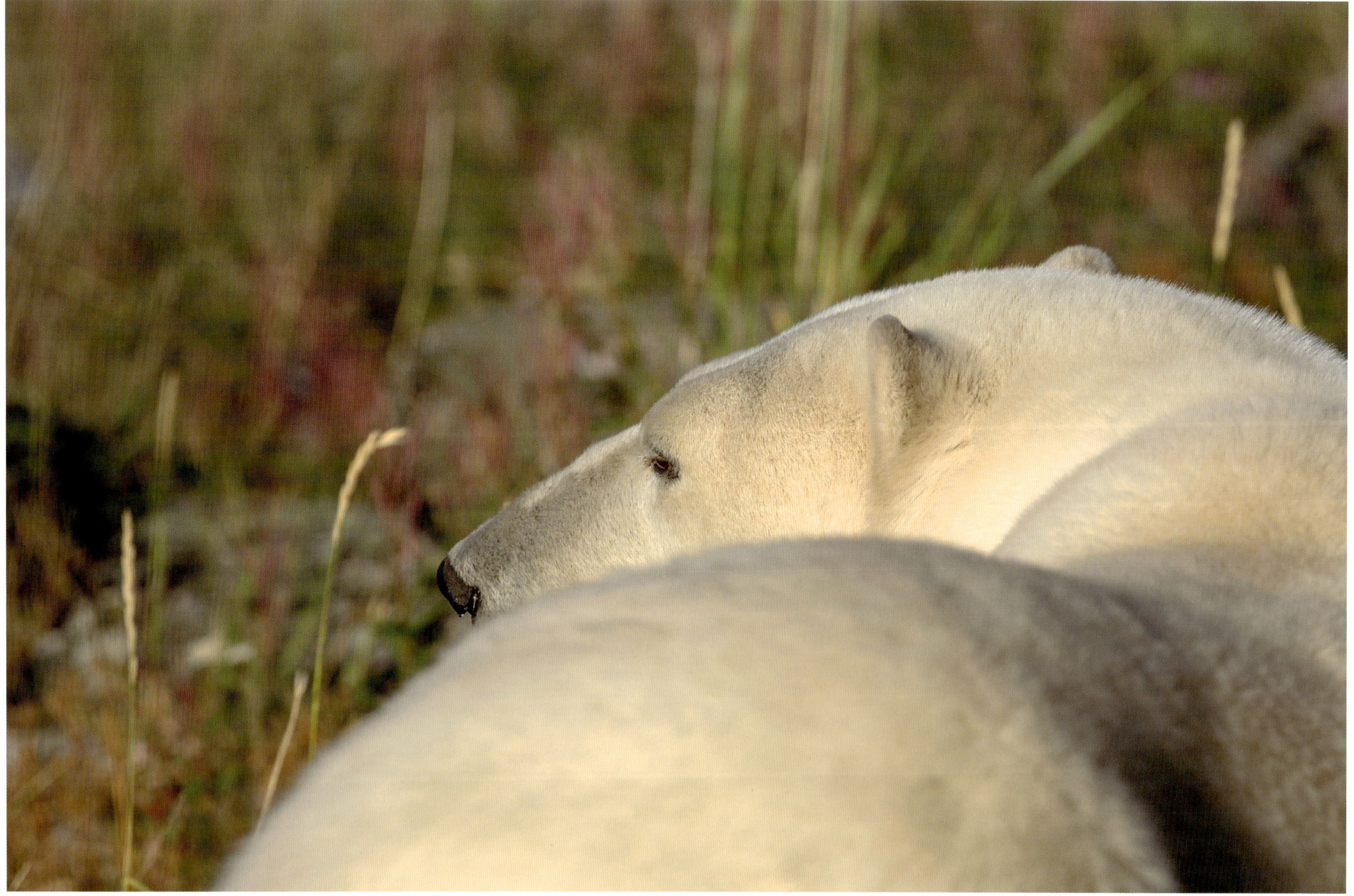

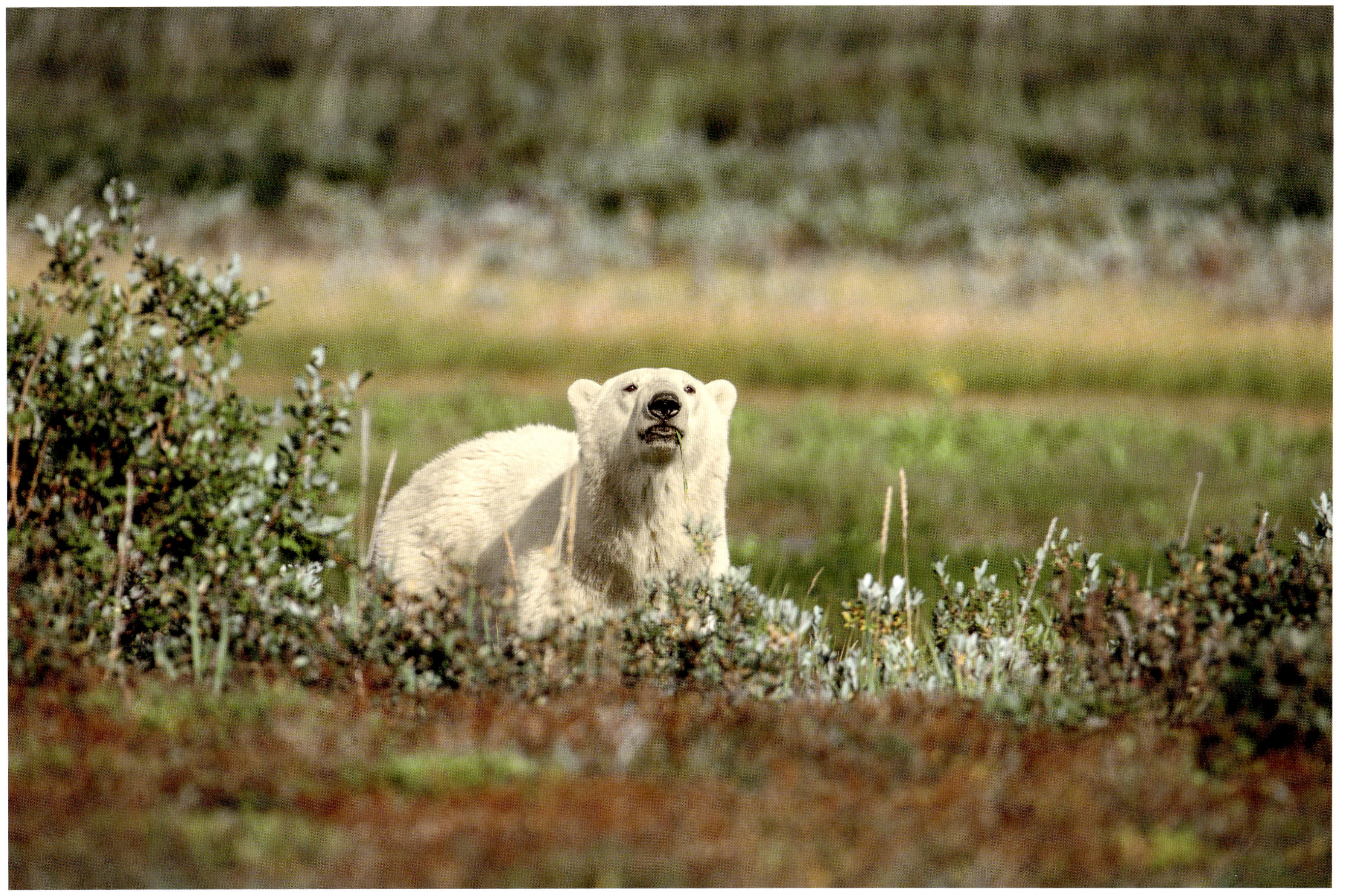

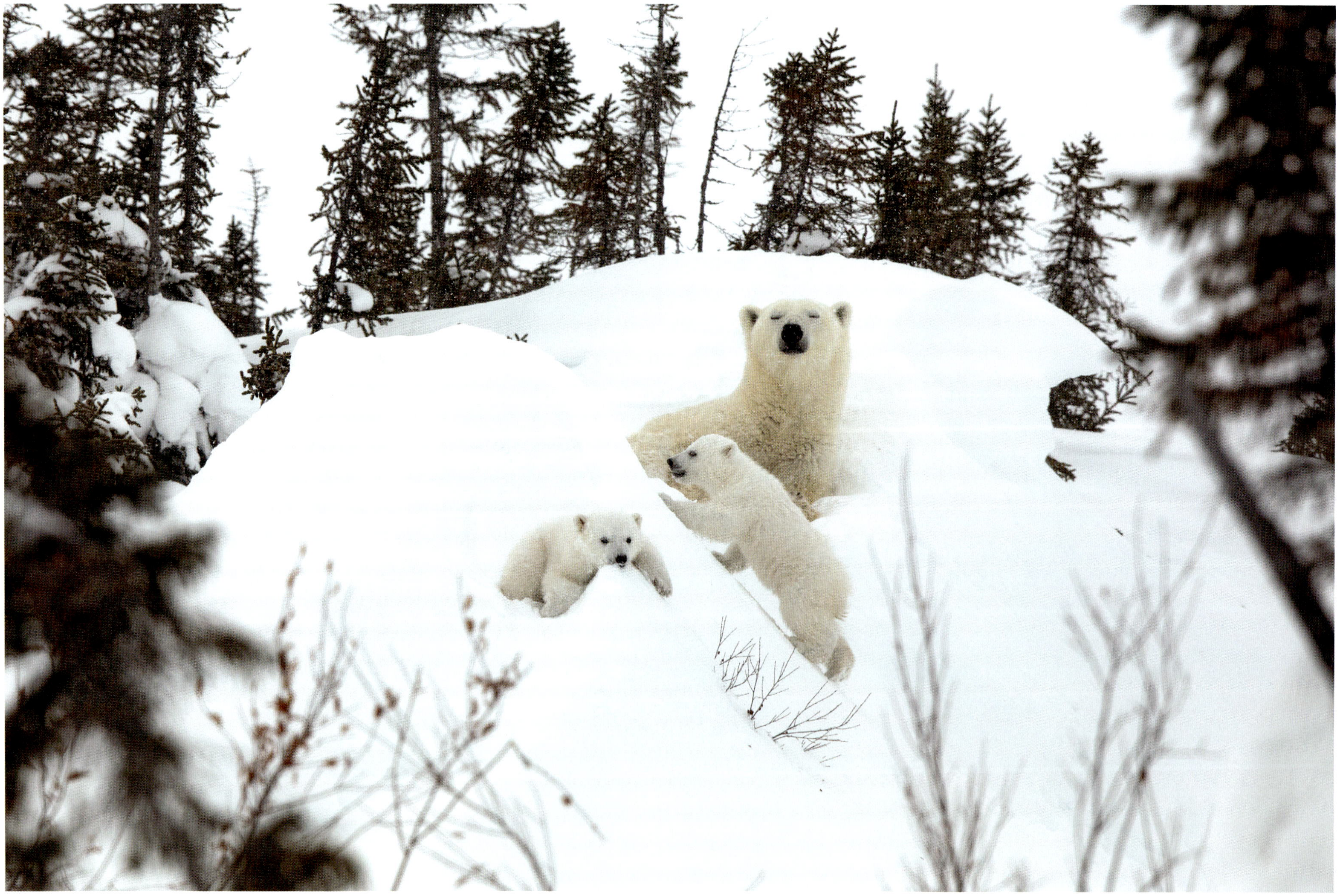

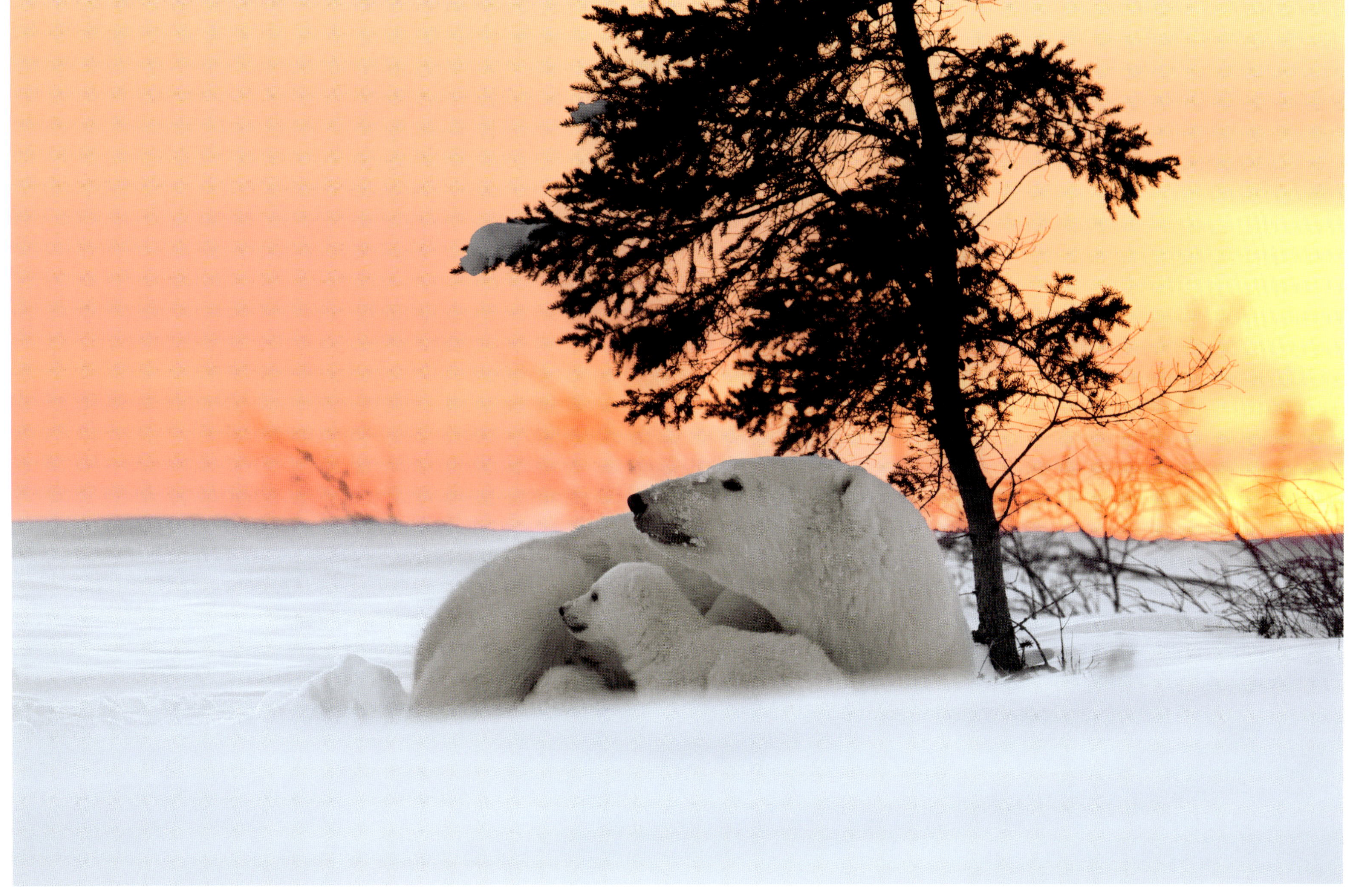

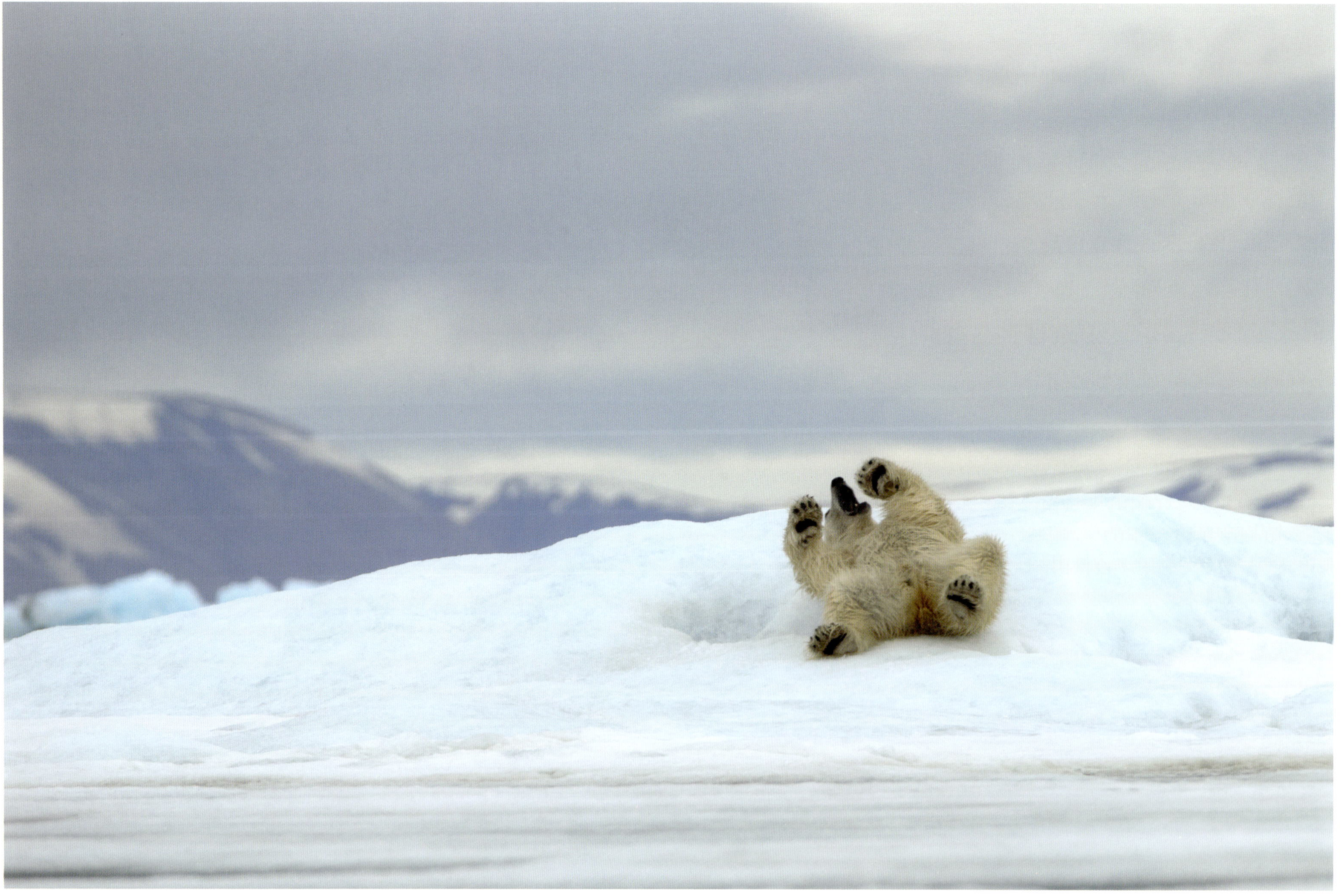

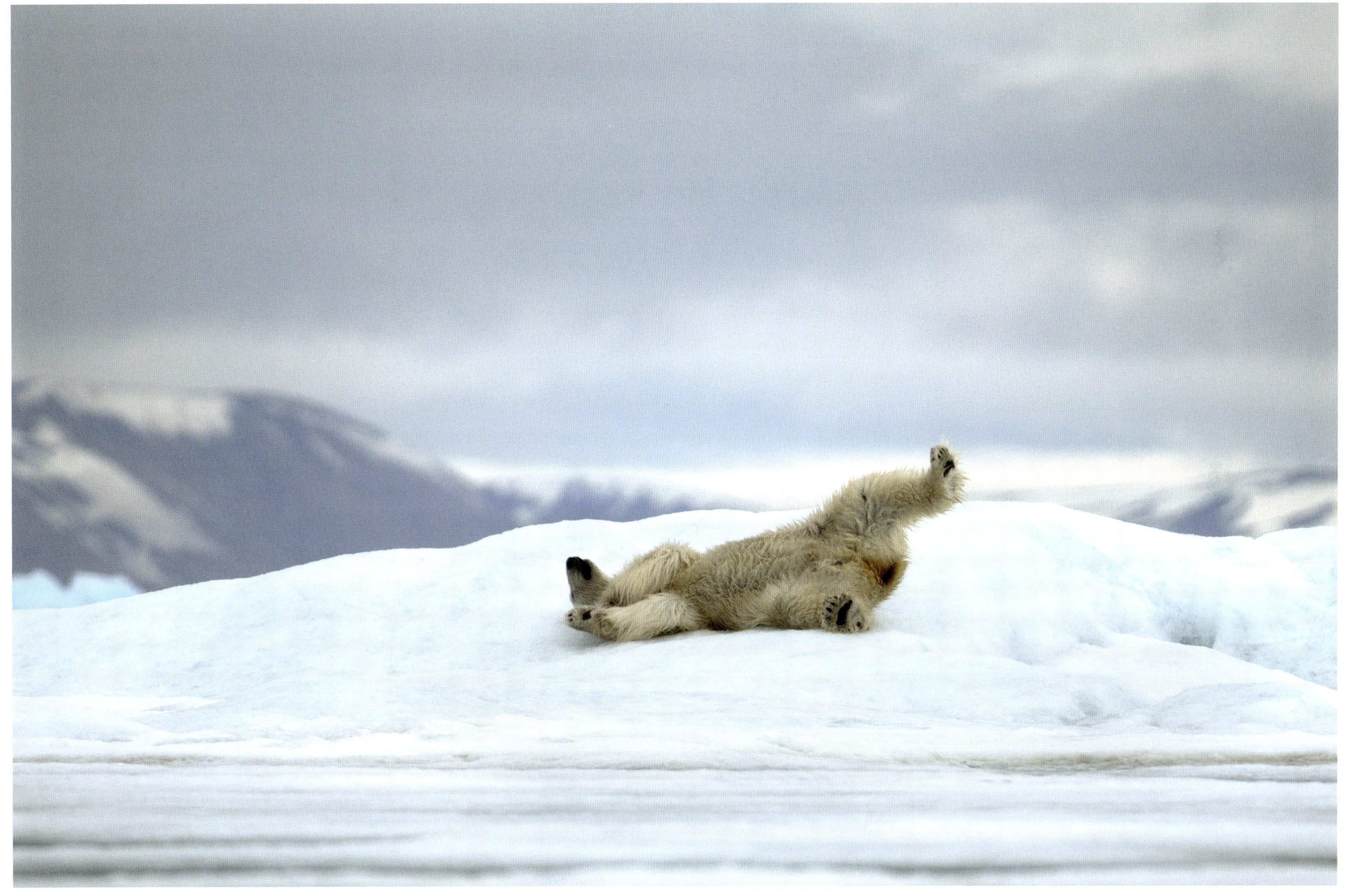

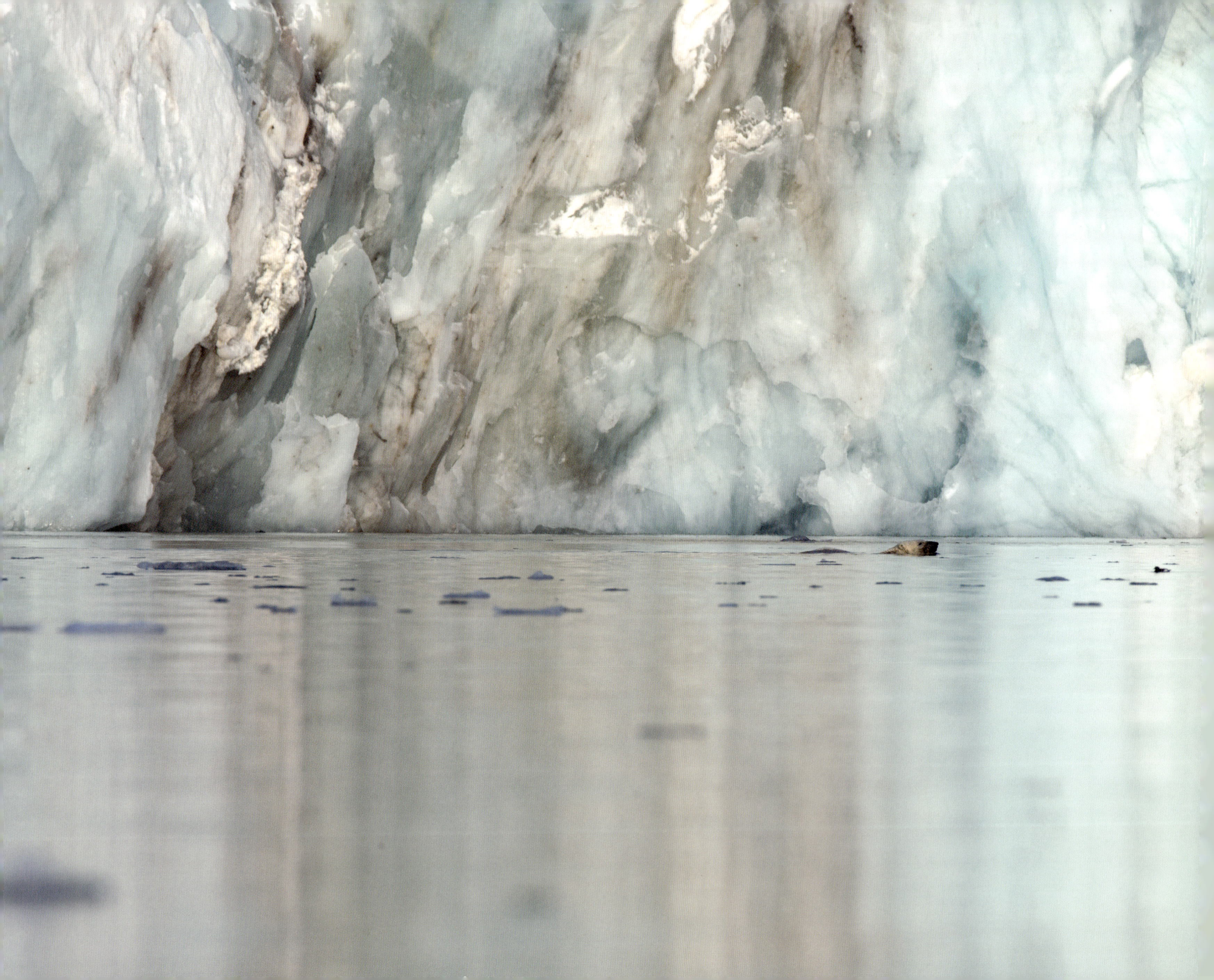

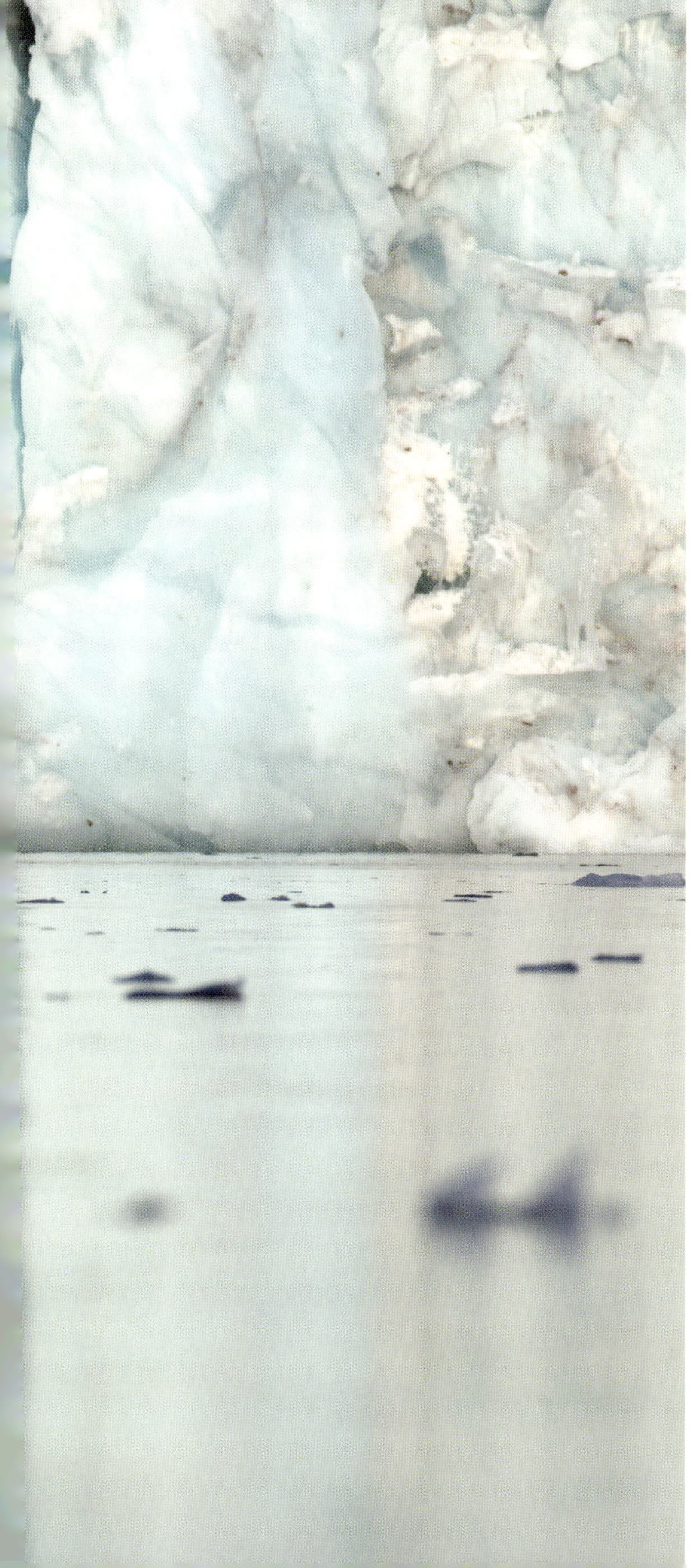

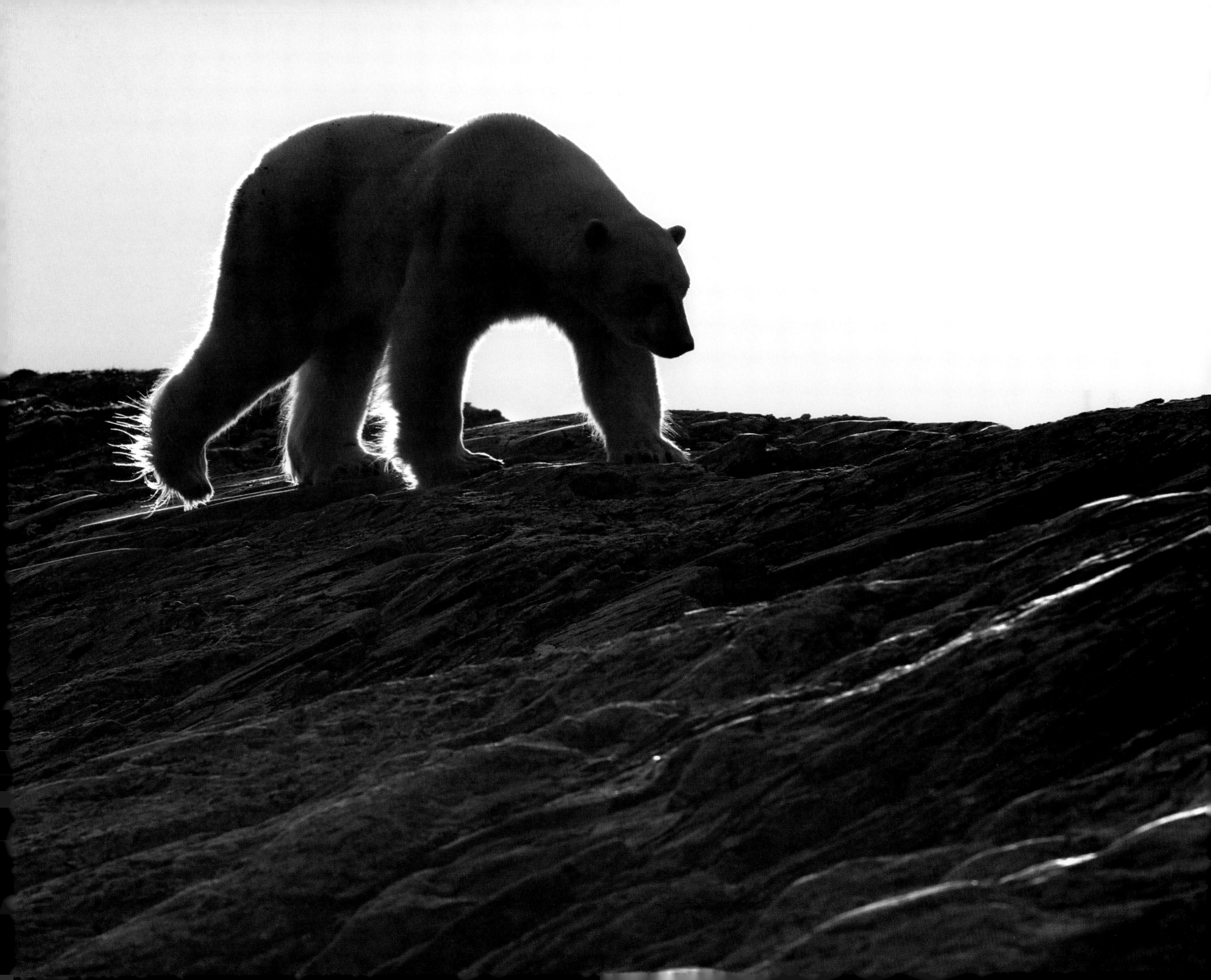

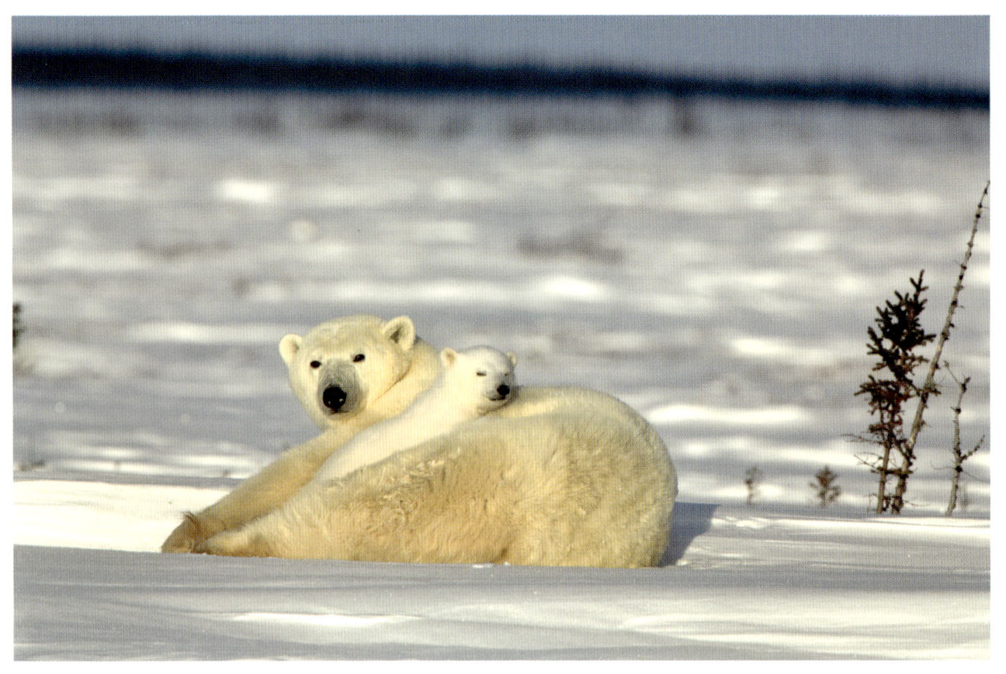
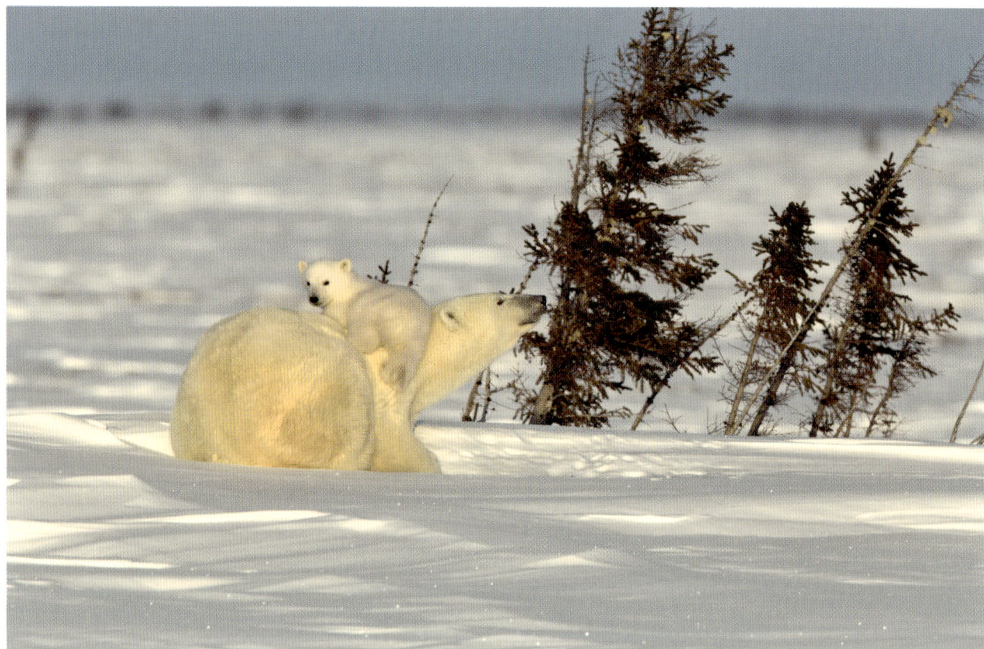
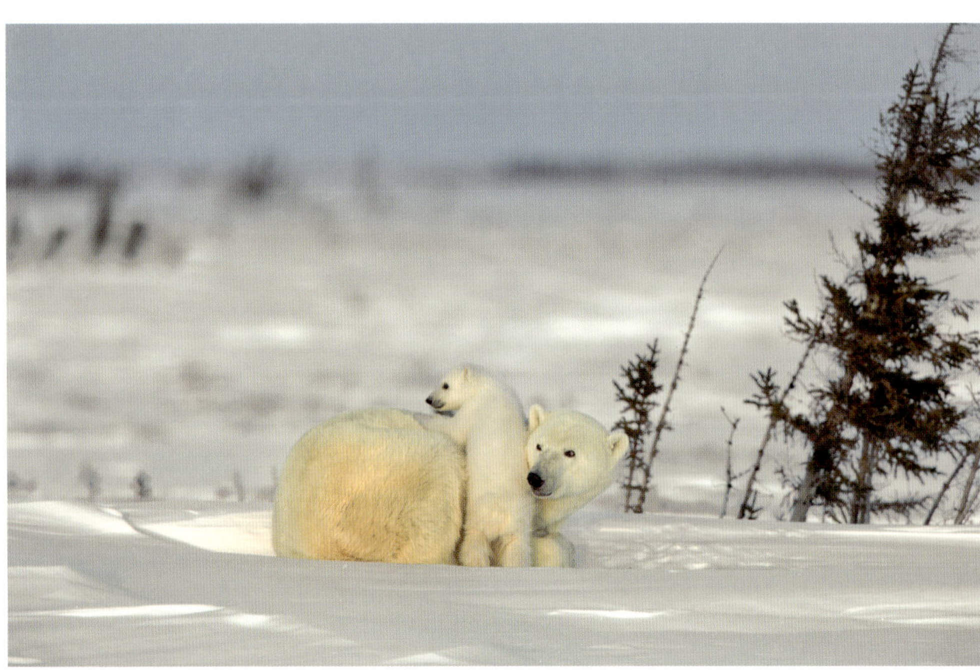
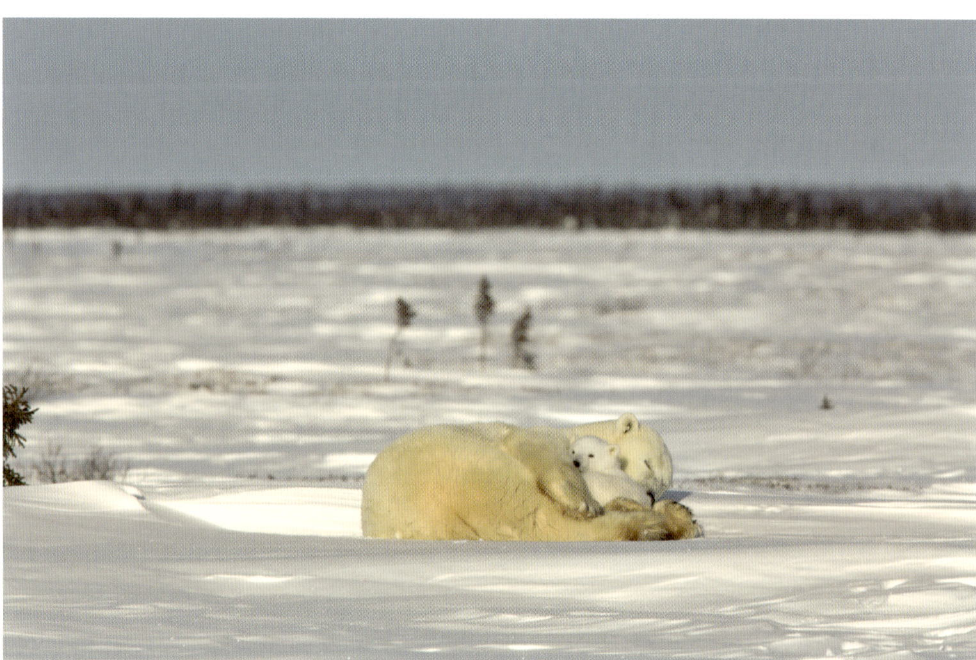

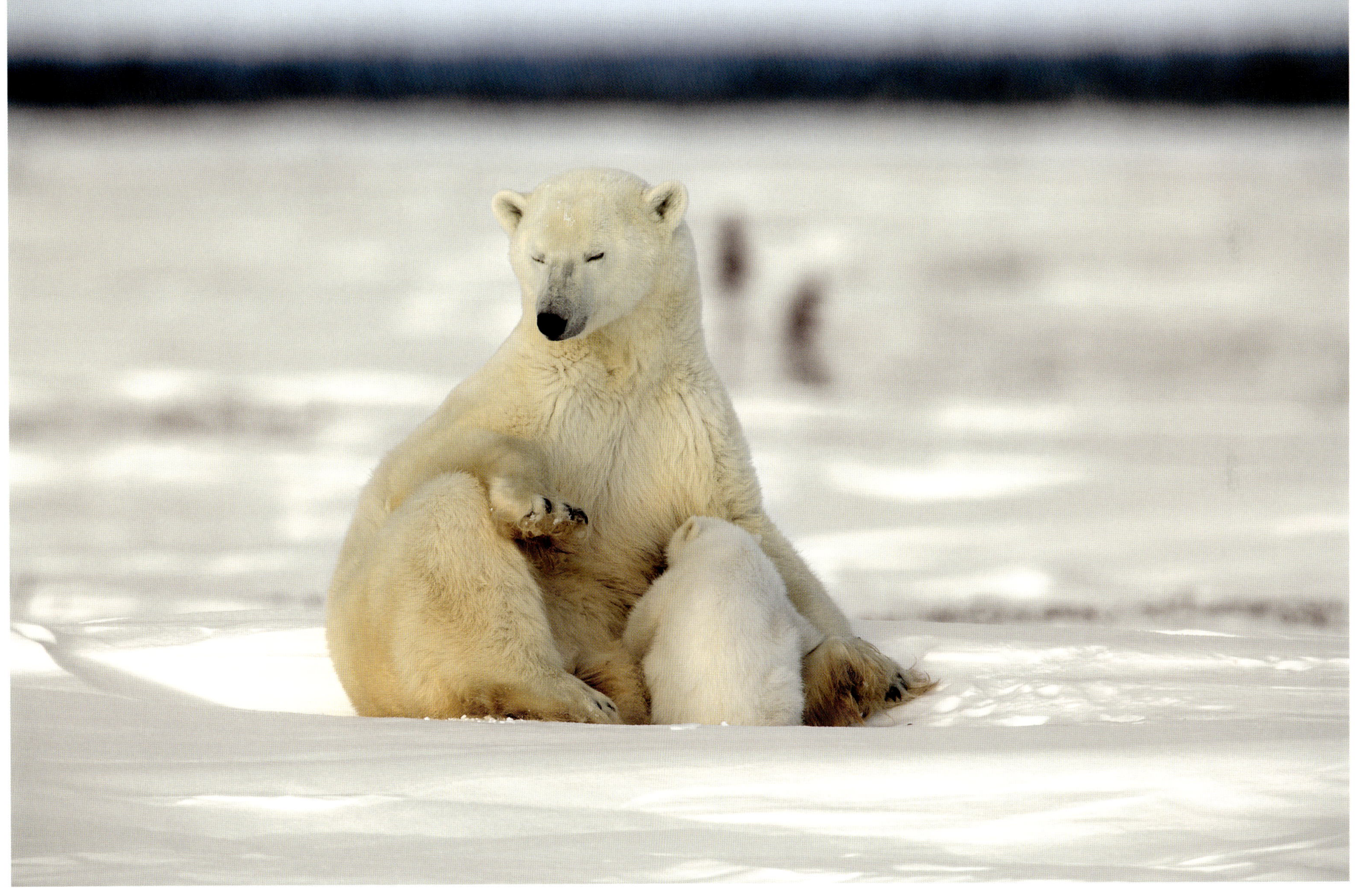

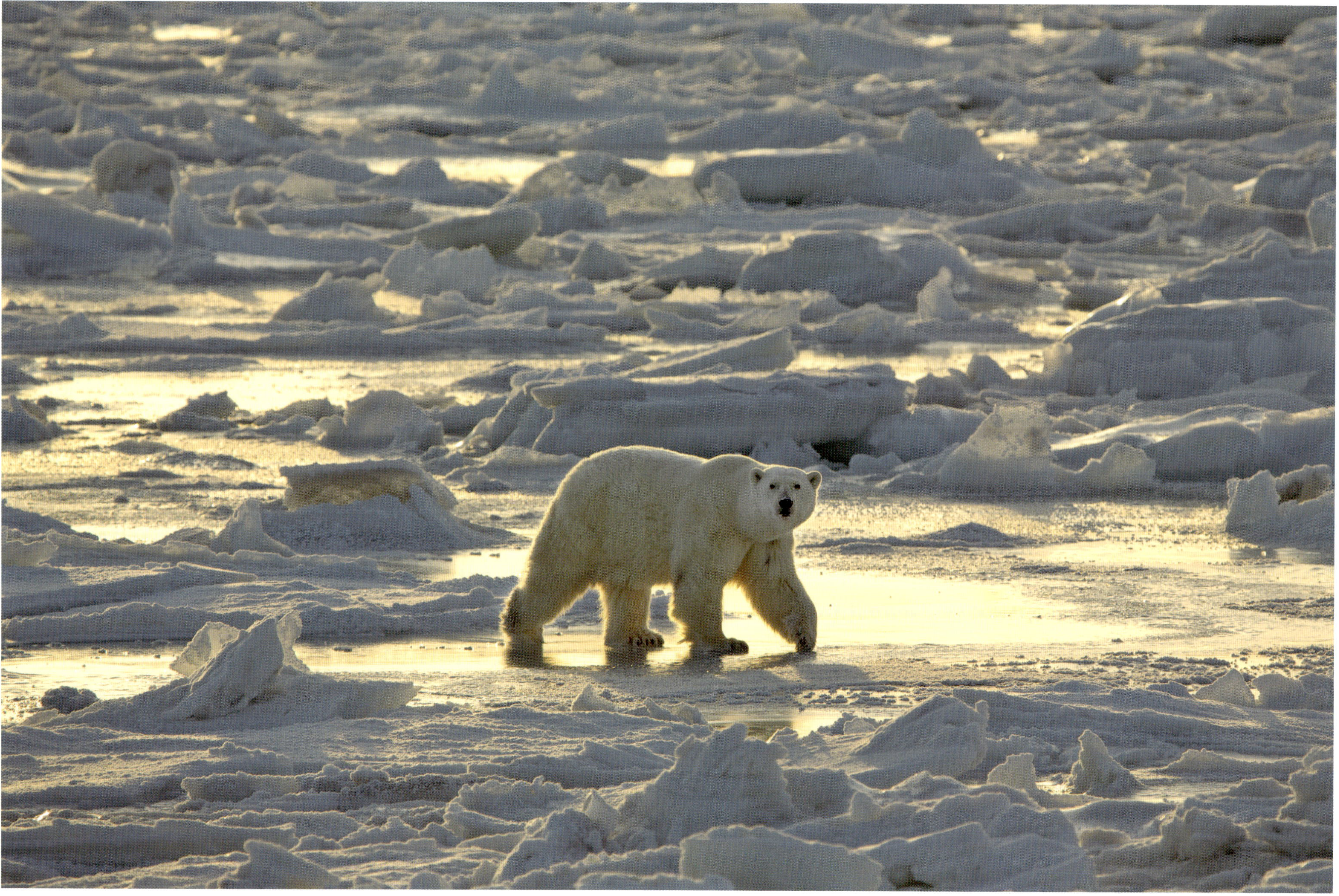

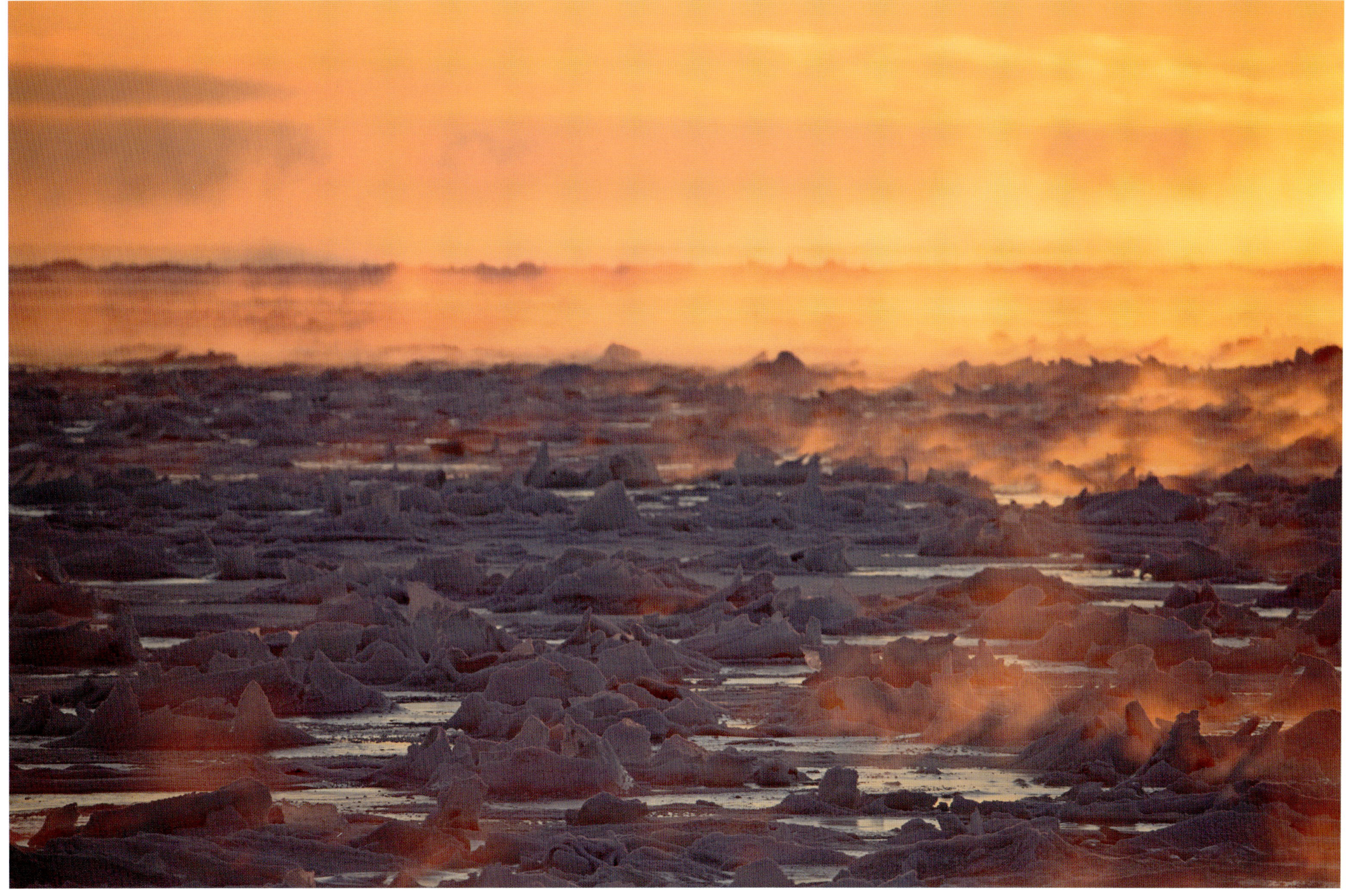

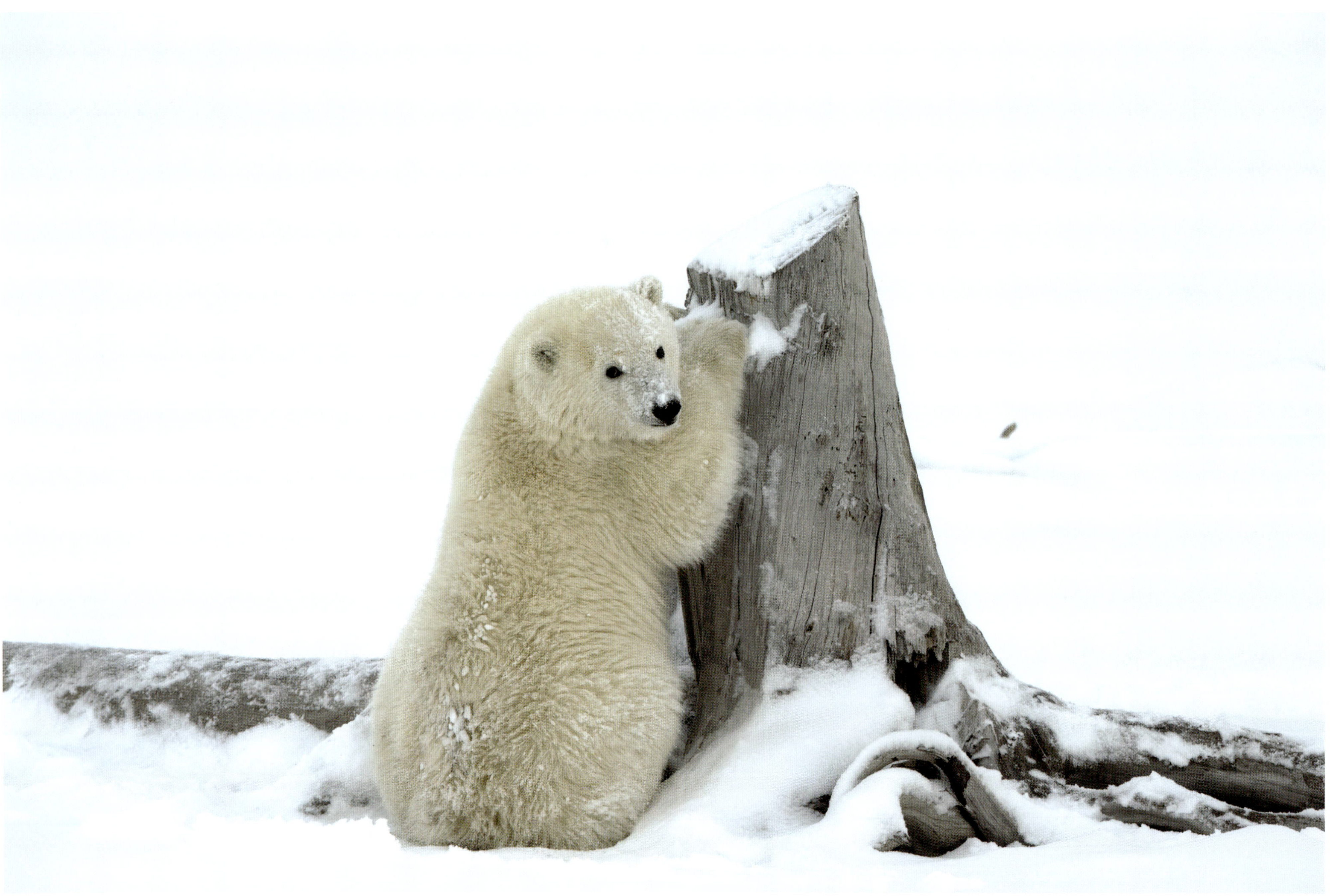

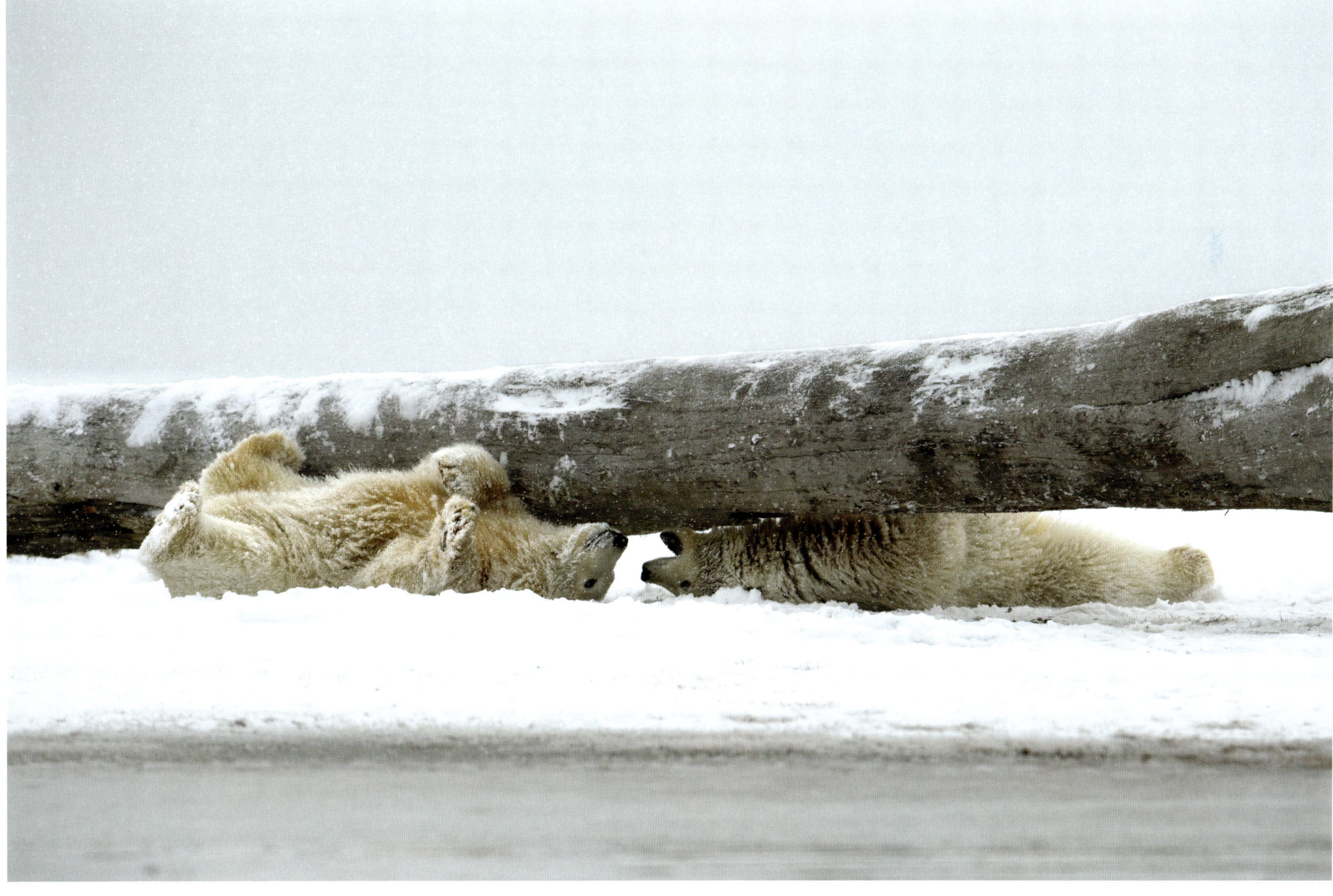

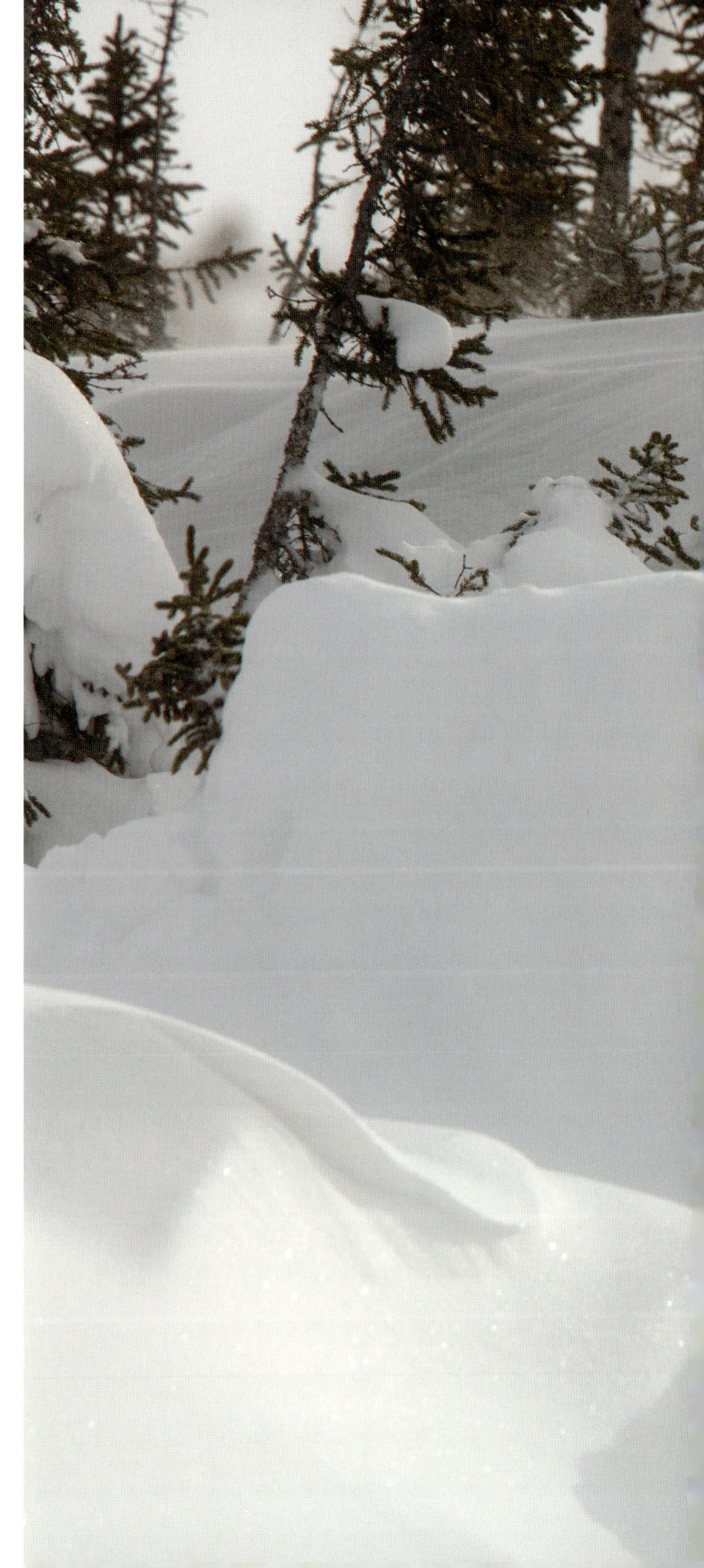

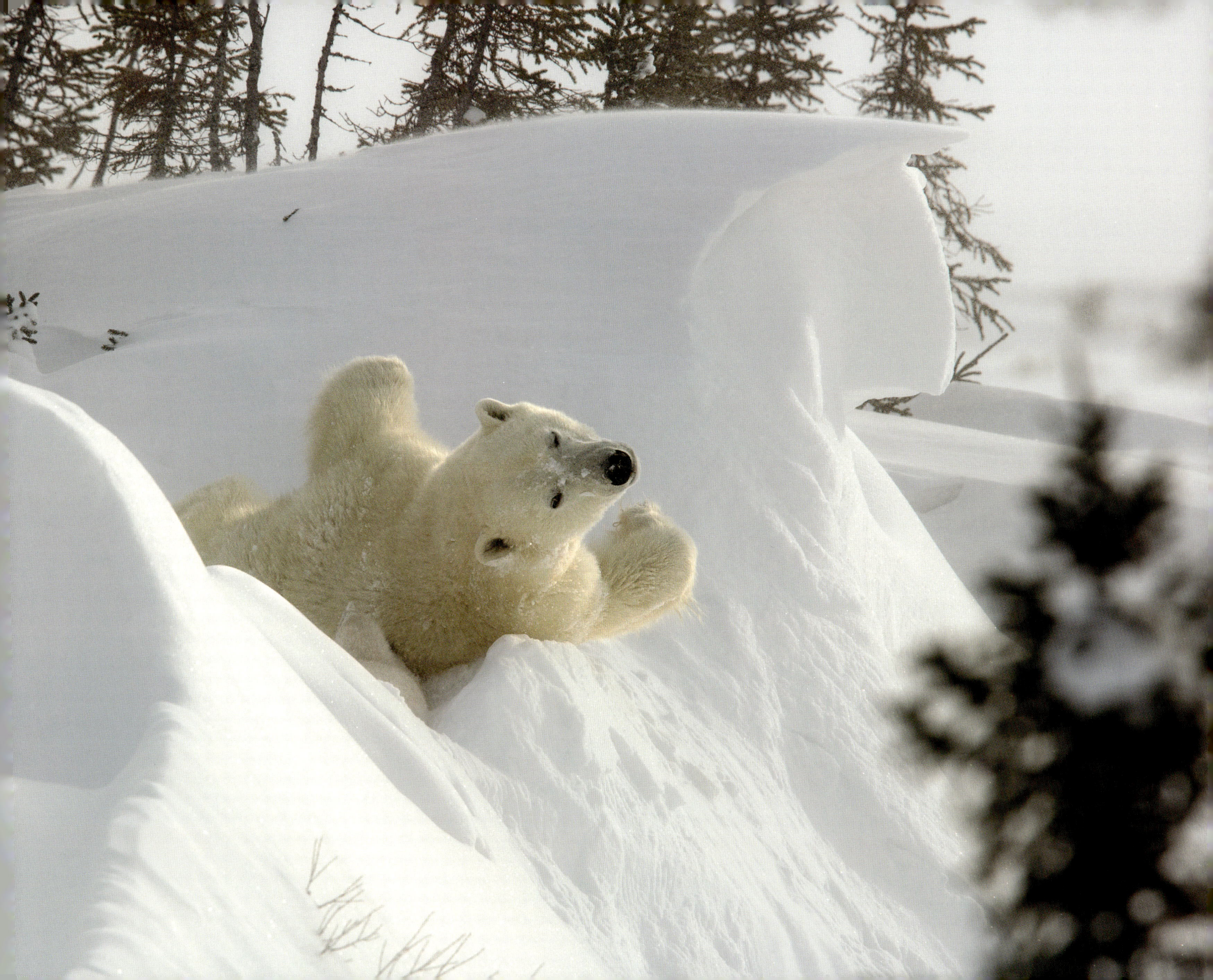

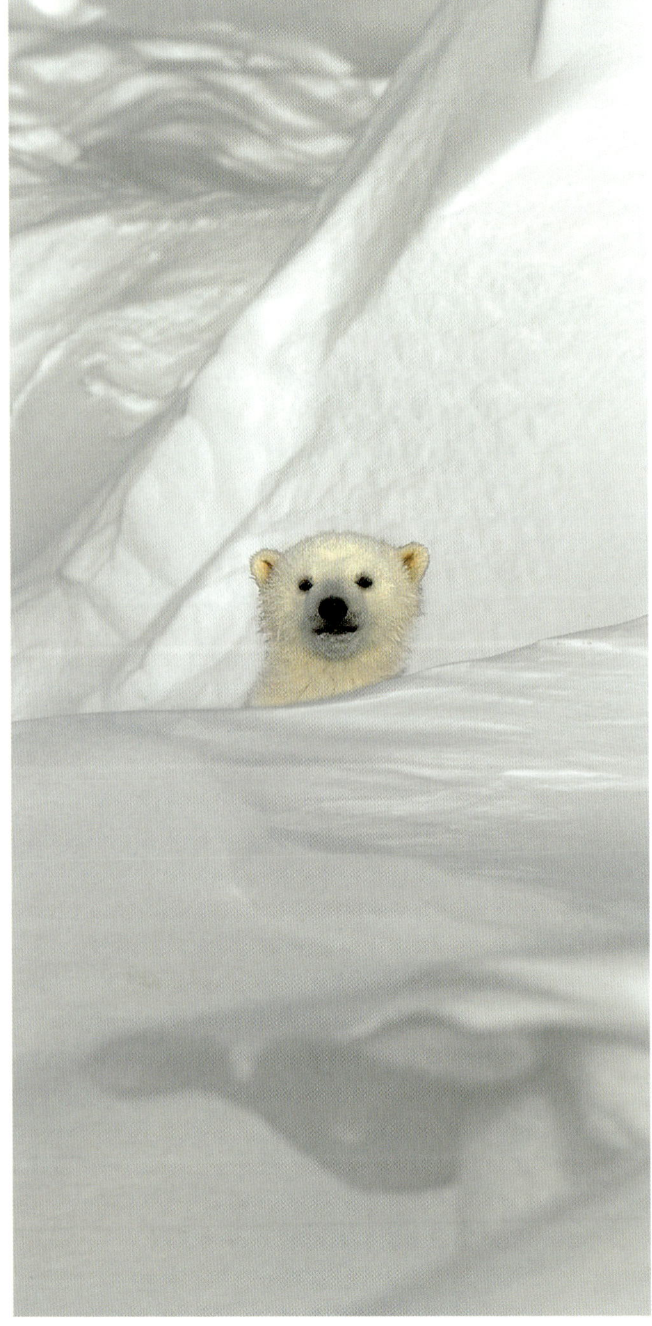
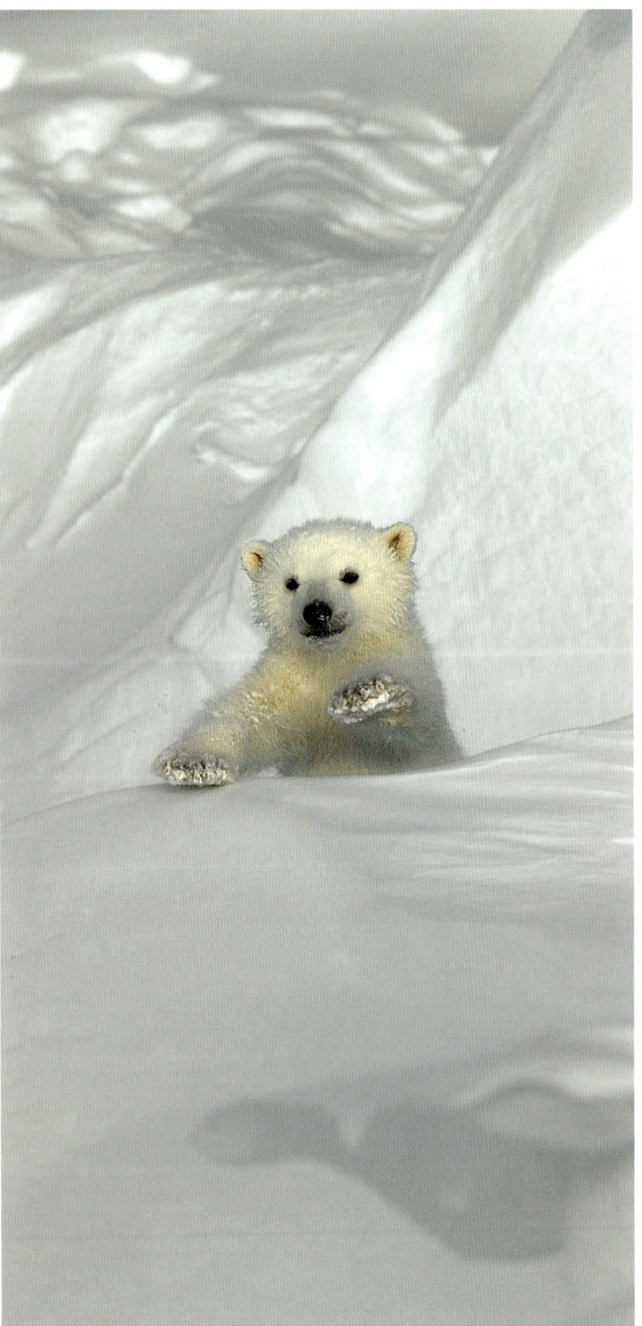
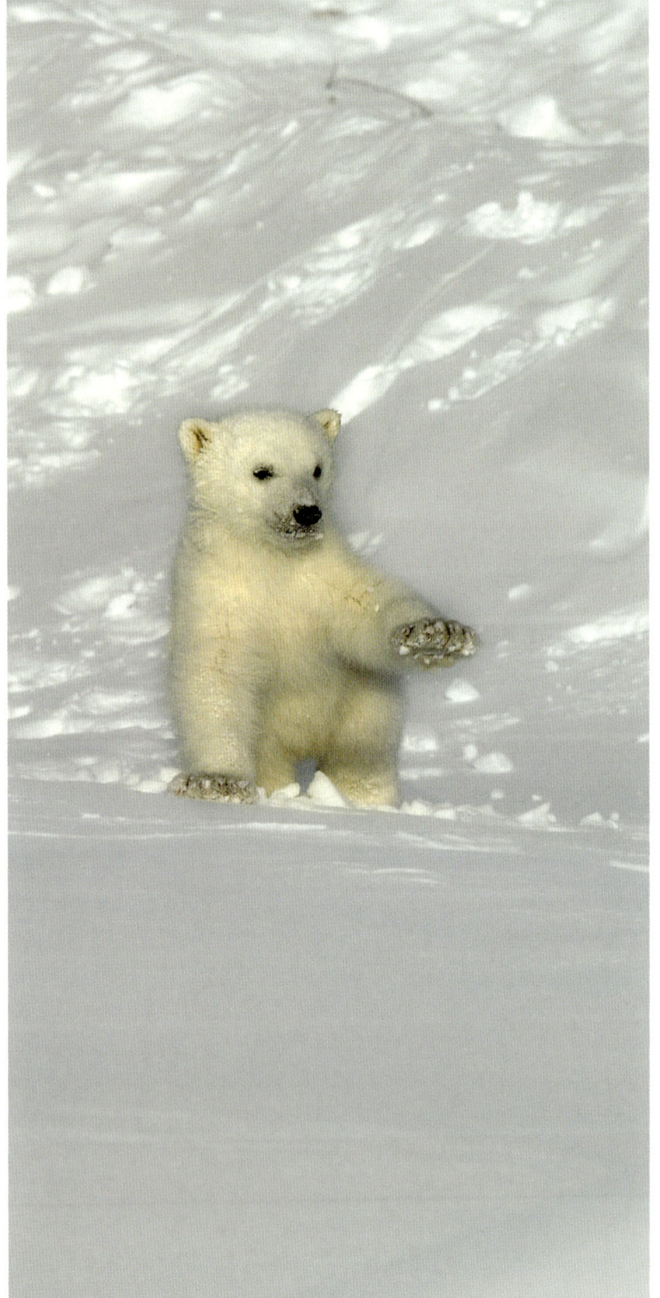

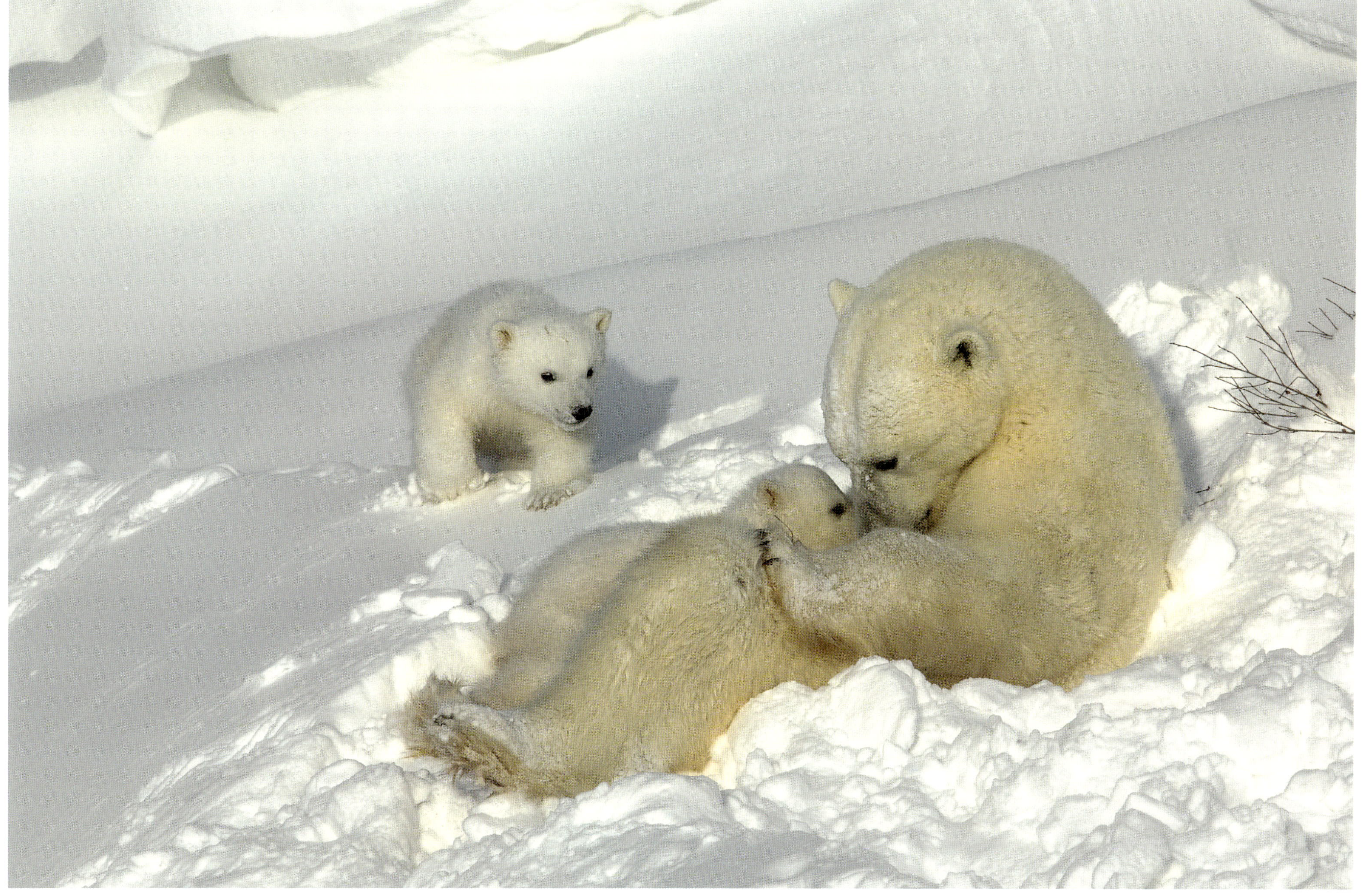

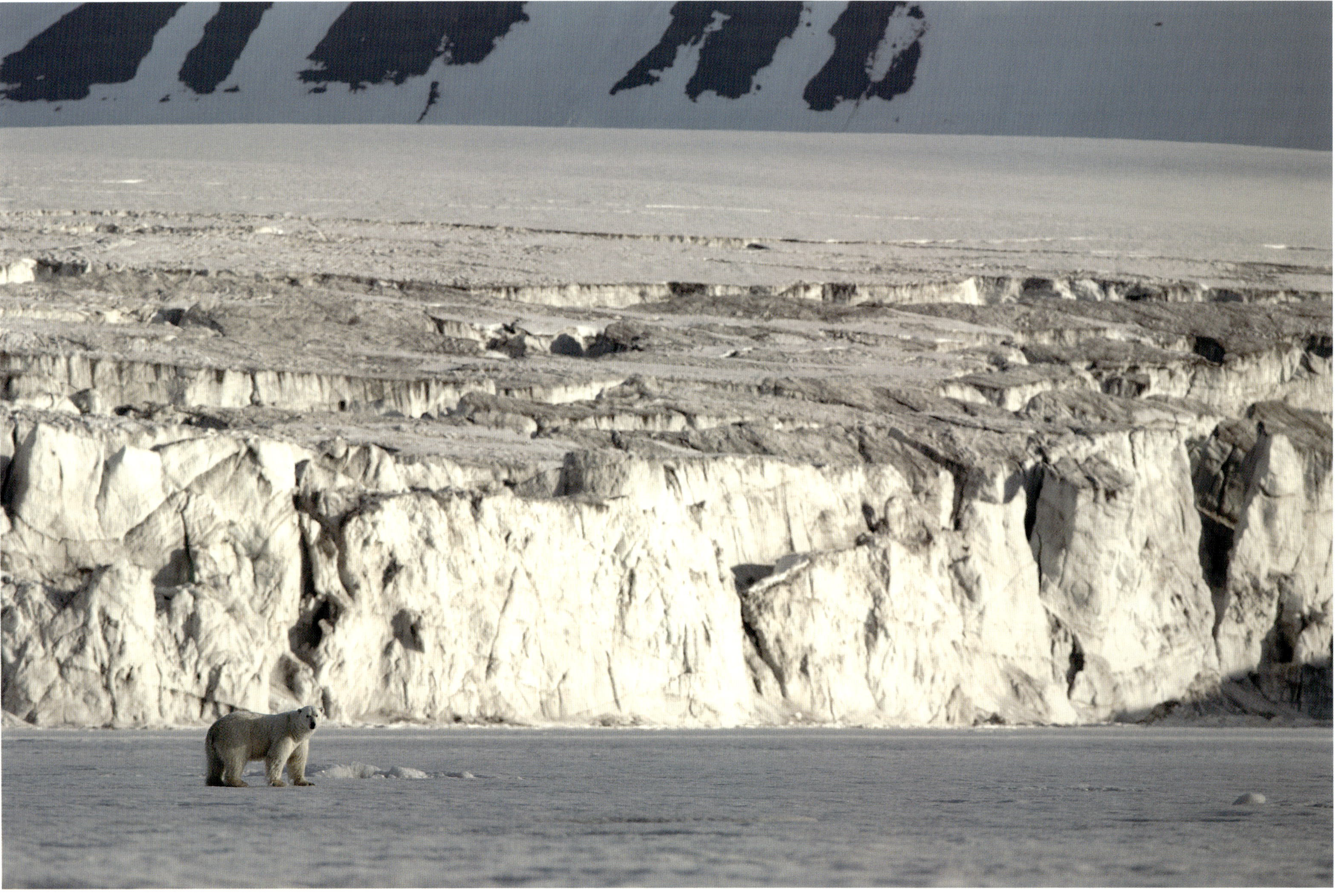

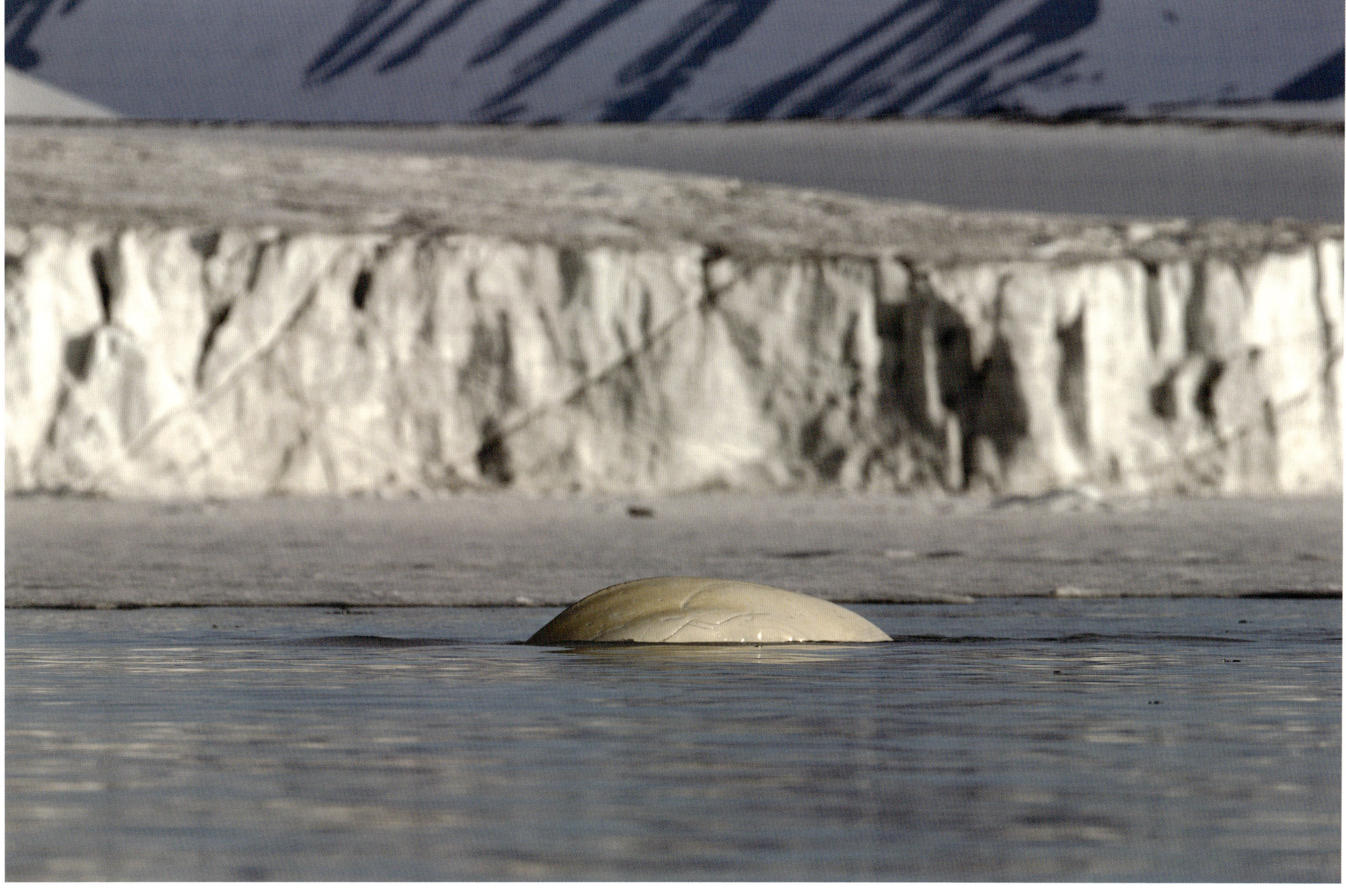

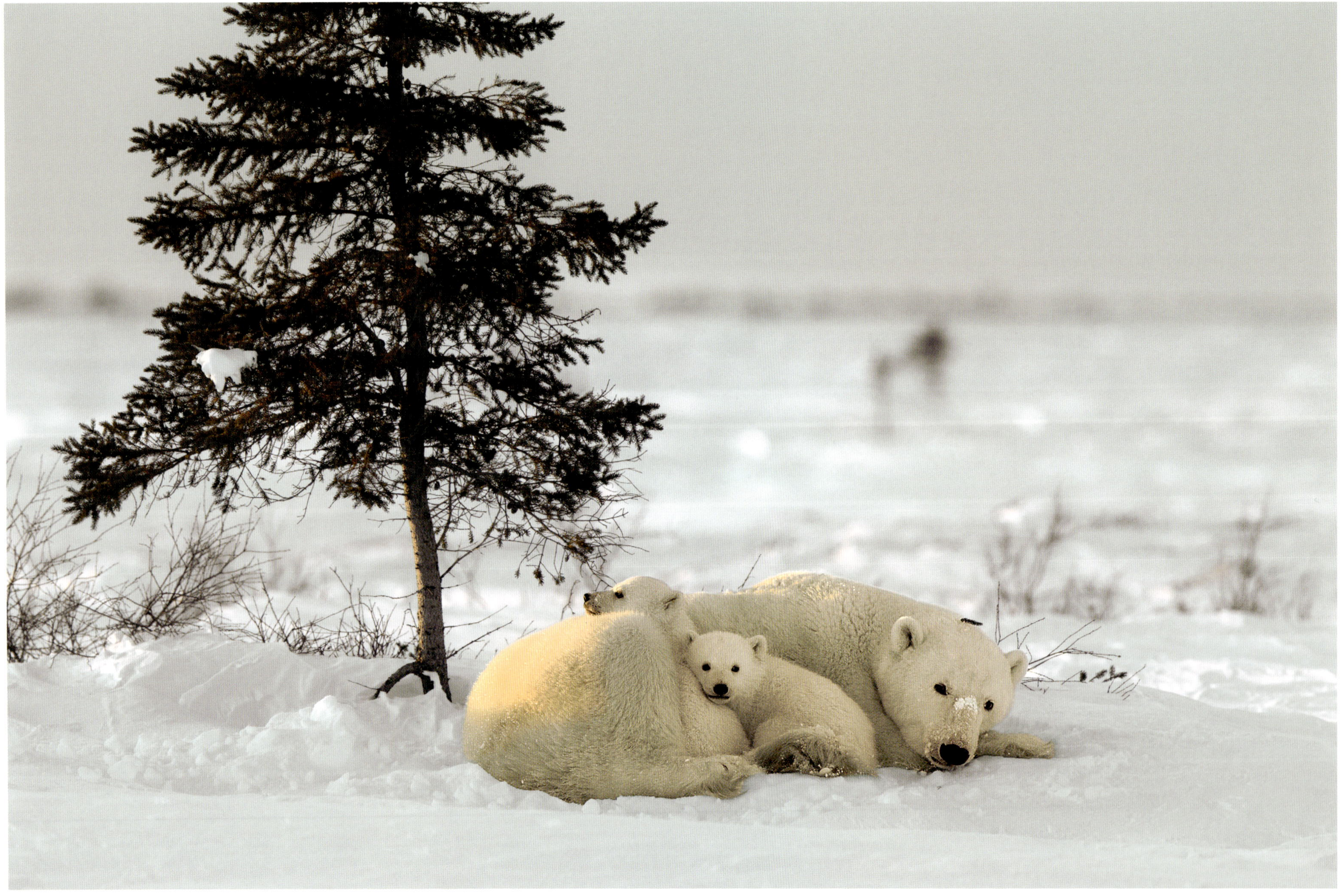

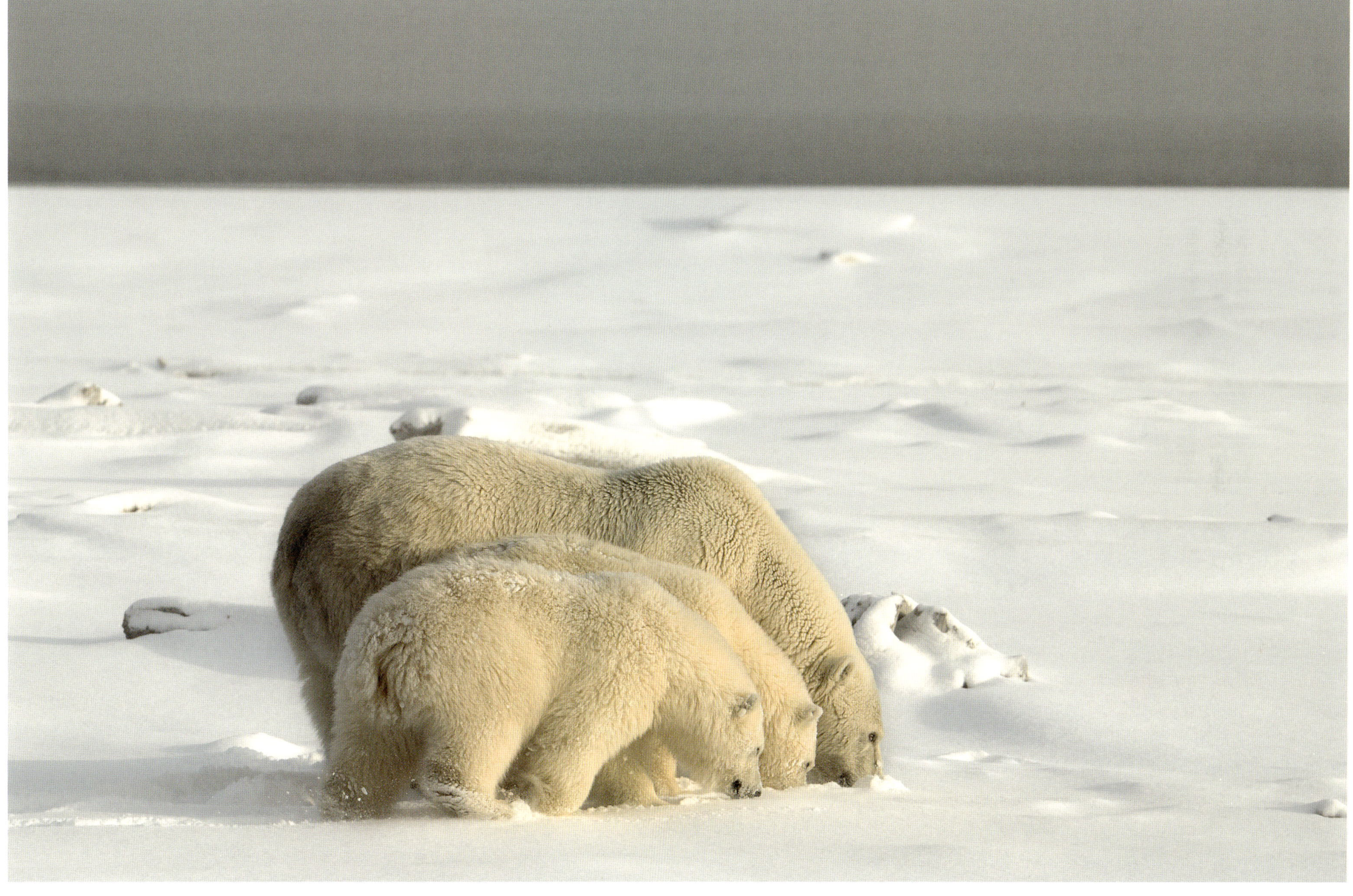

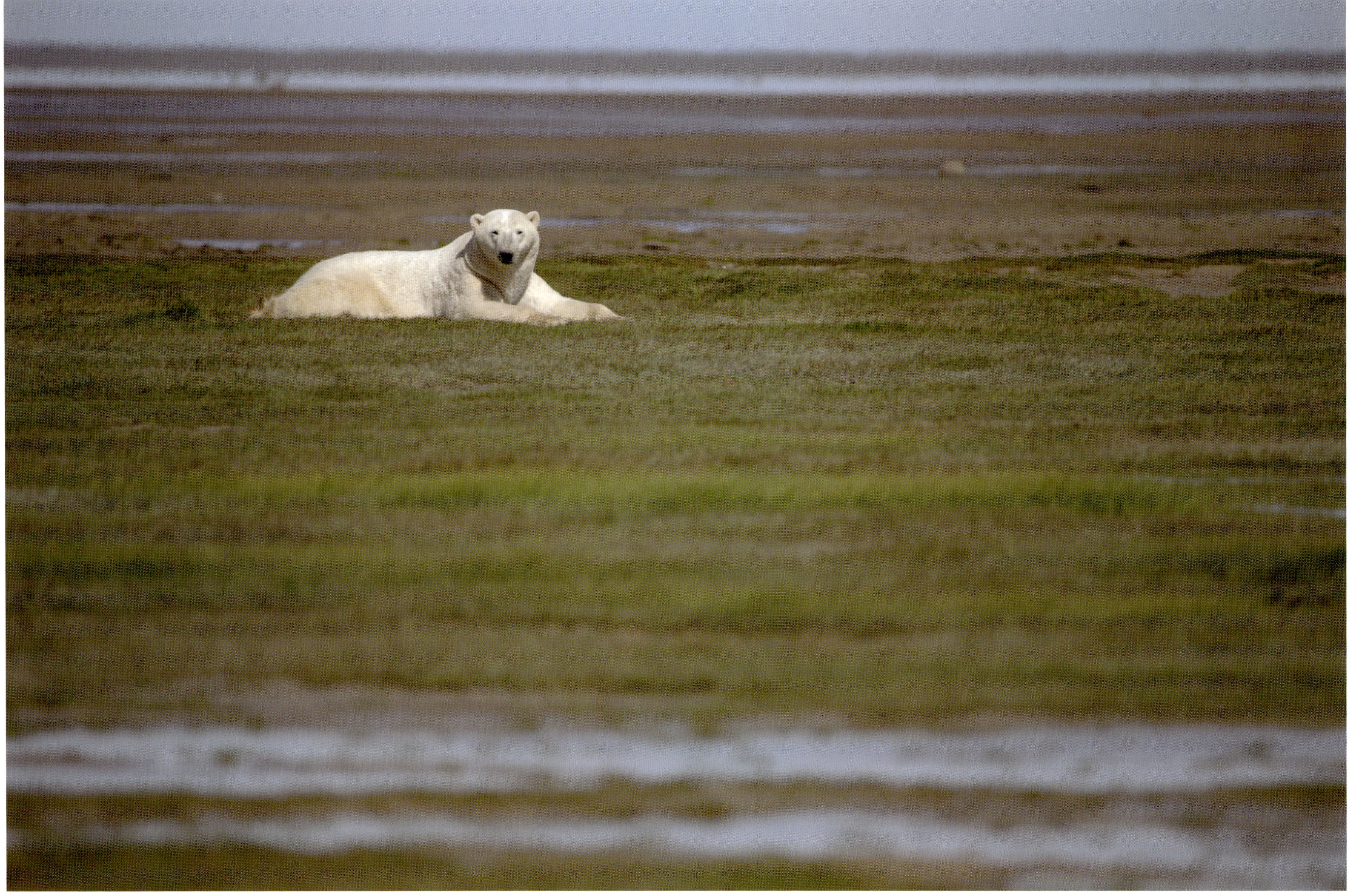

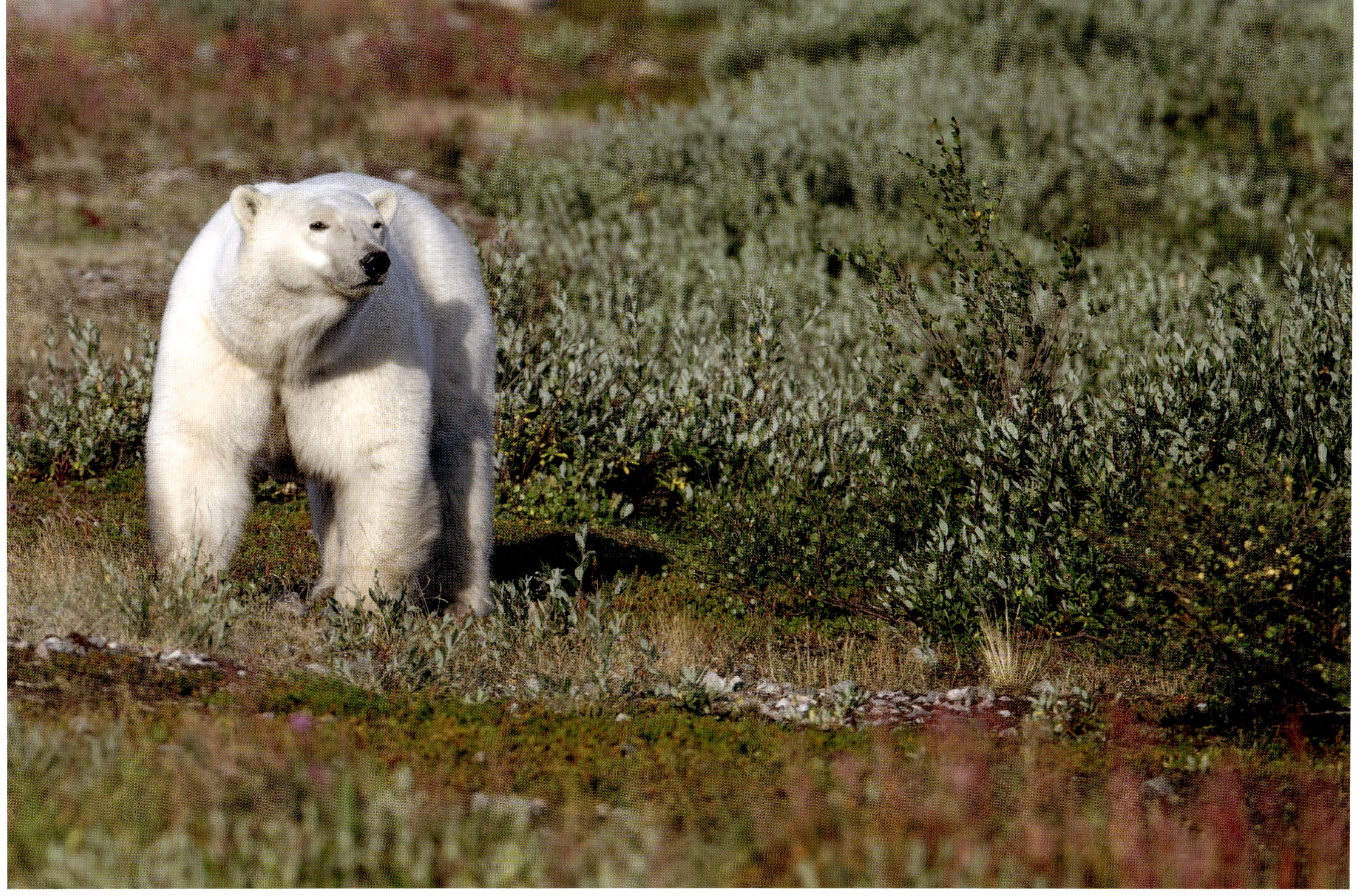

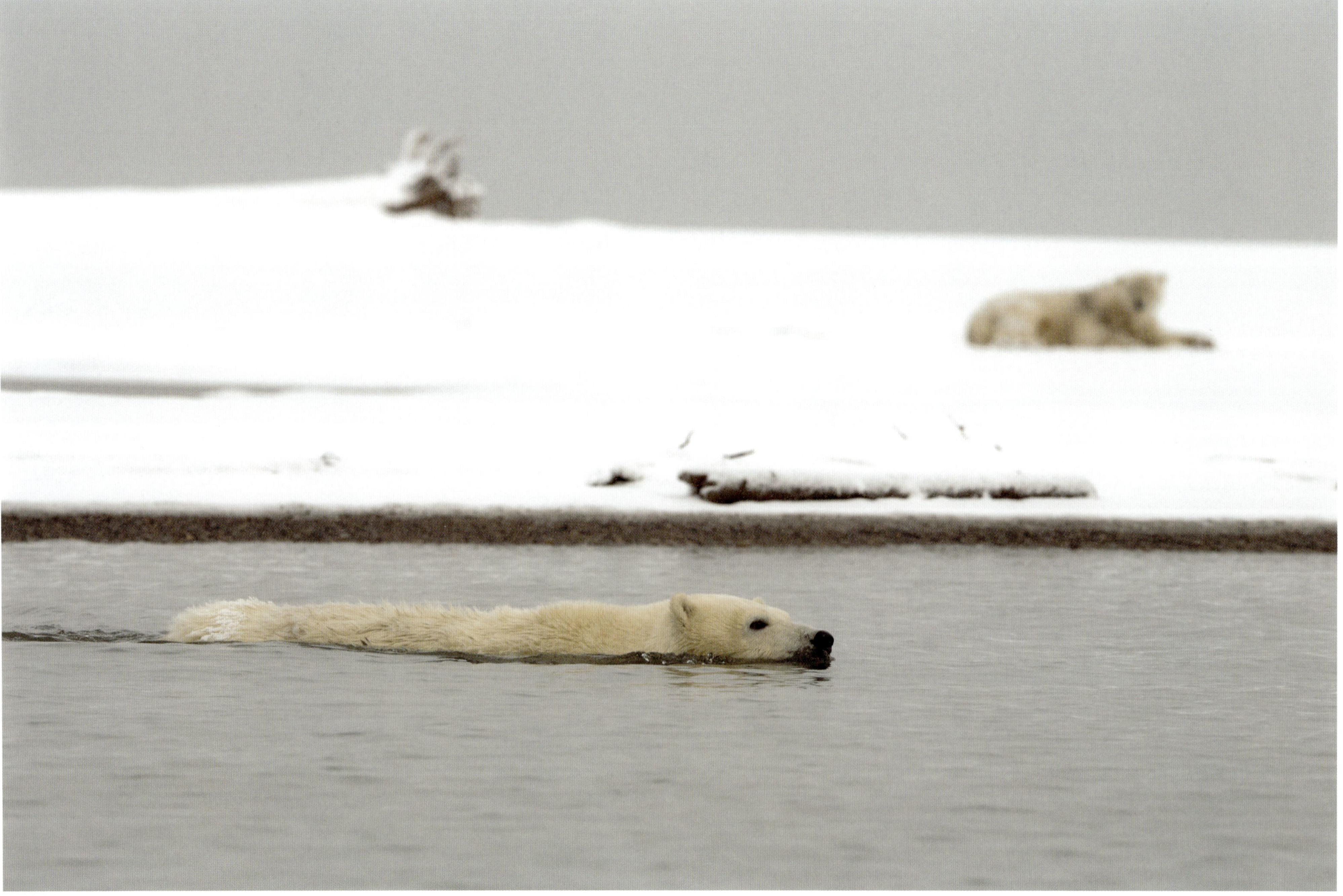

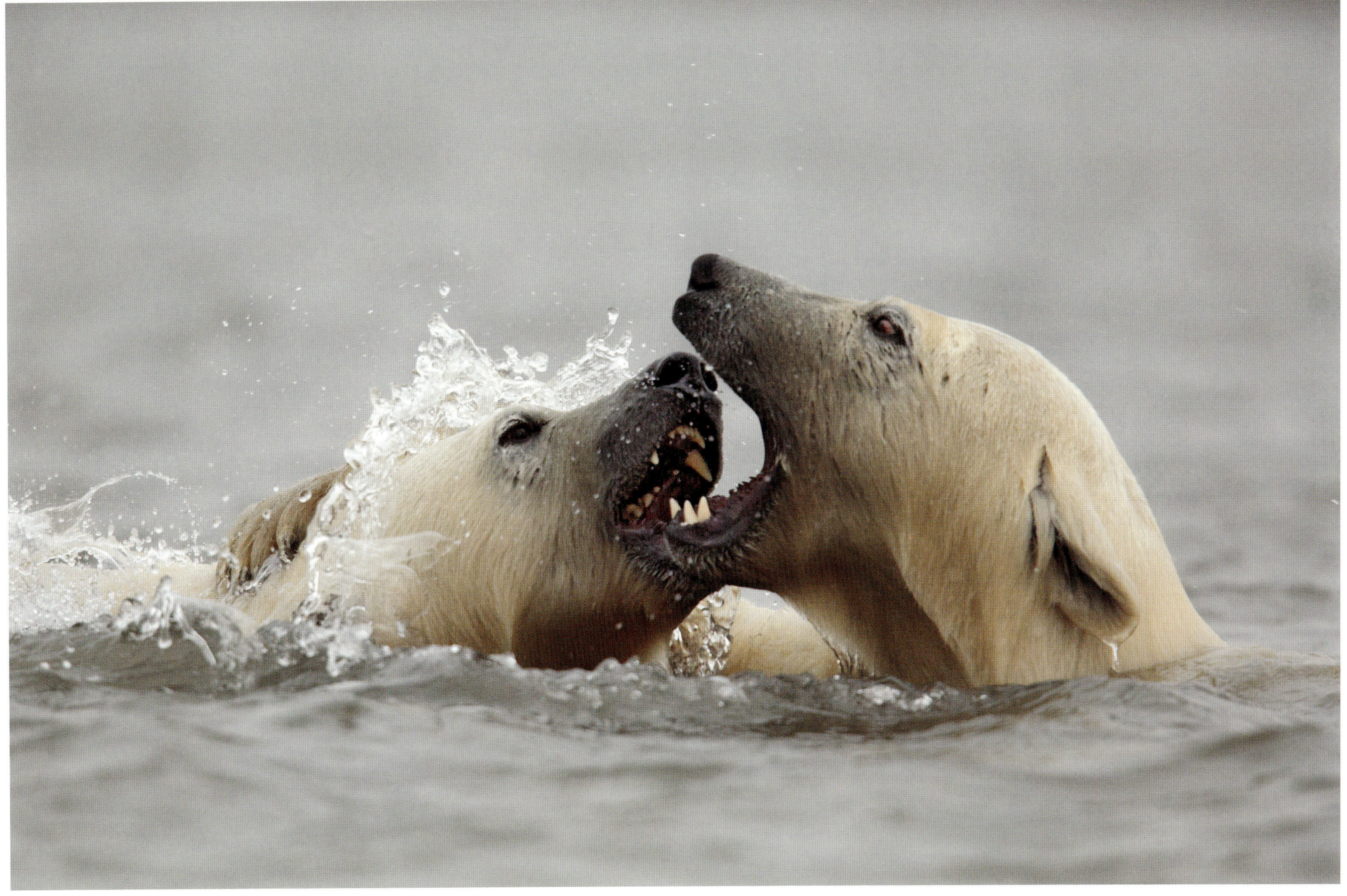

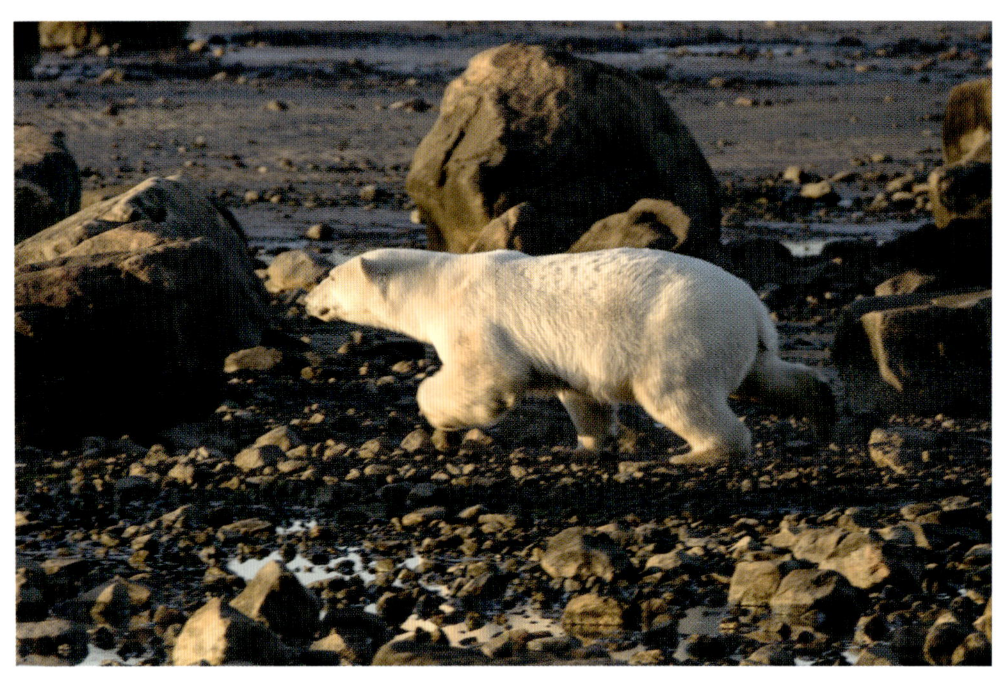
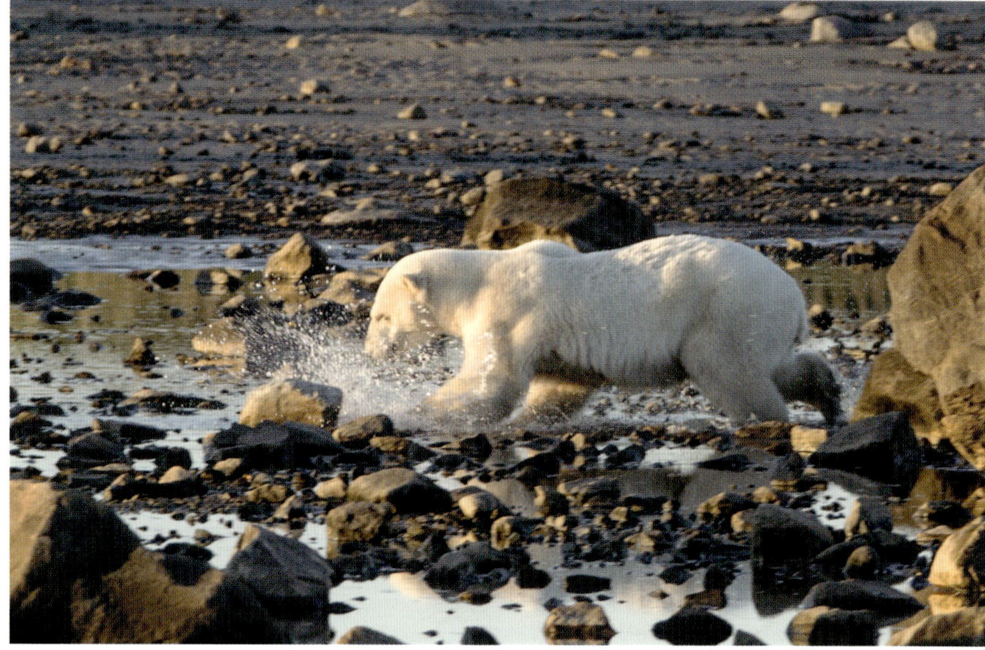
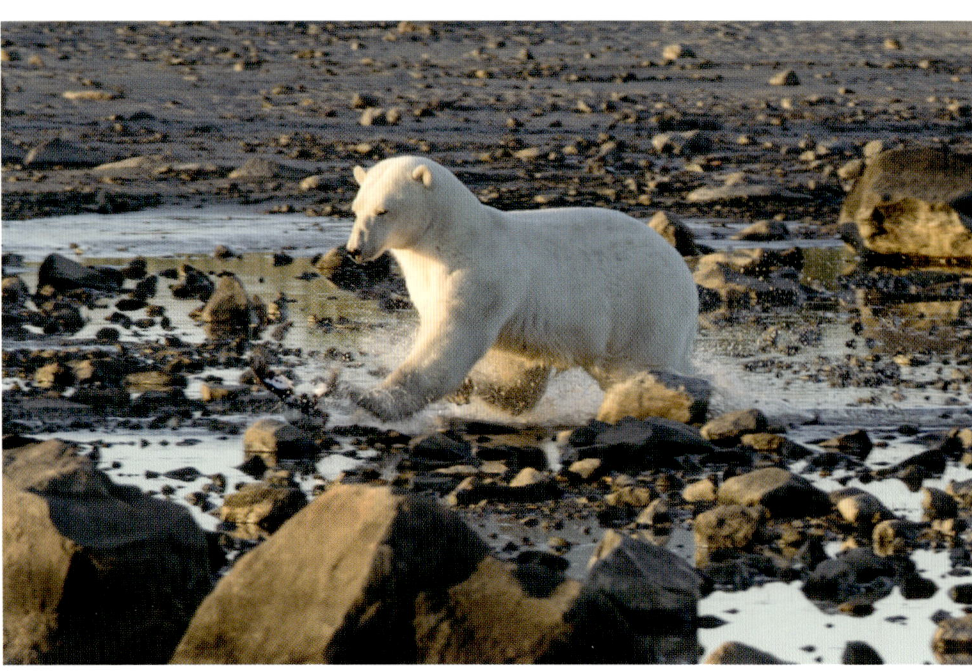
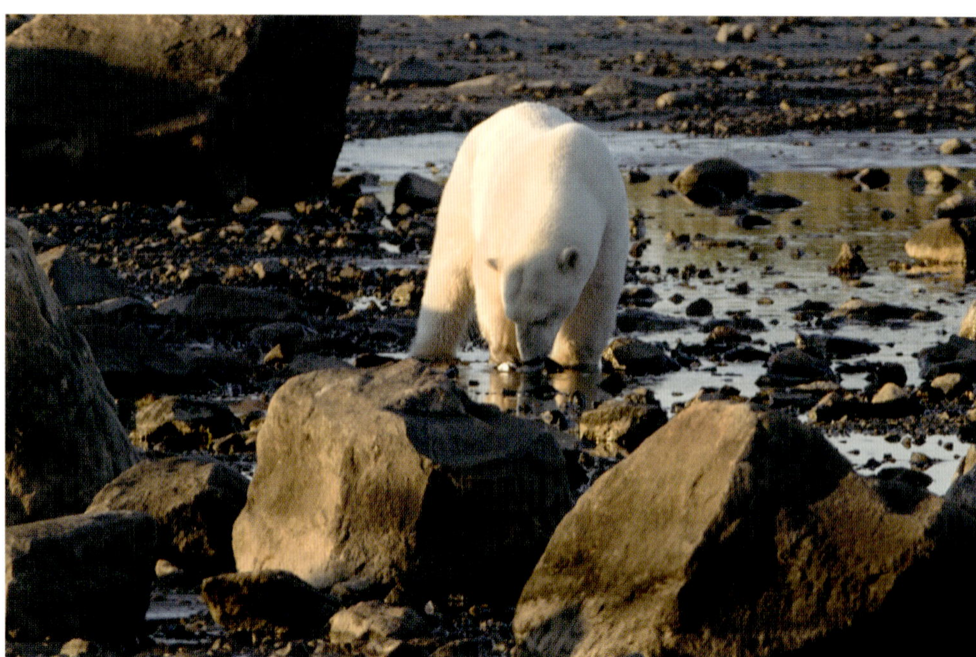

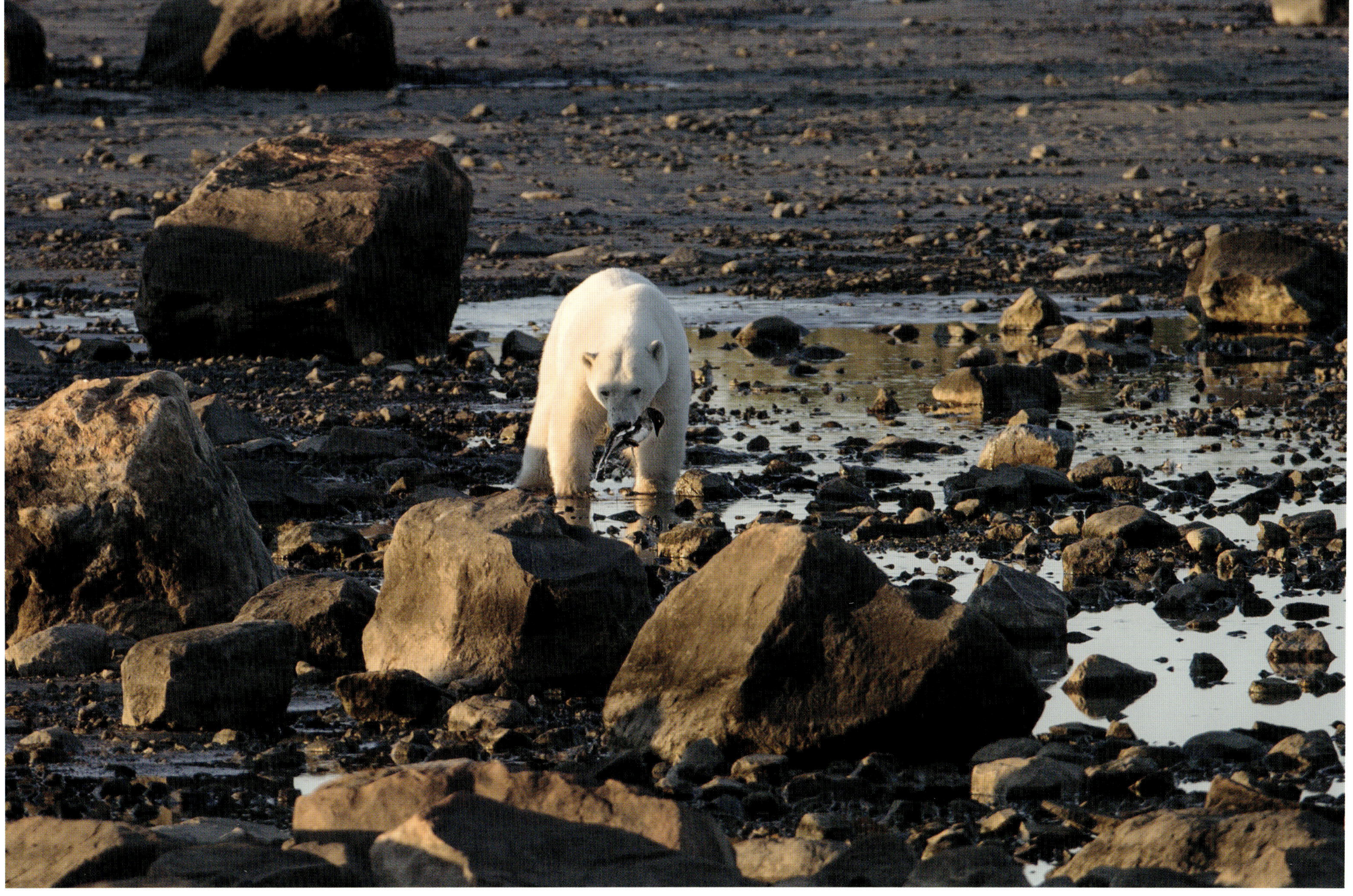

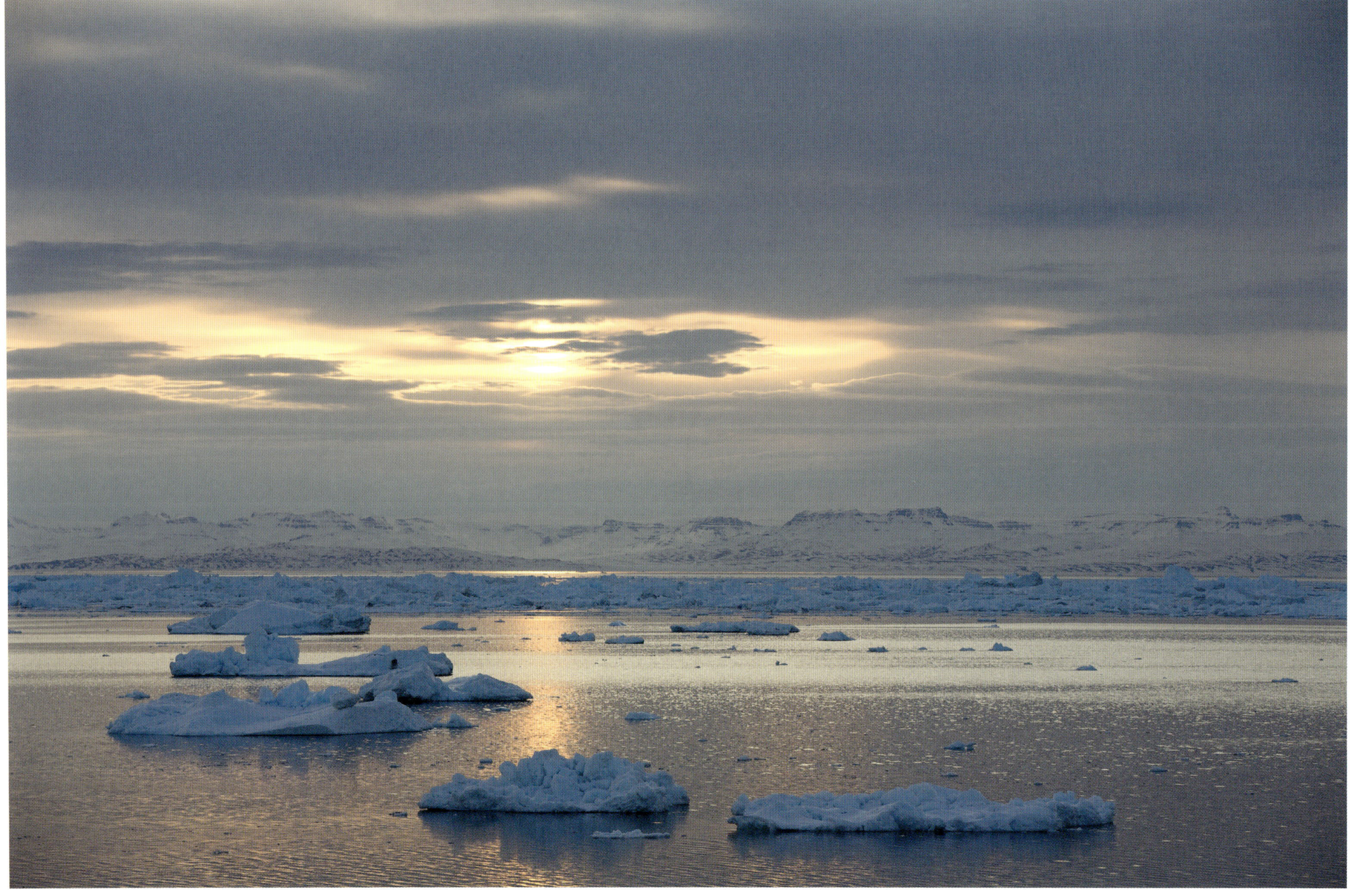

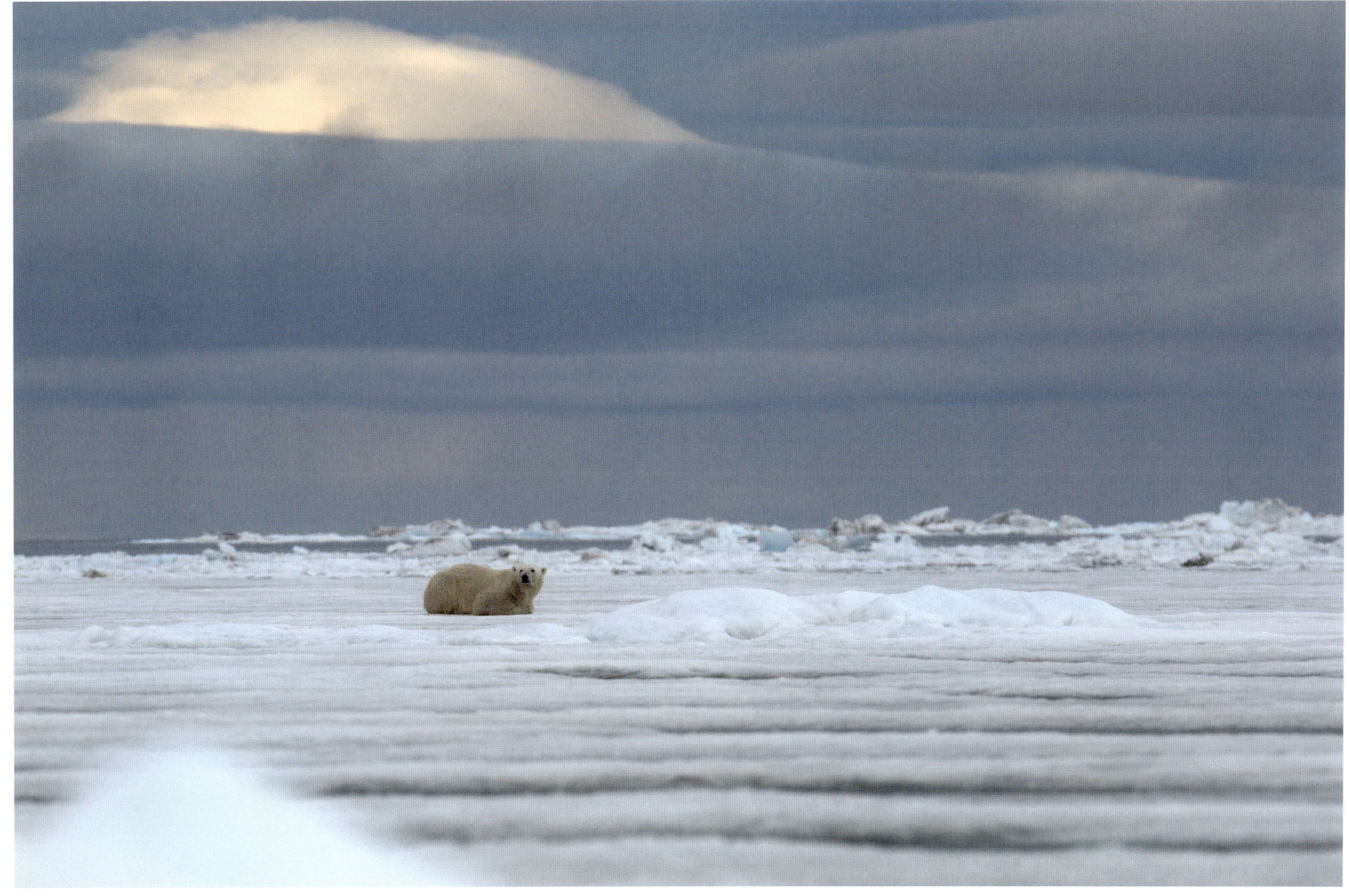

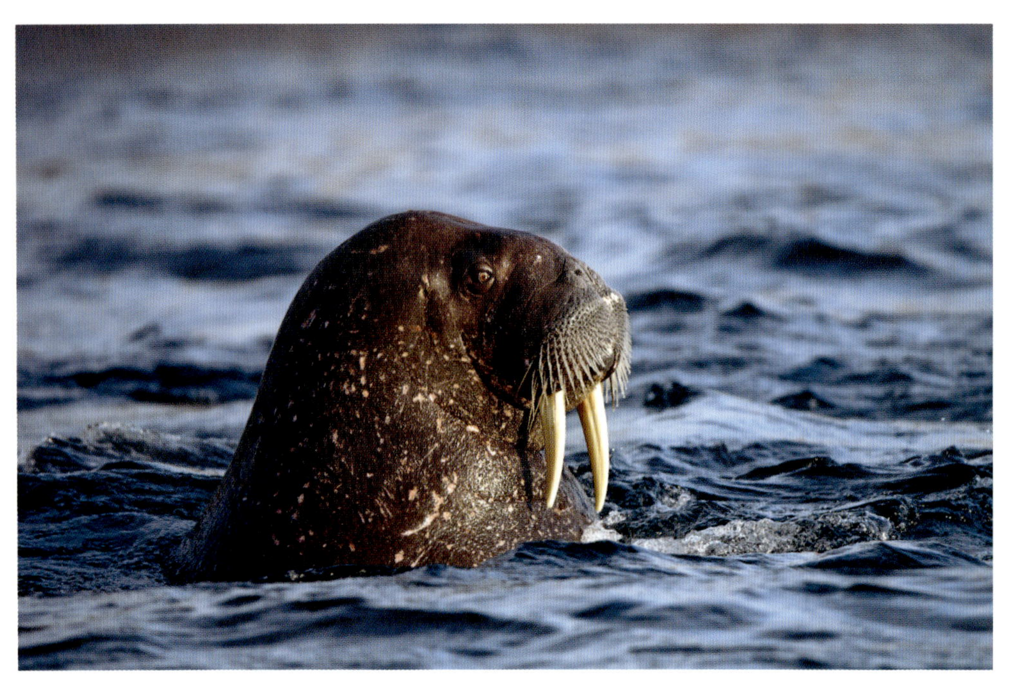
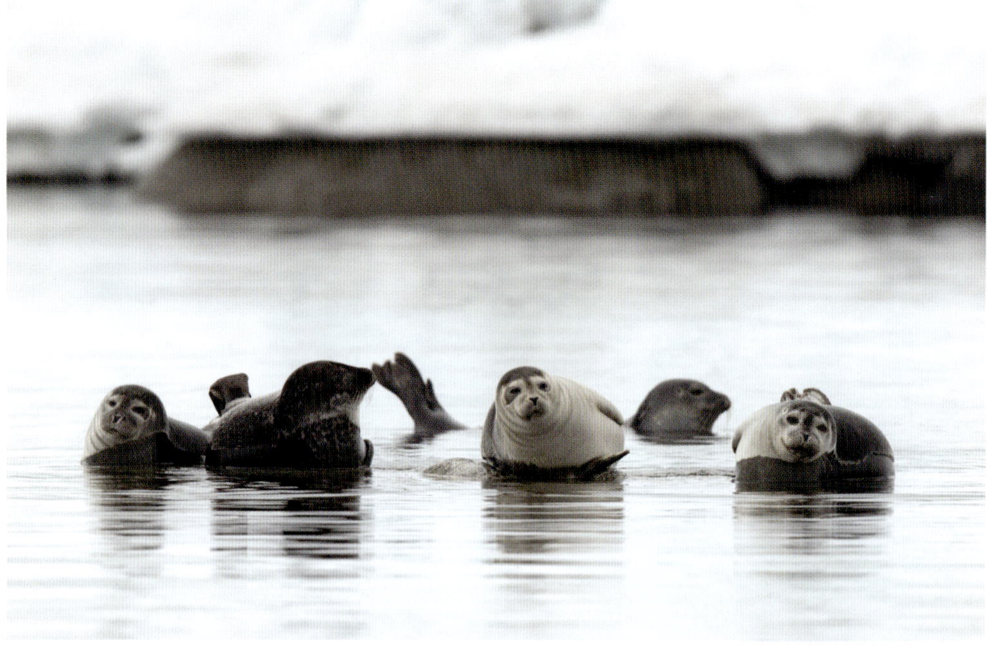
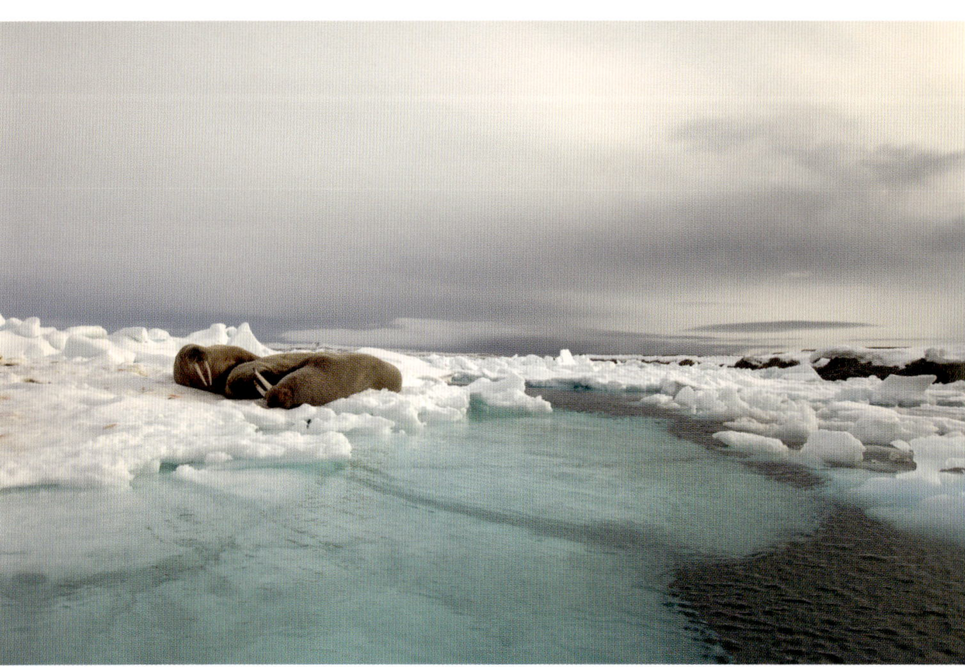
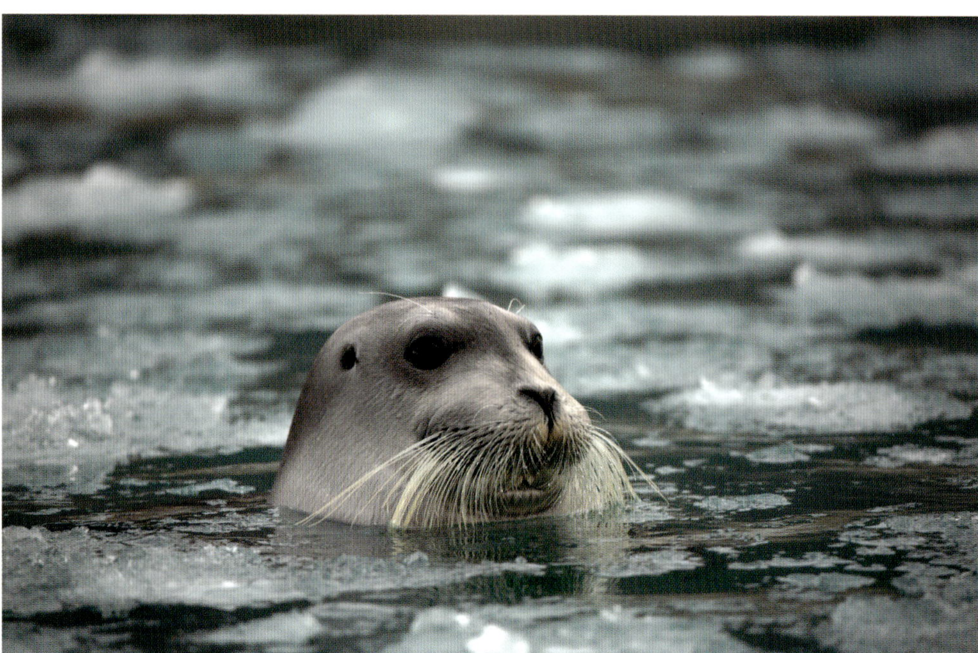

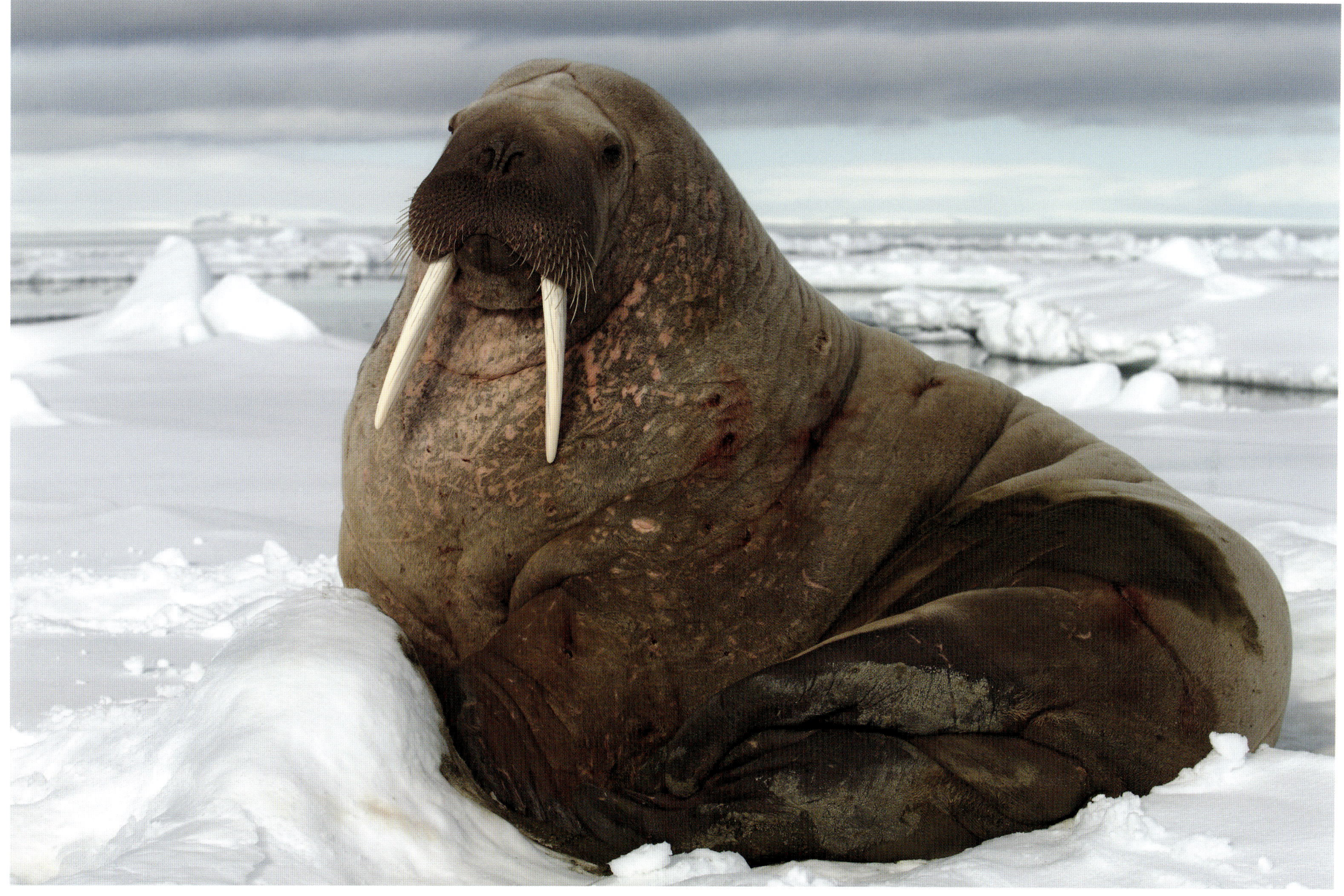

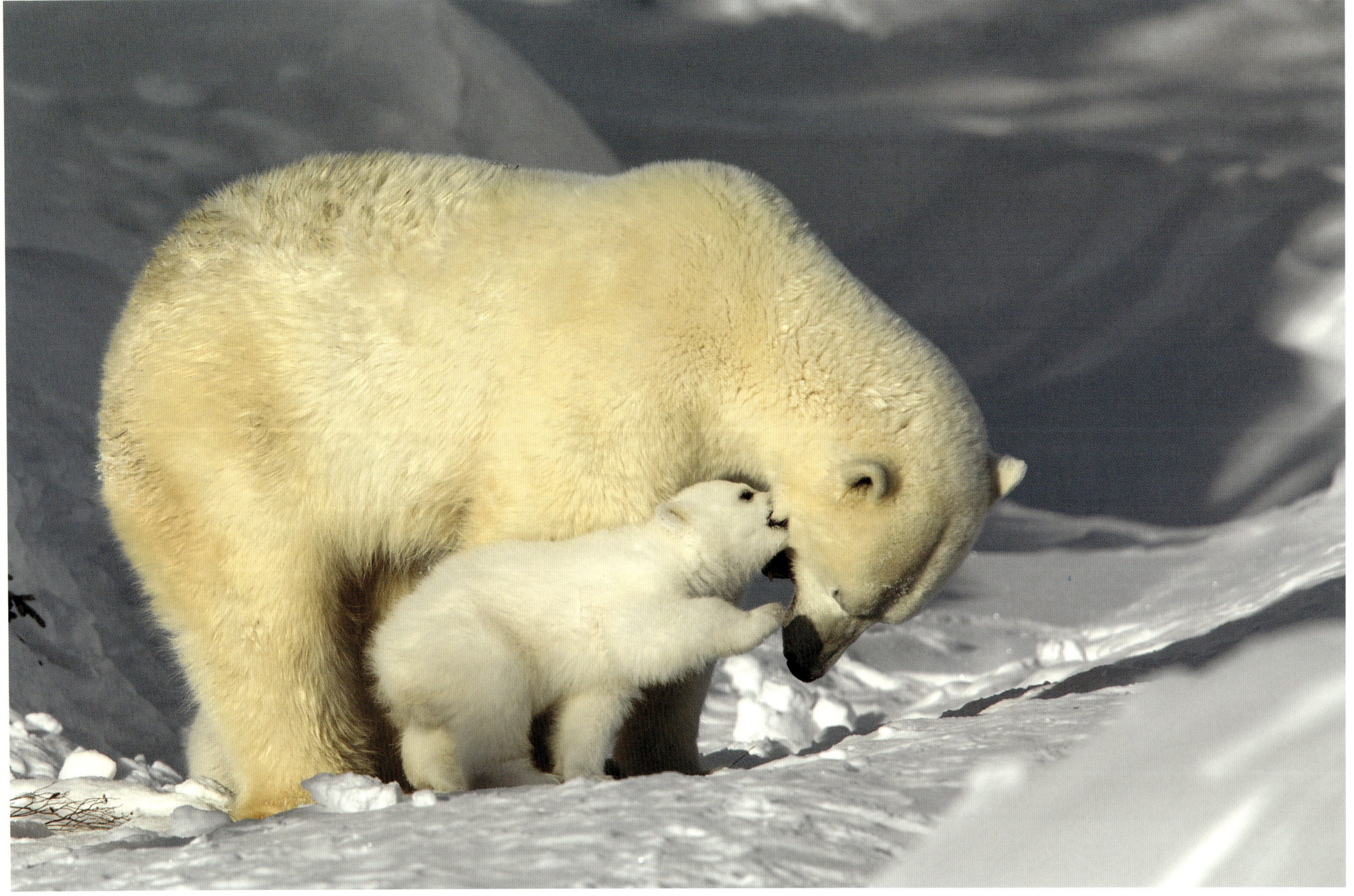

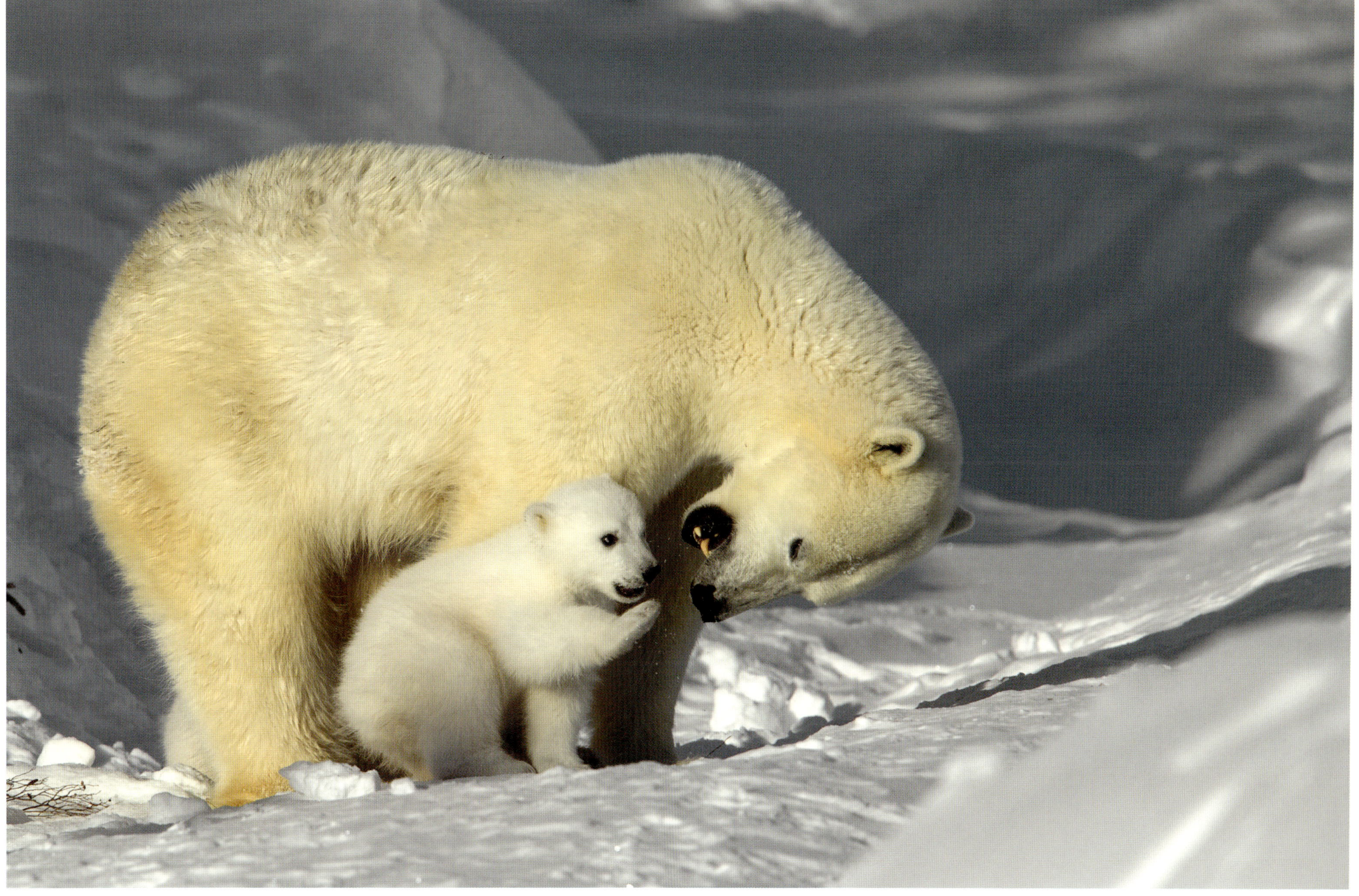

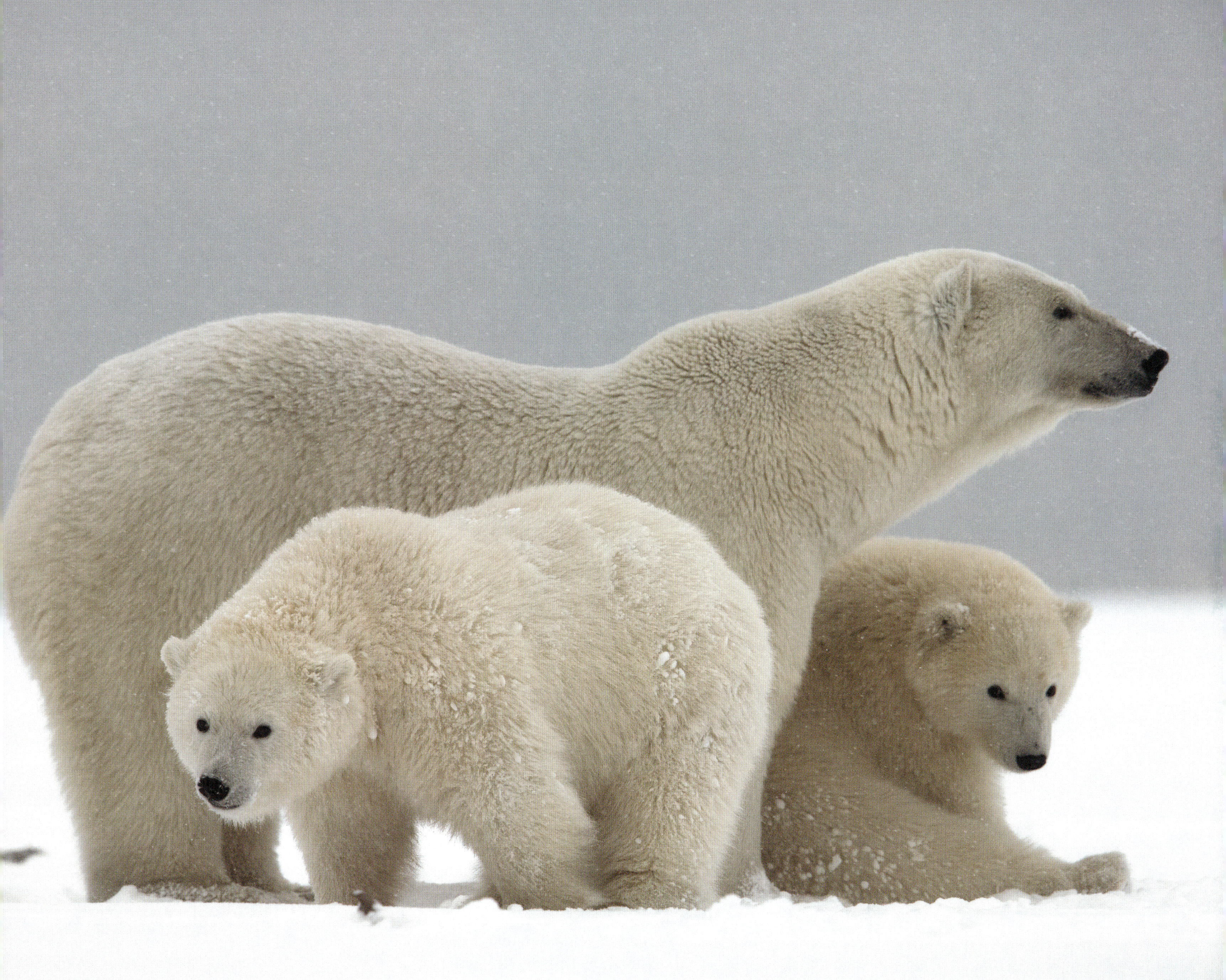

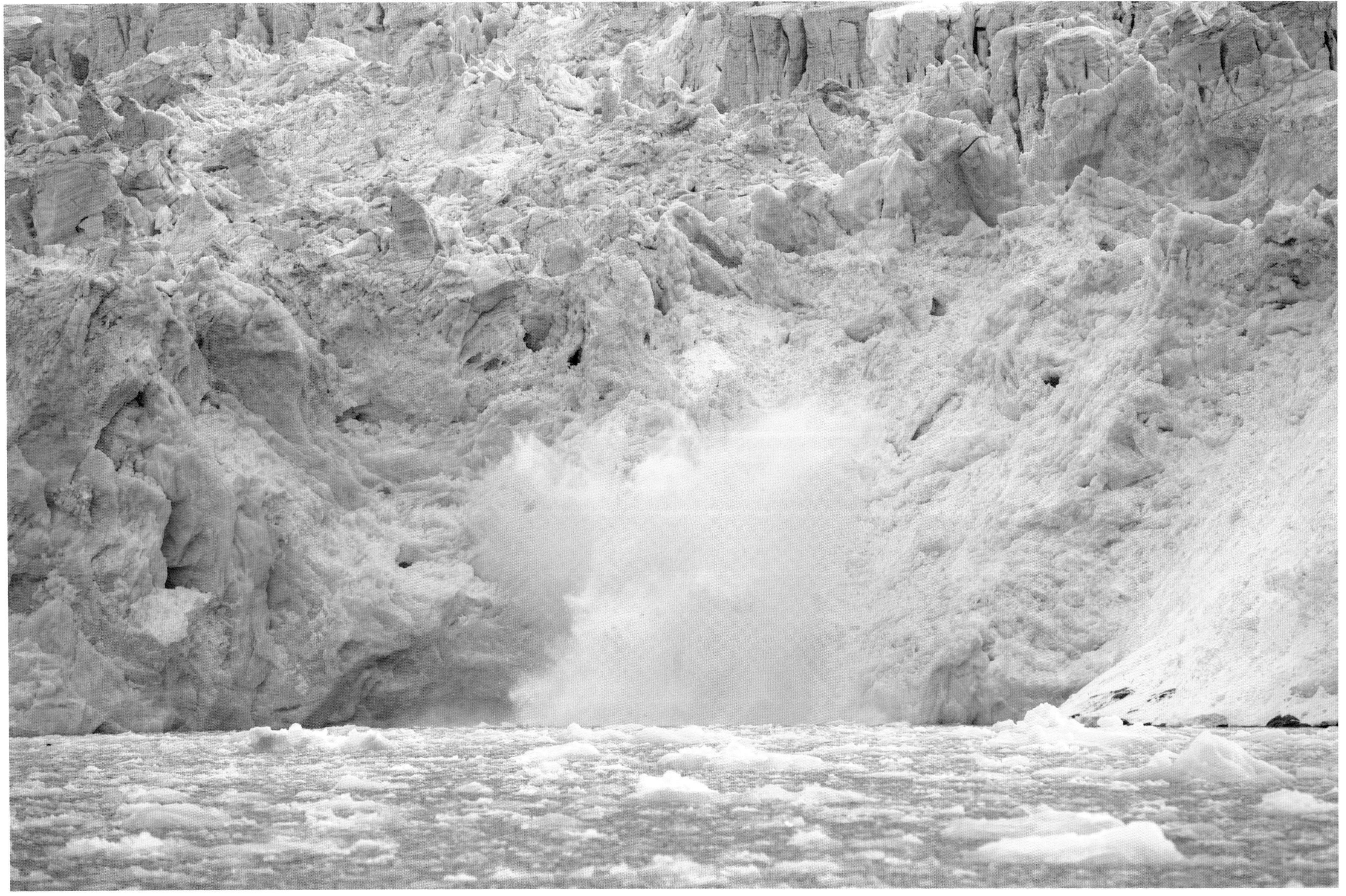

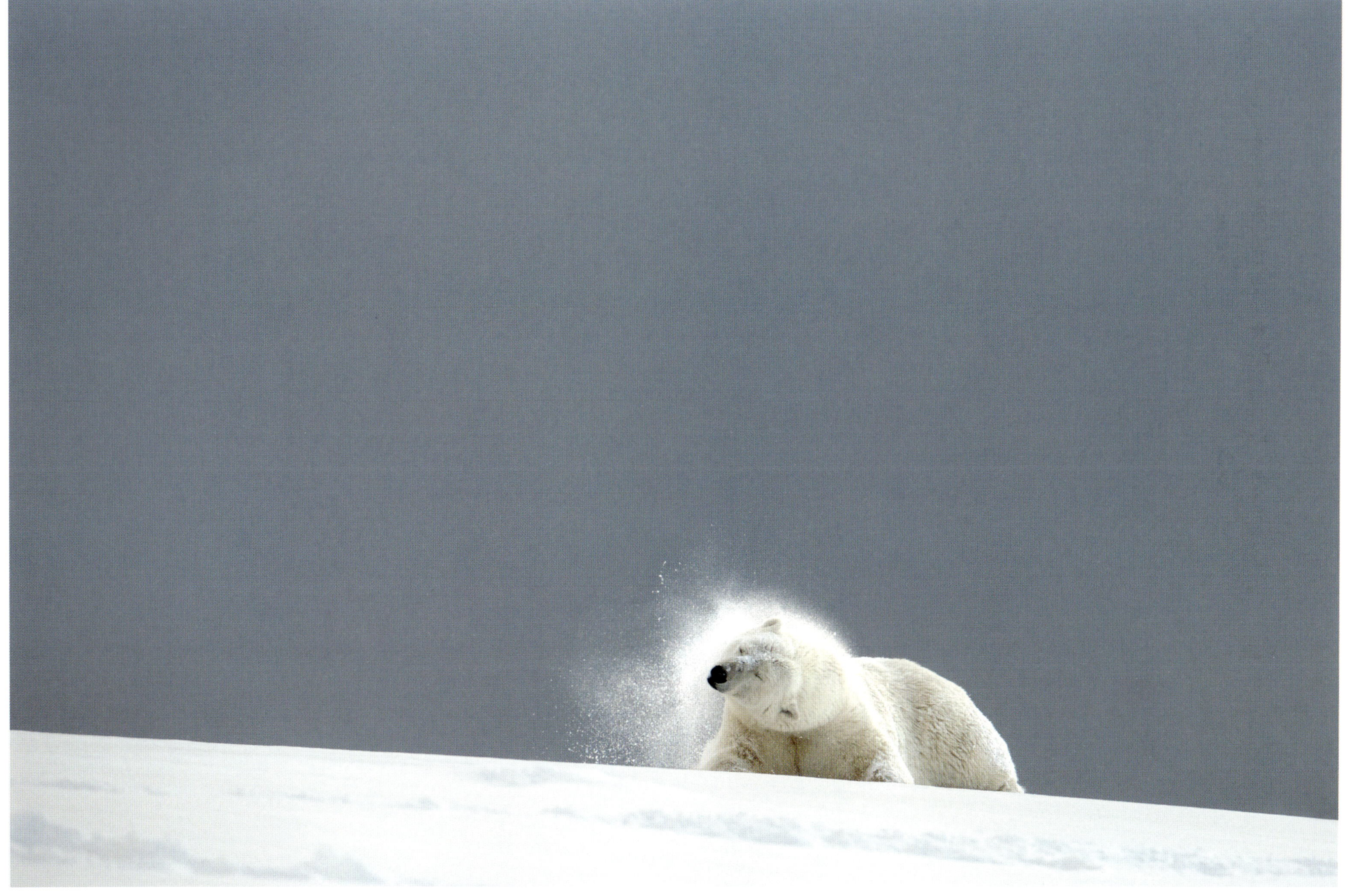

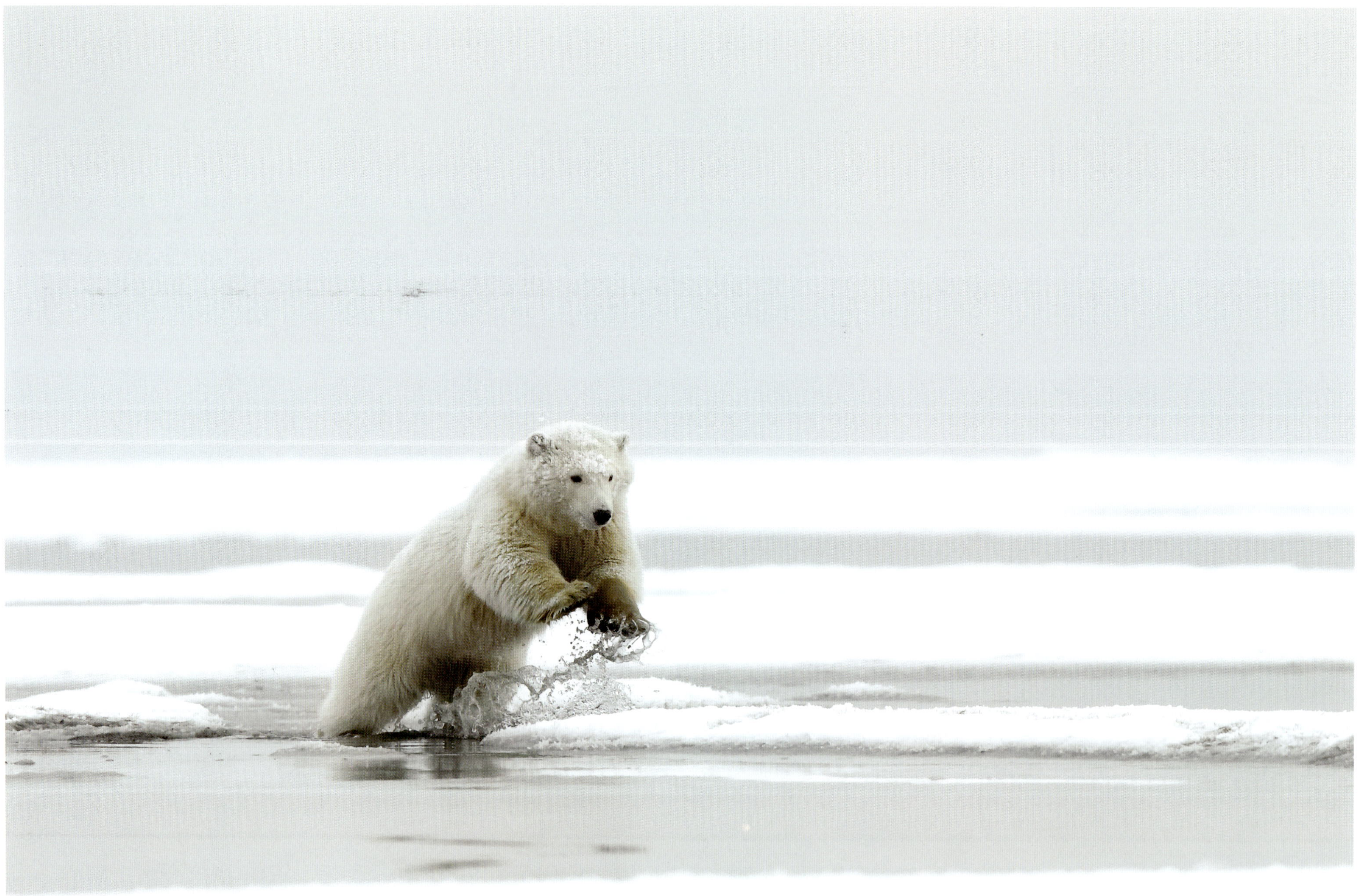

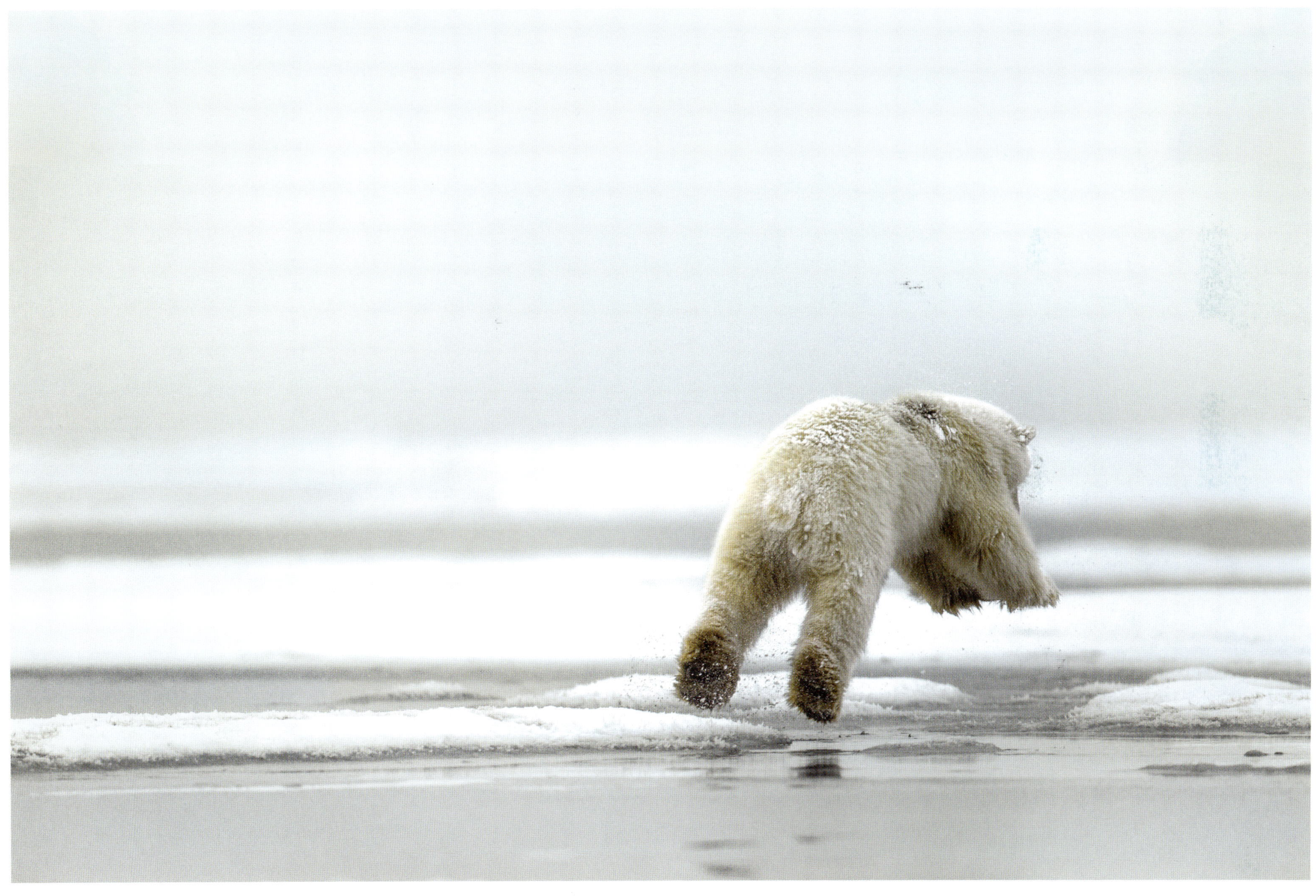

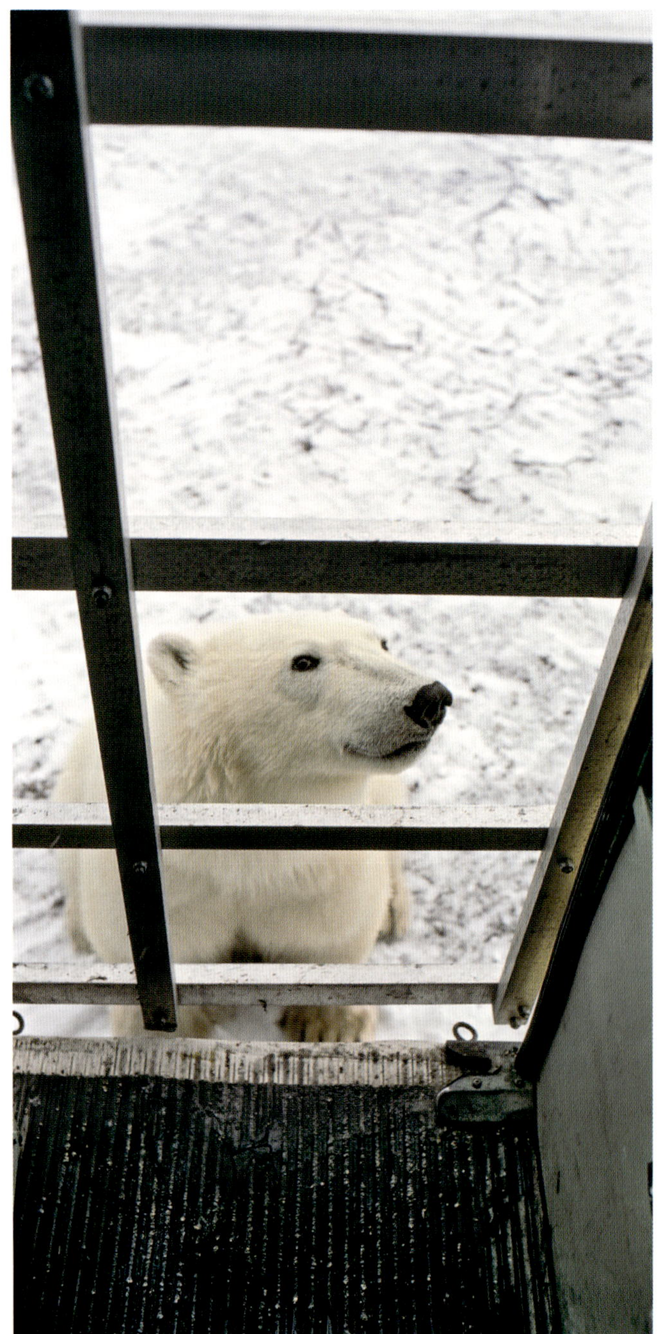
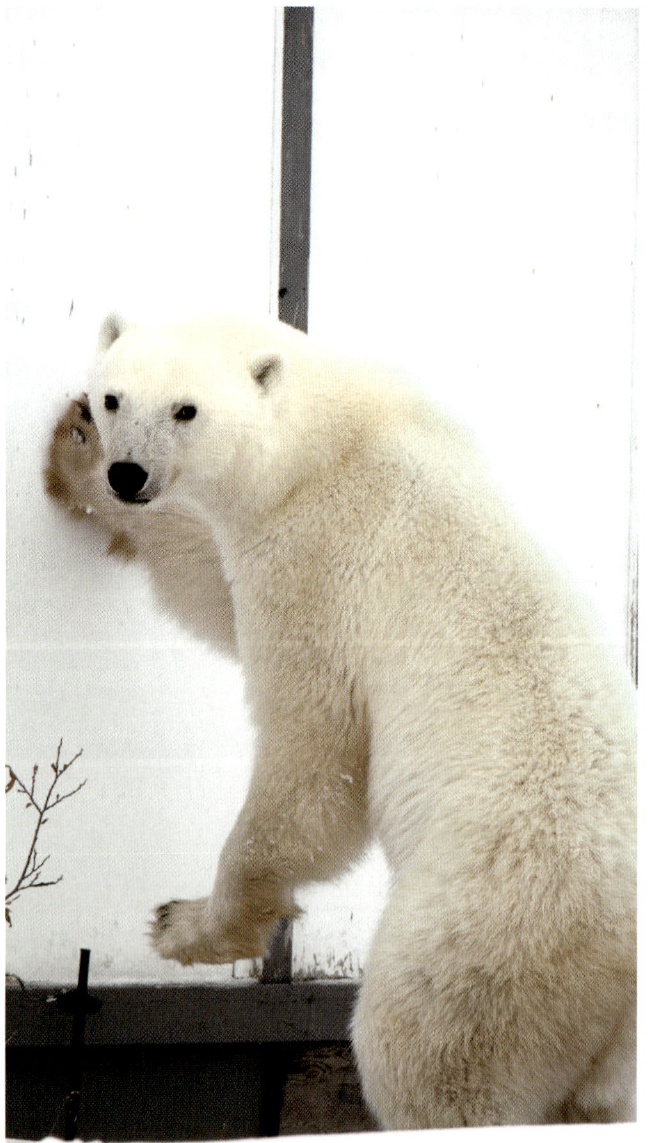
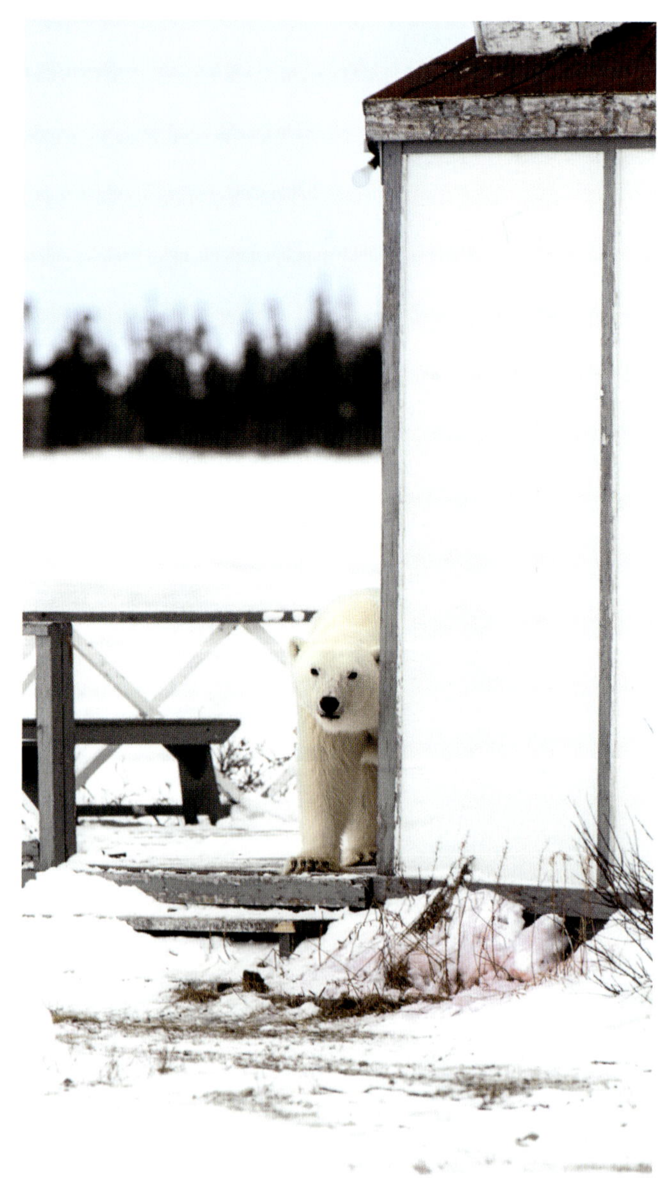

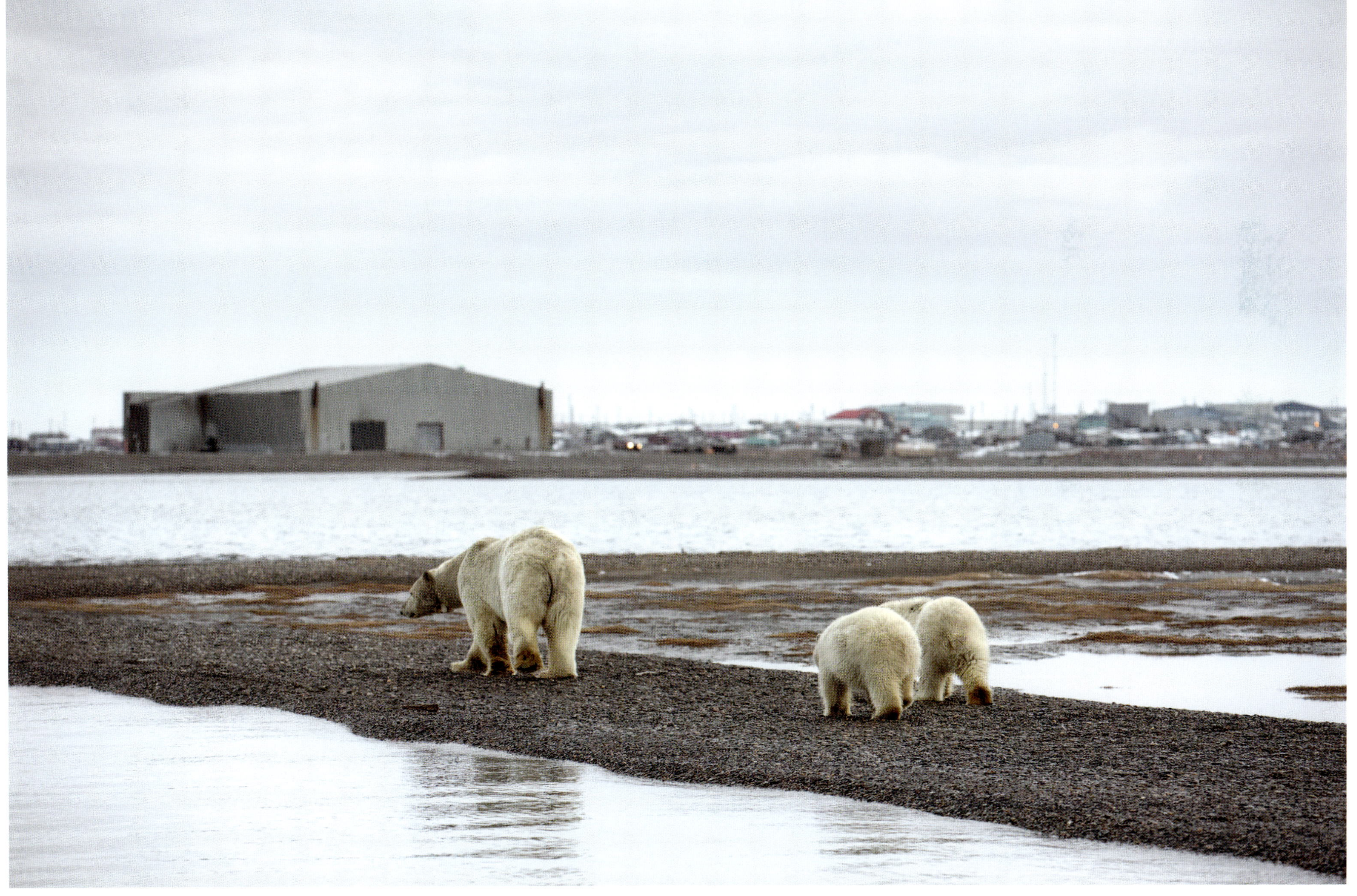

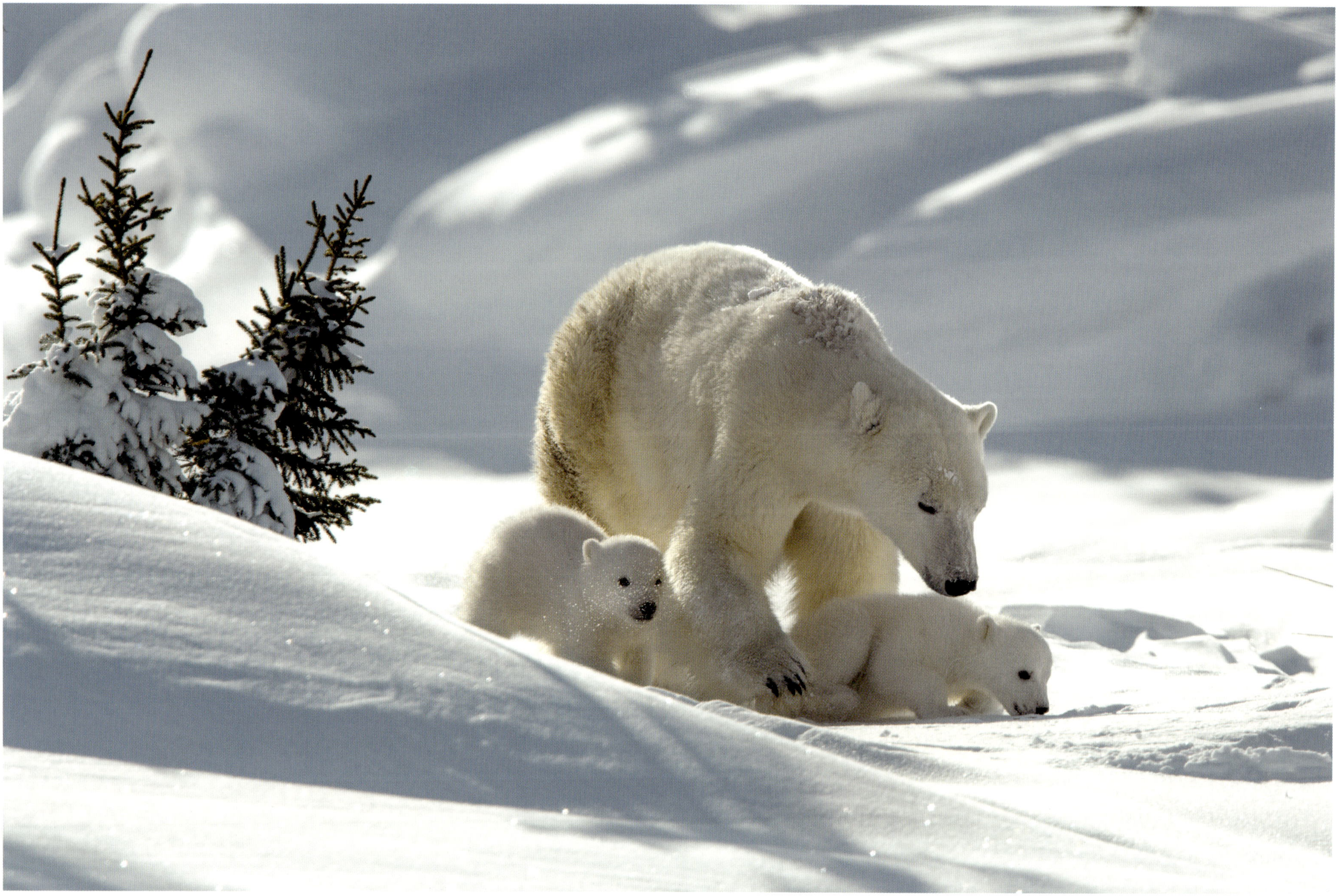

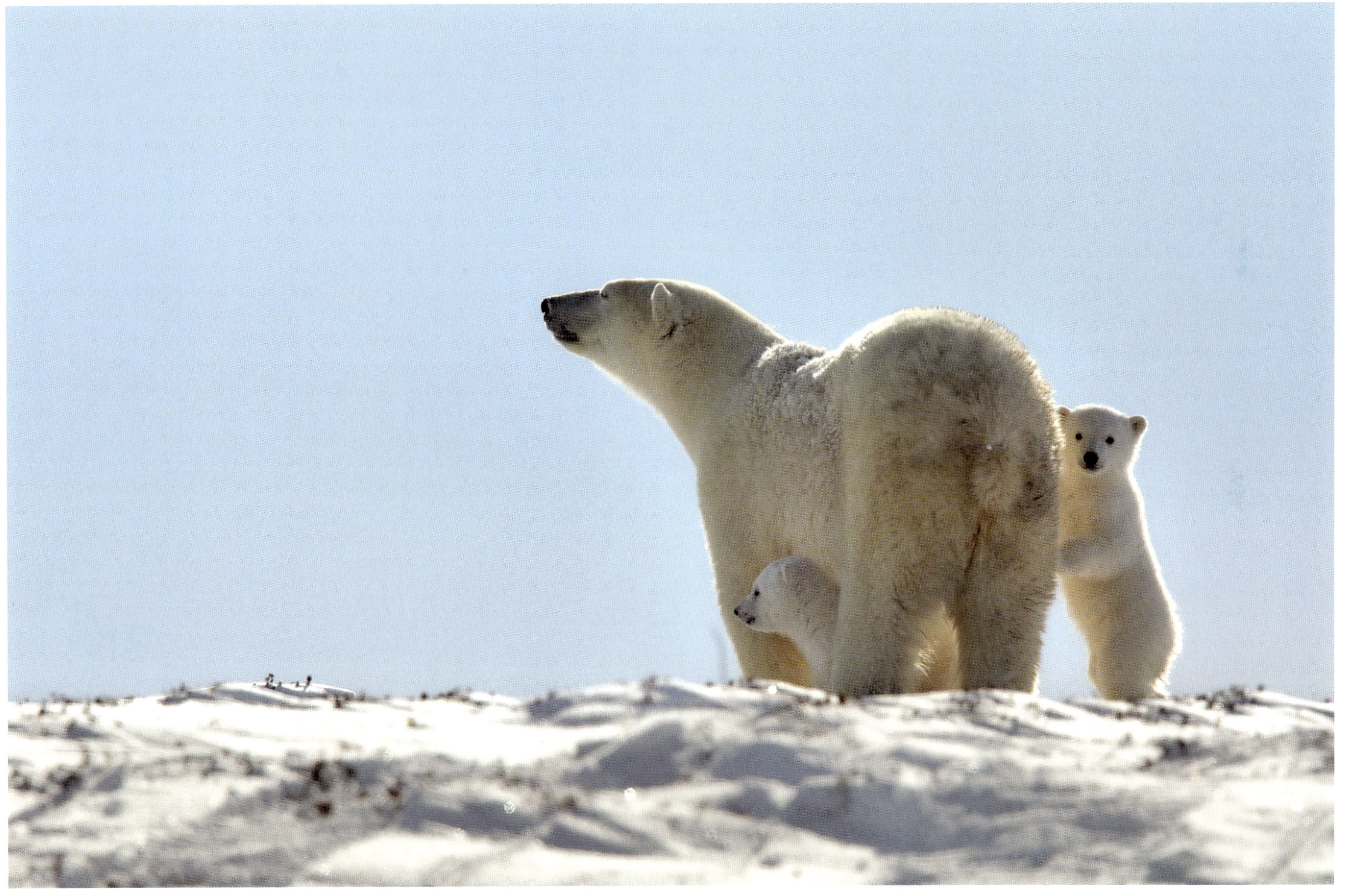

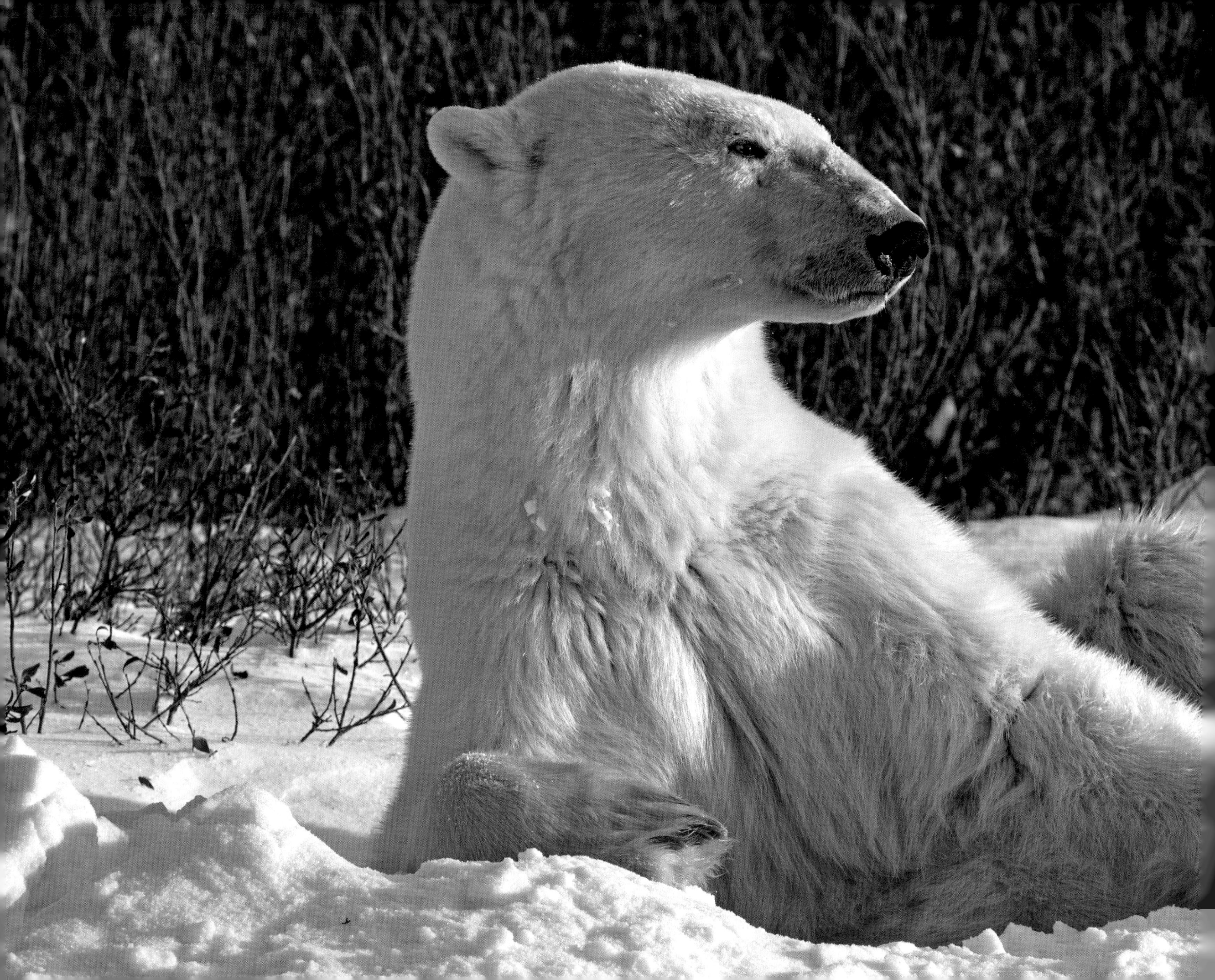

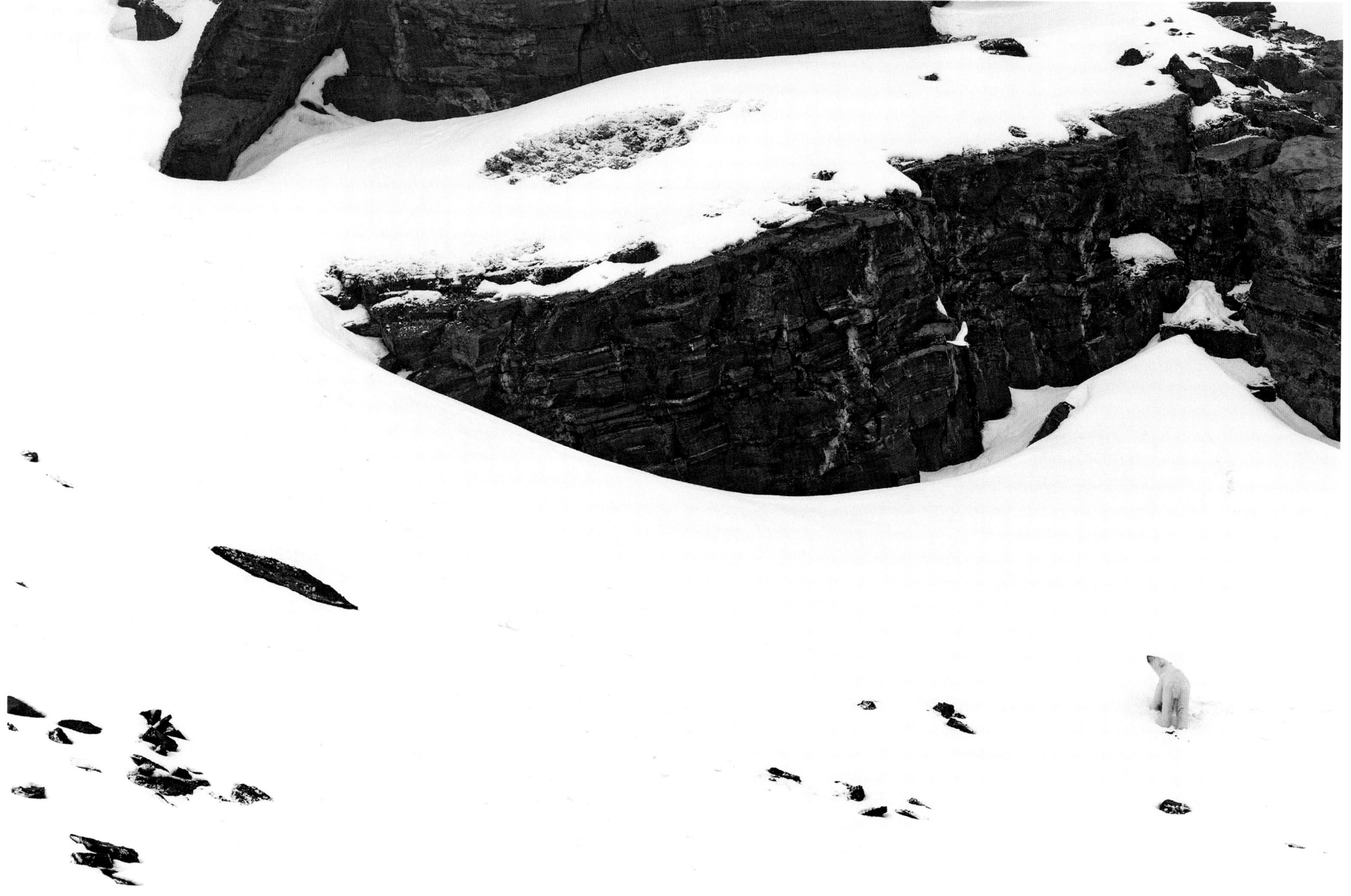

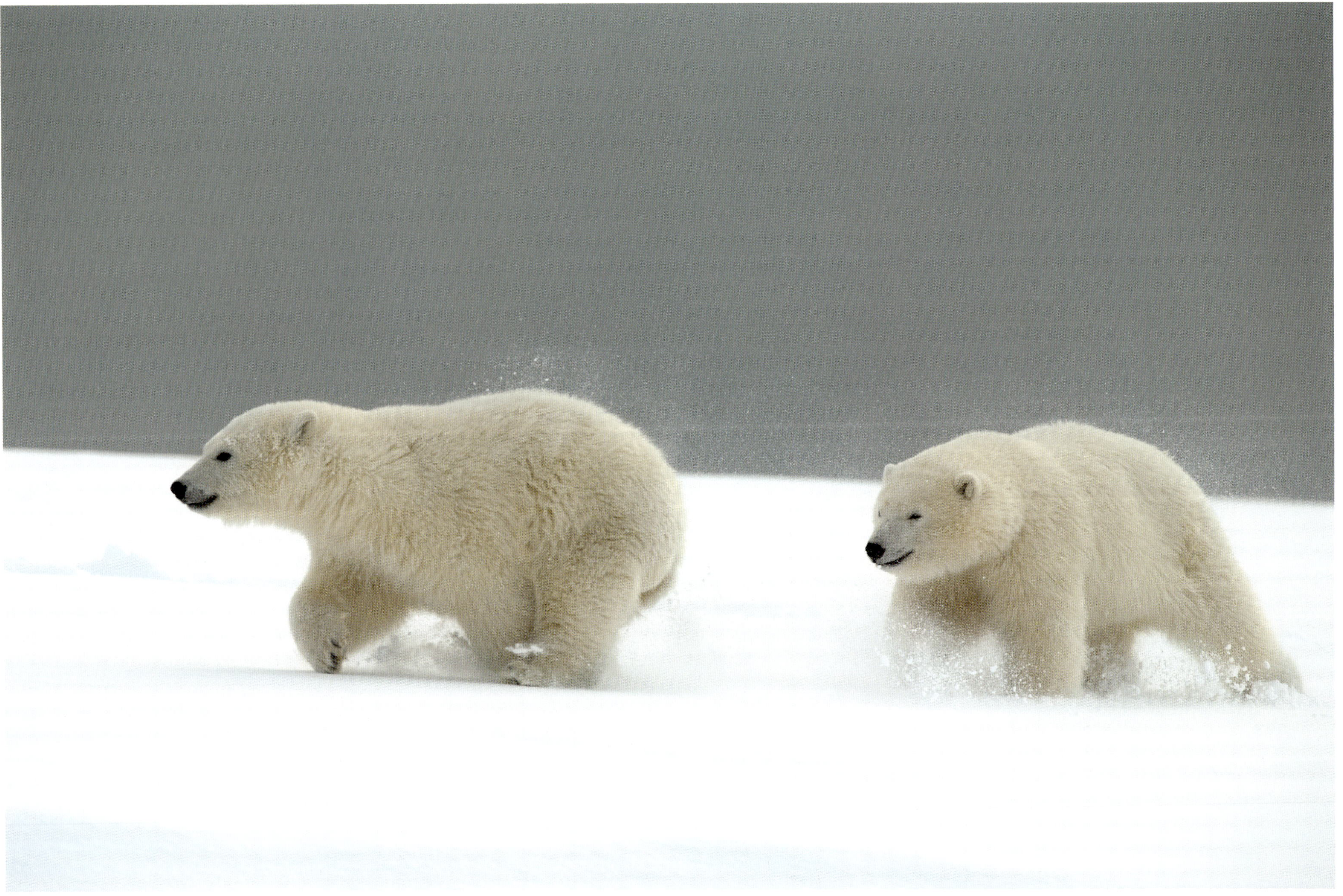

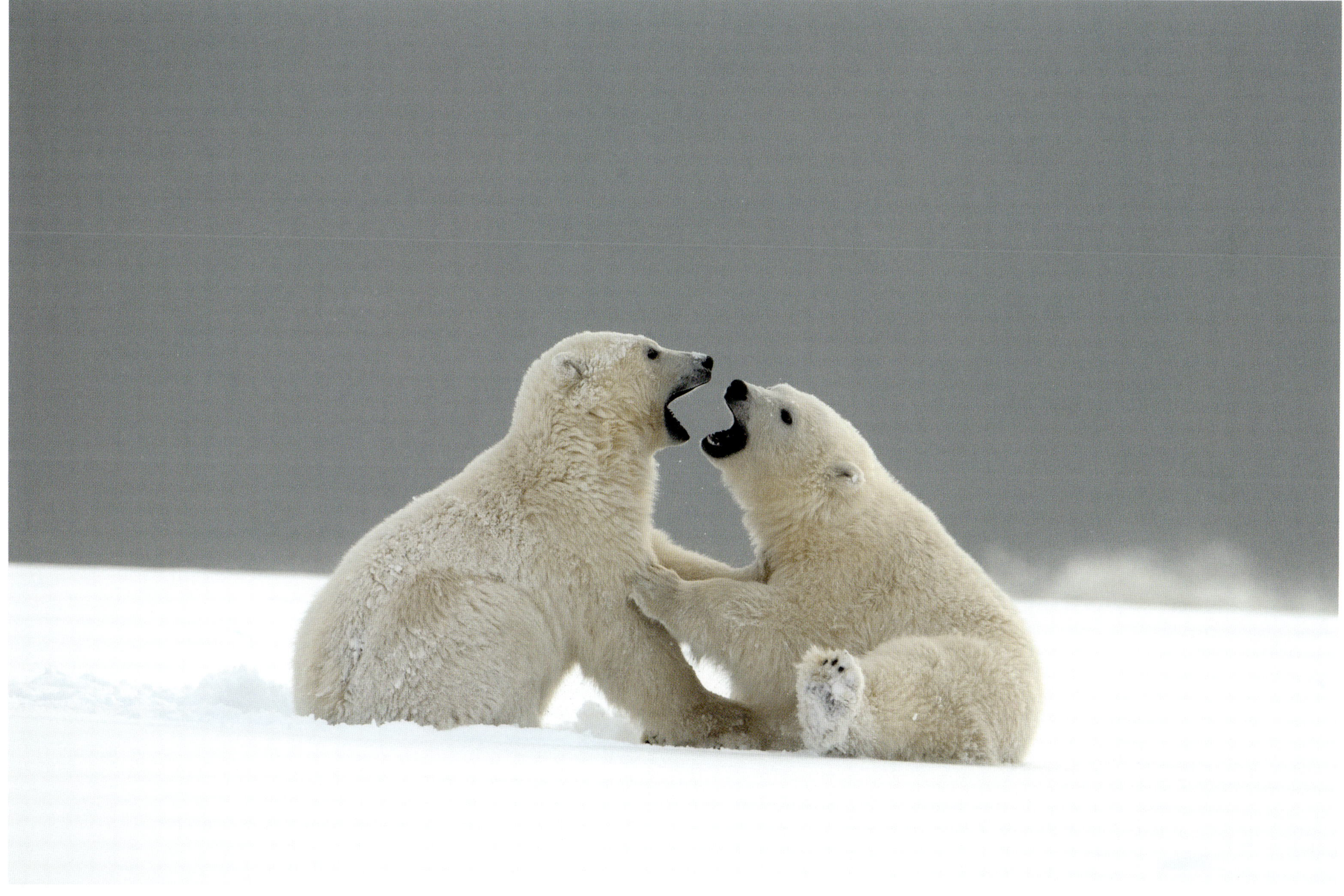

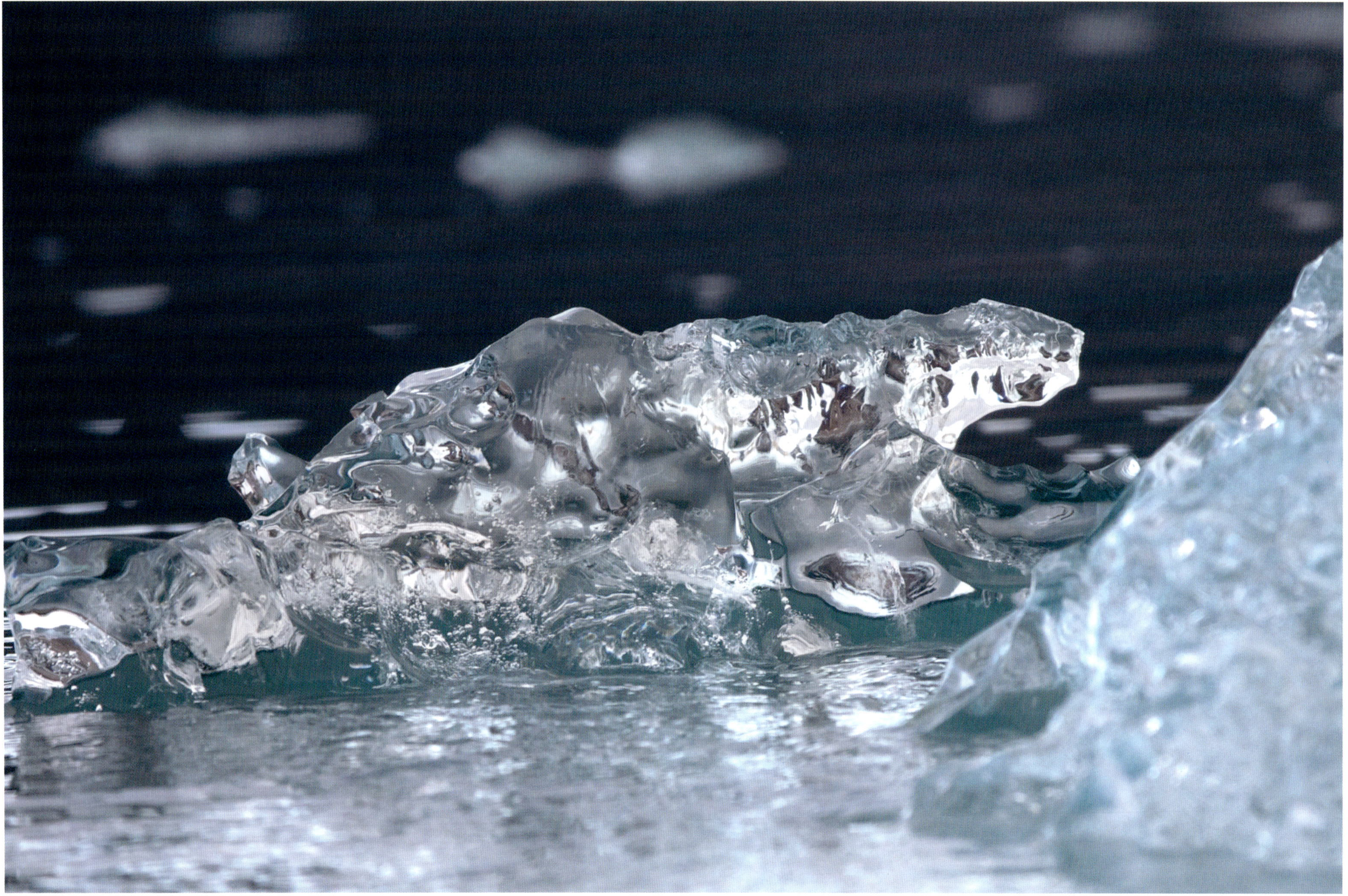

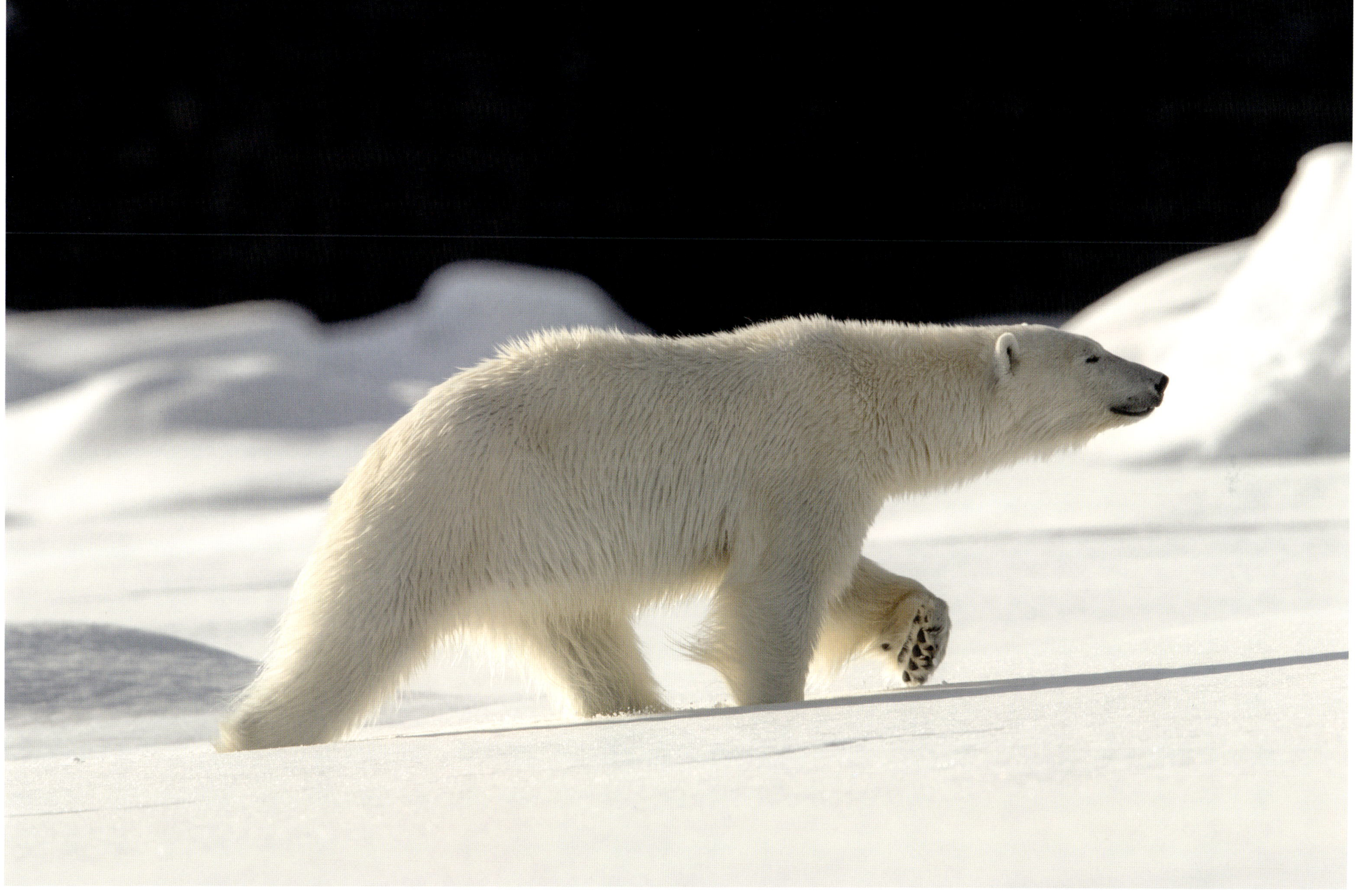

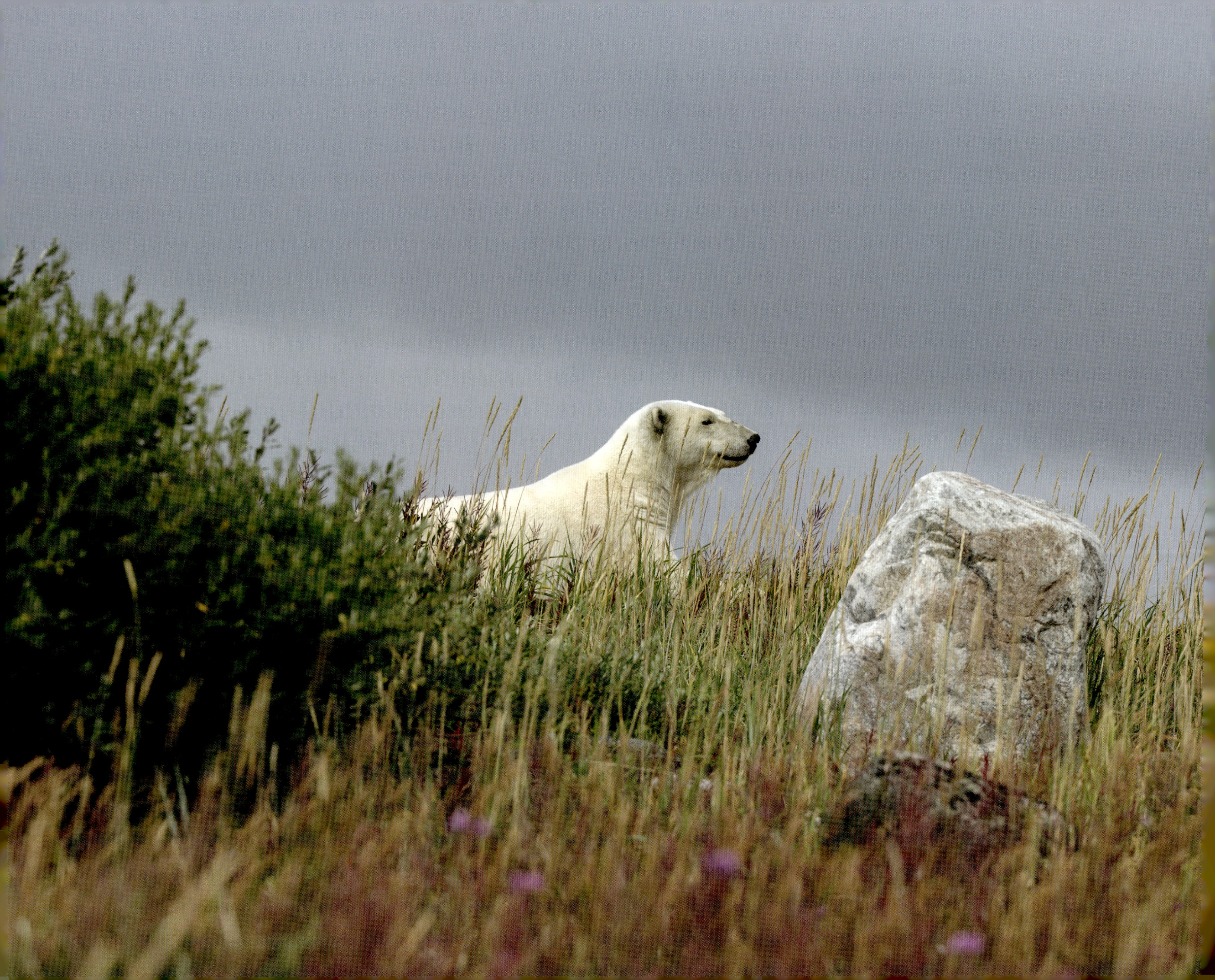

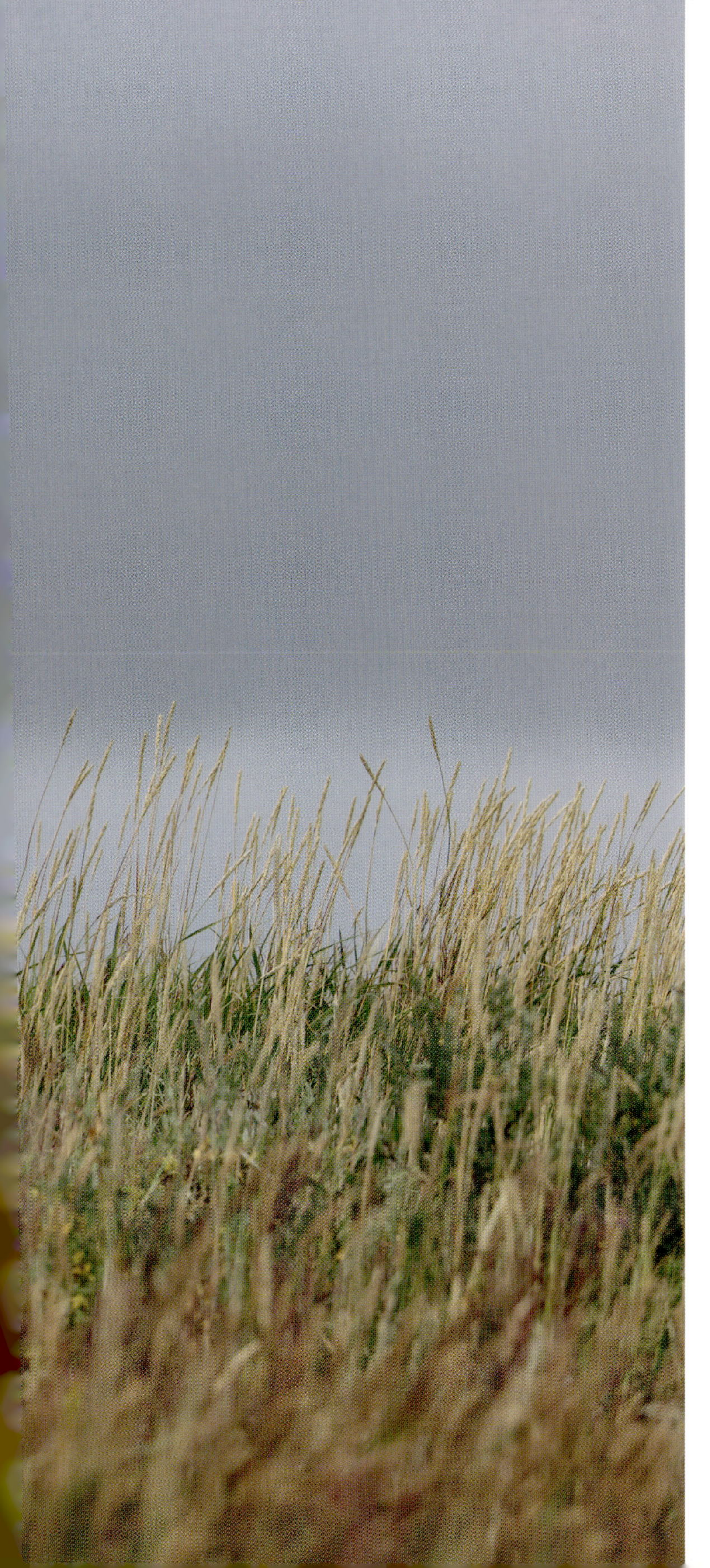

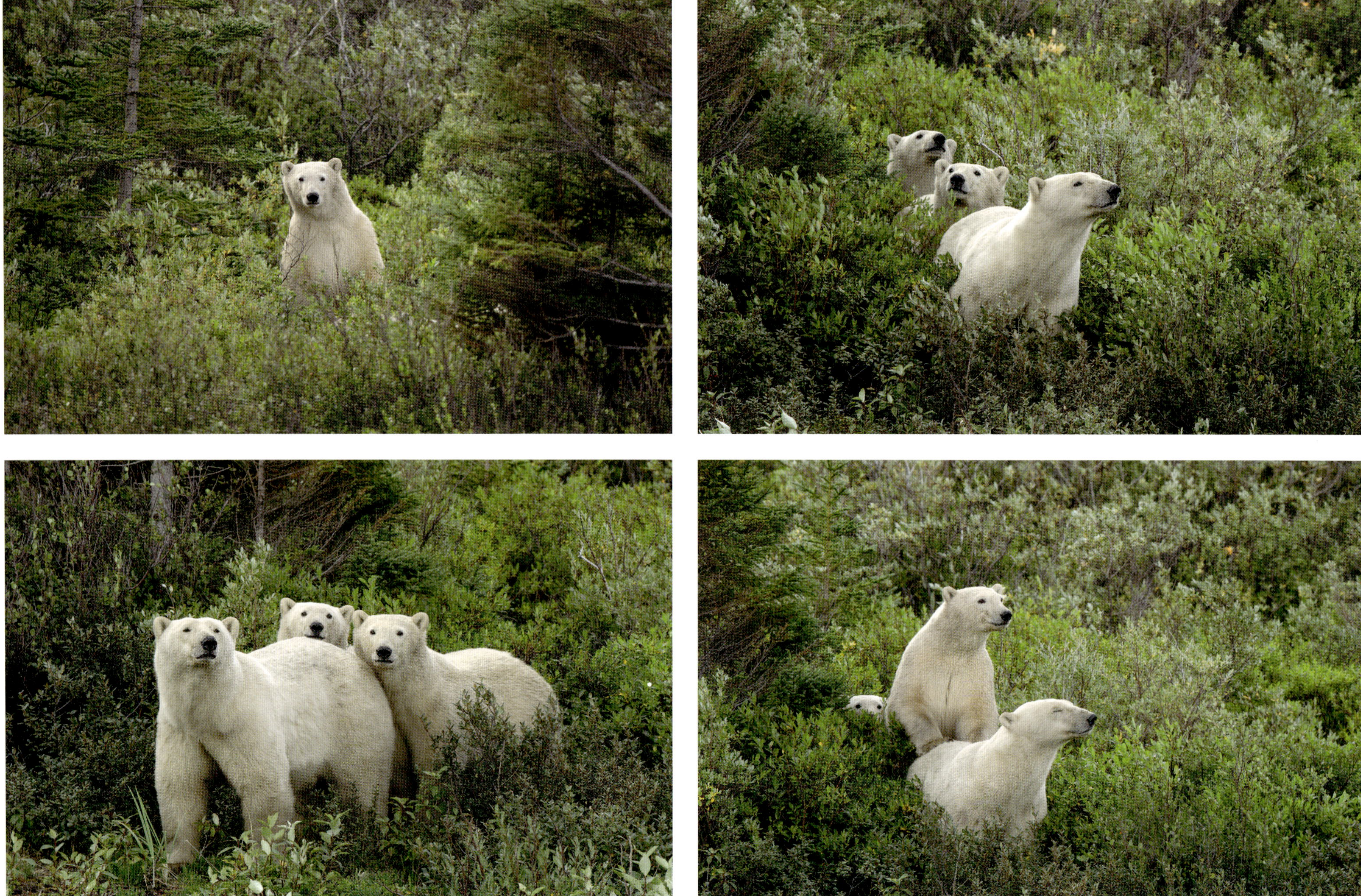

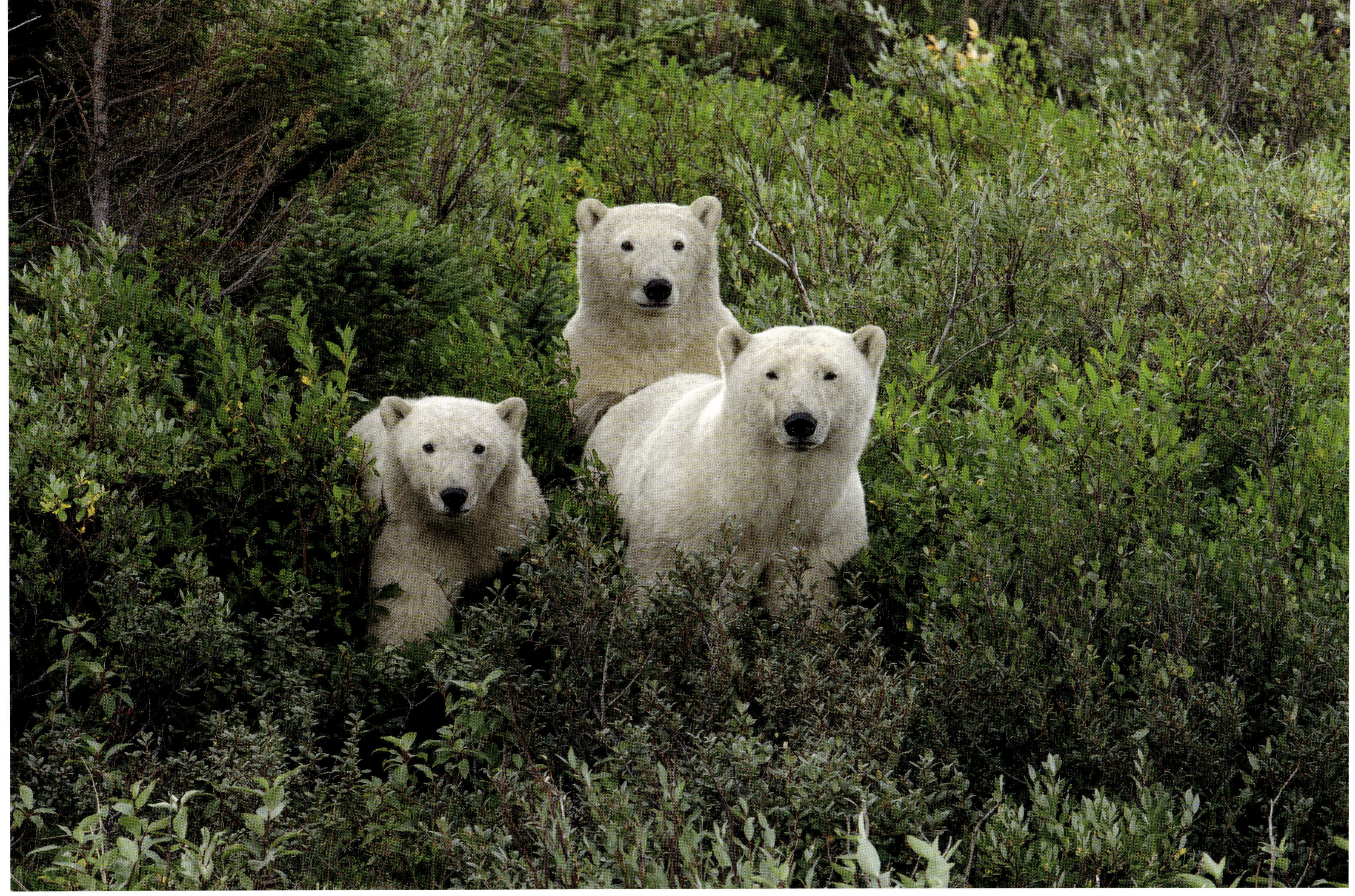

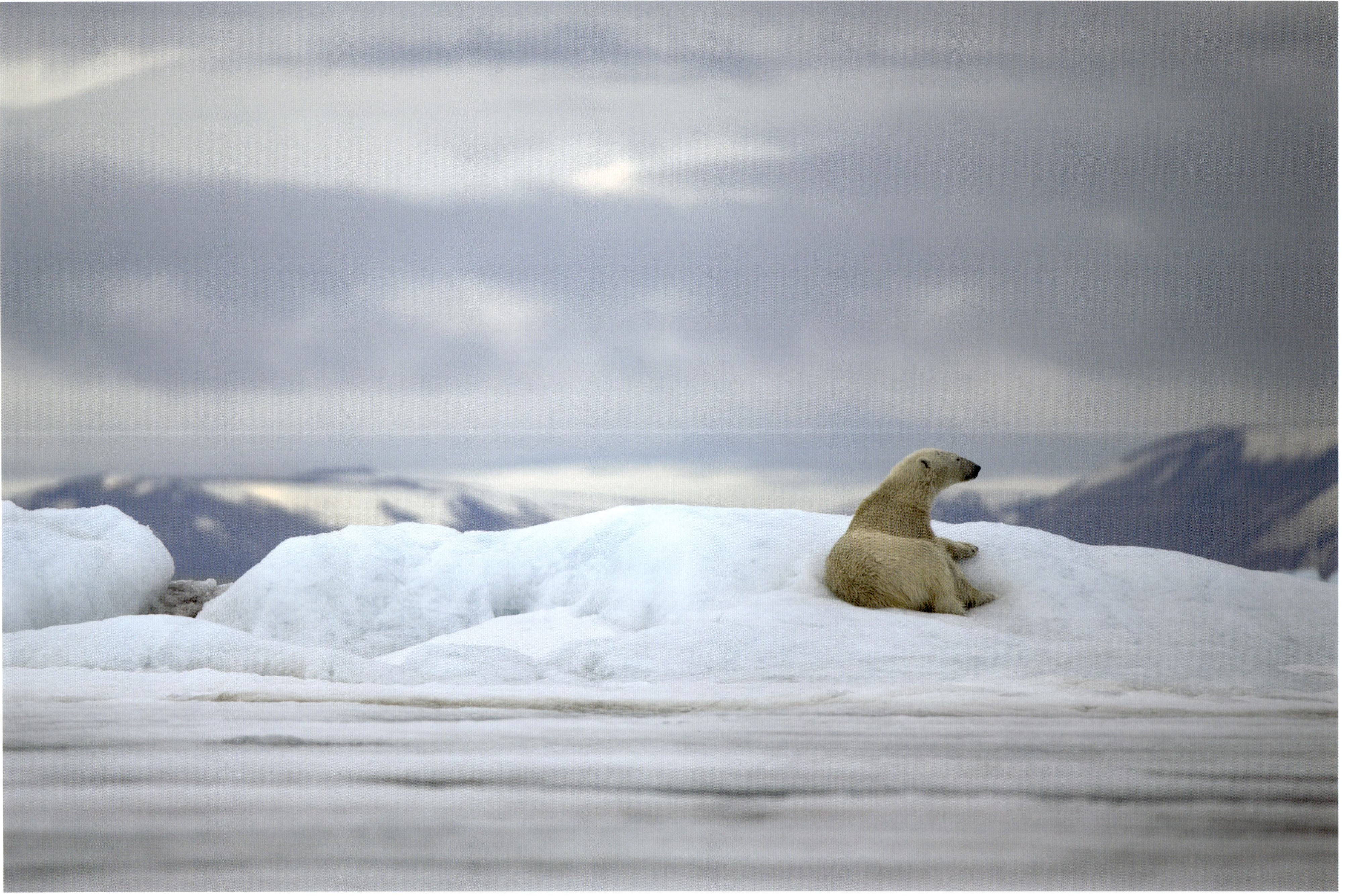

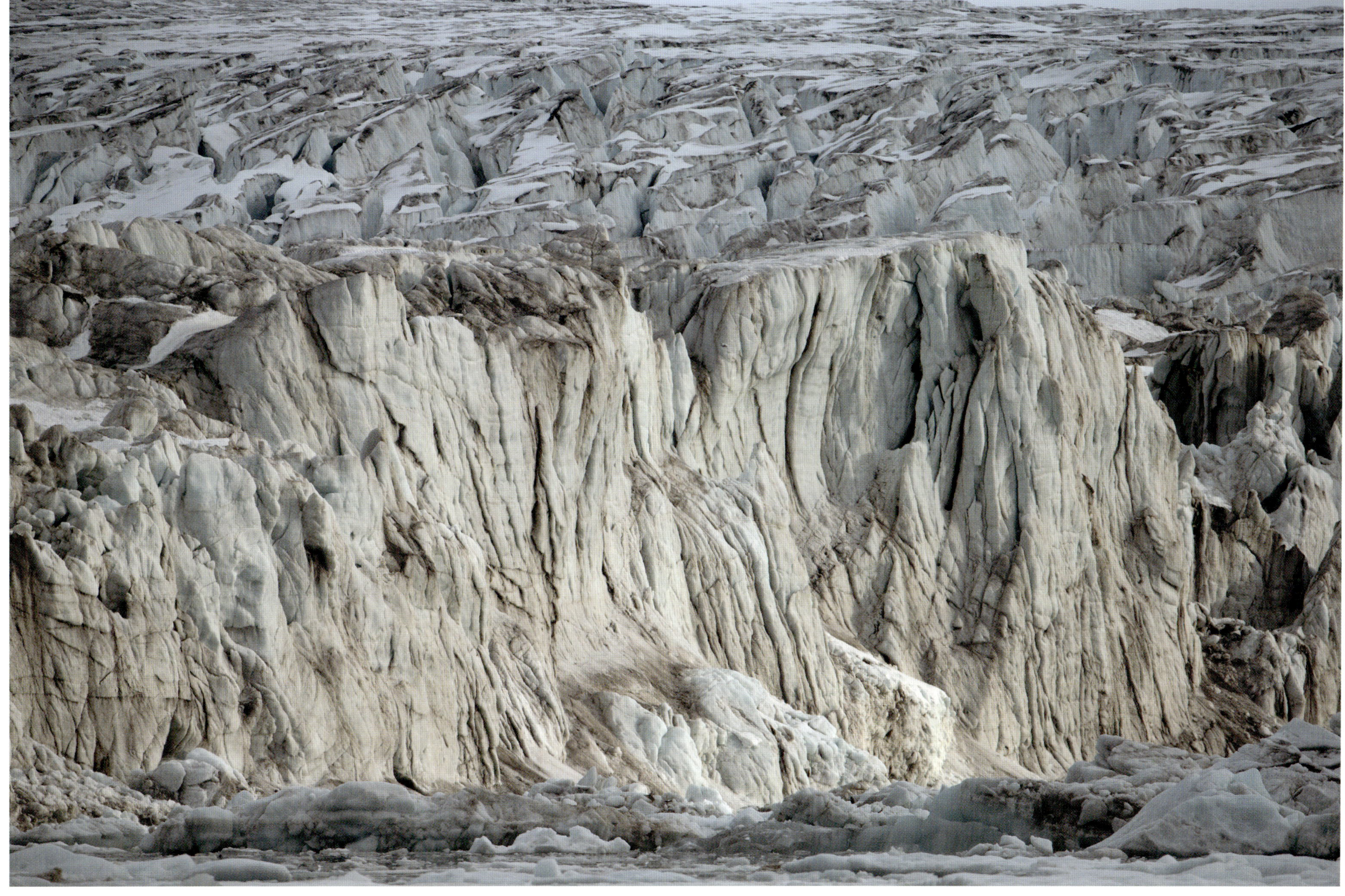

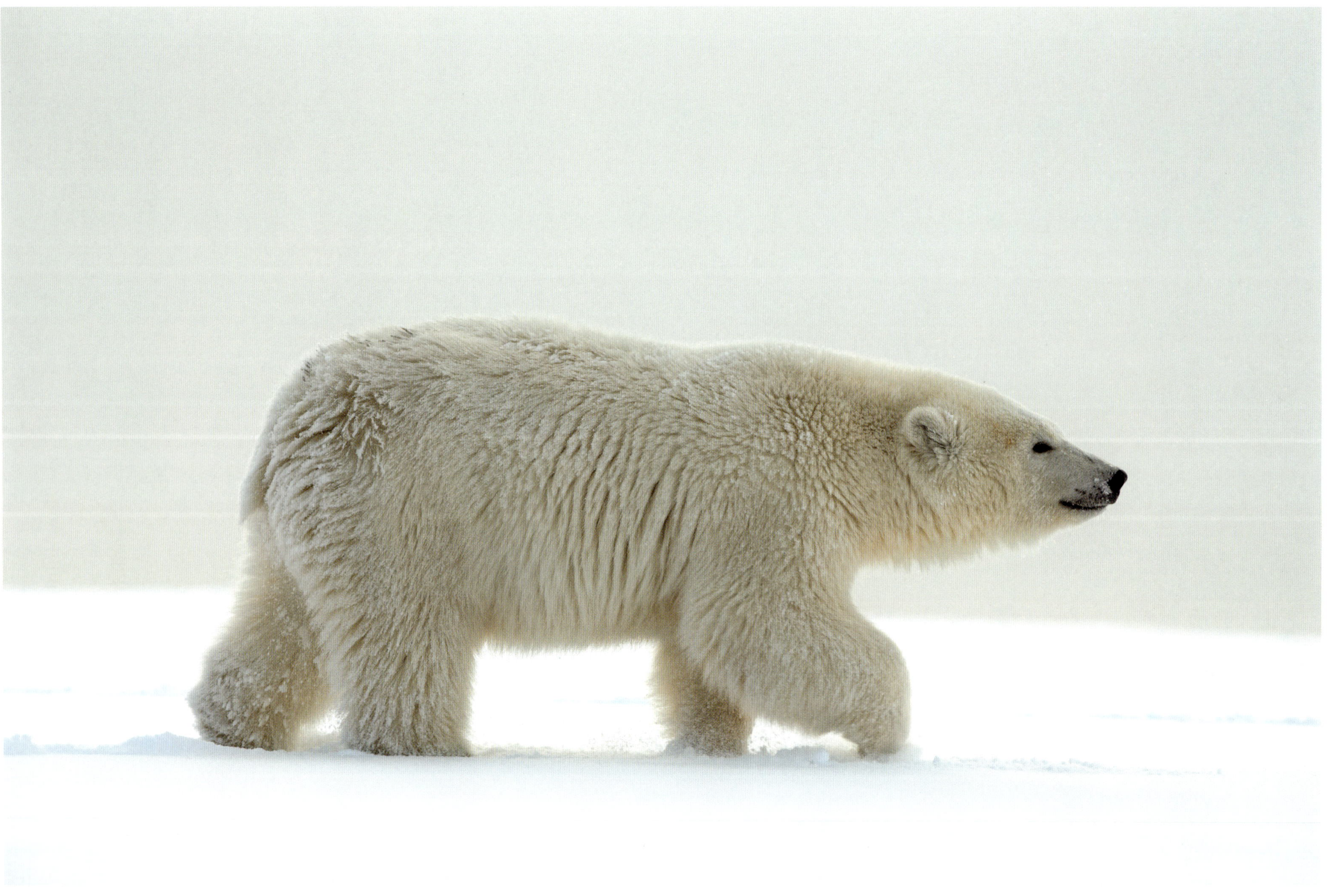

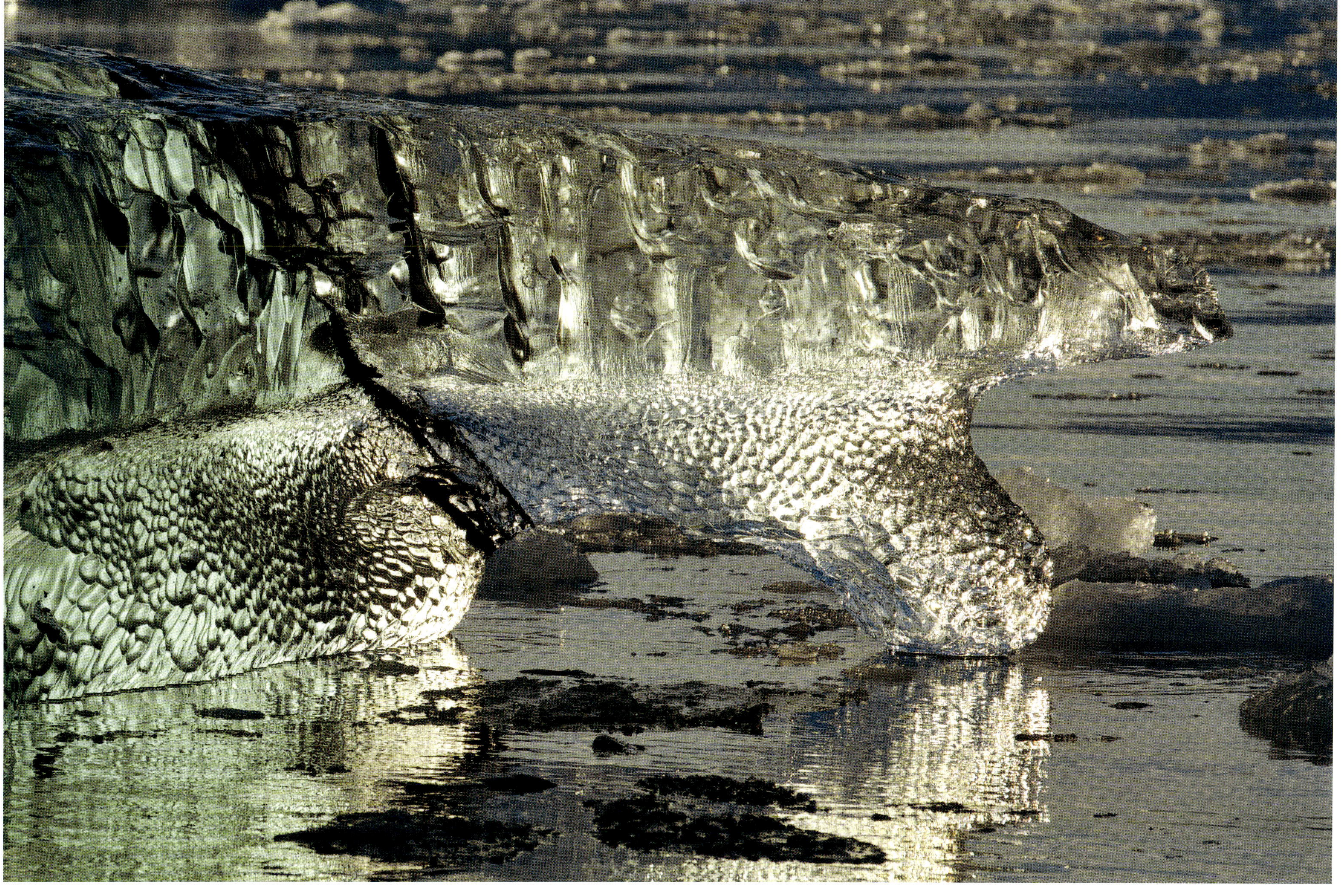

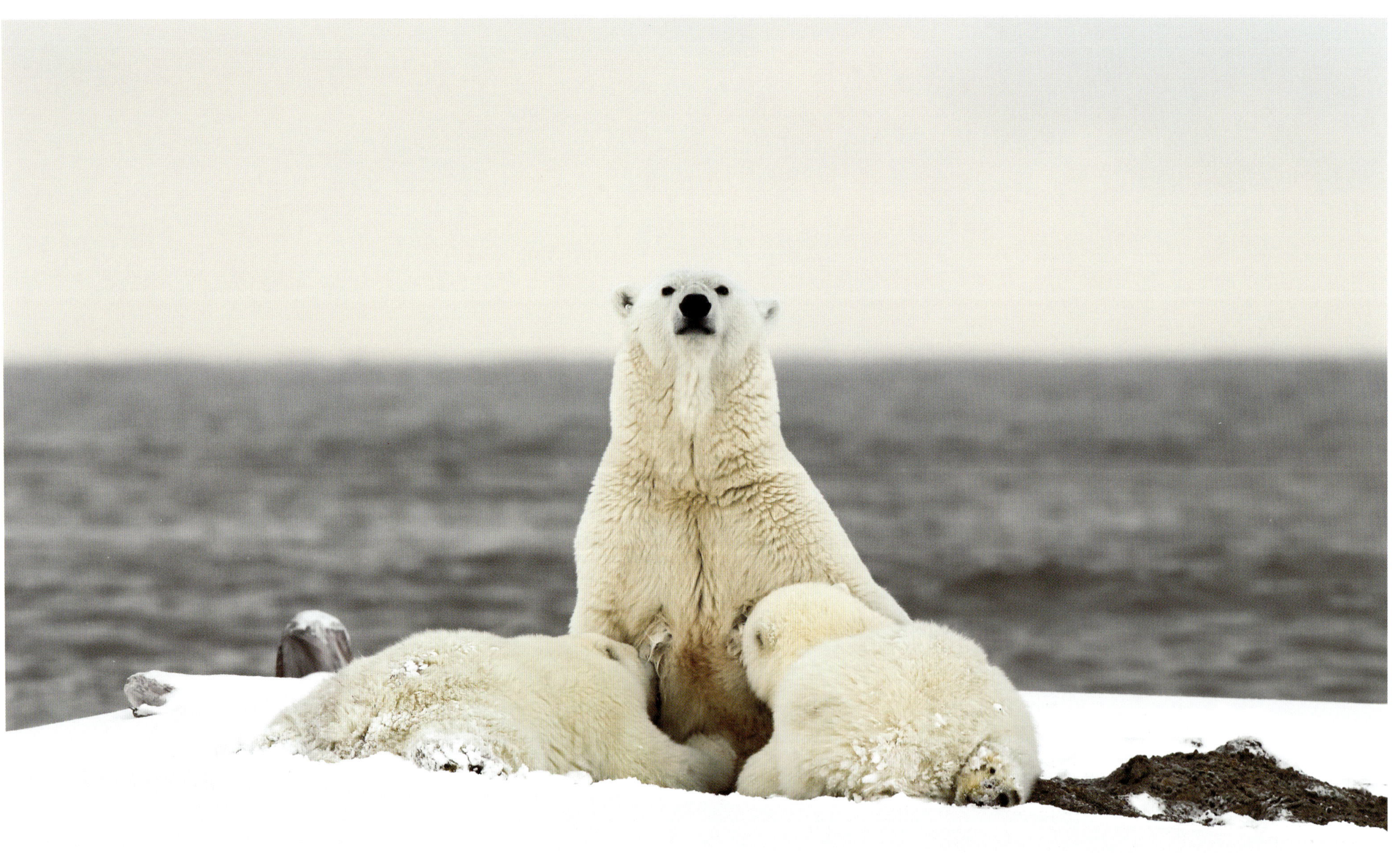

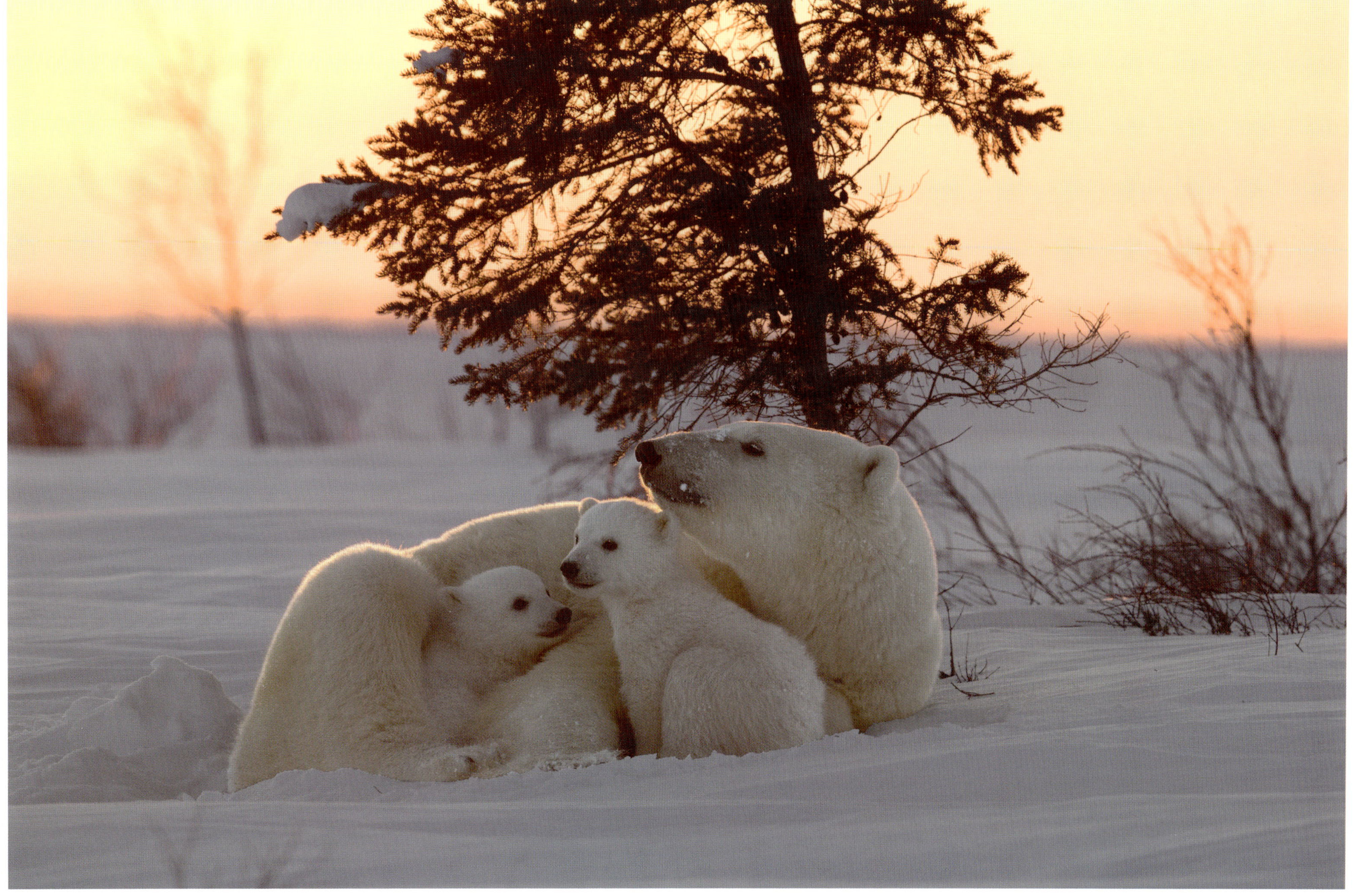

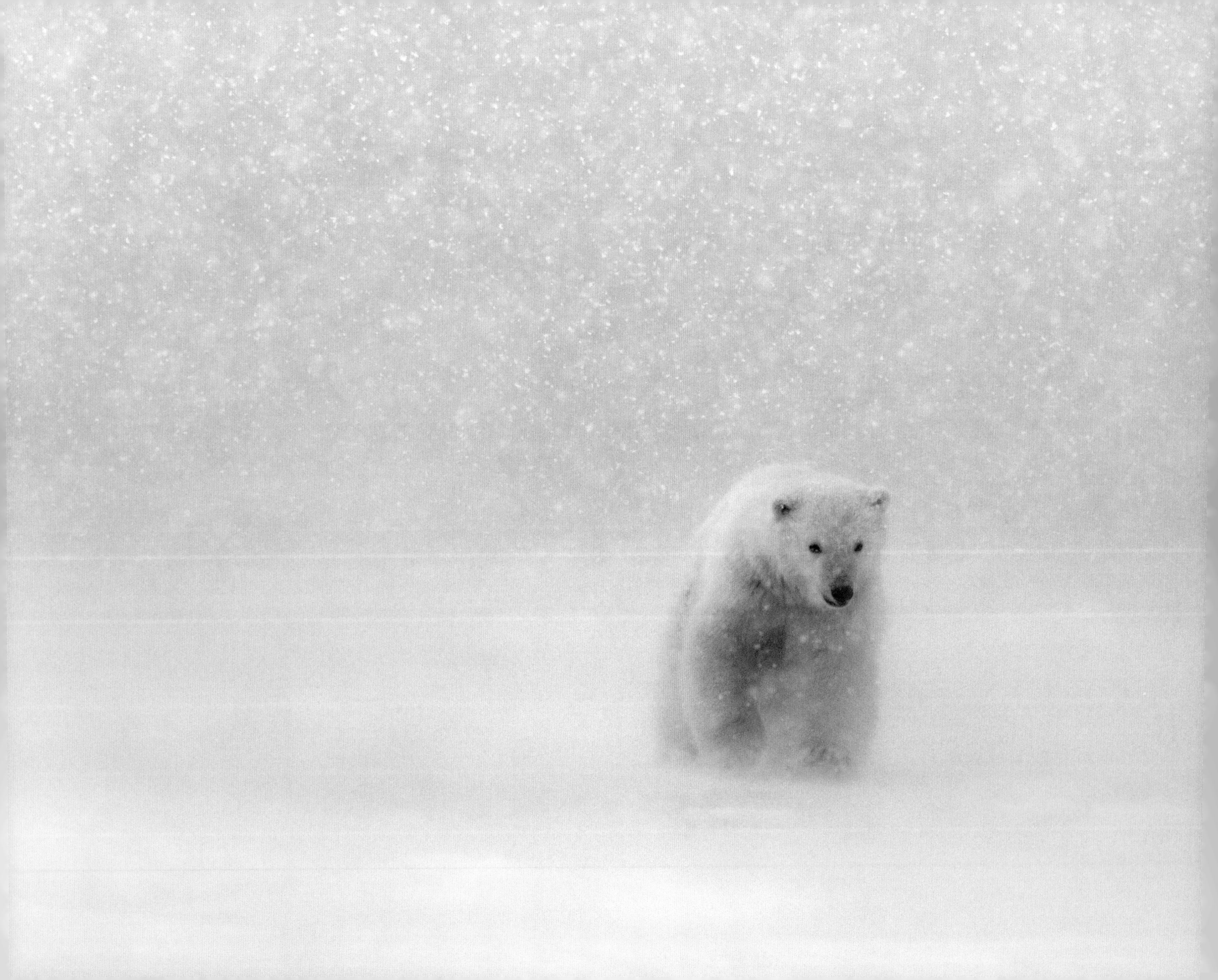

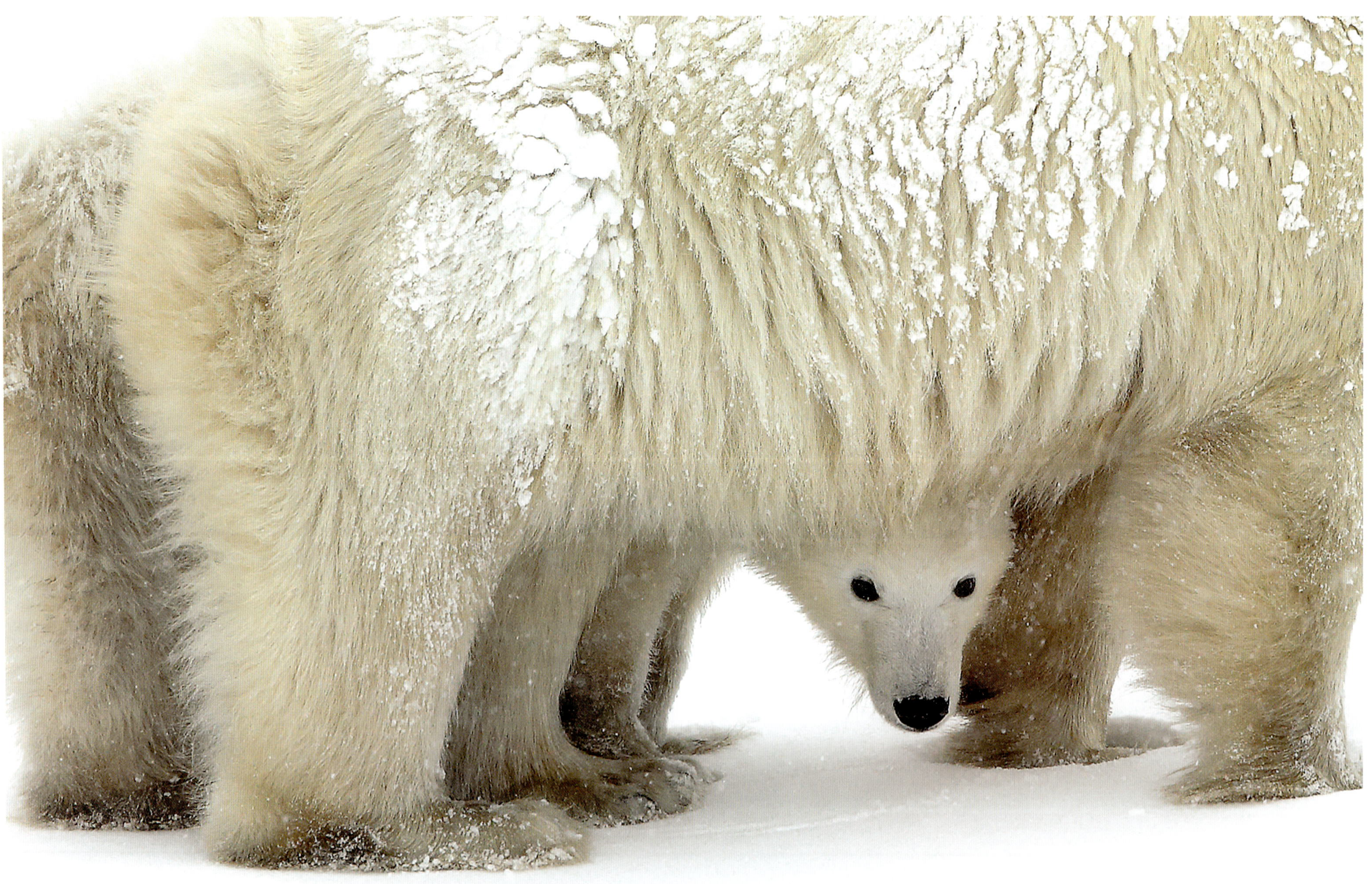

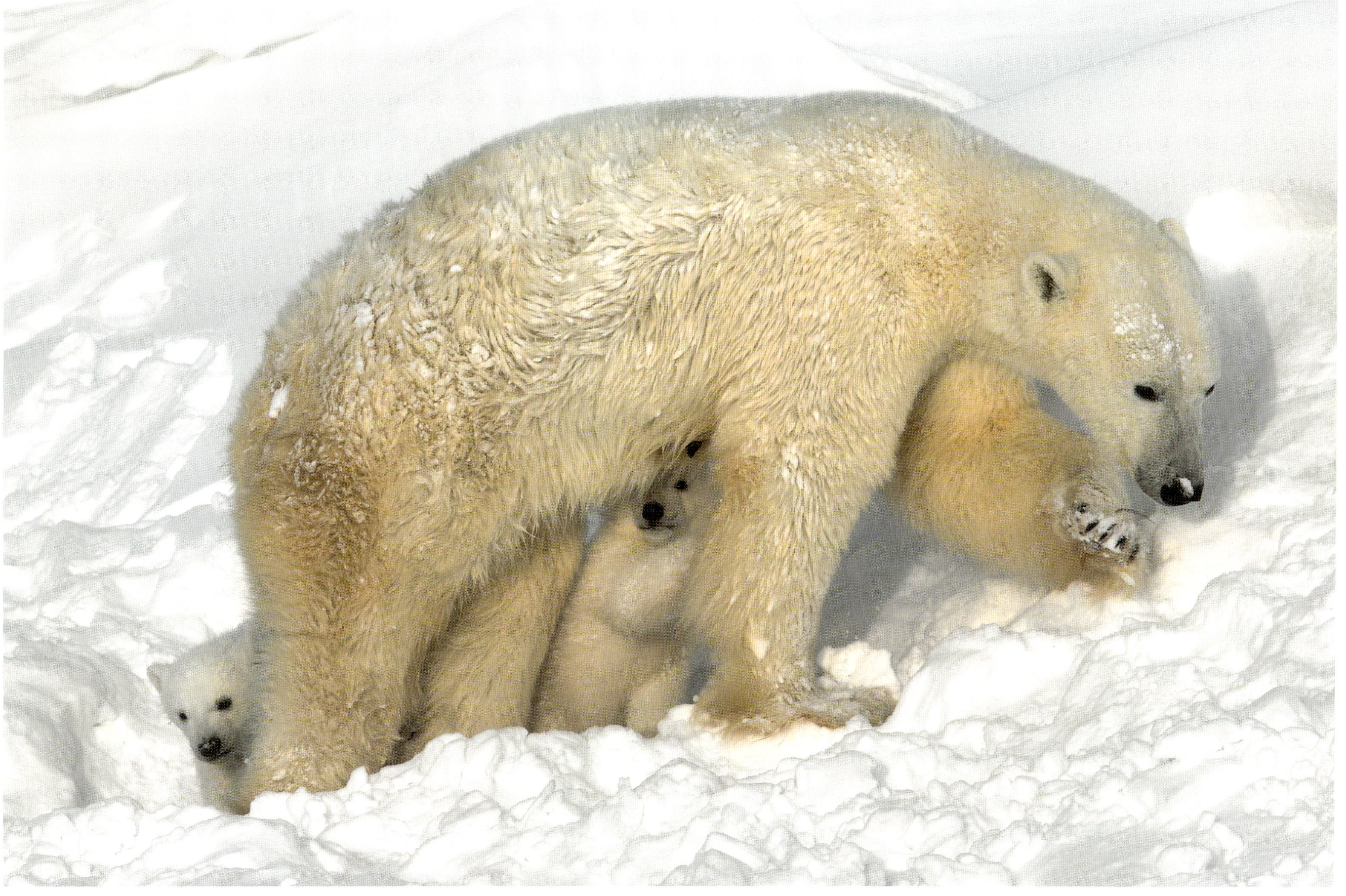

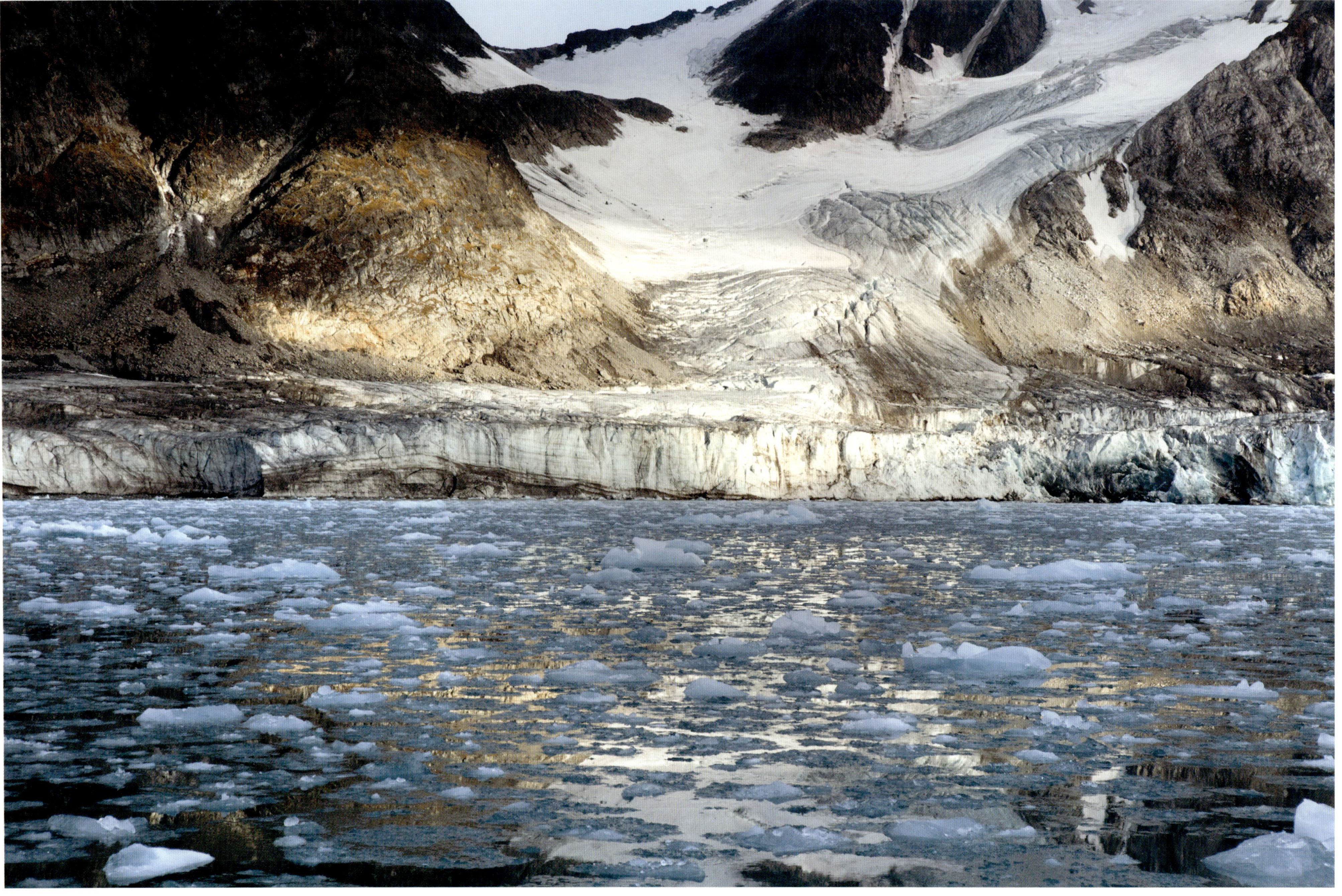

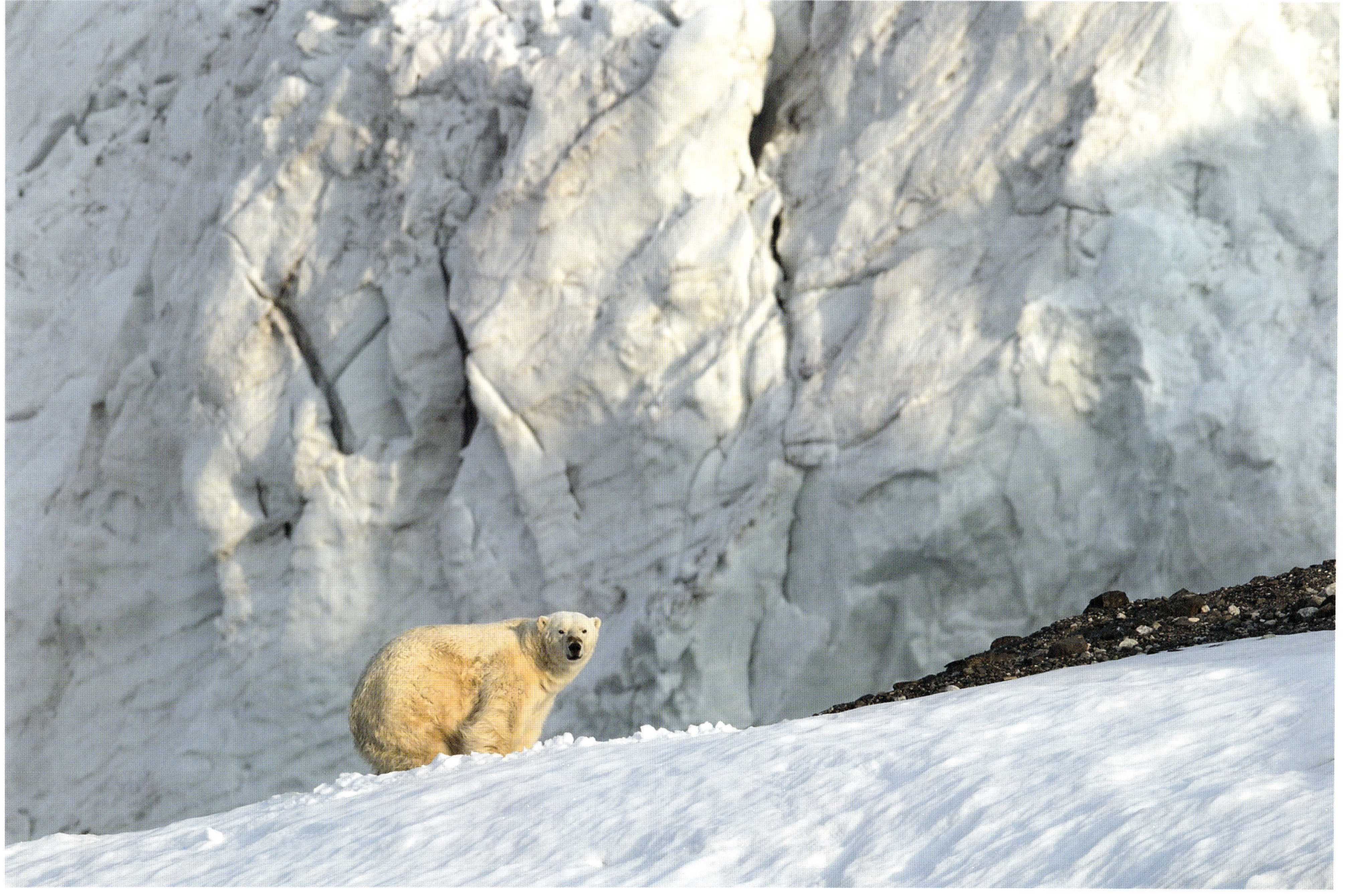

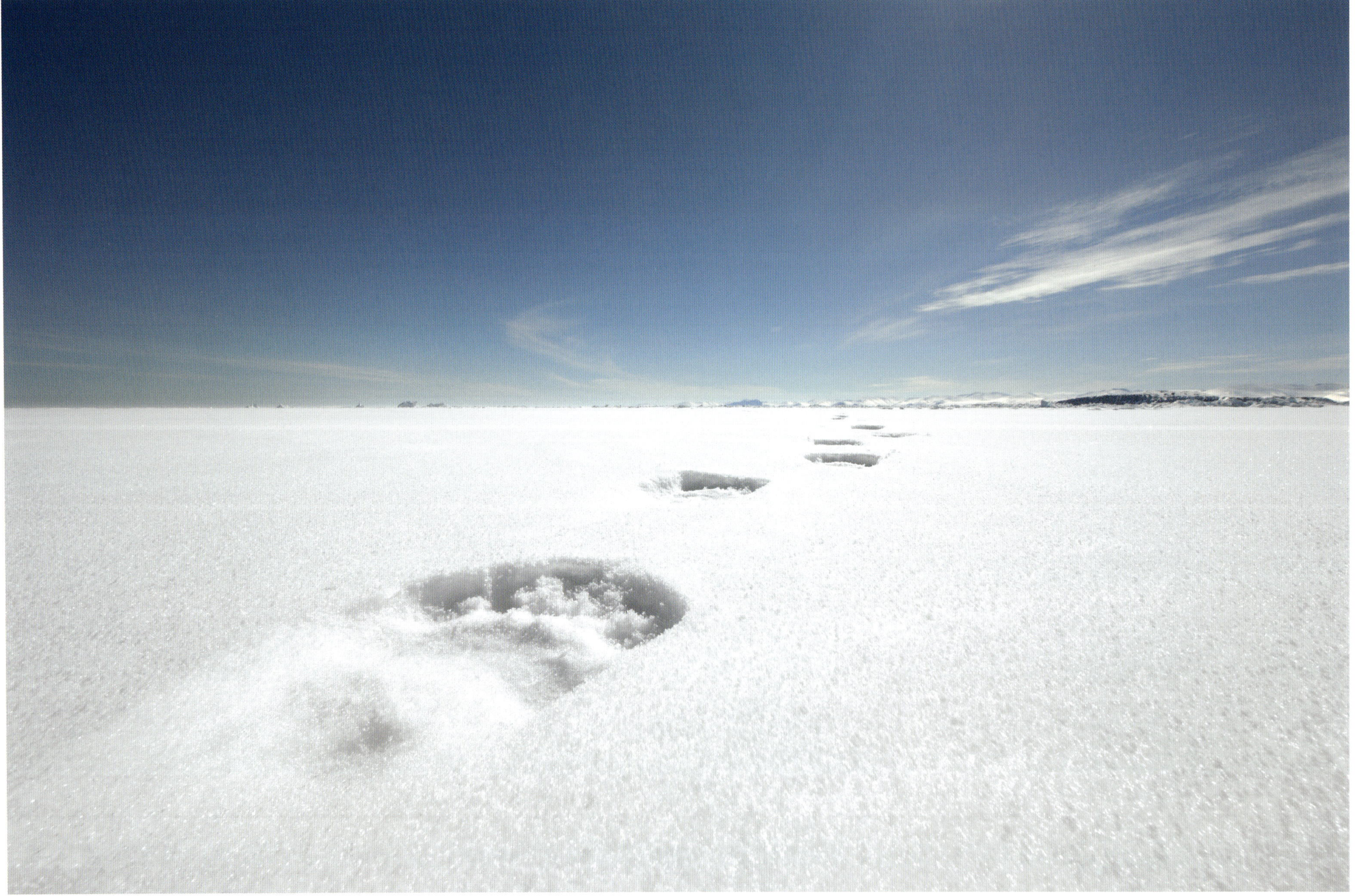

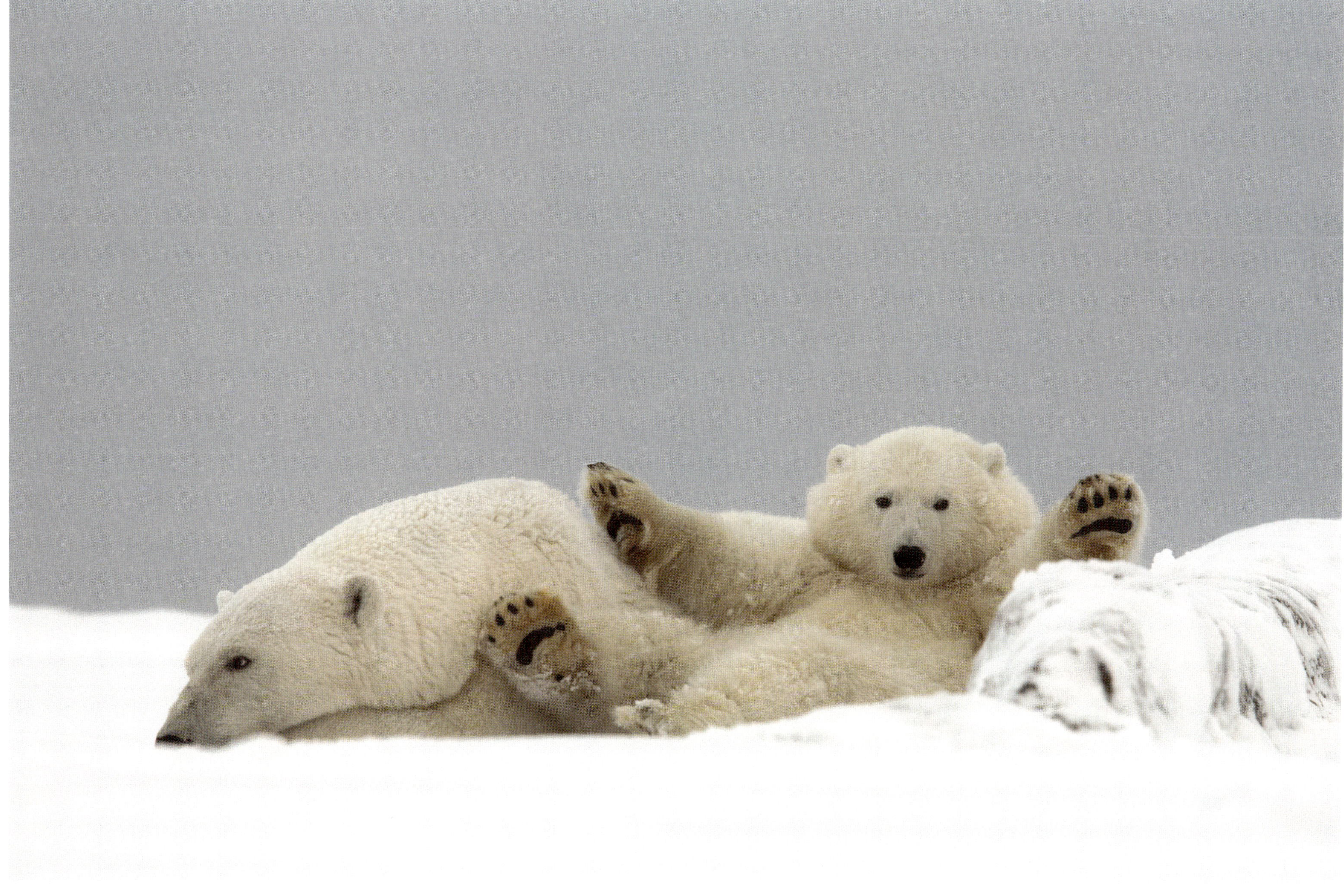

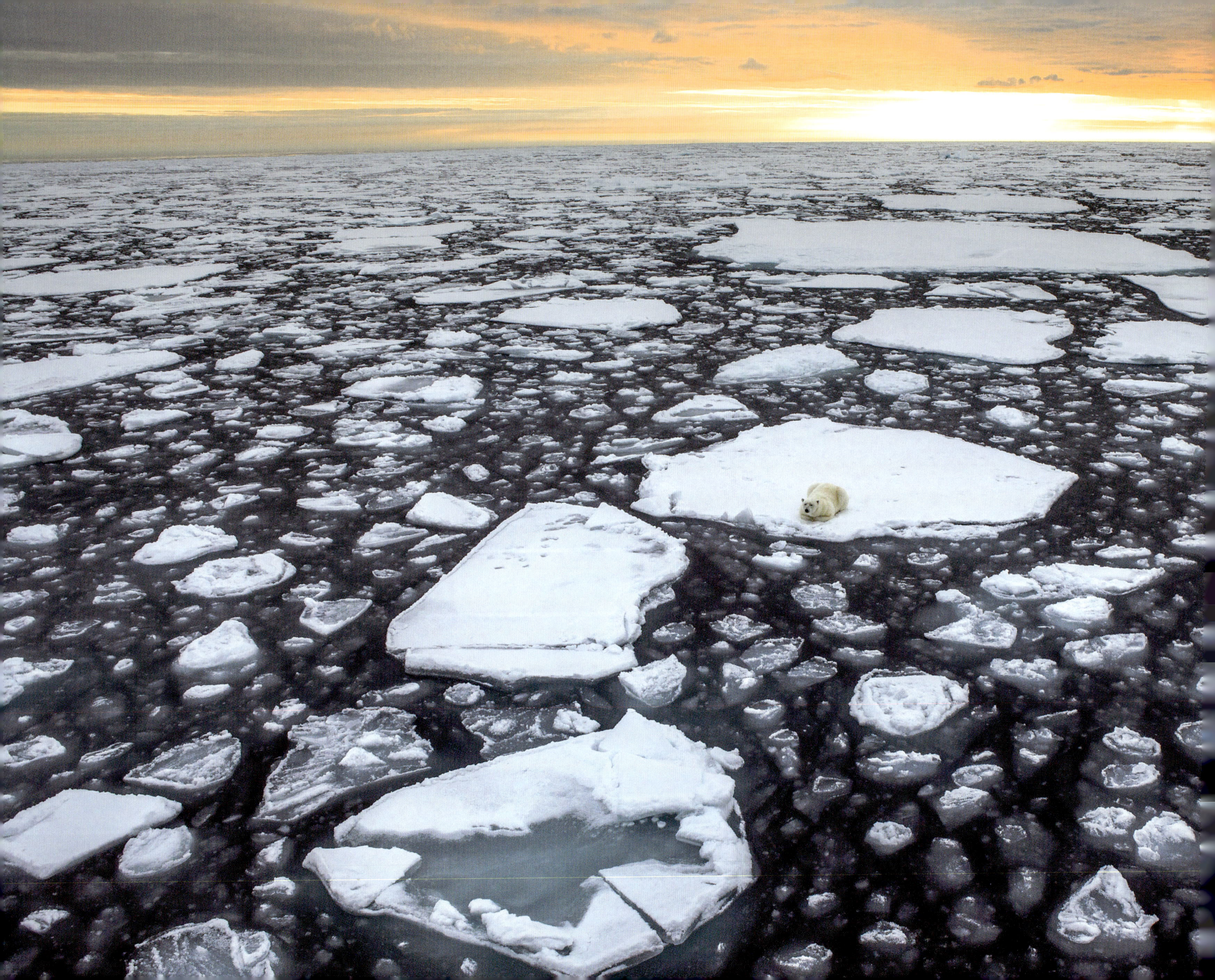

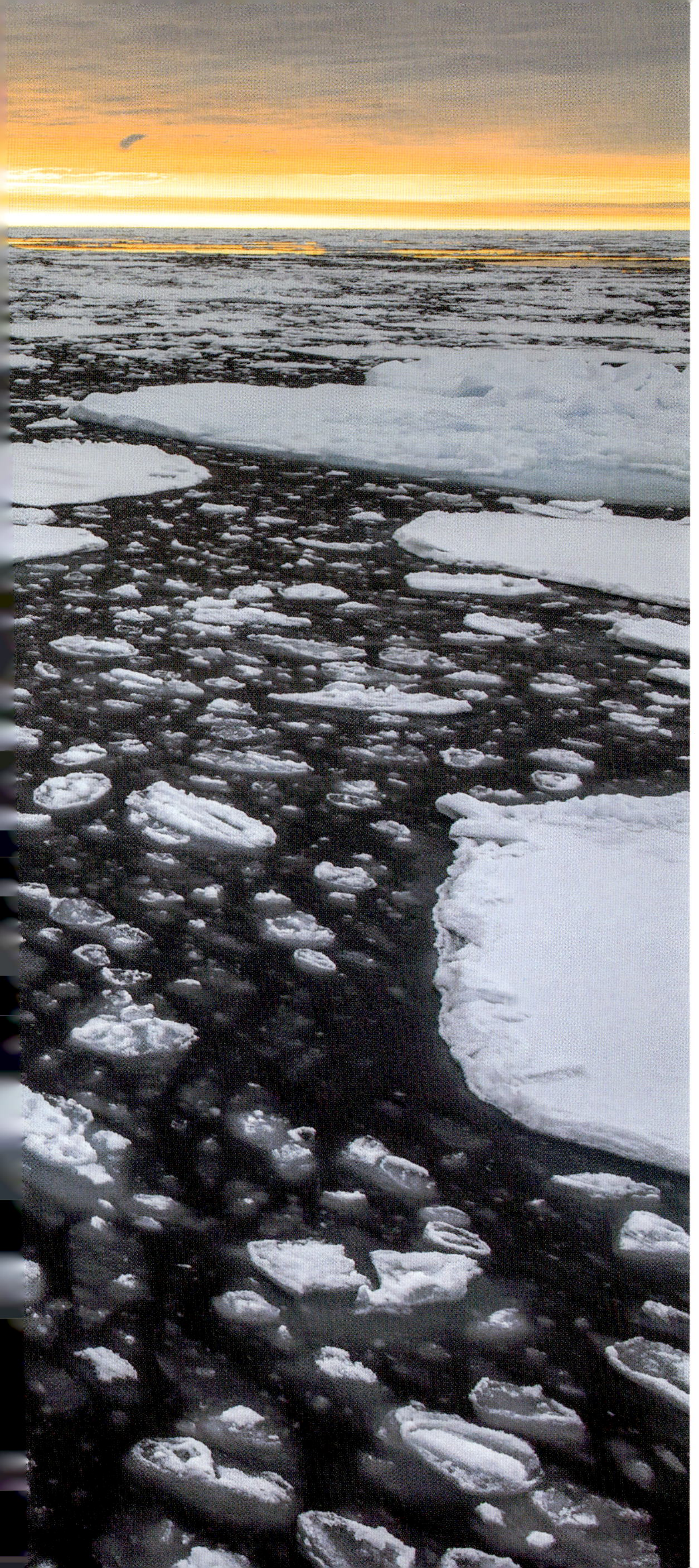

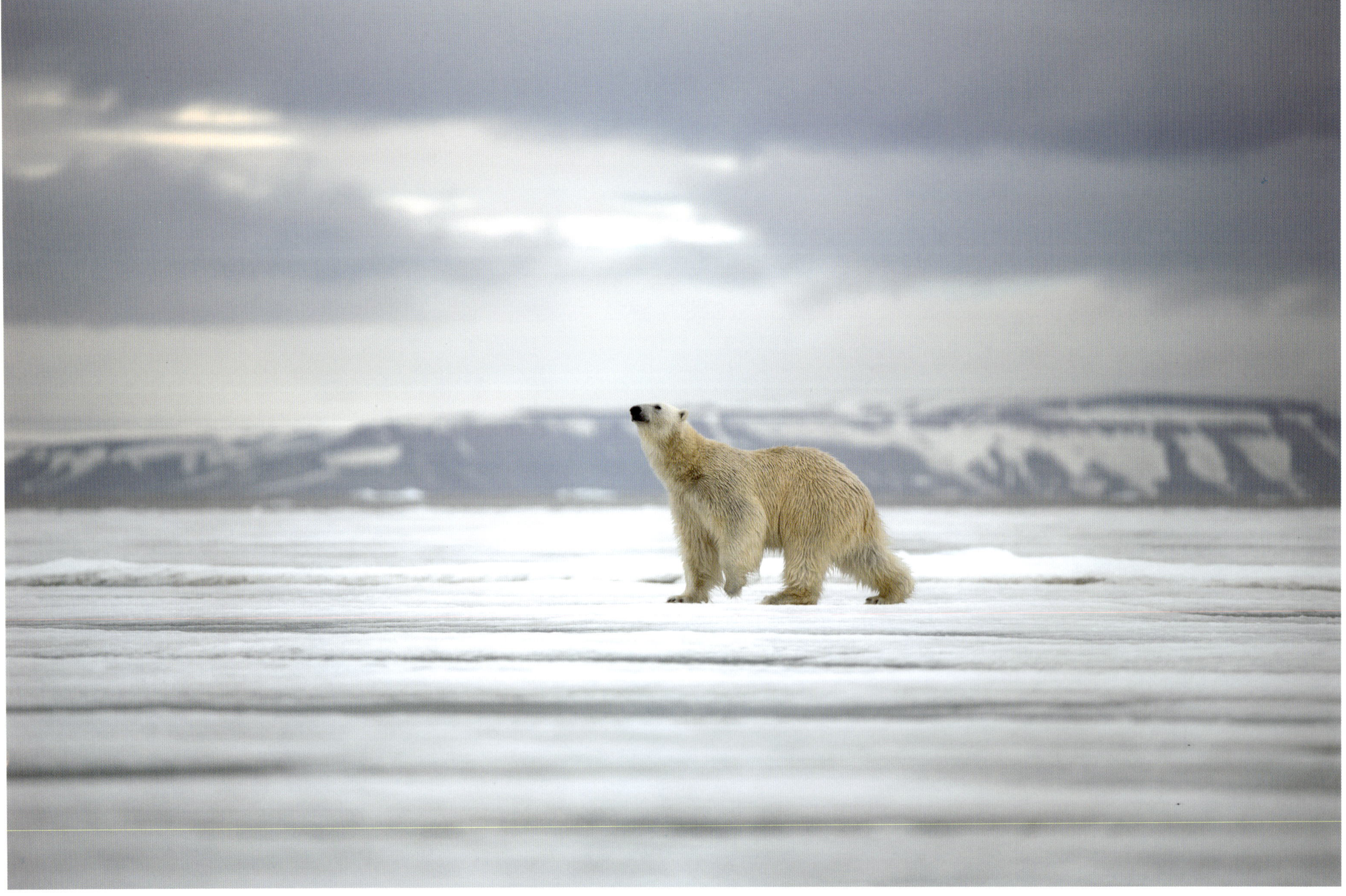

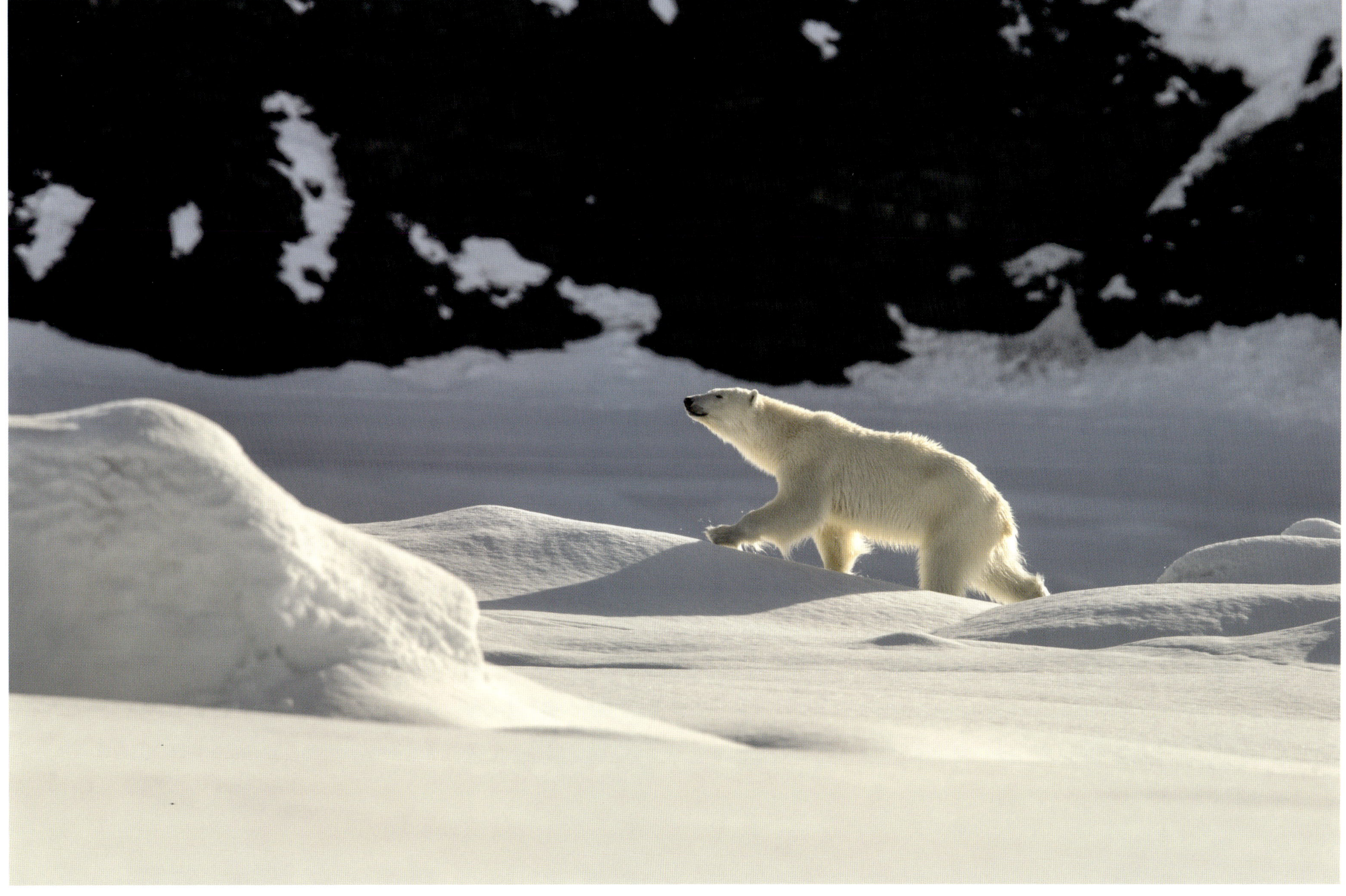

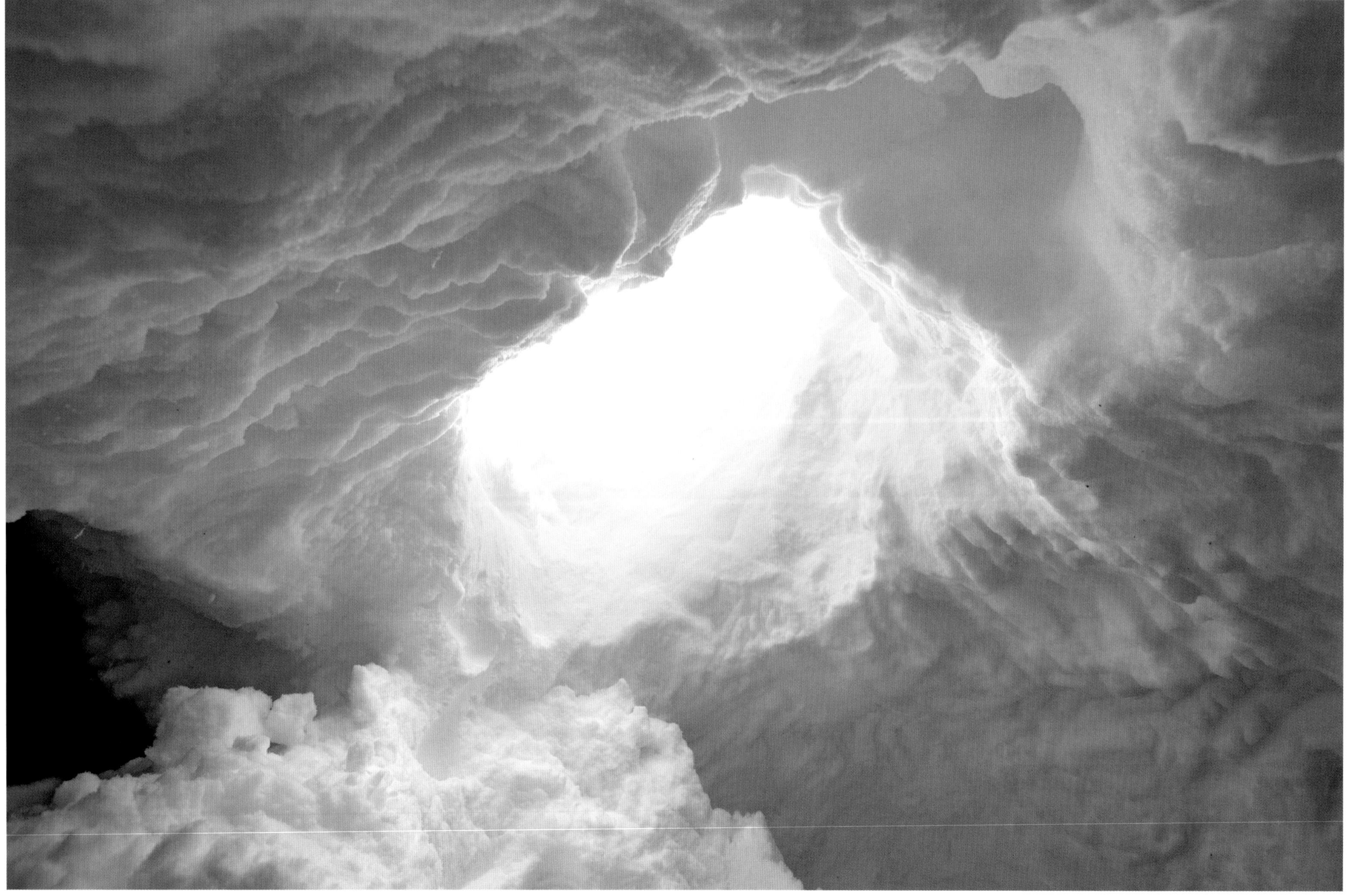

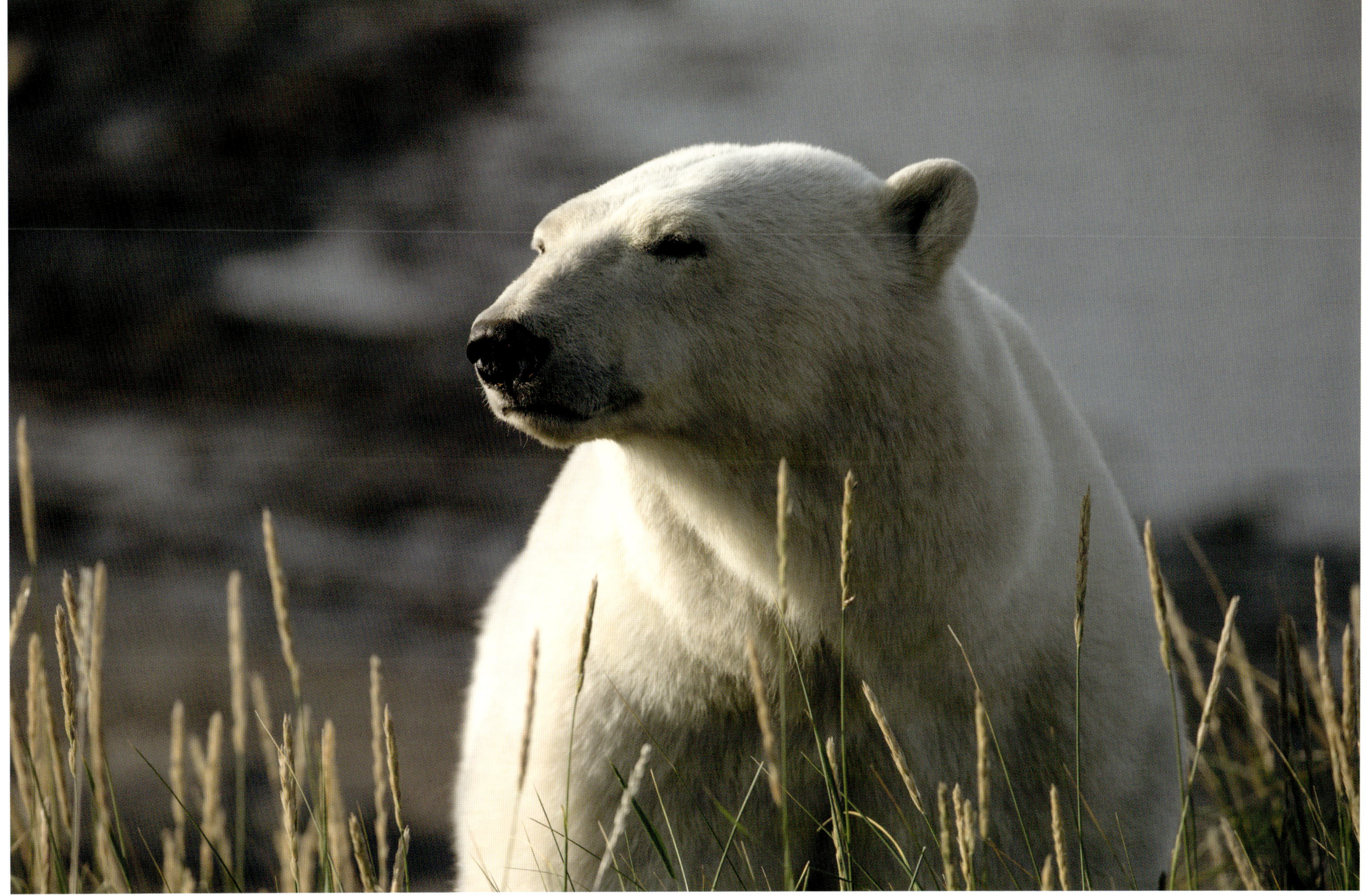

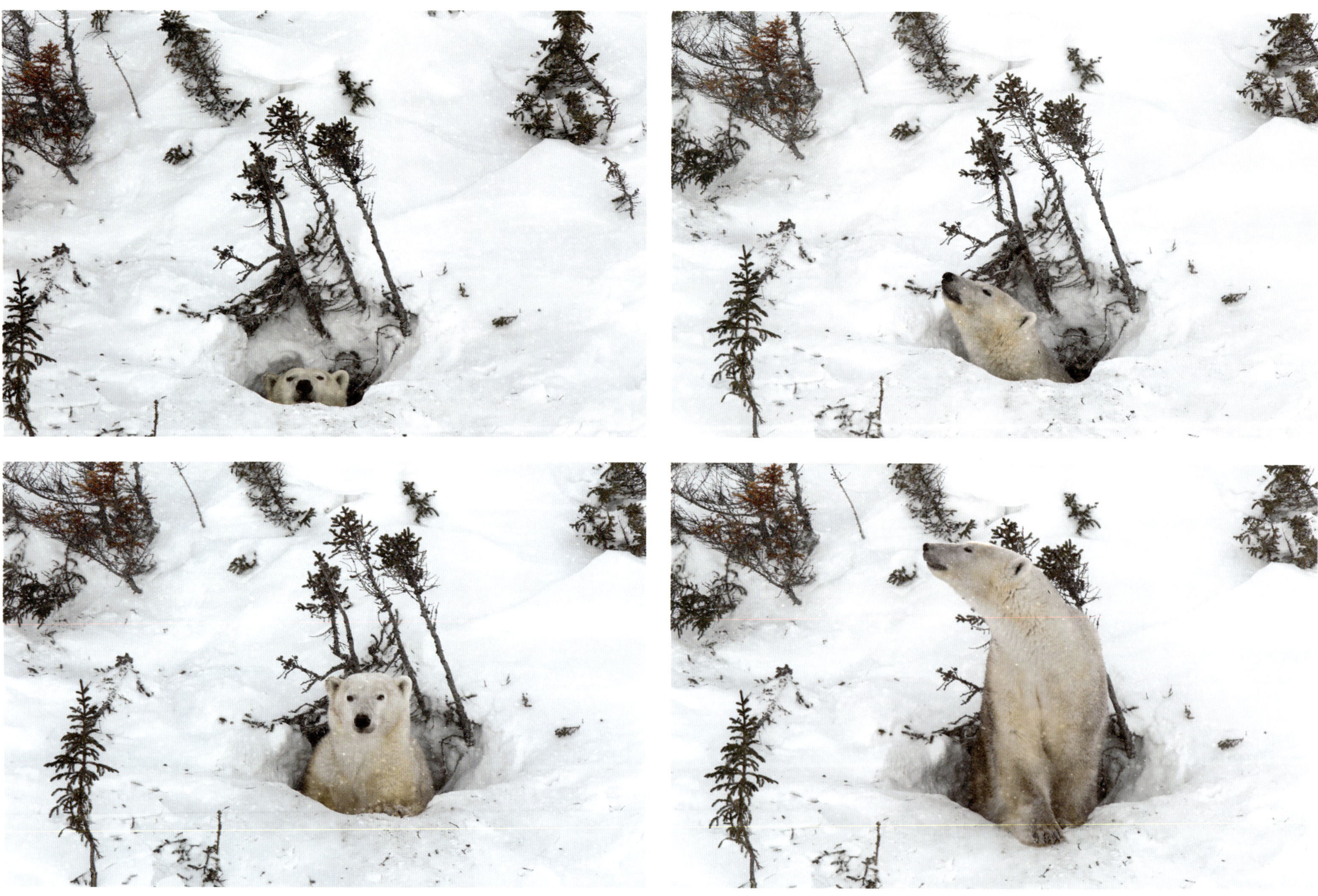

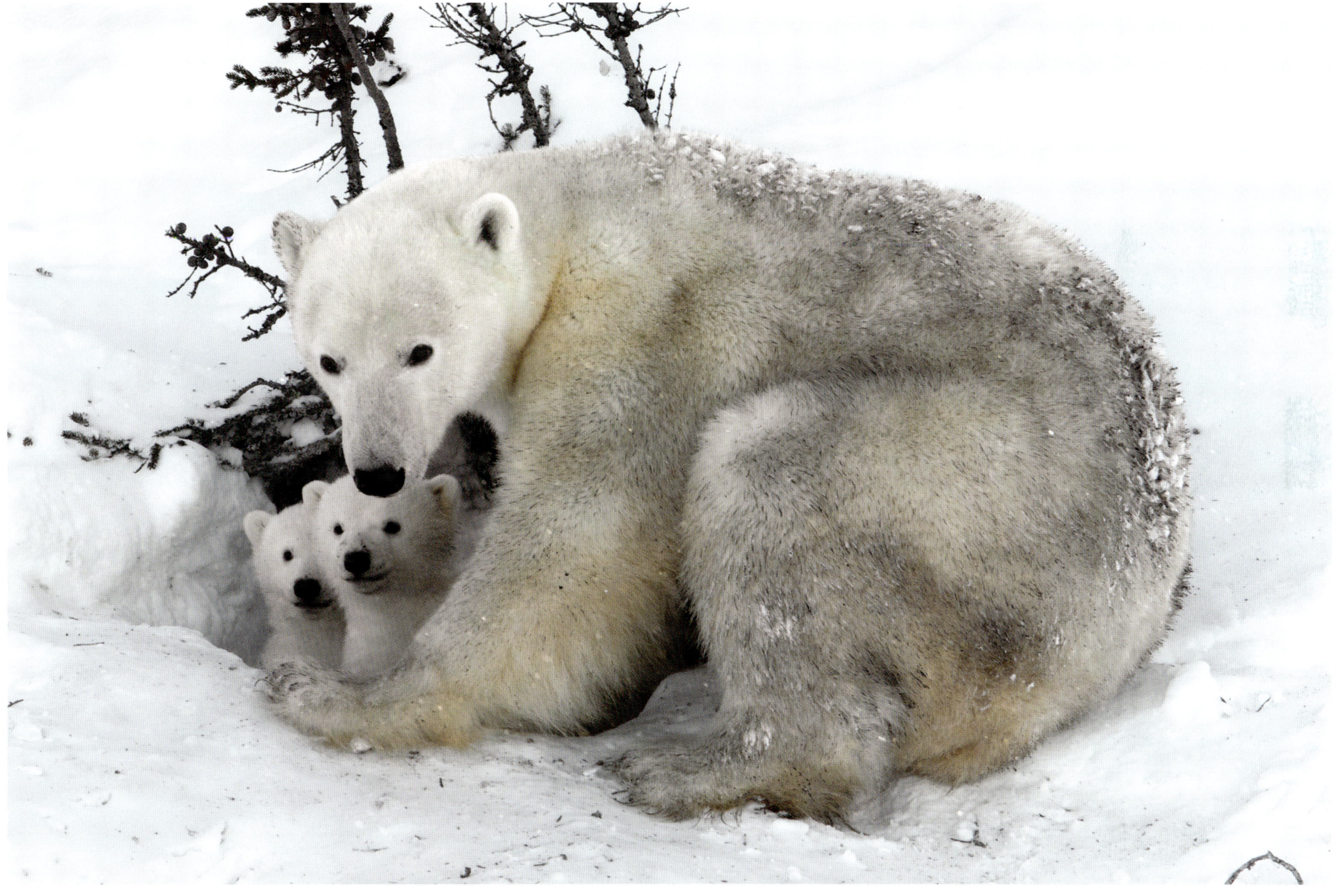

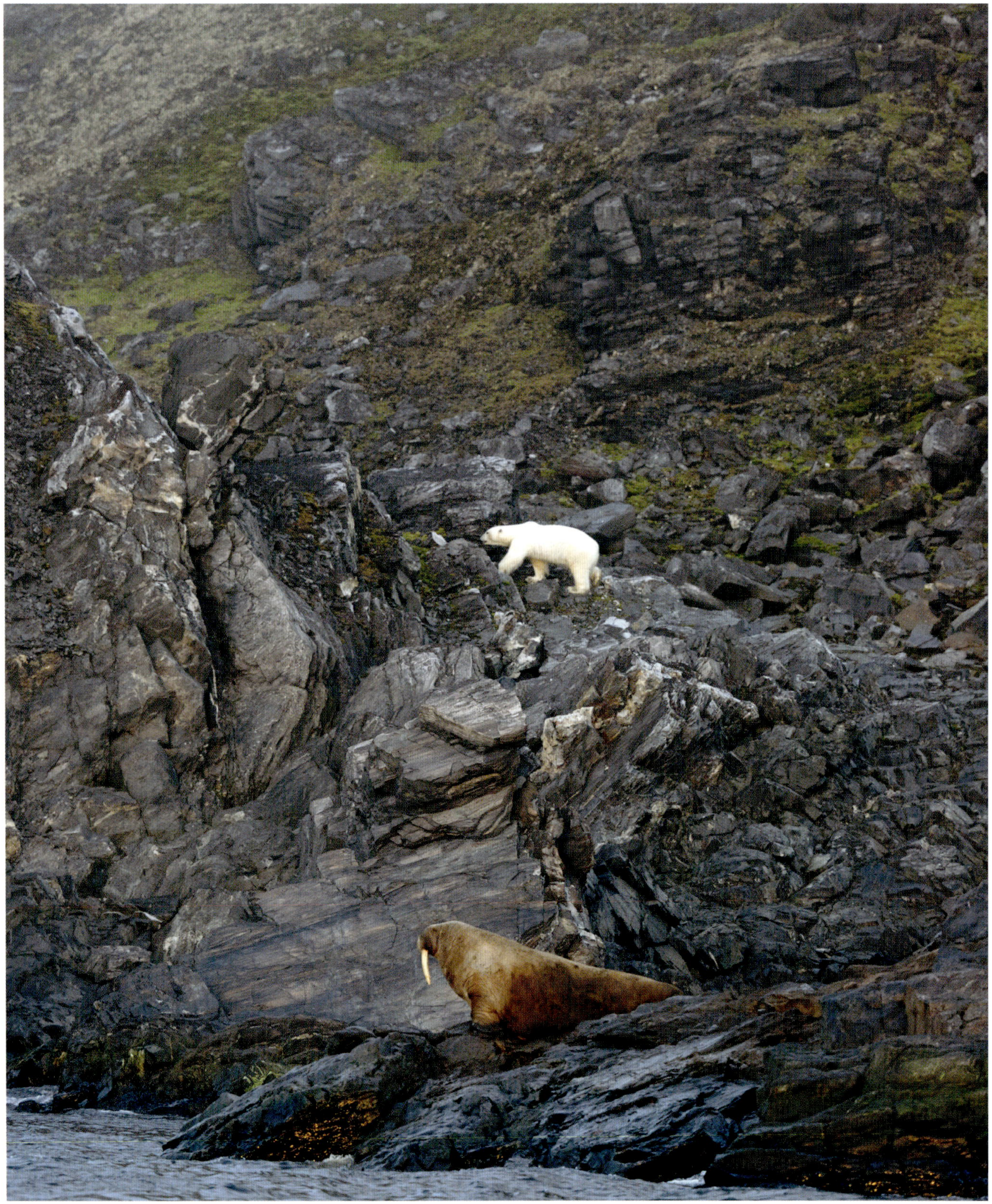

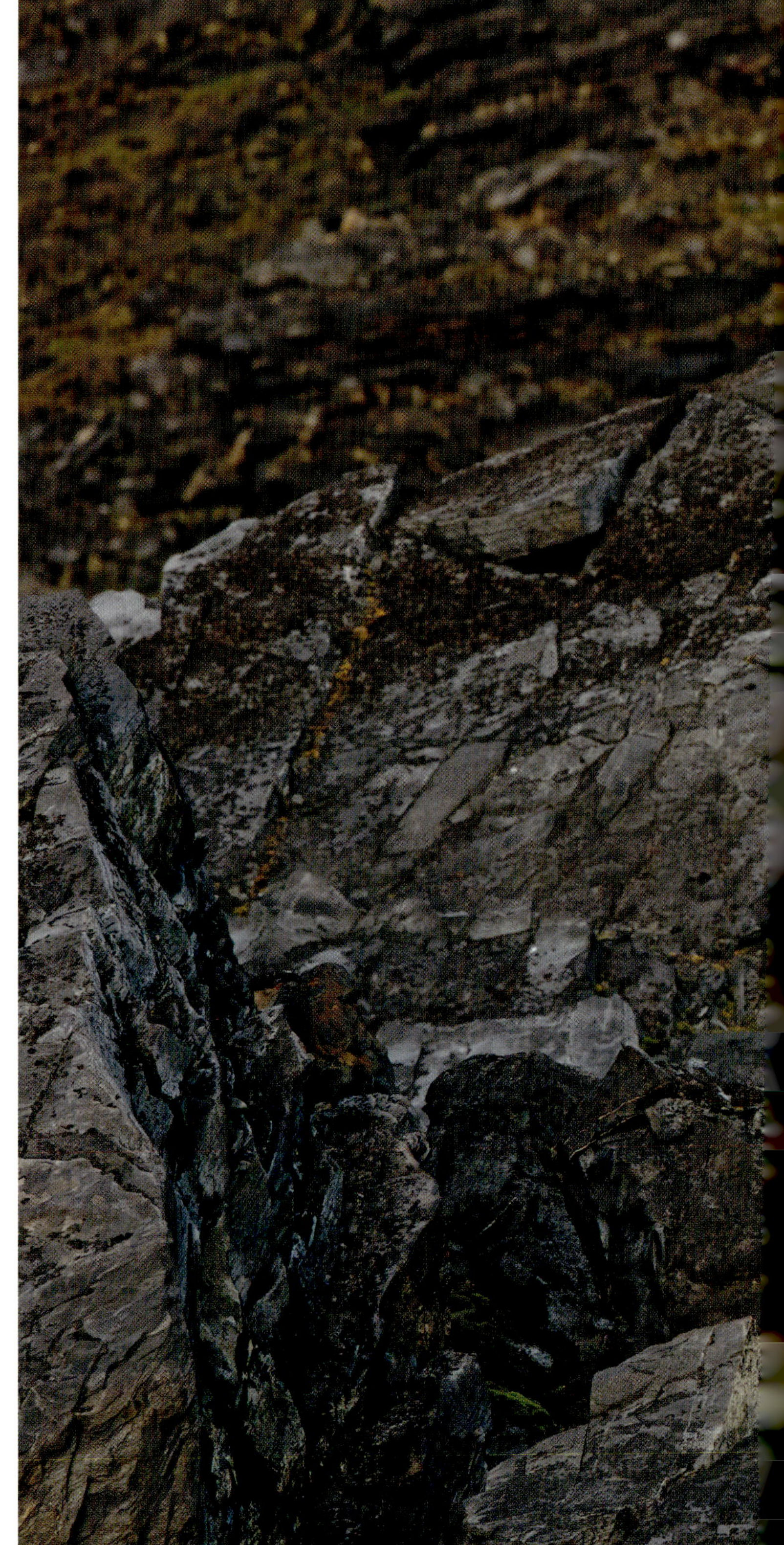

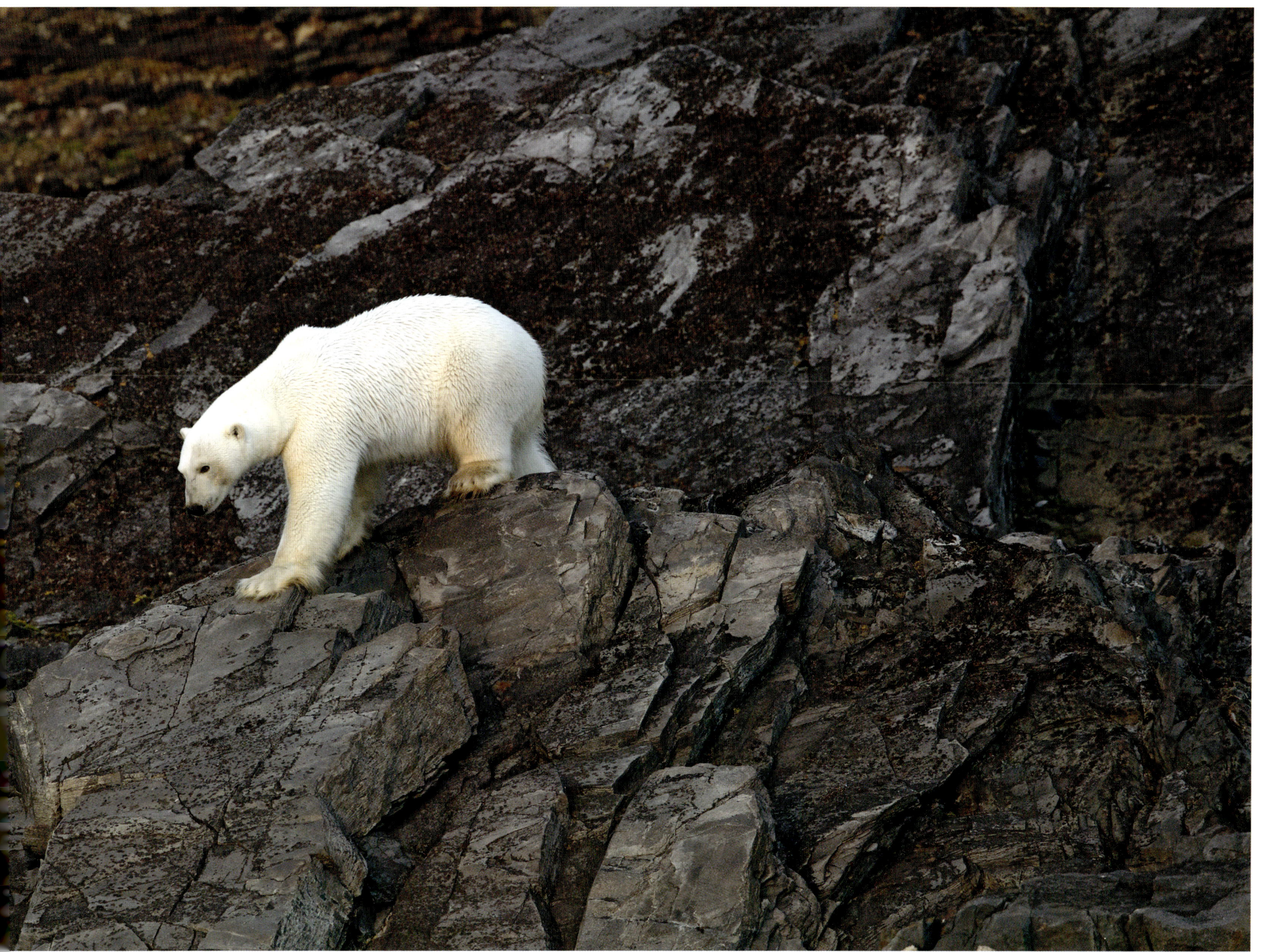

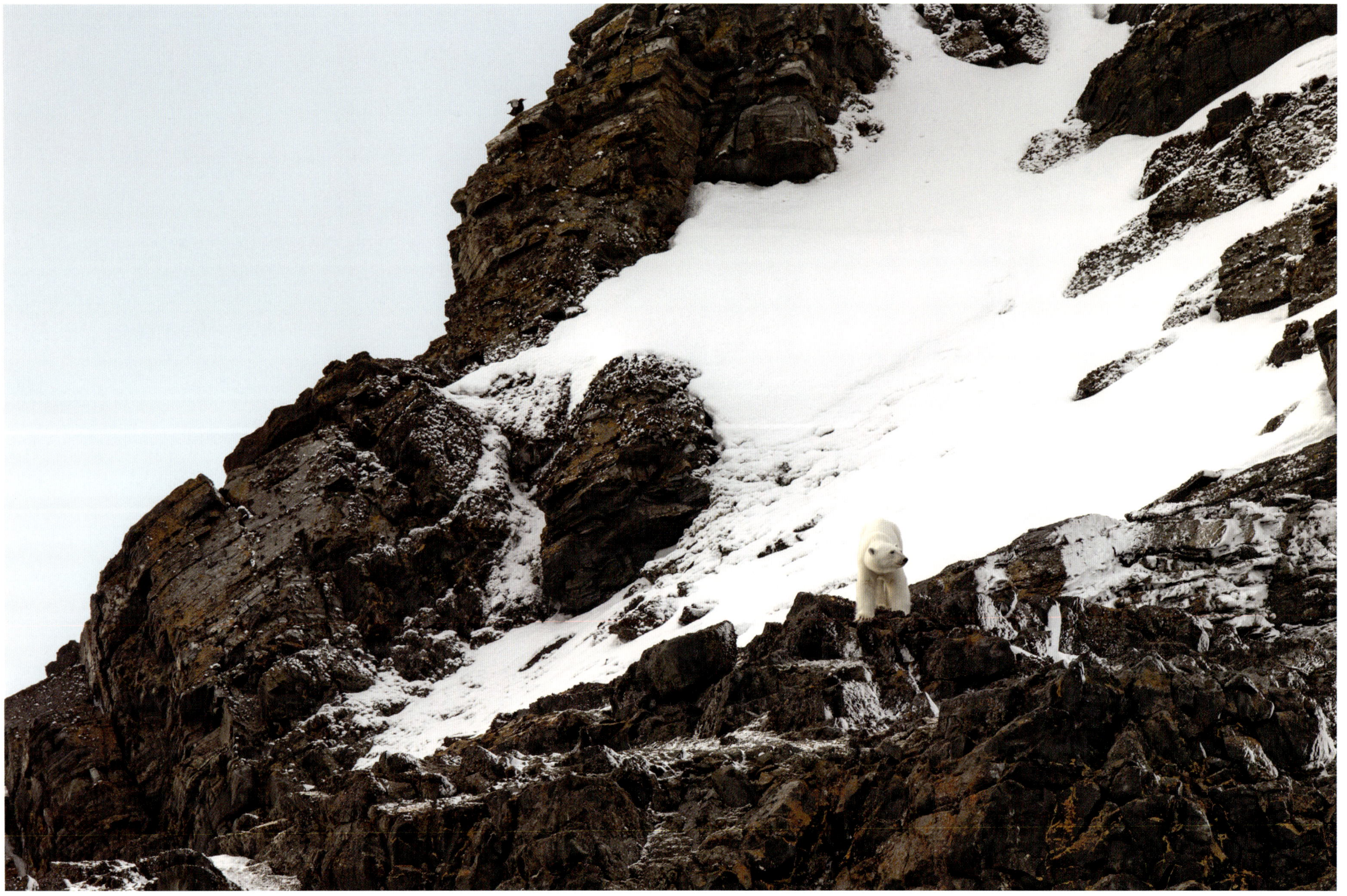

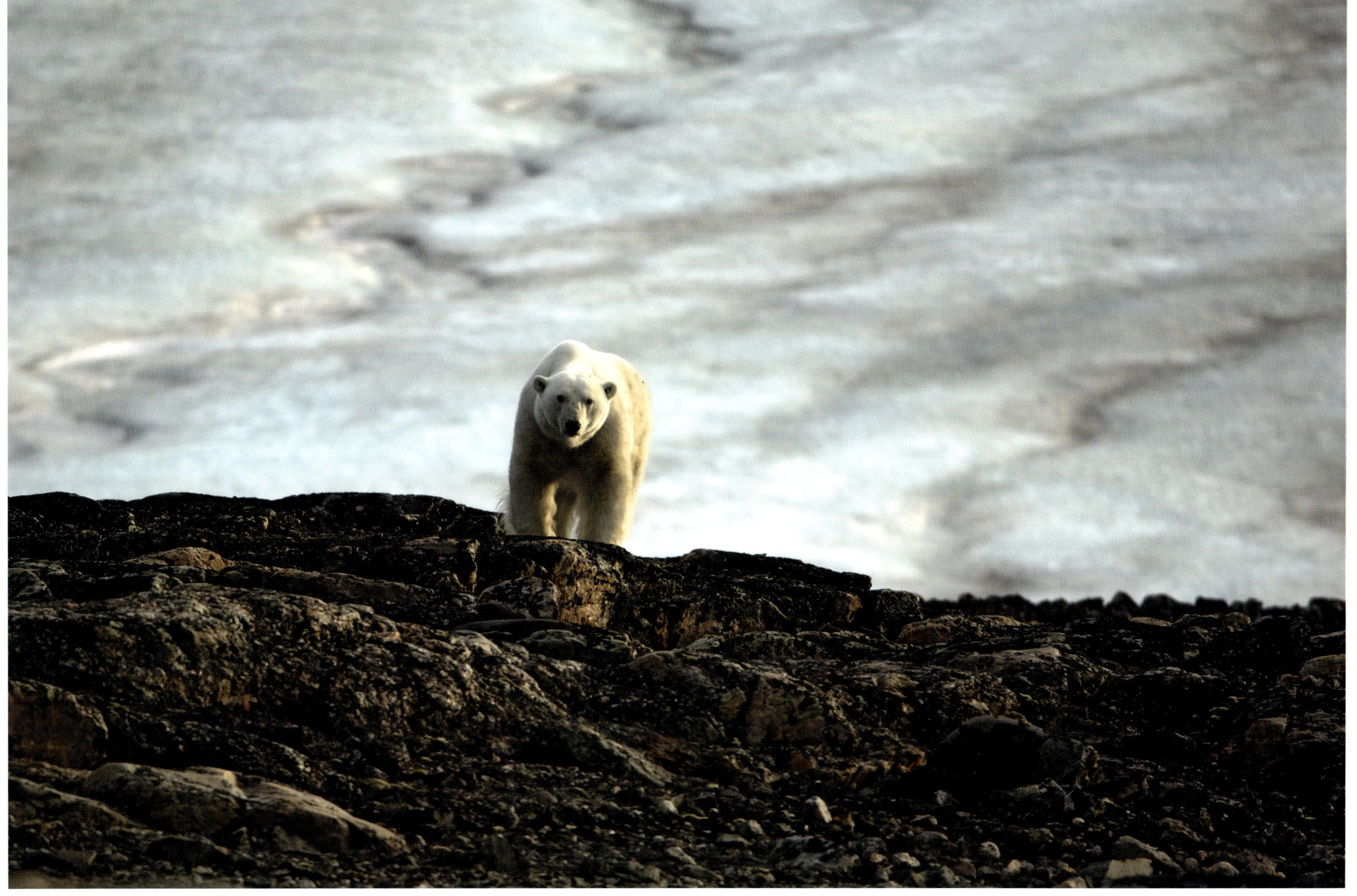

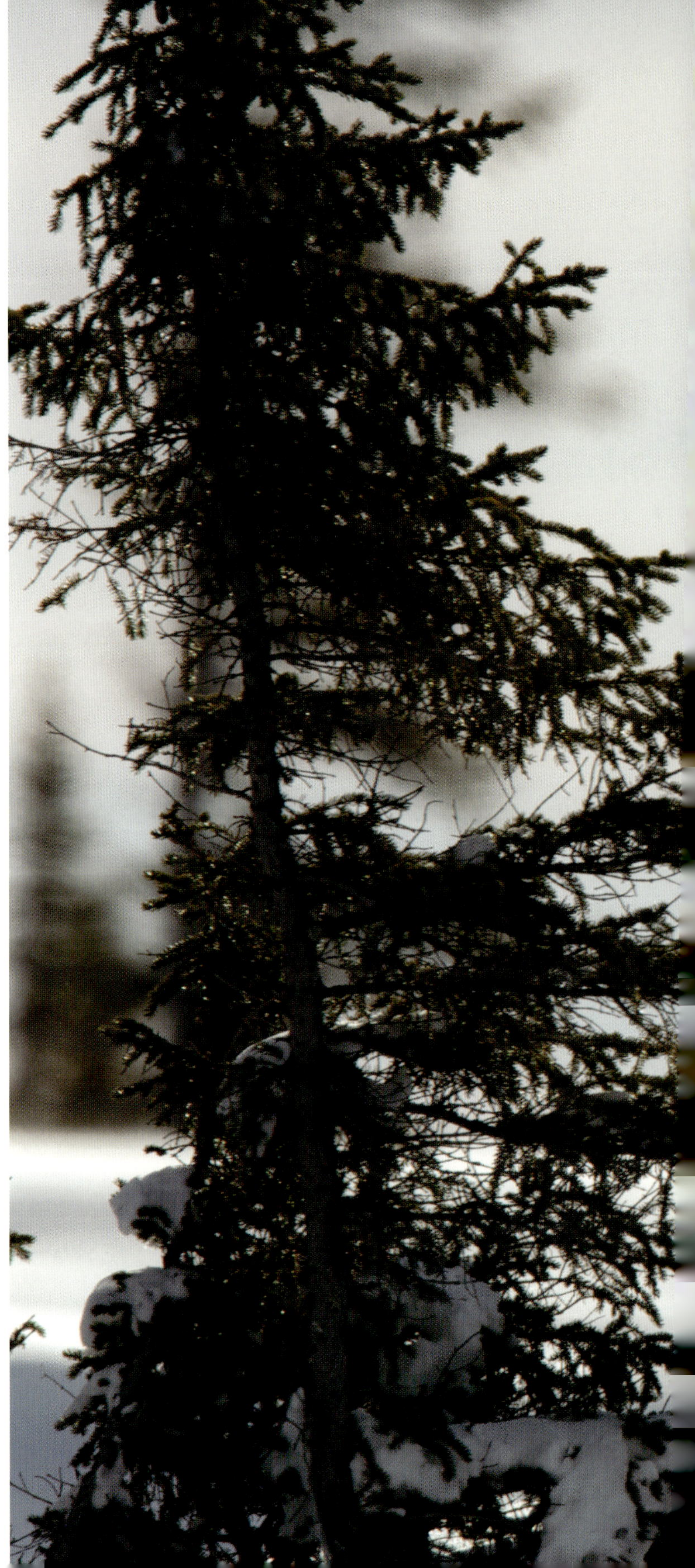

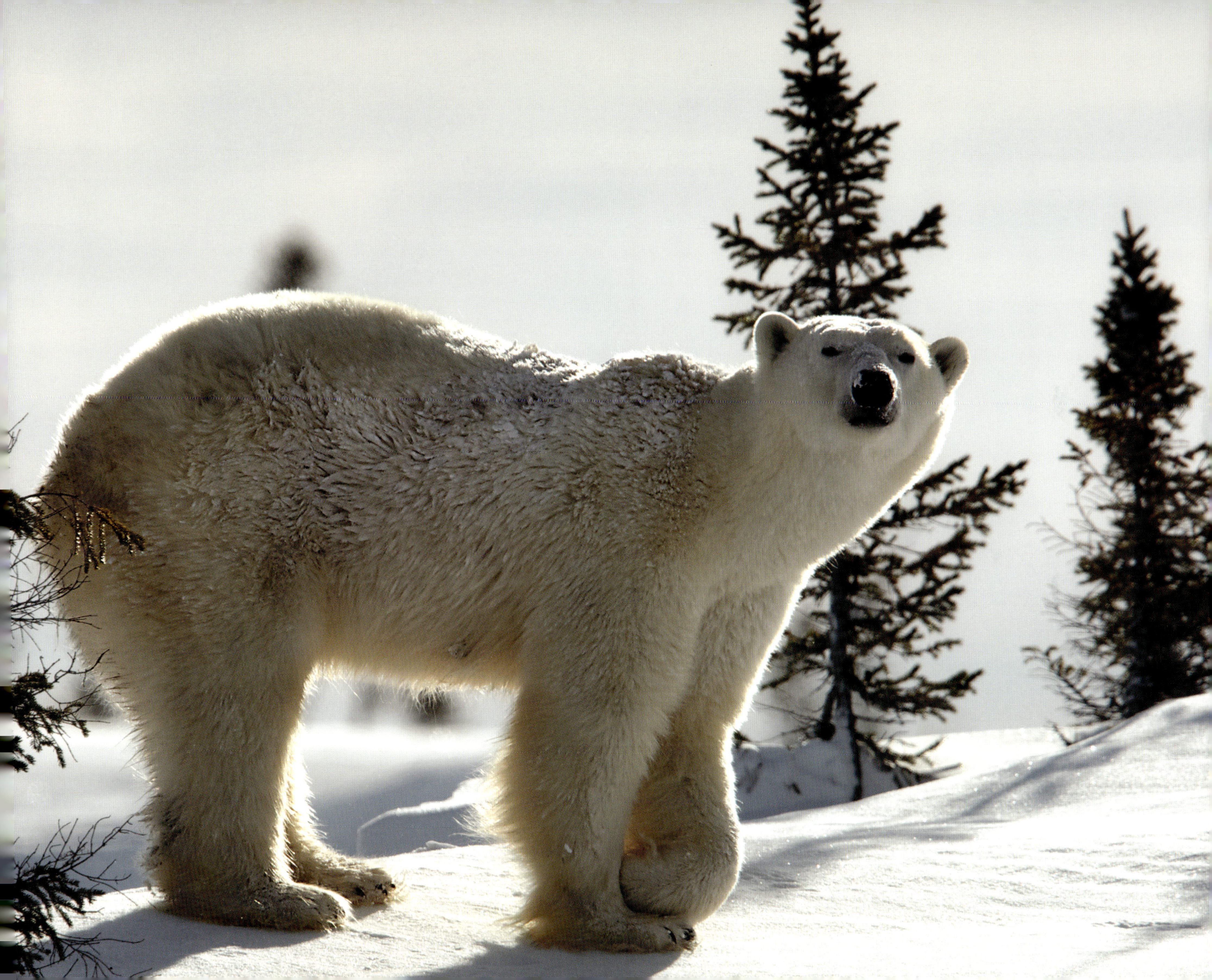

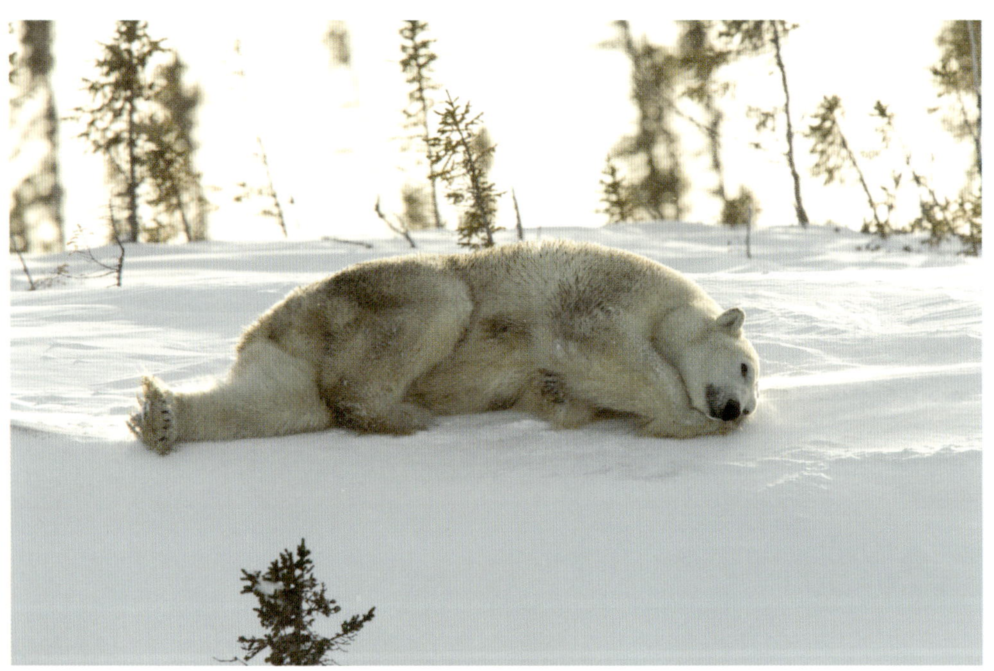
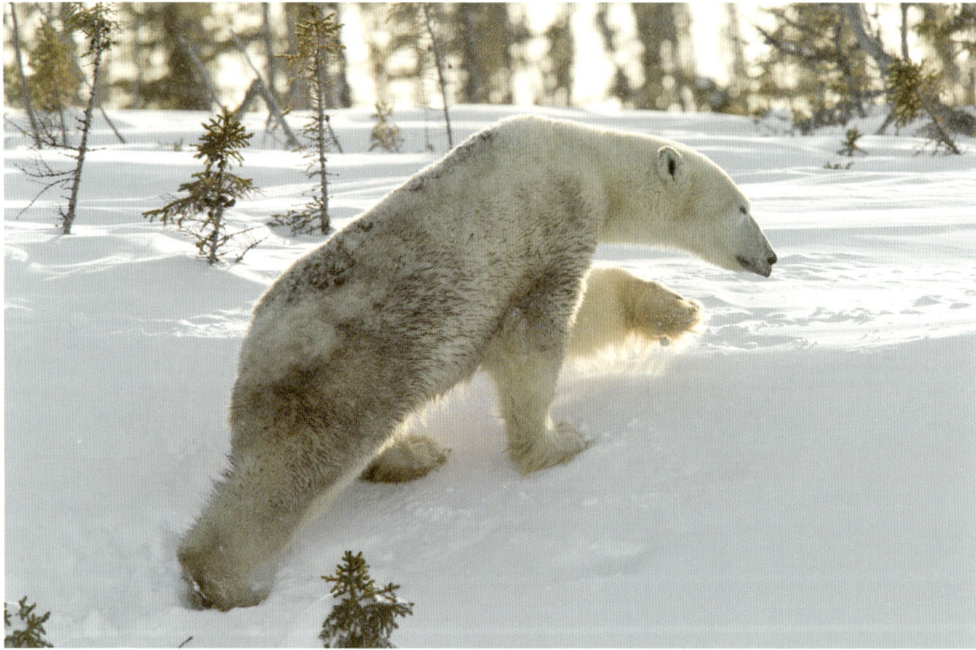
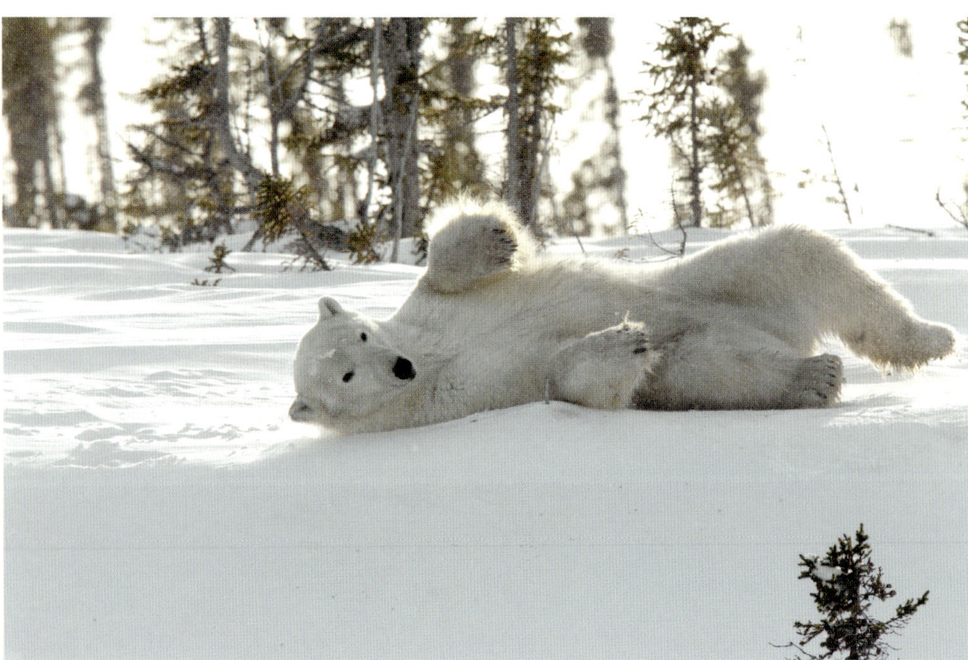
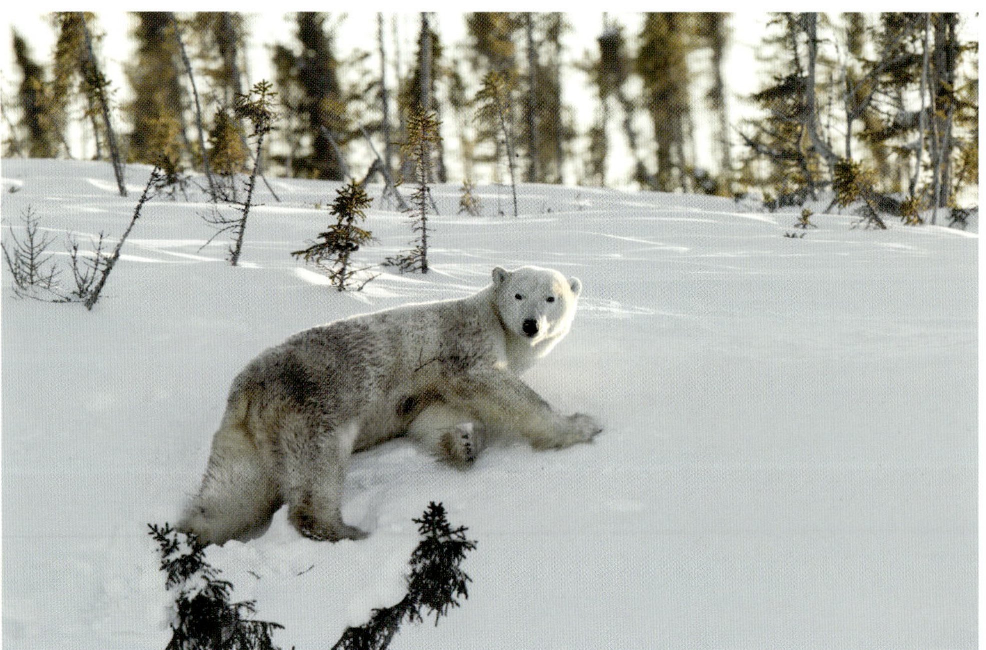

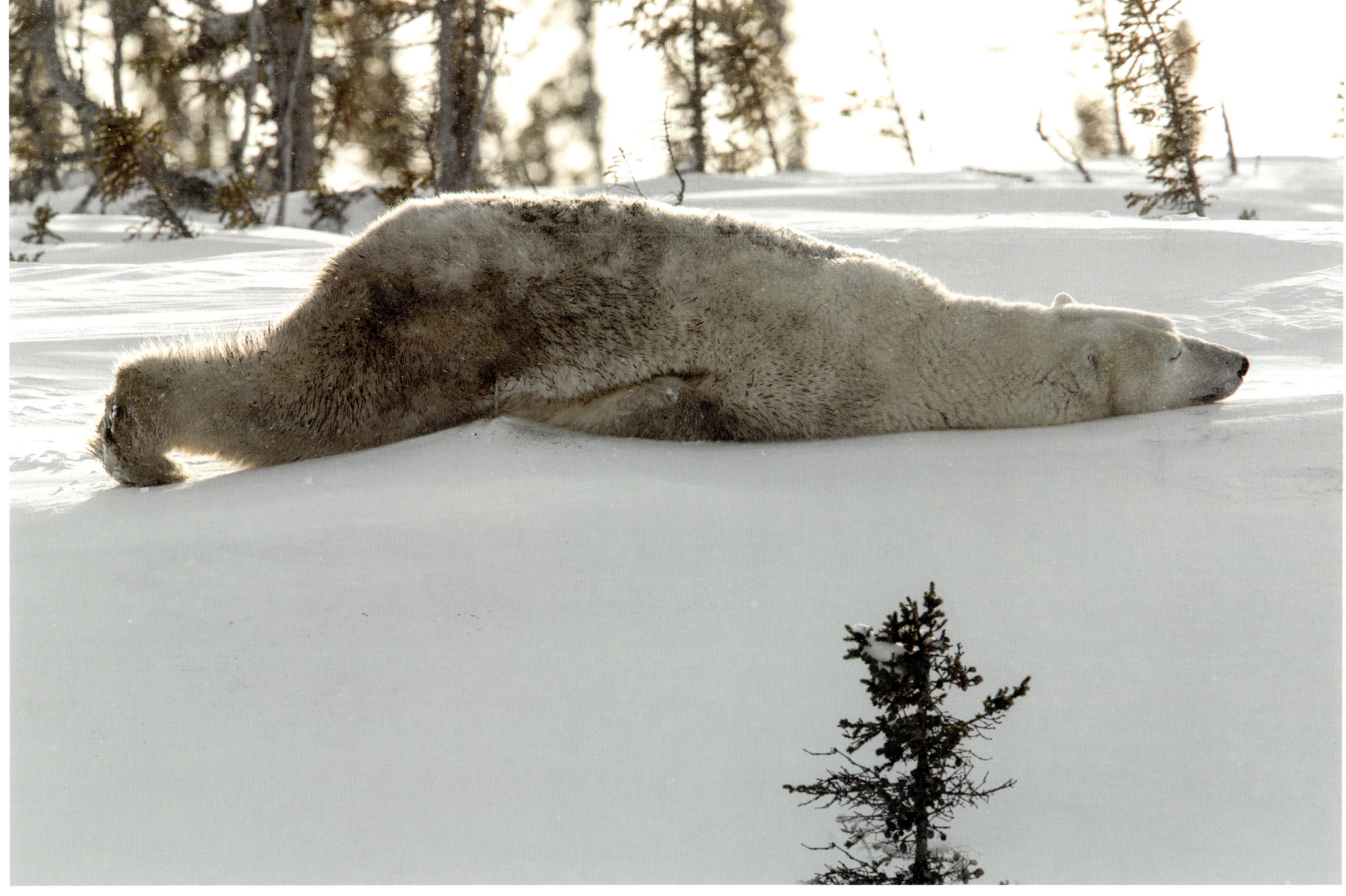

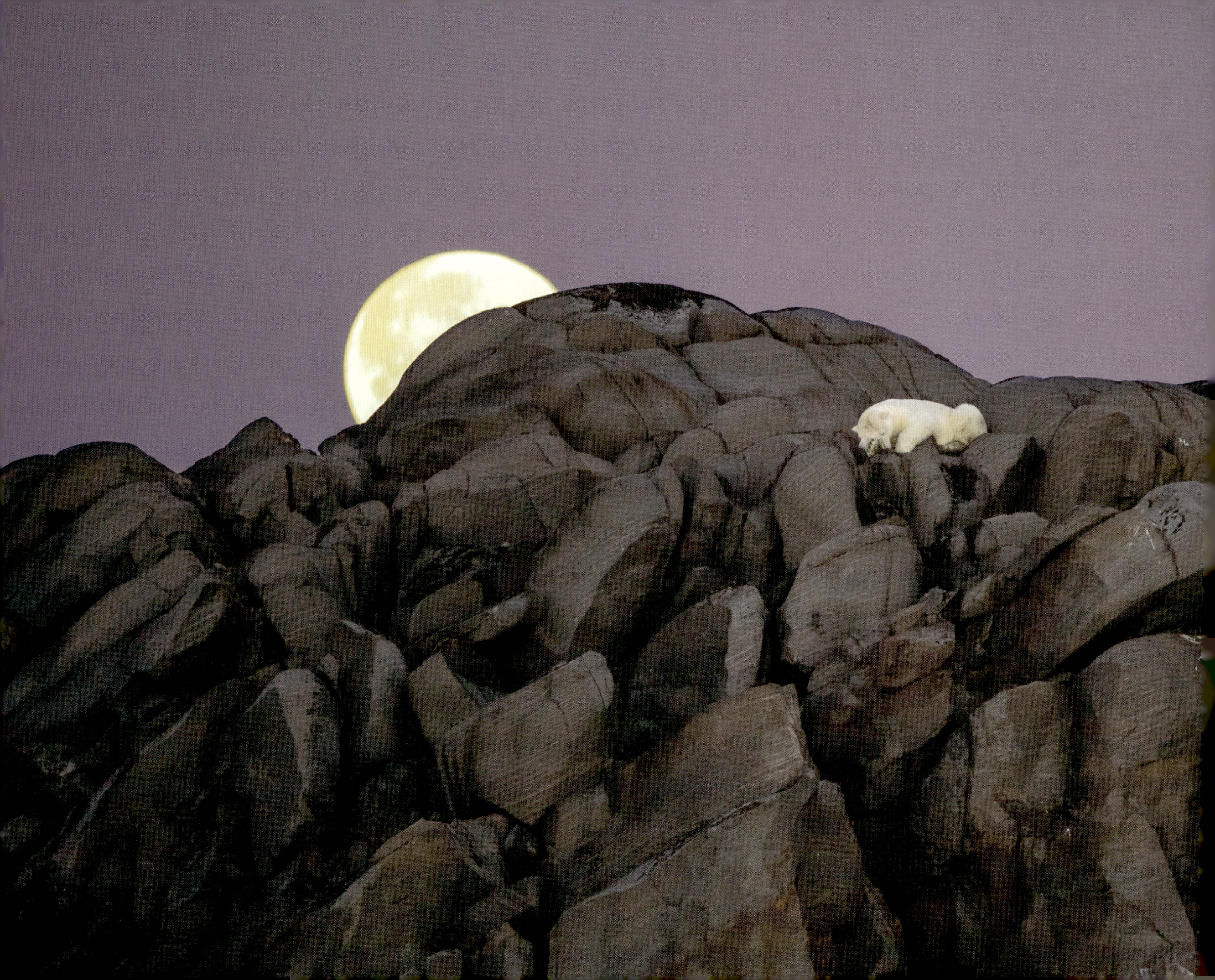

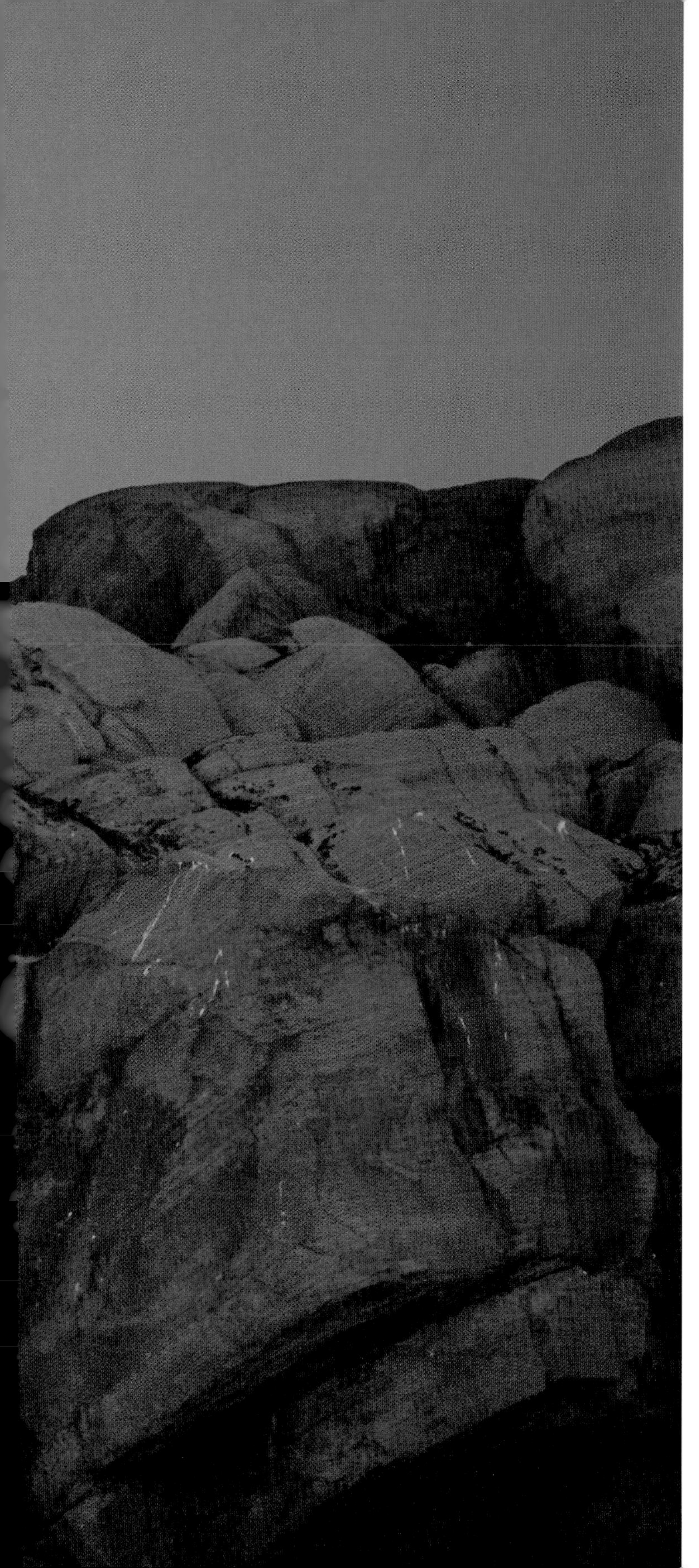

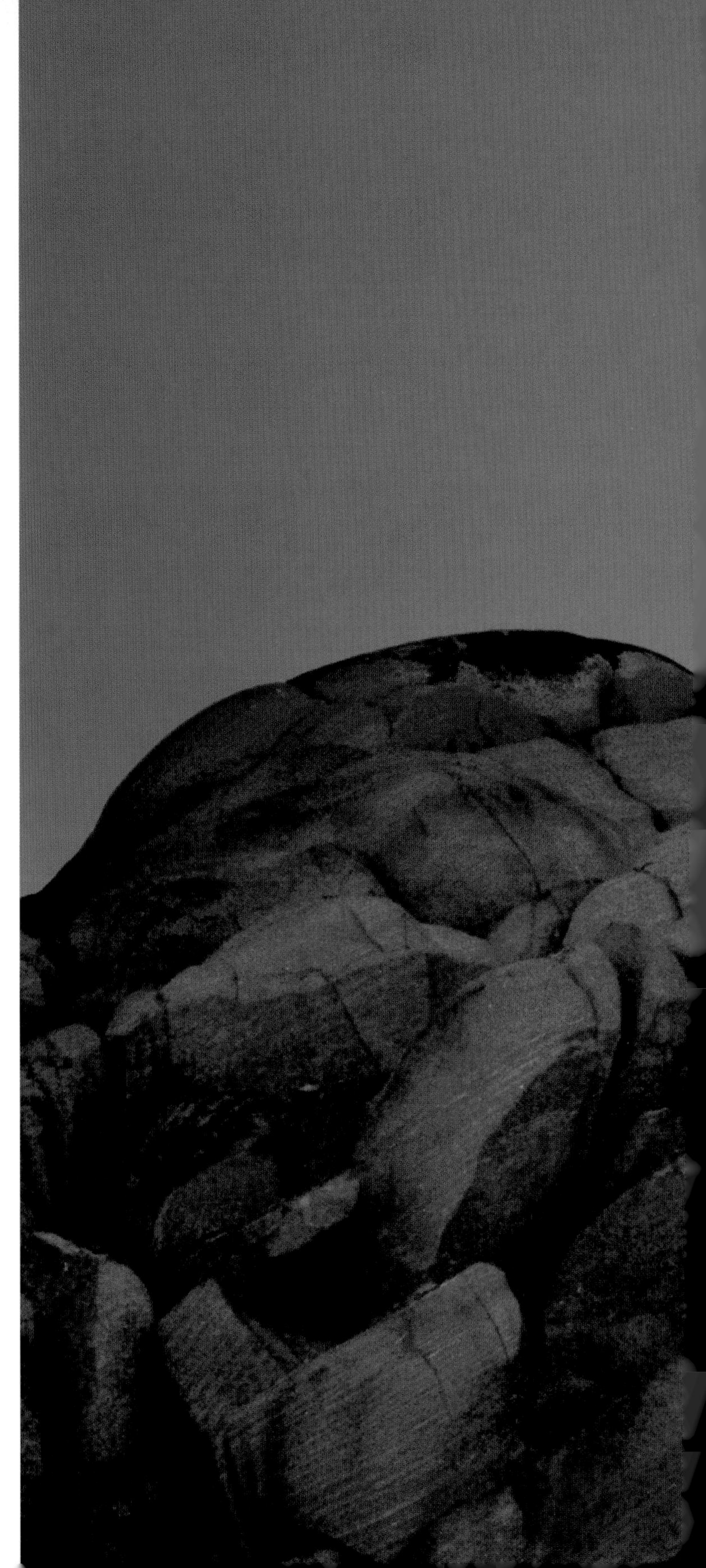

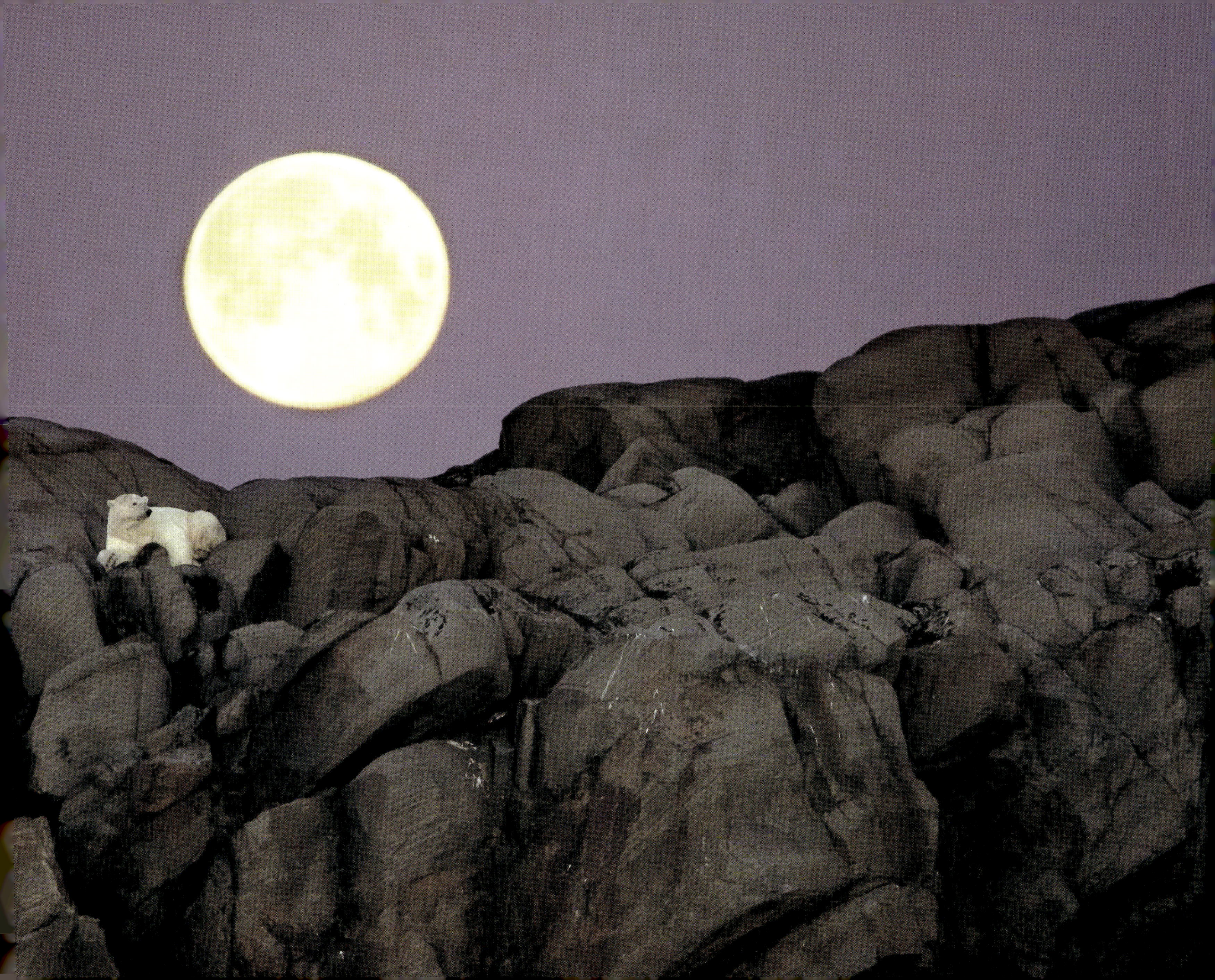

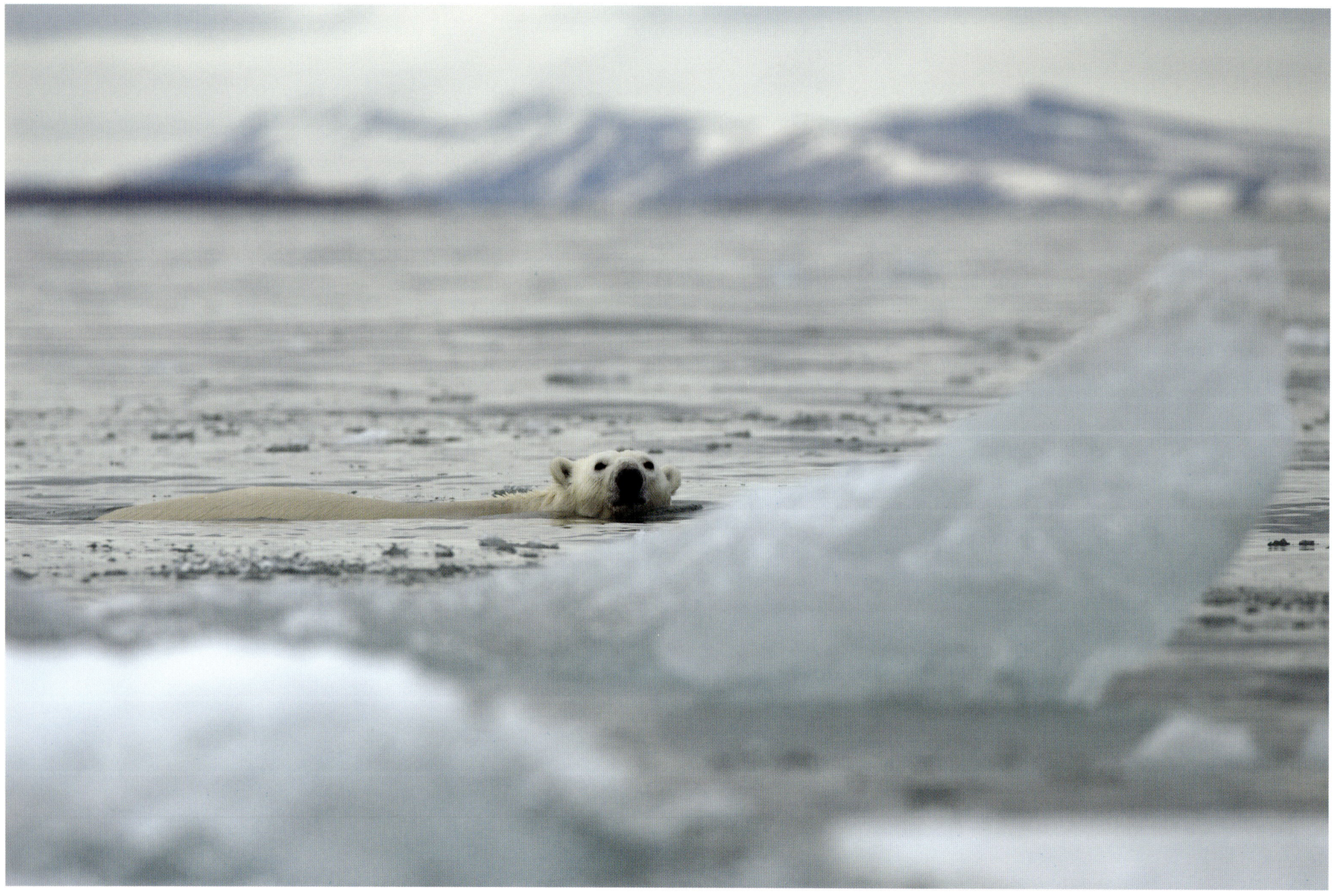

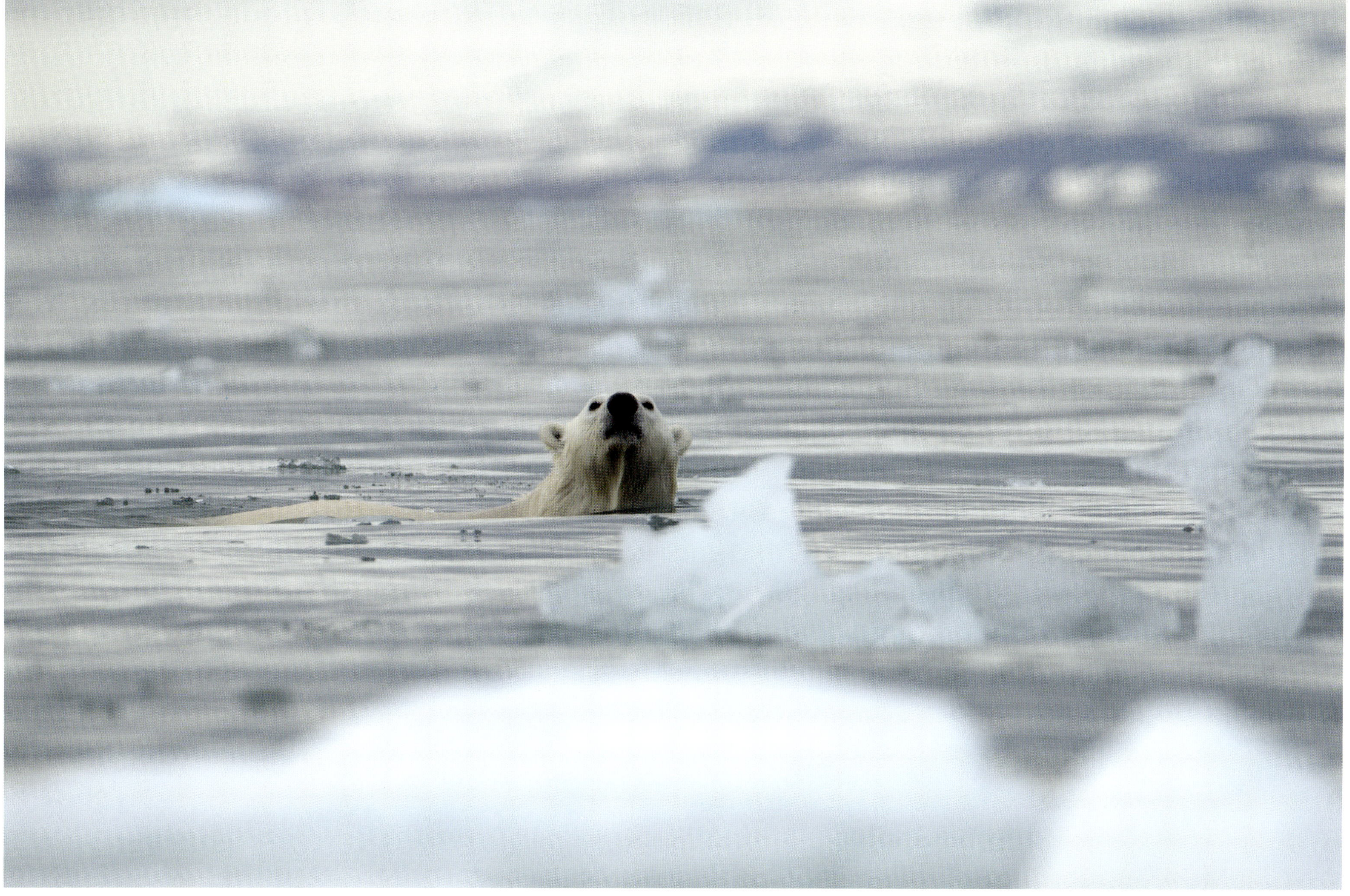

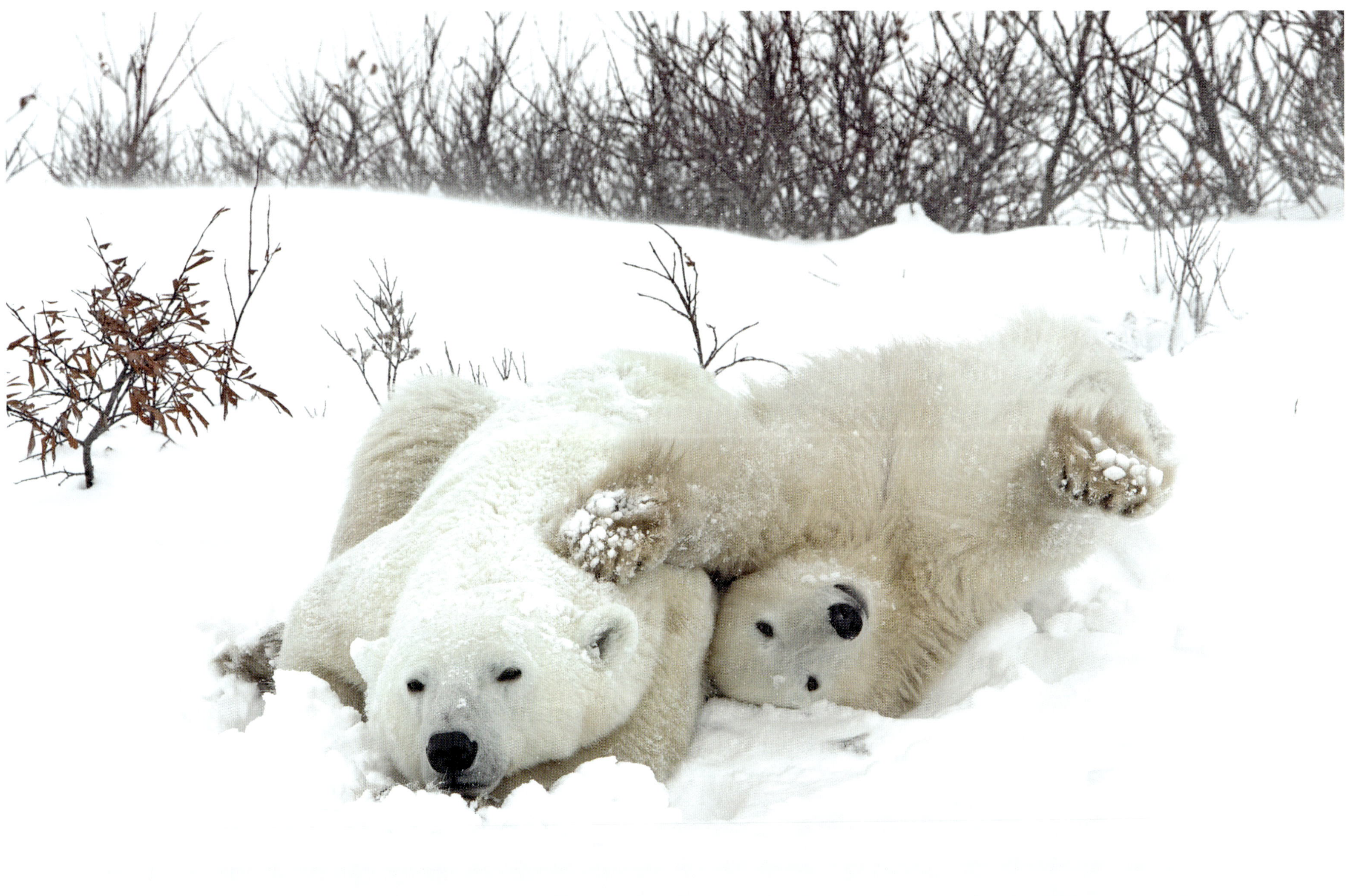

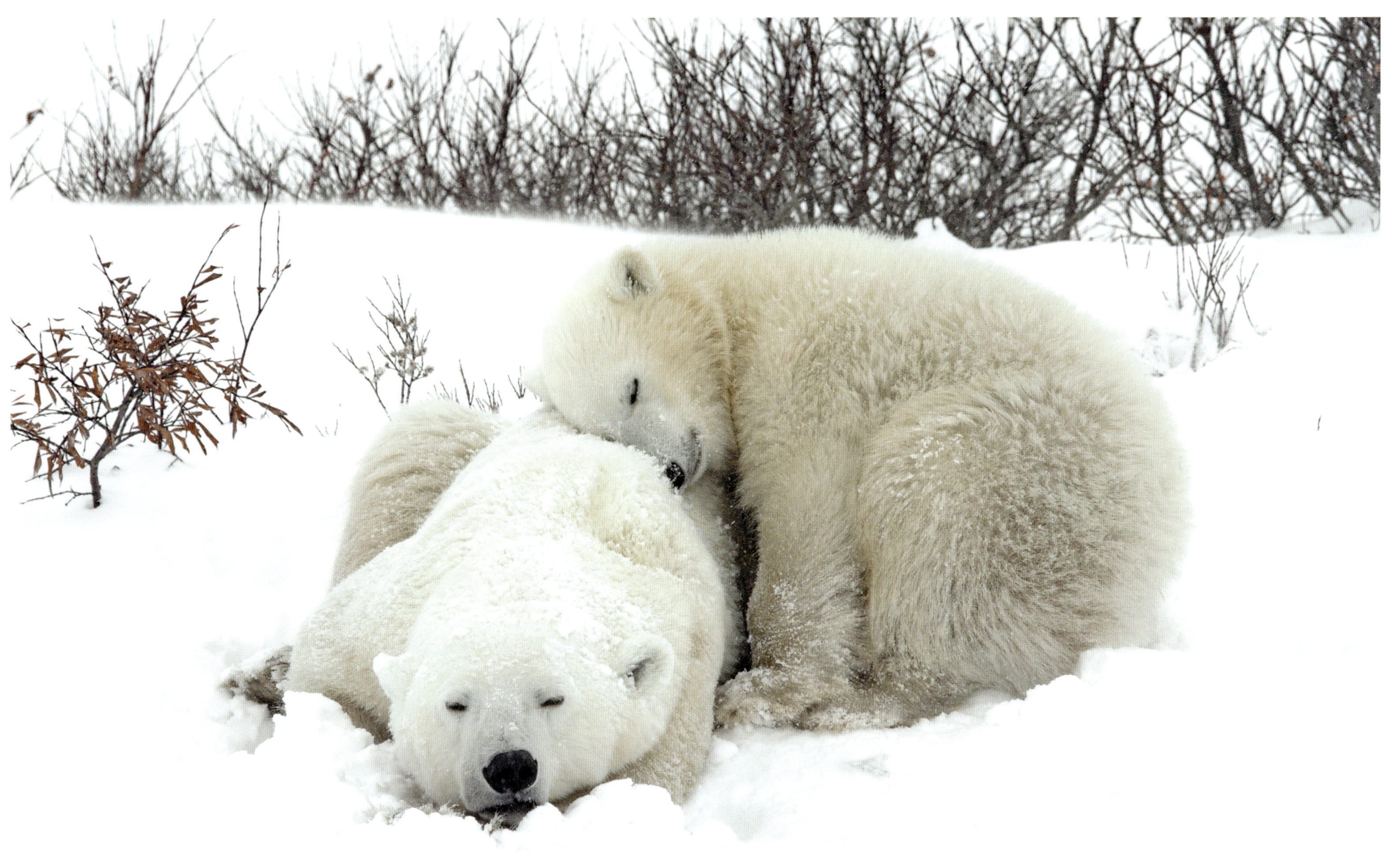

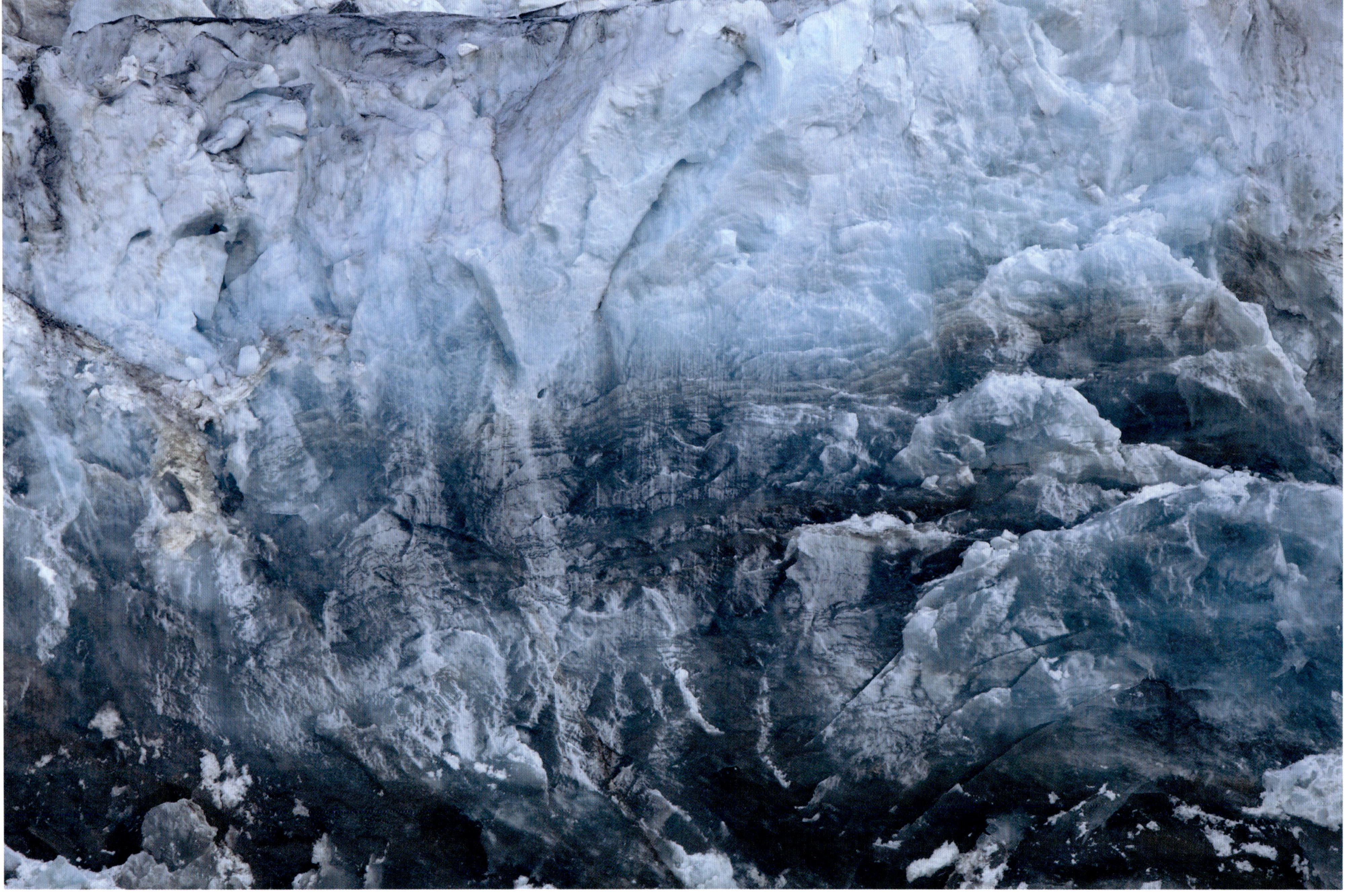

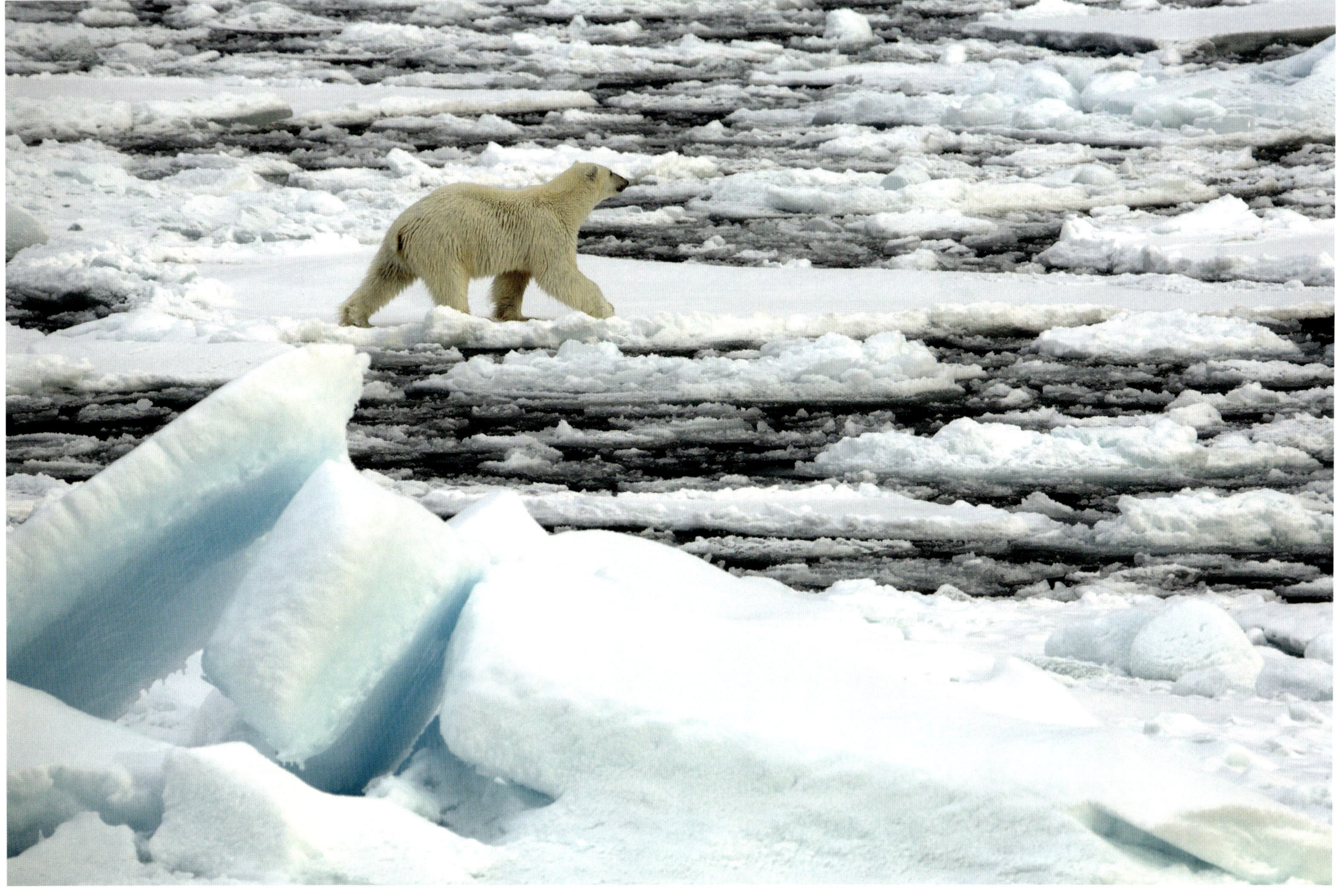

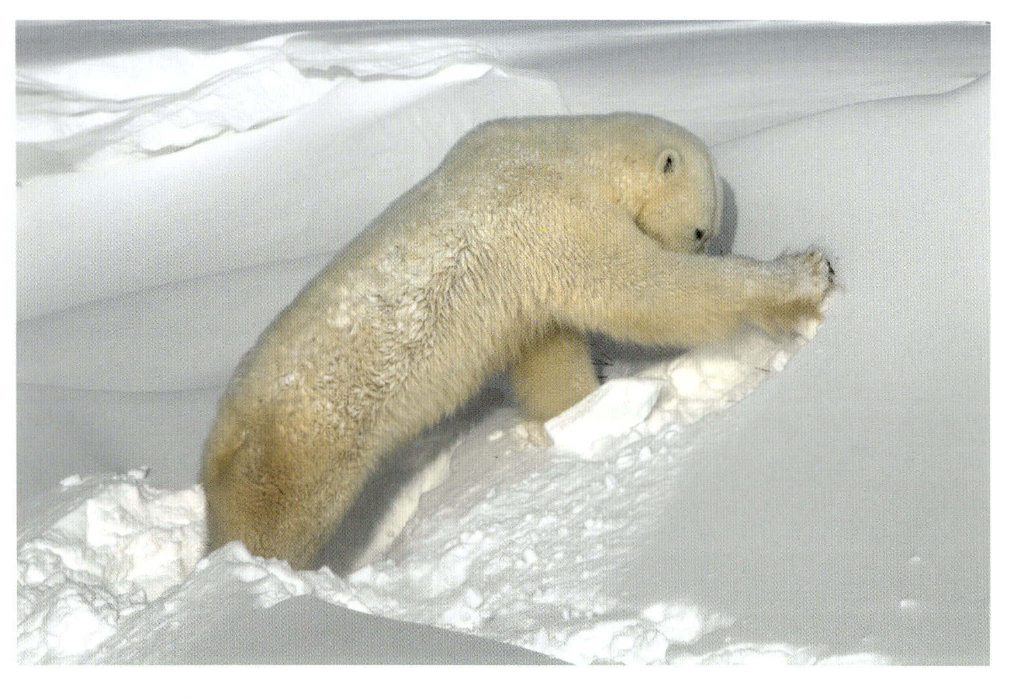
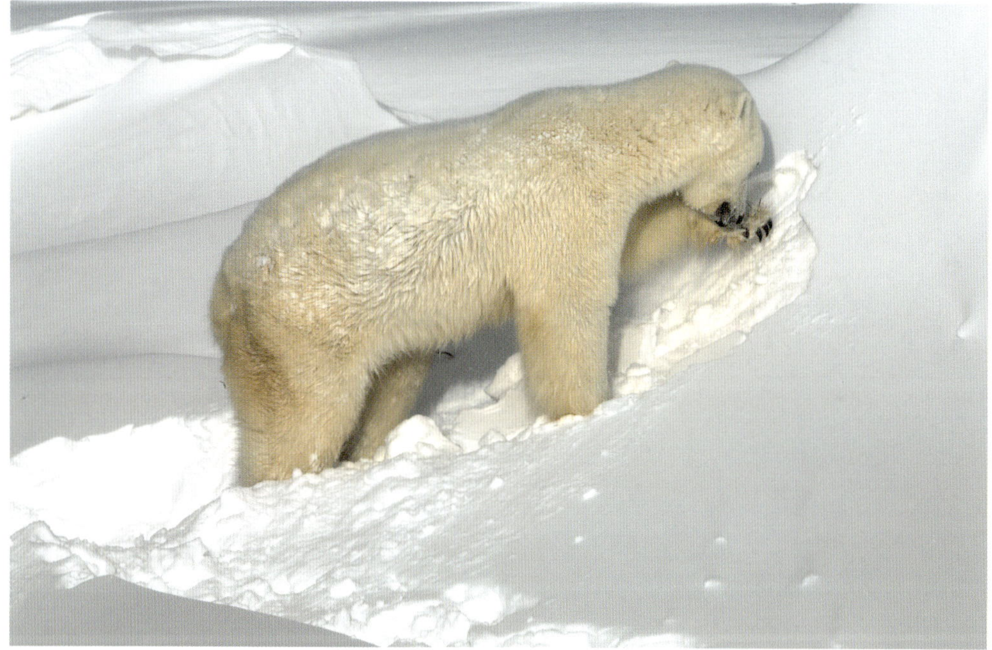
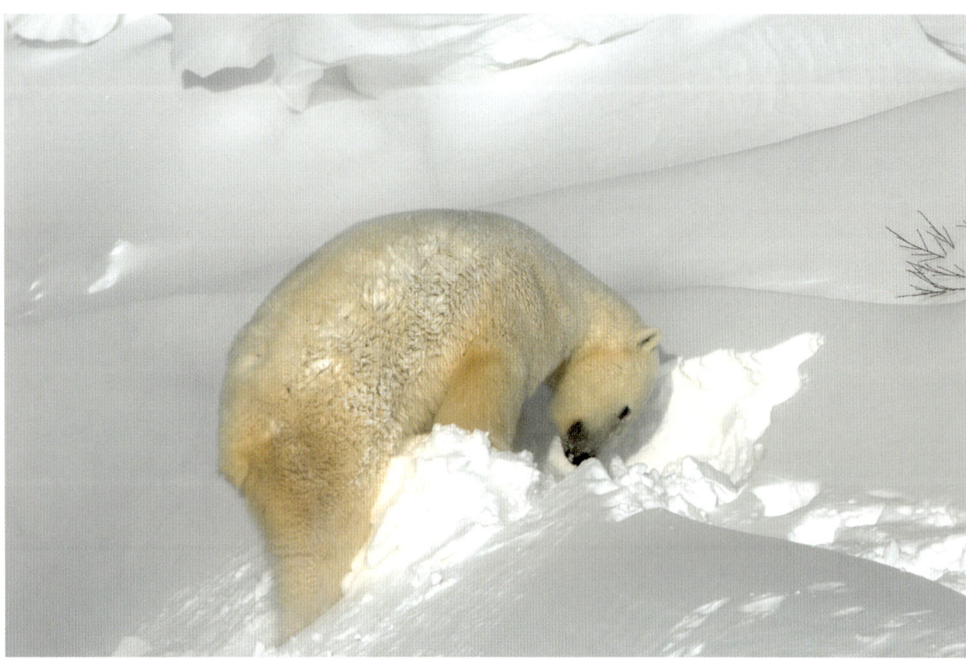
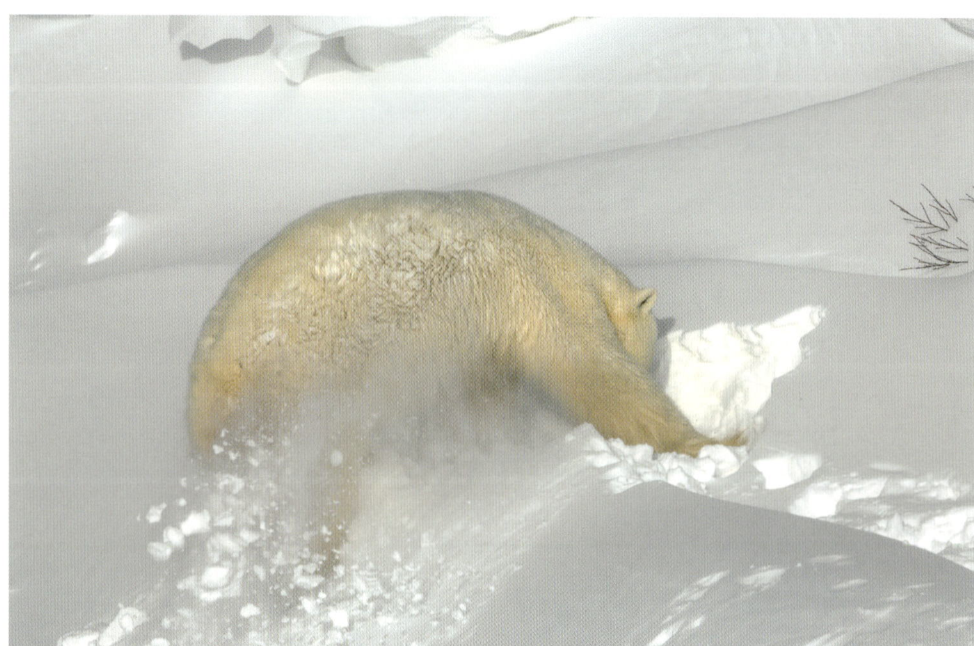

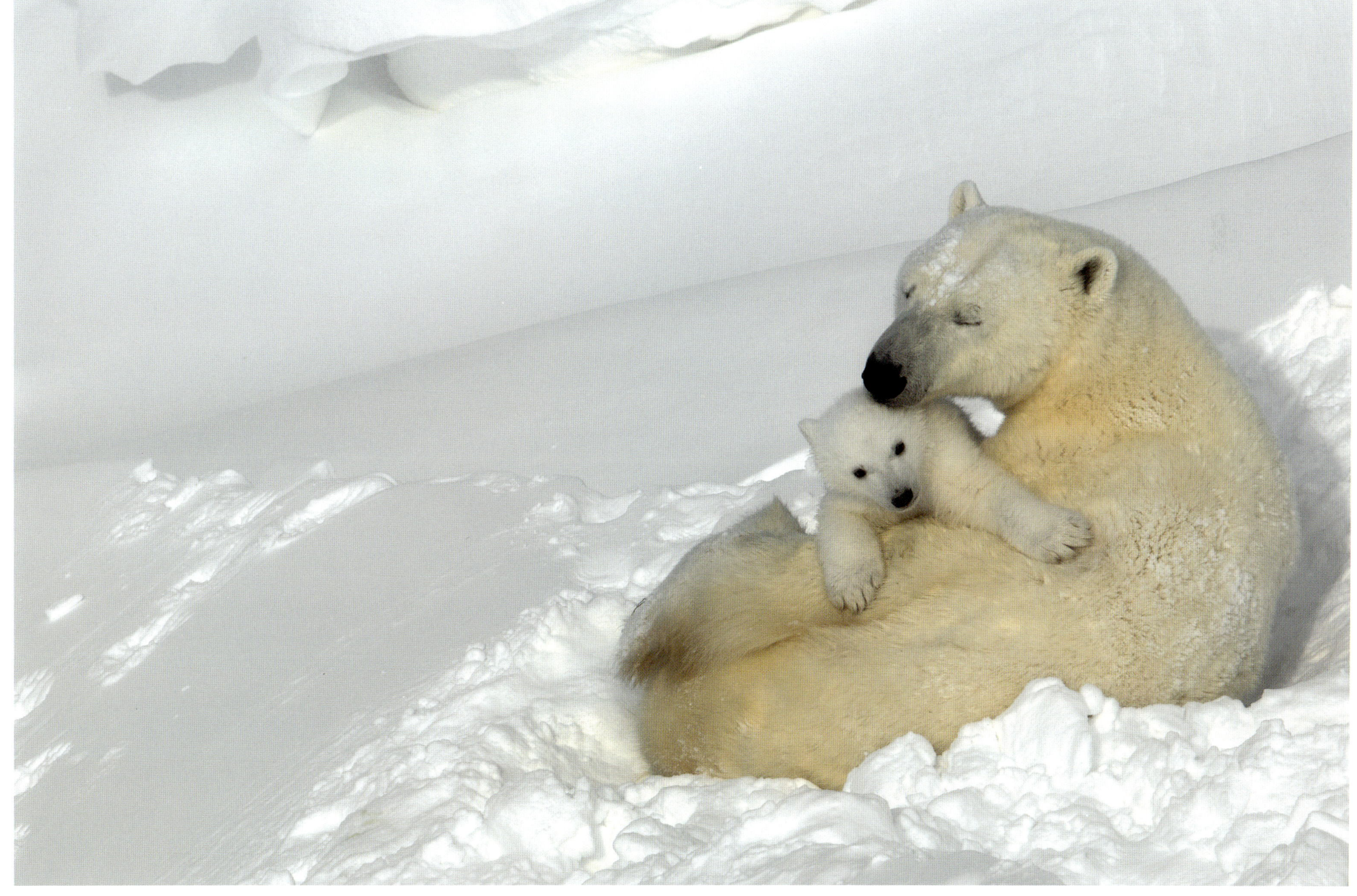

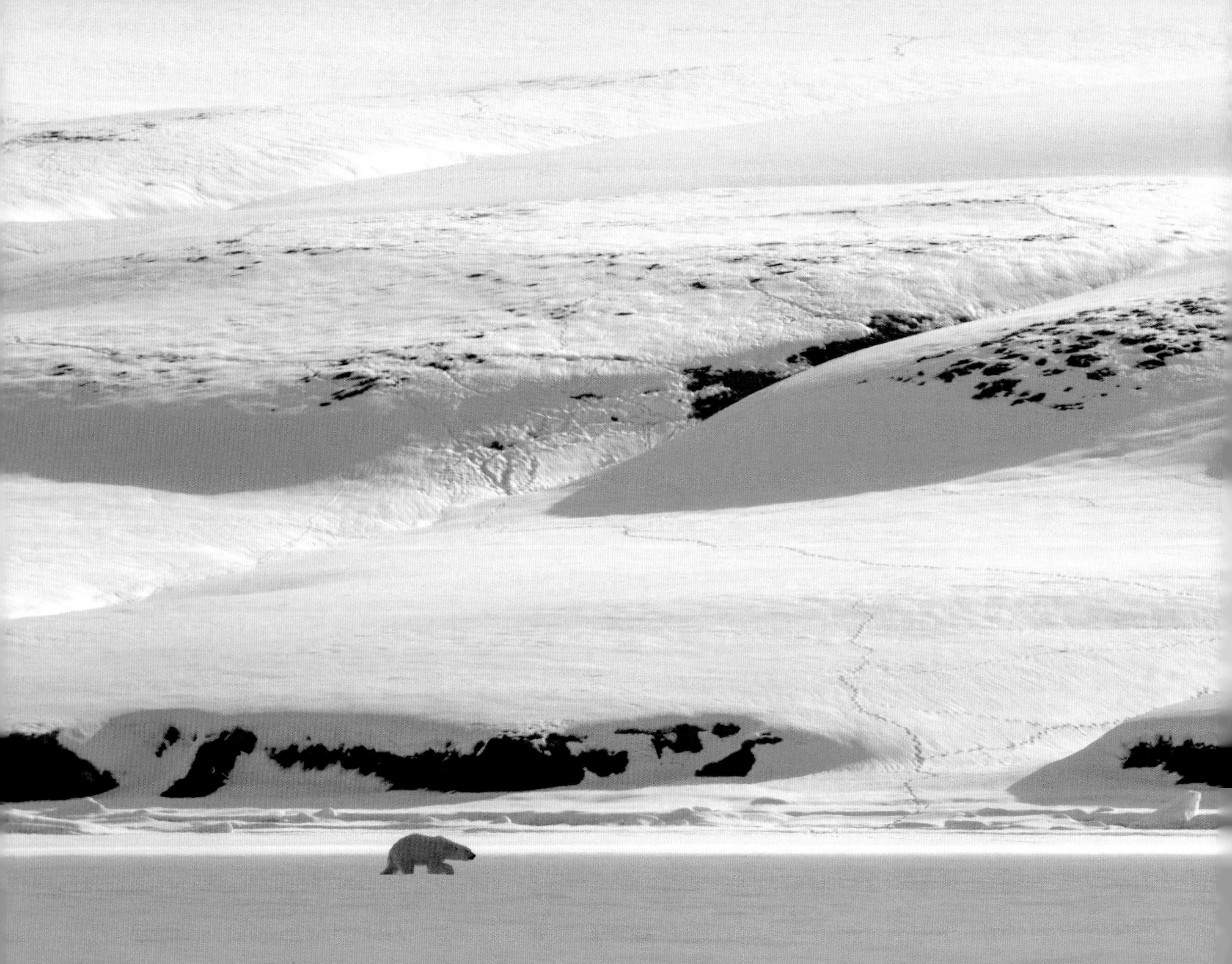

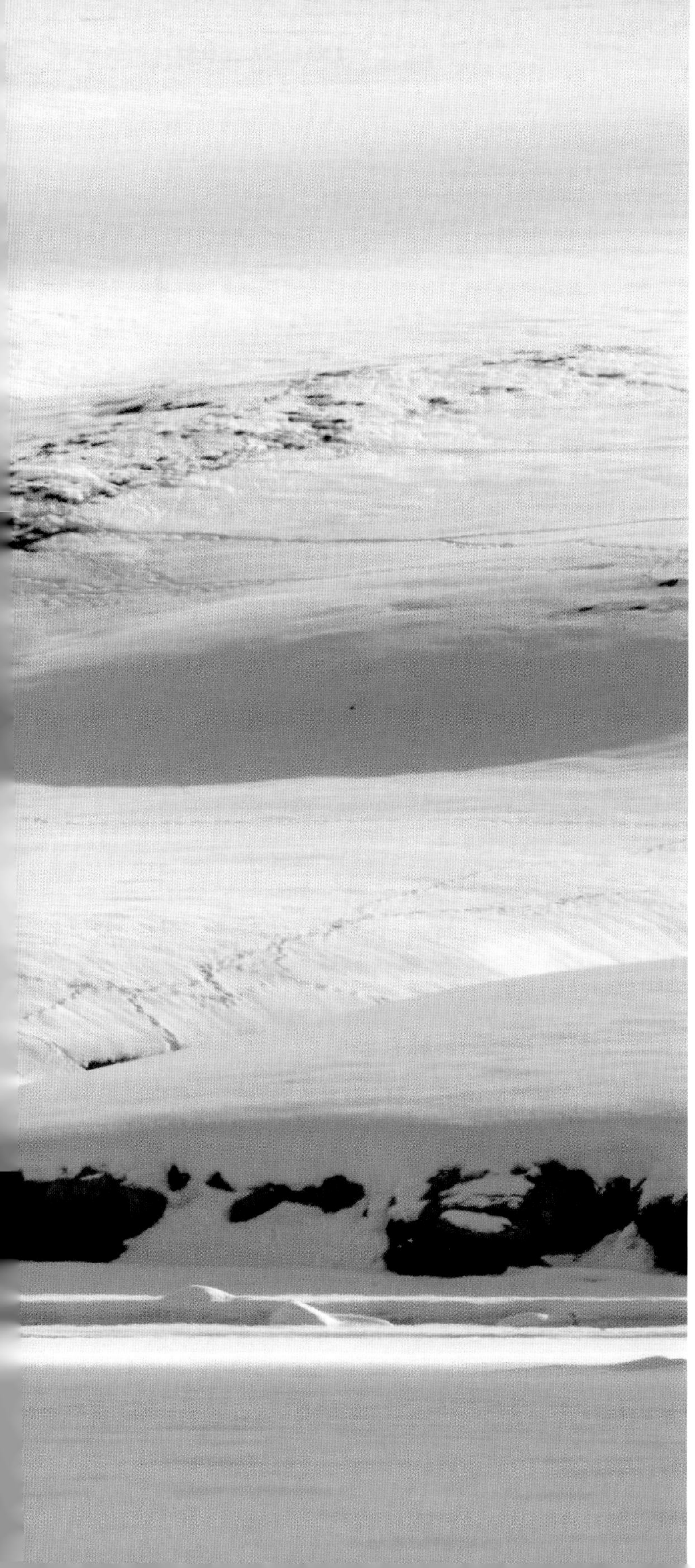

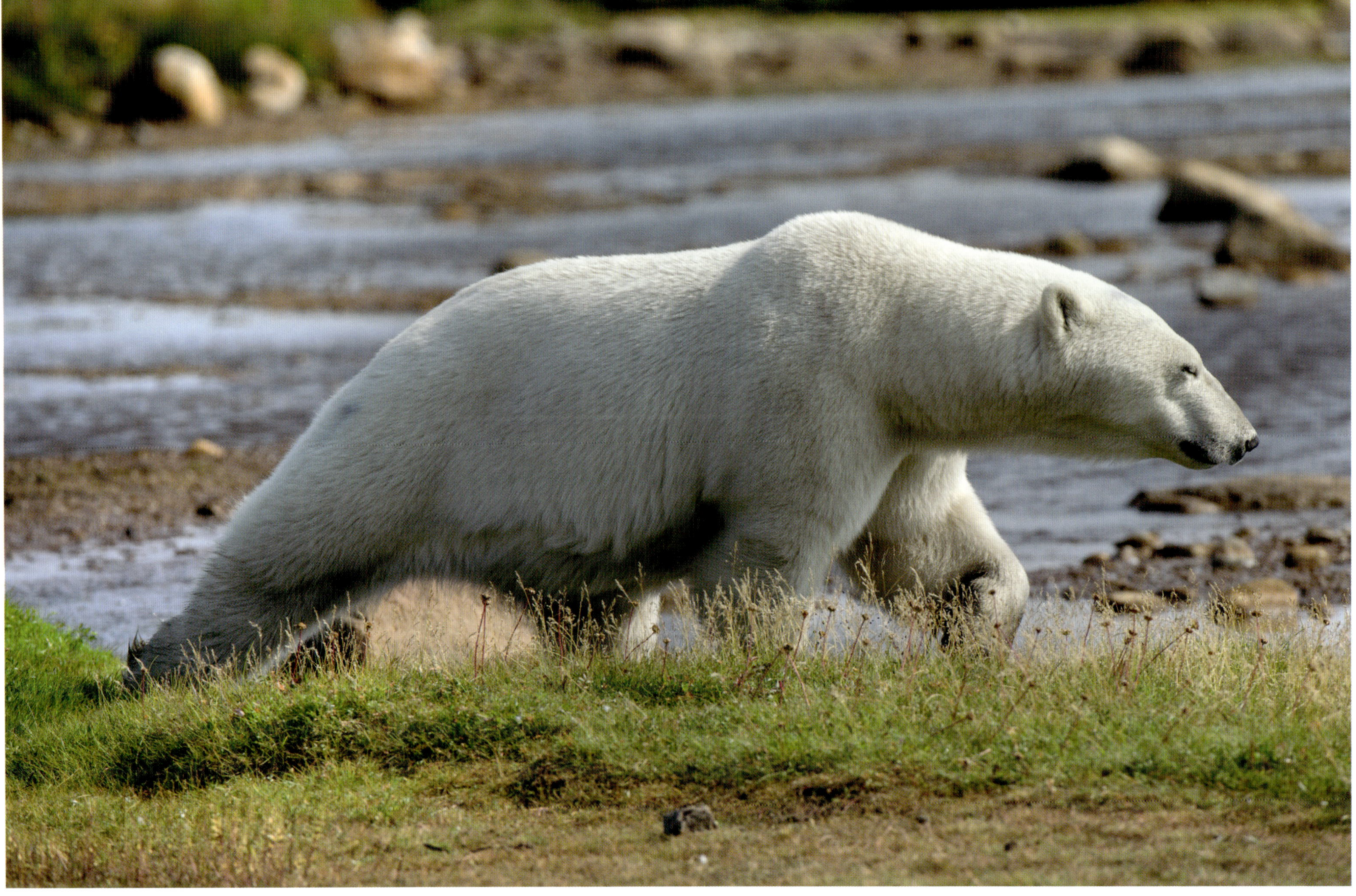

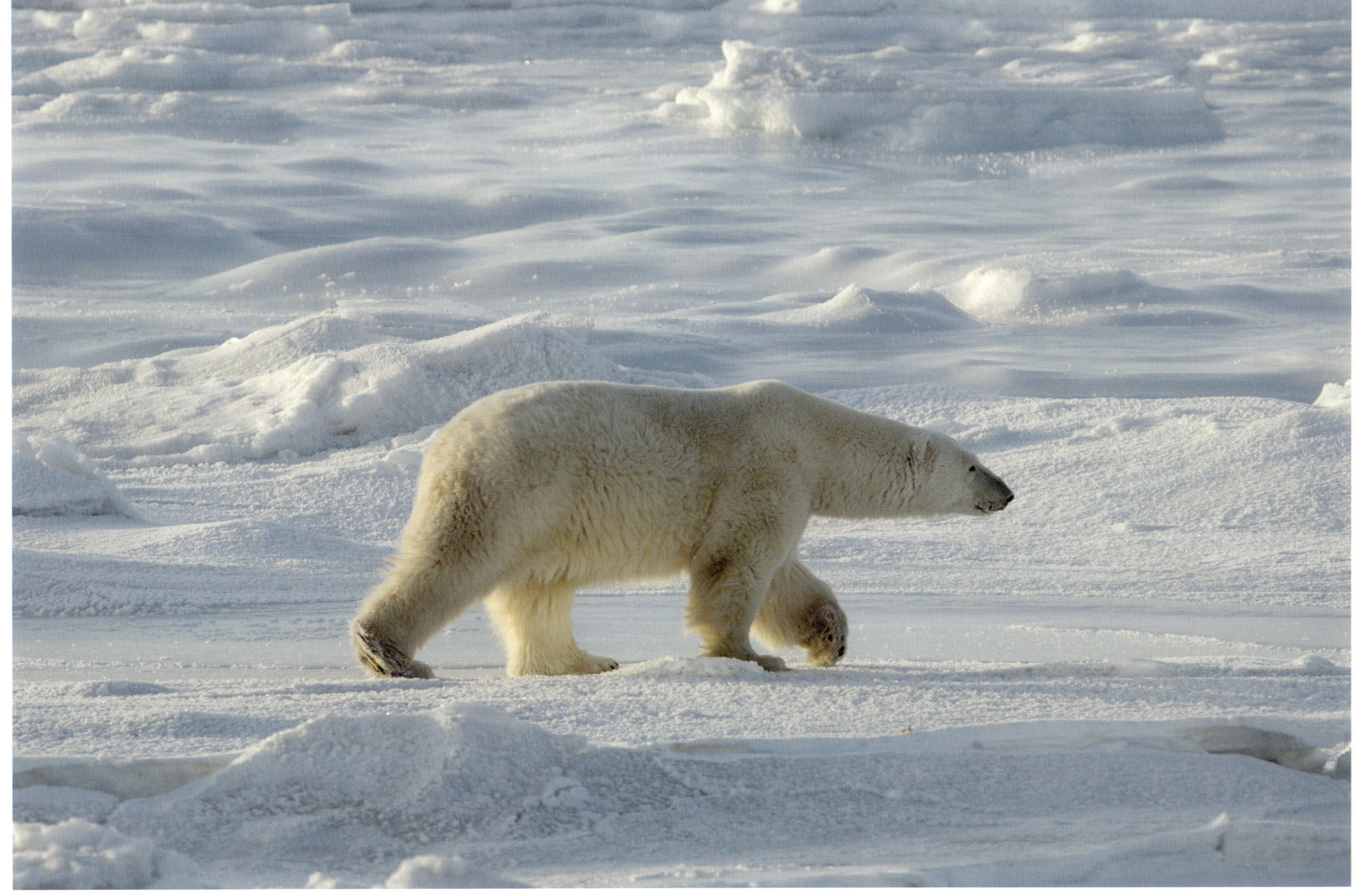

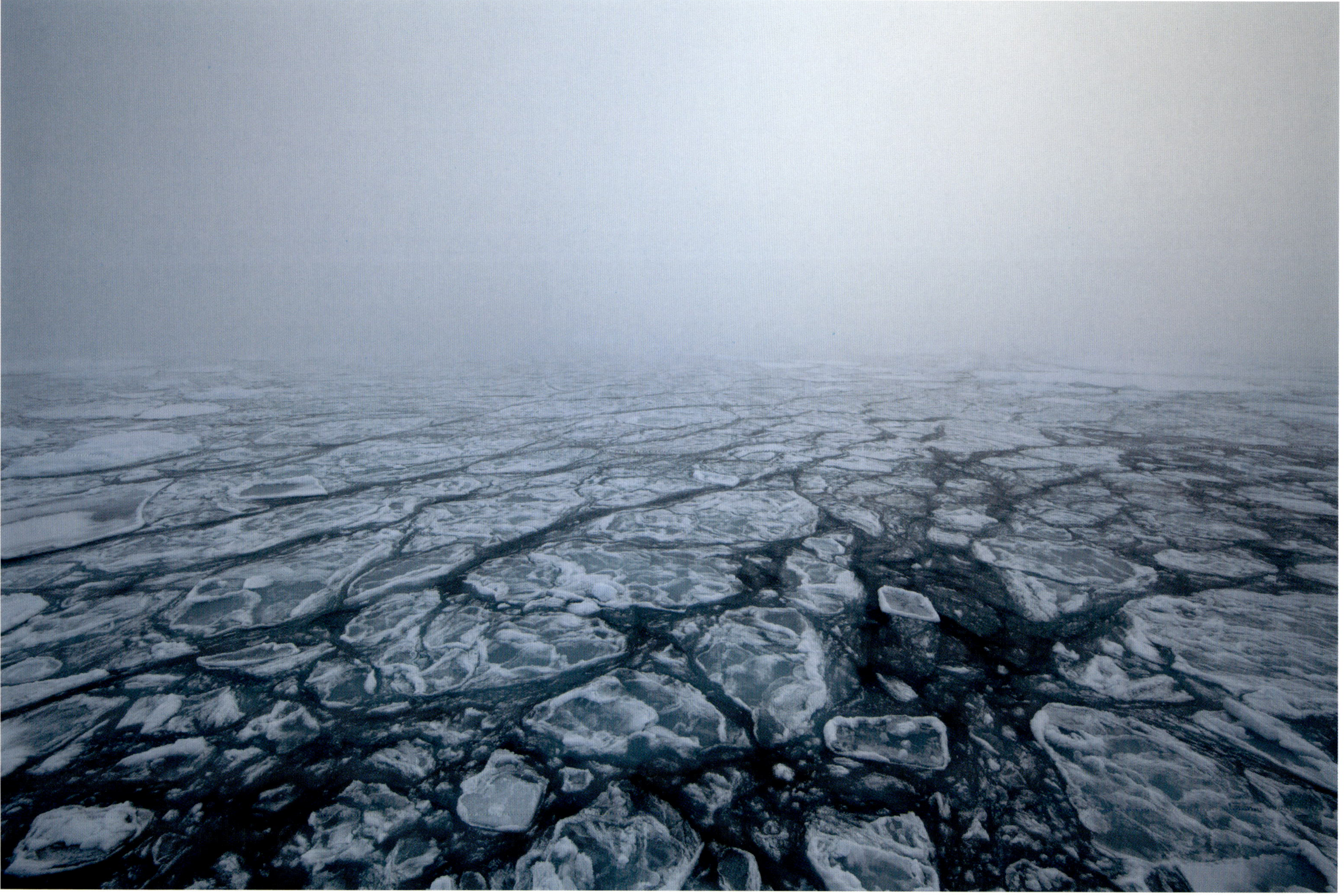

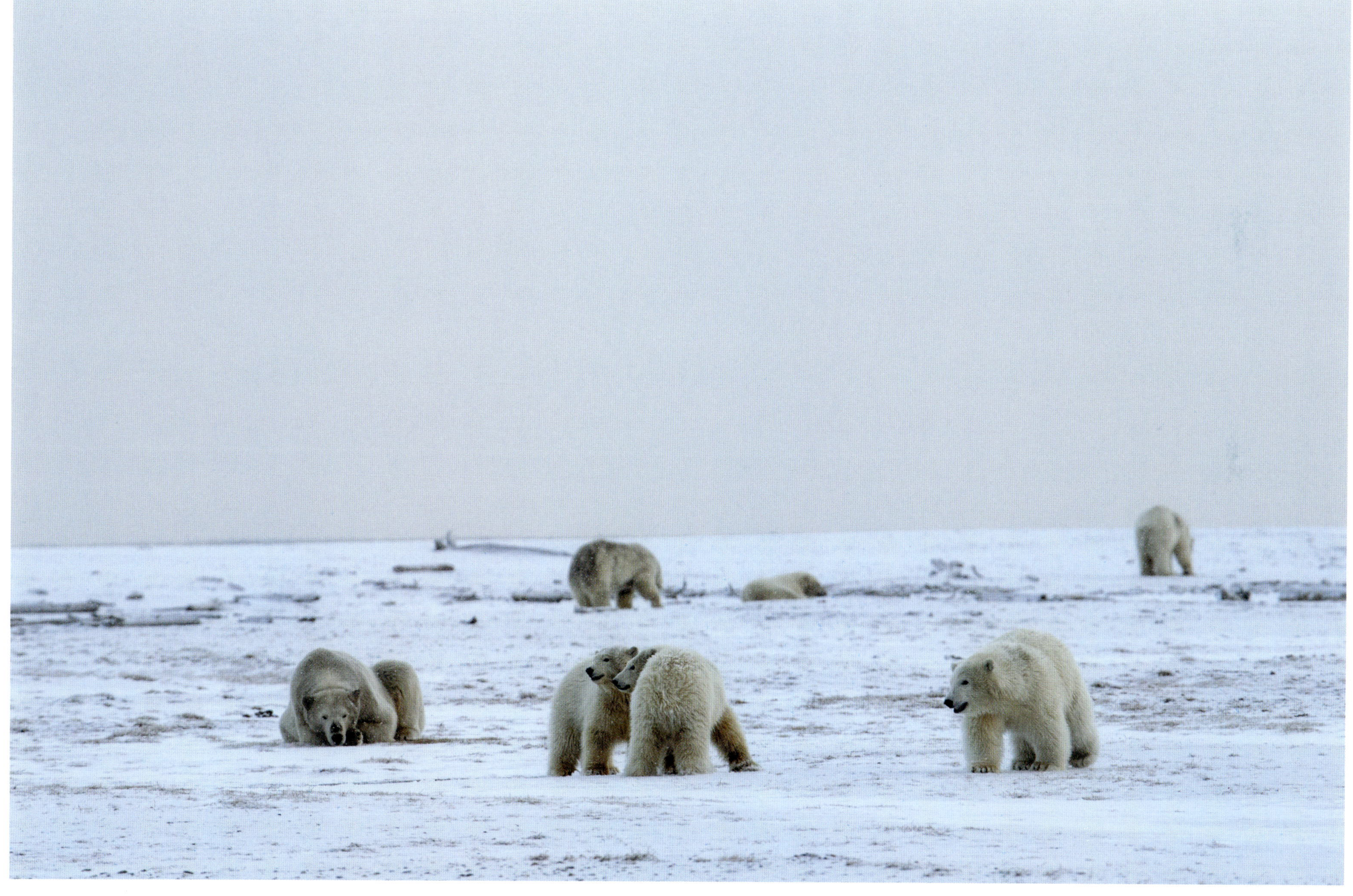

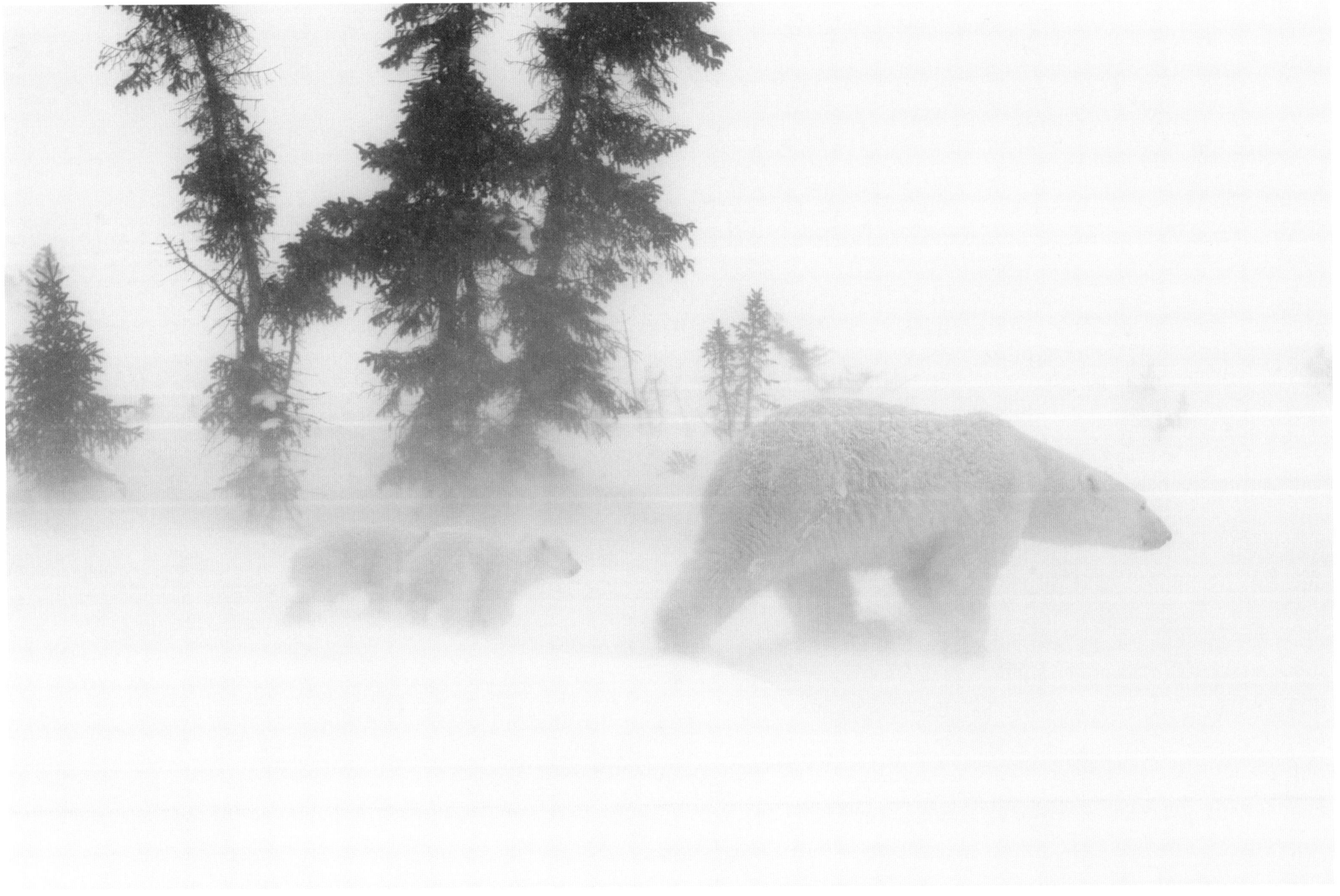

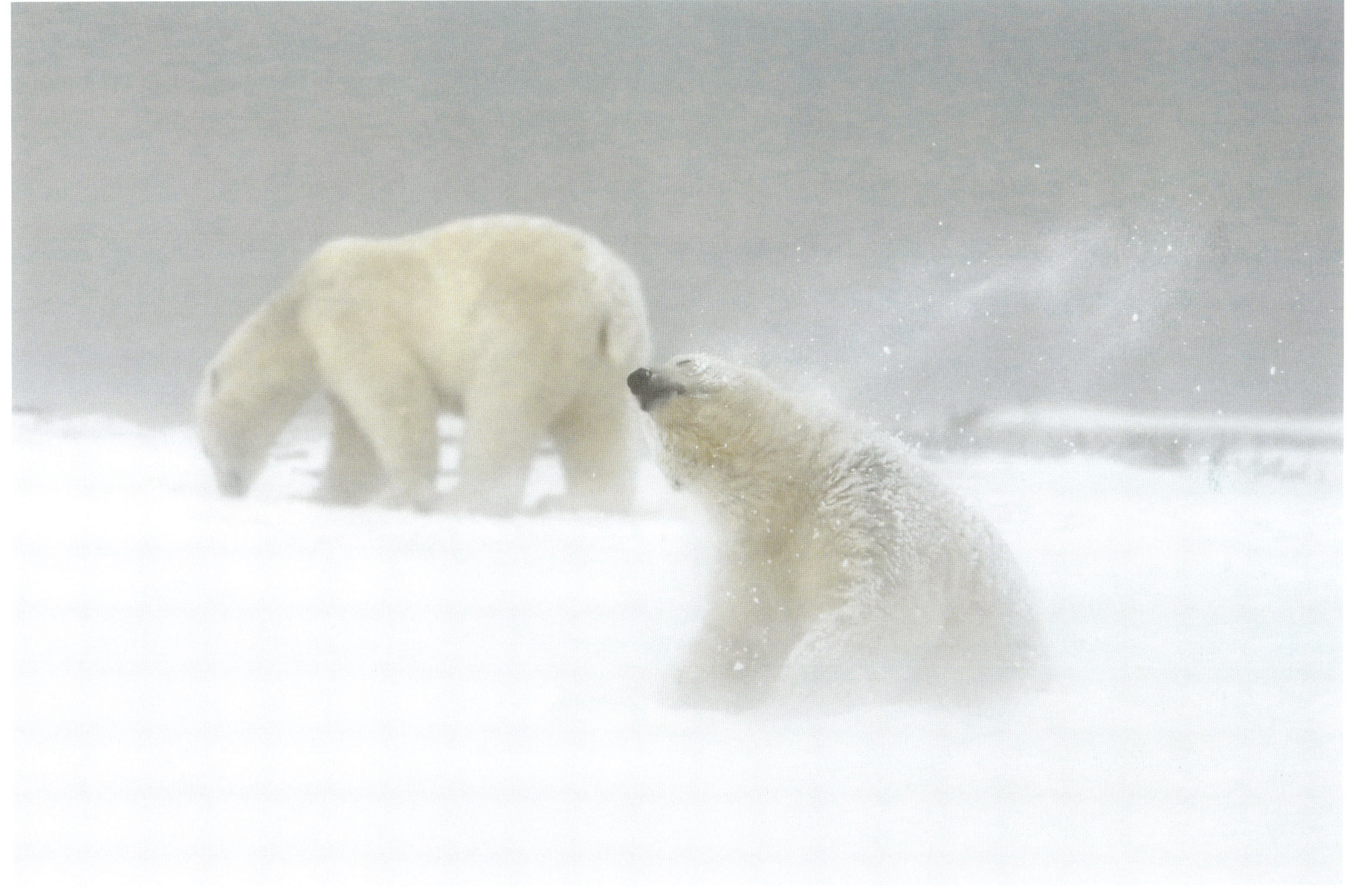

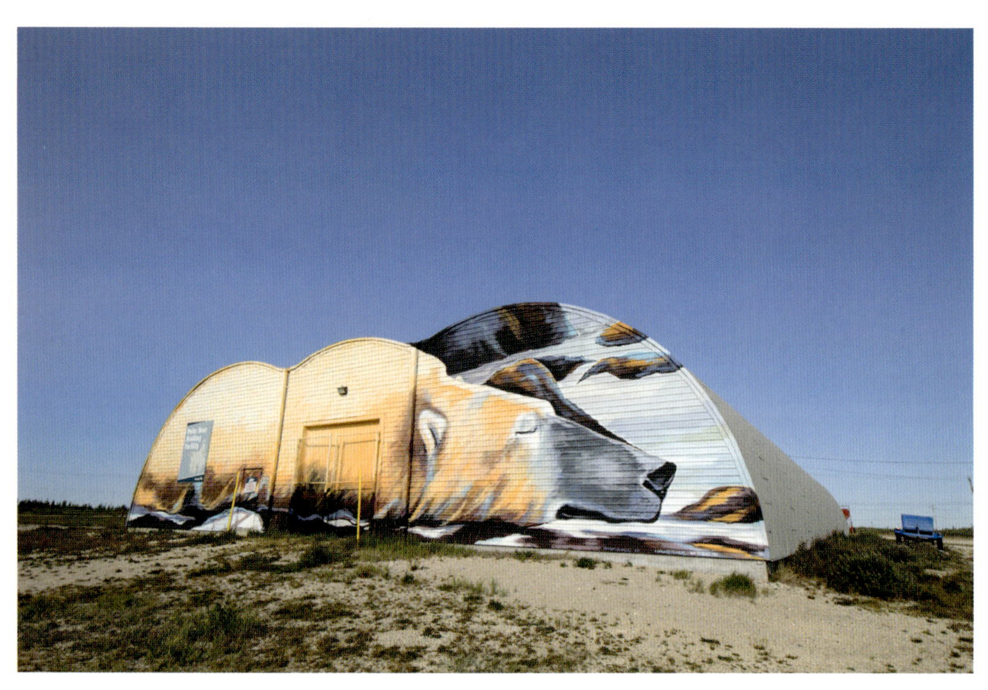

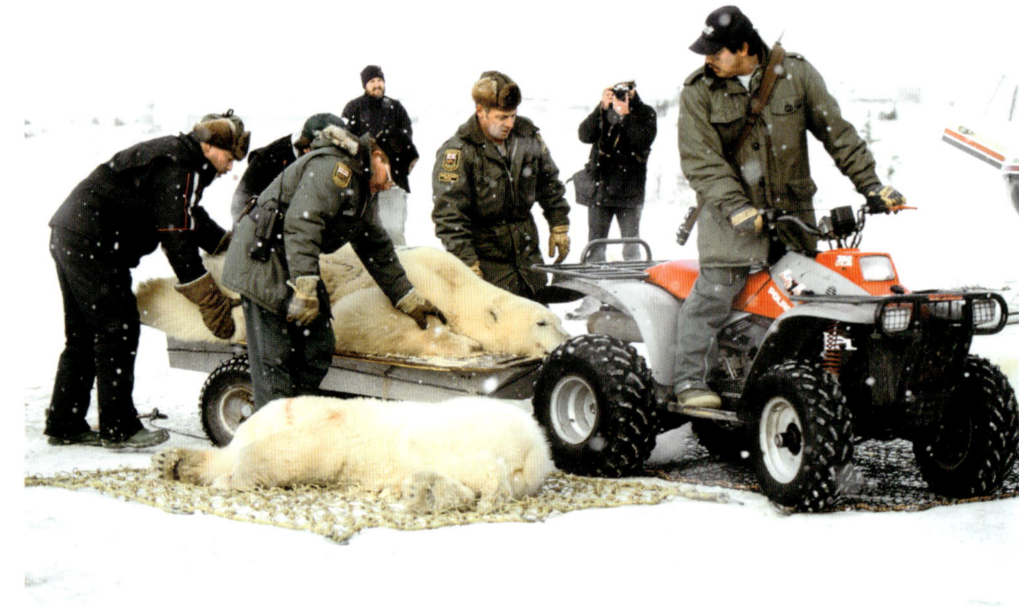

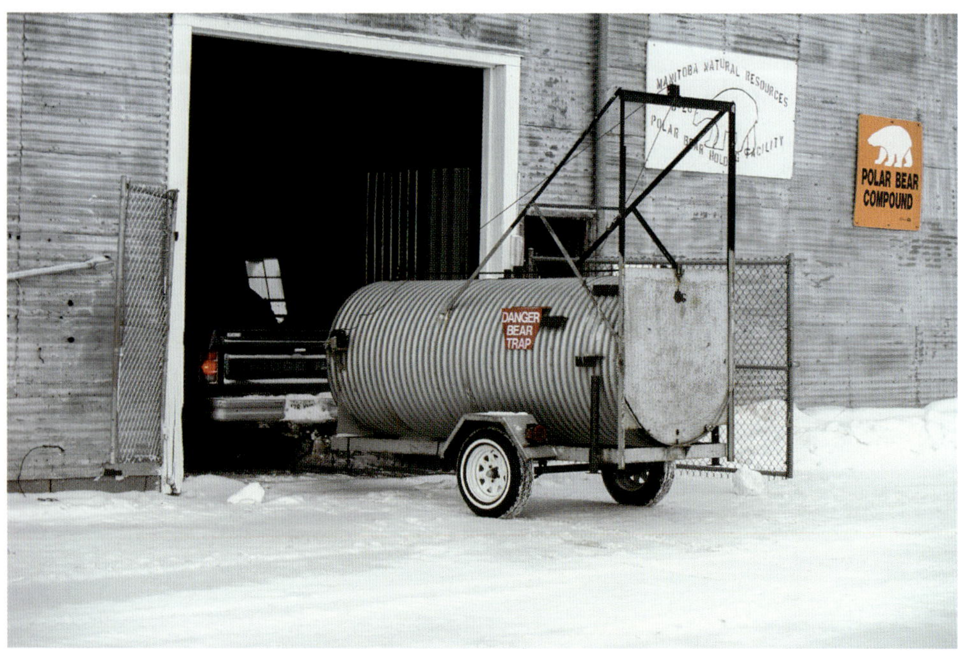
MANITOBA NATURAL RESOURCES
POLAR BEAR HOLDING FACILITY
POLAR BEAR COMPOUND
DANGER BEAR TRAP

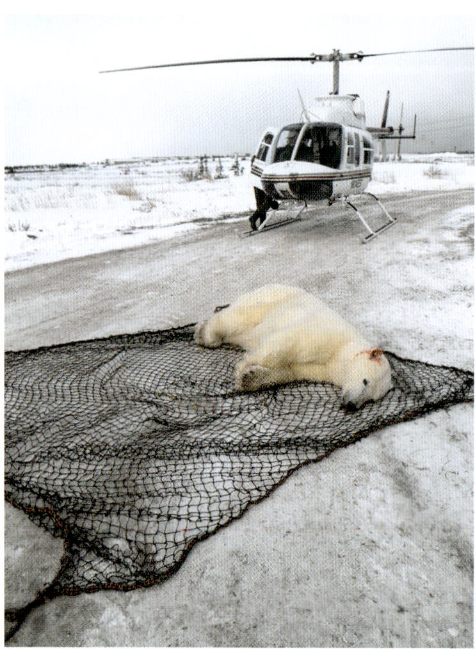

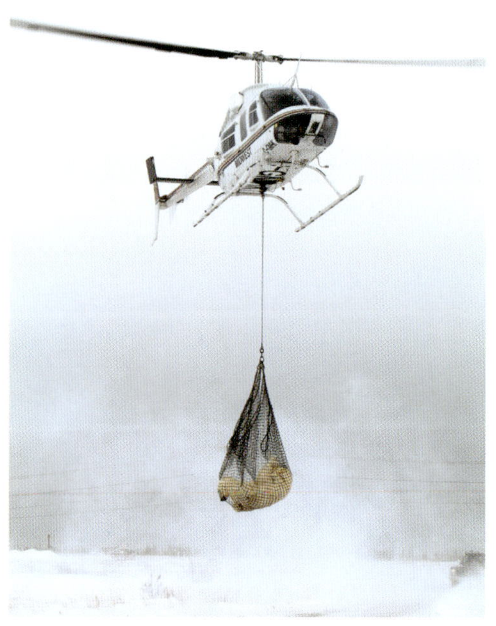

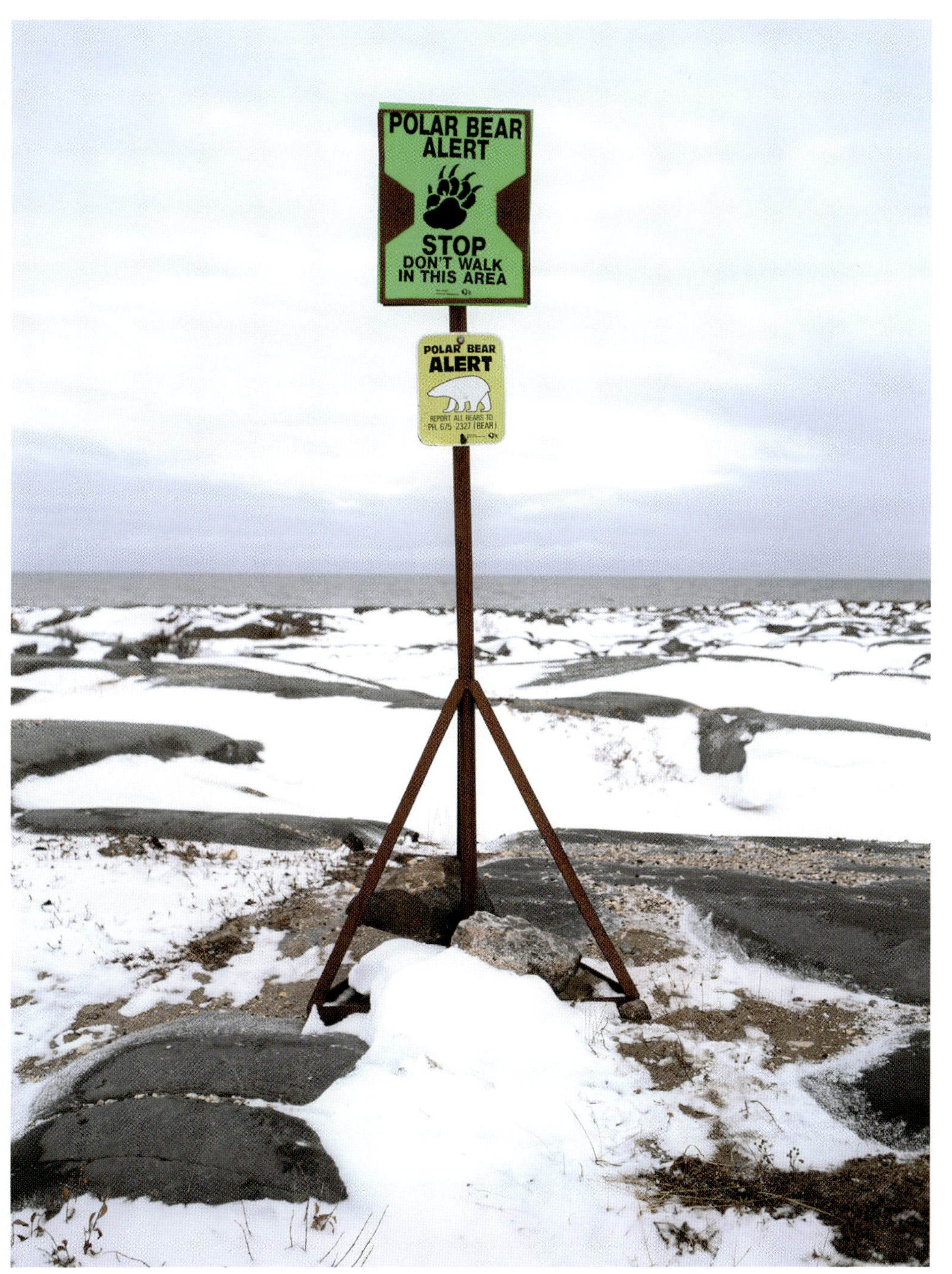
POLAR BEAR
ALERT
STOP
DON'T WALK
IN THIS AREA

POLAR BEAR
ALERT
REPORT ALL BEARS TO
PH. 675-2327 (BEAR)

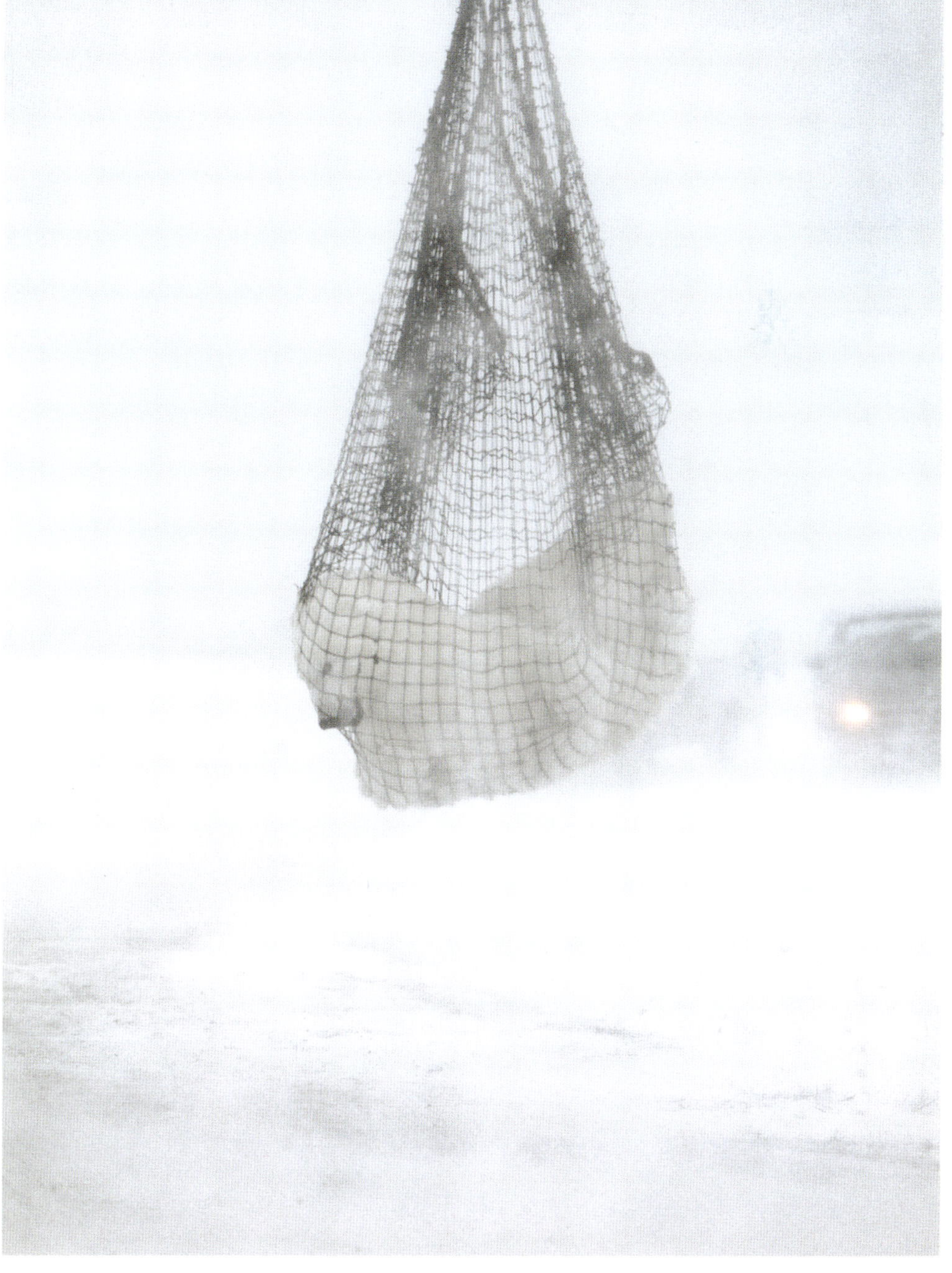

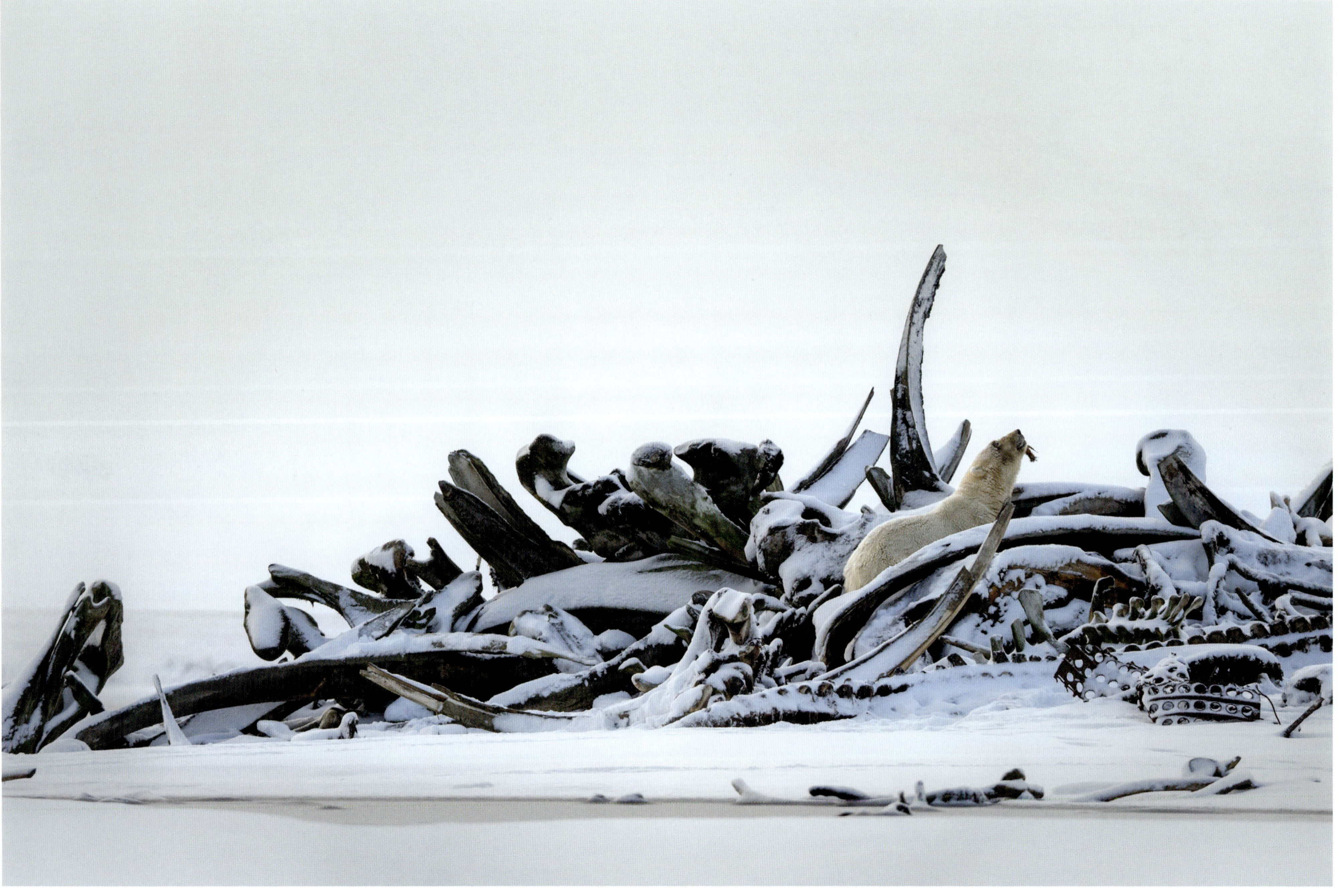

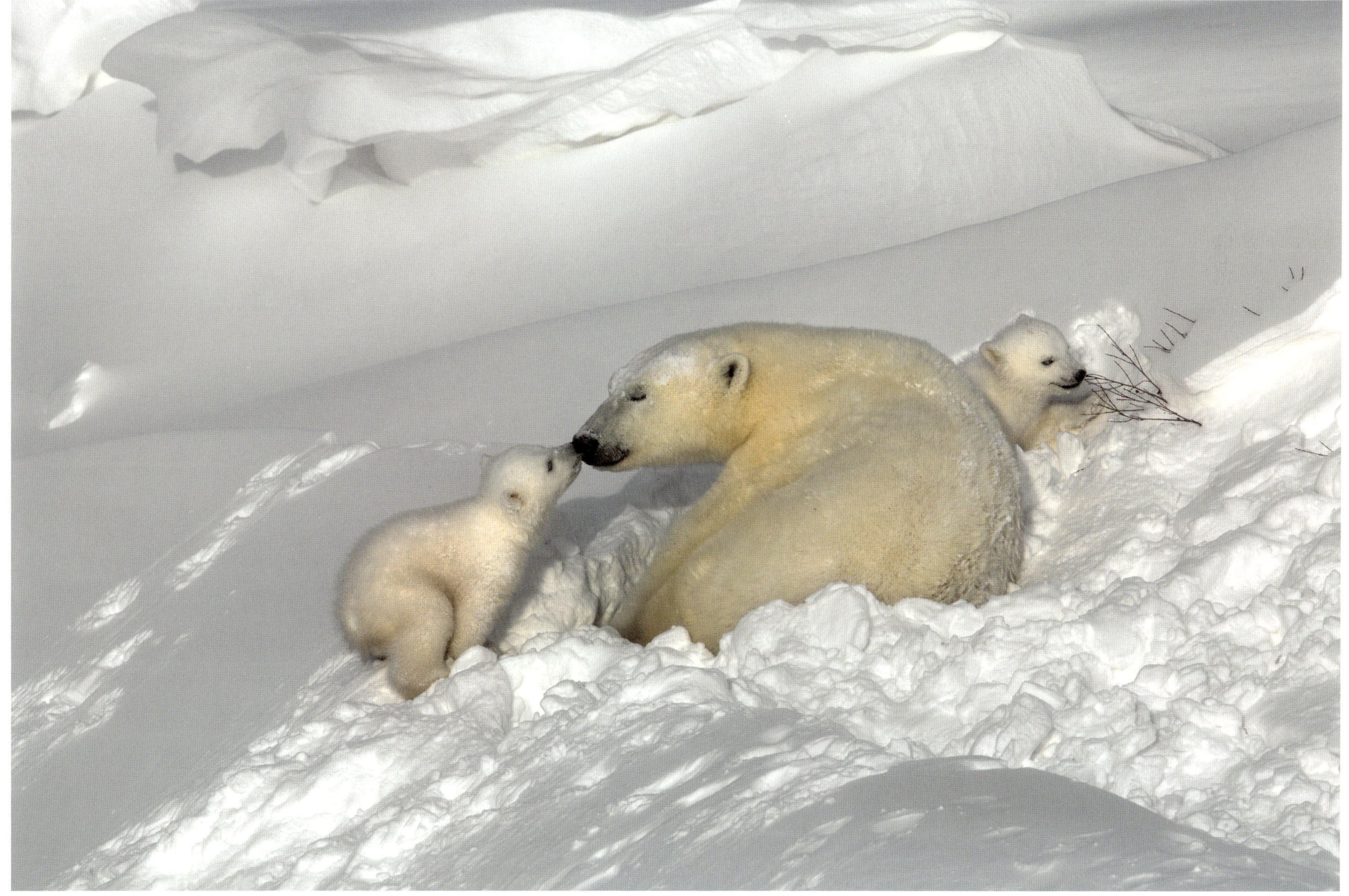

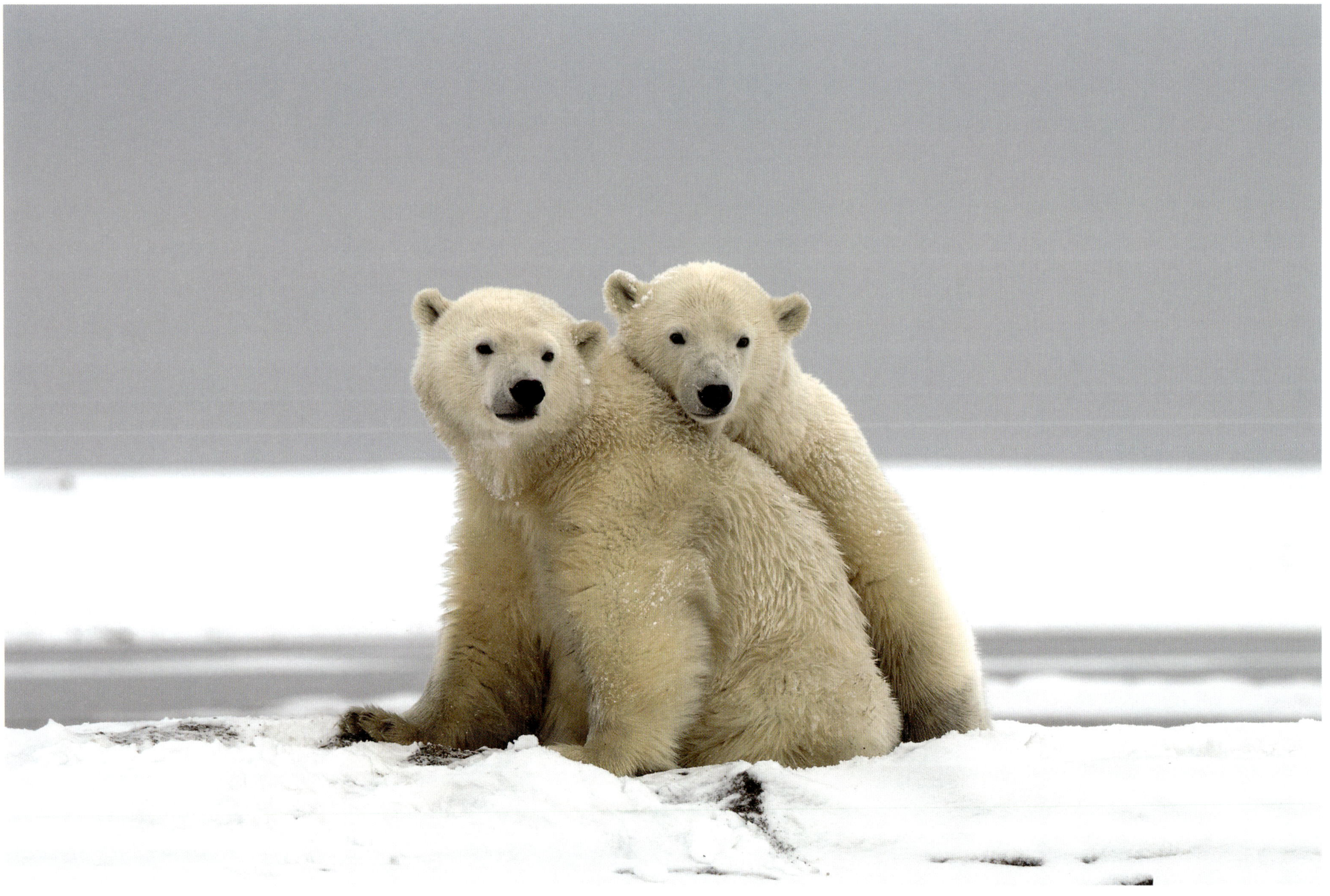

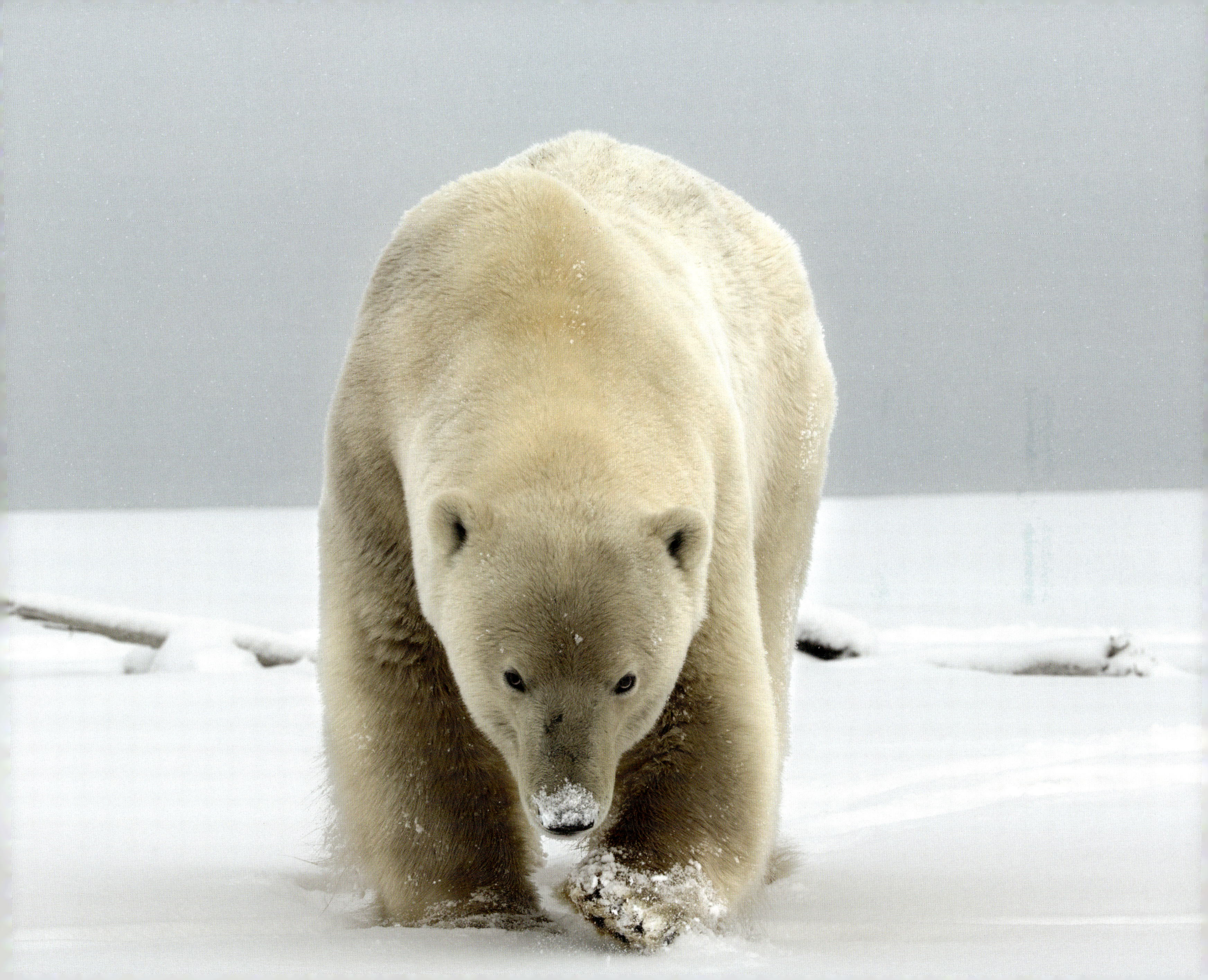

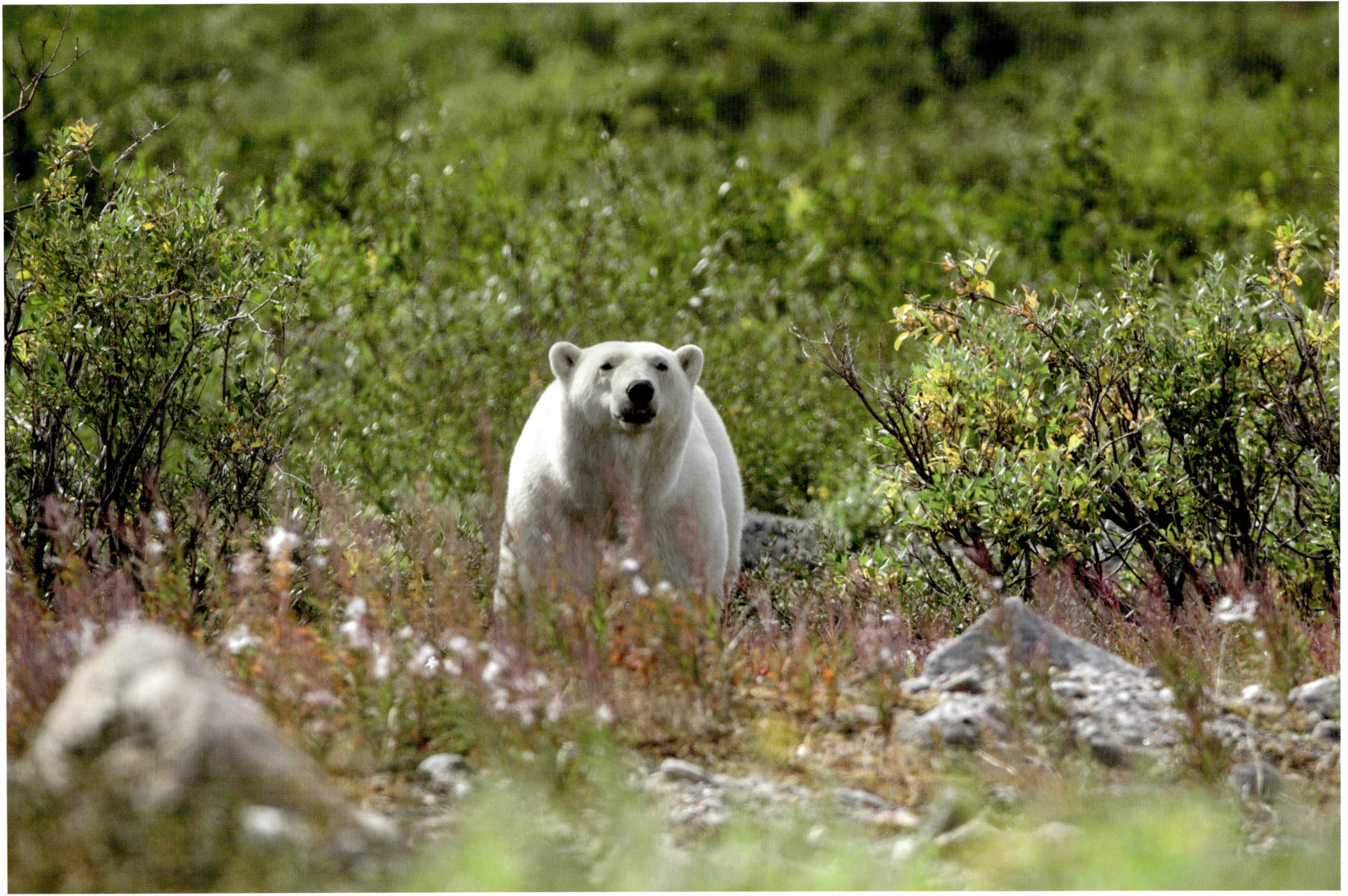

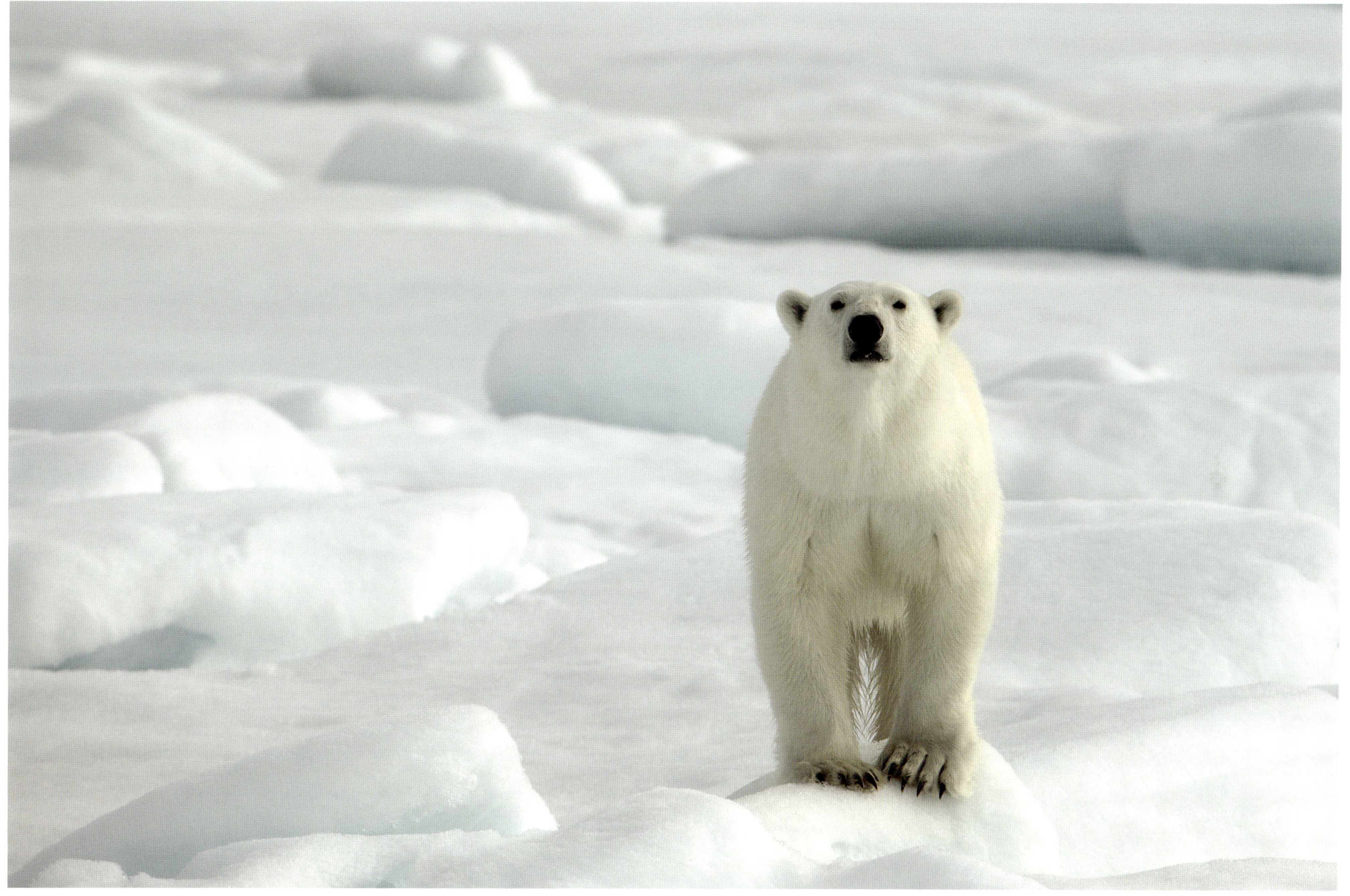

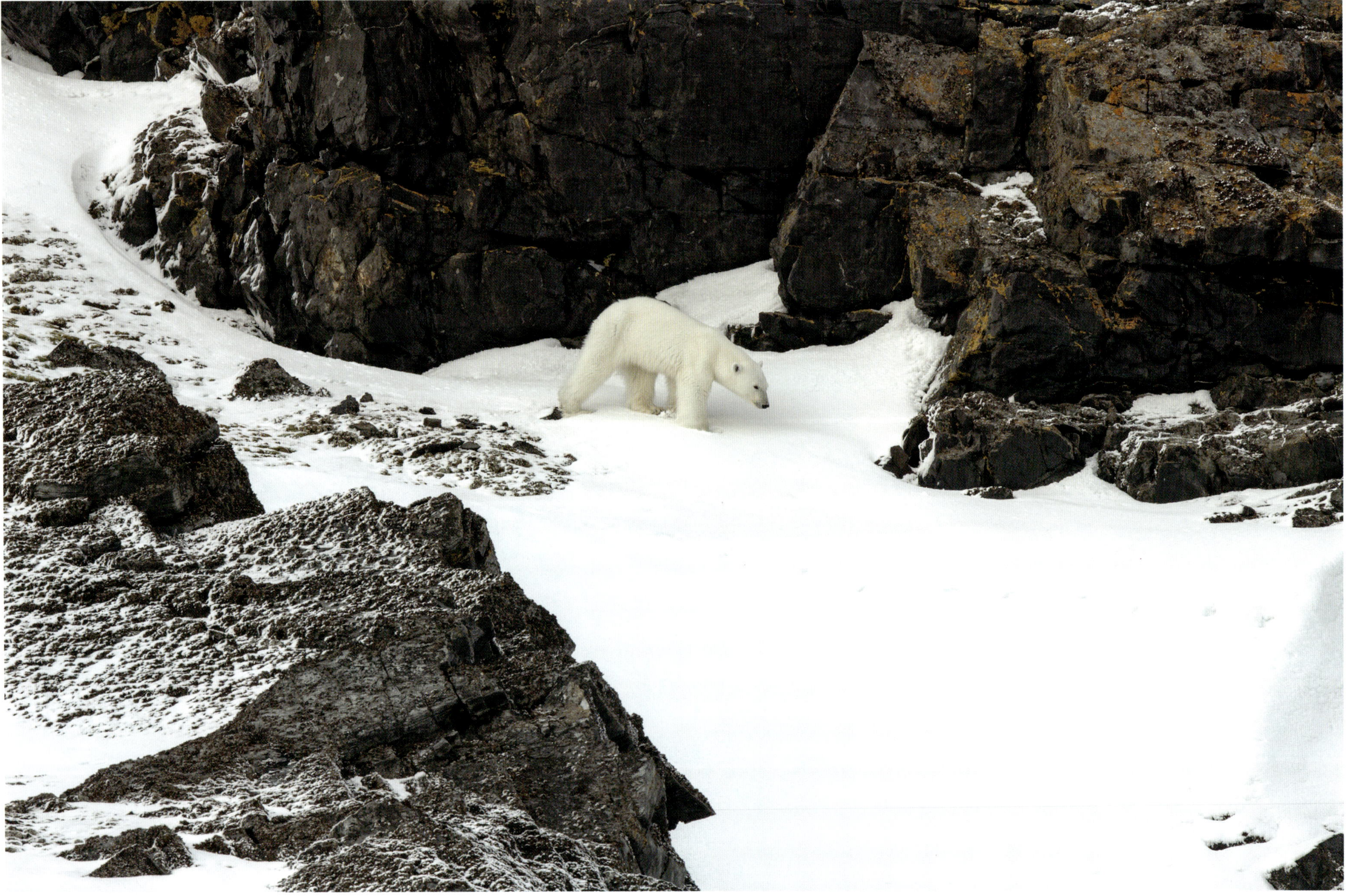

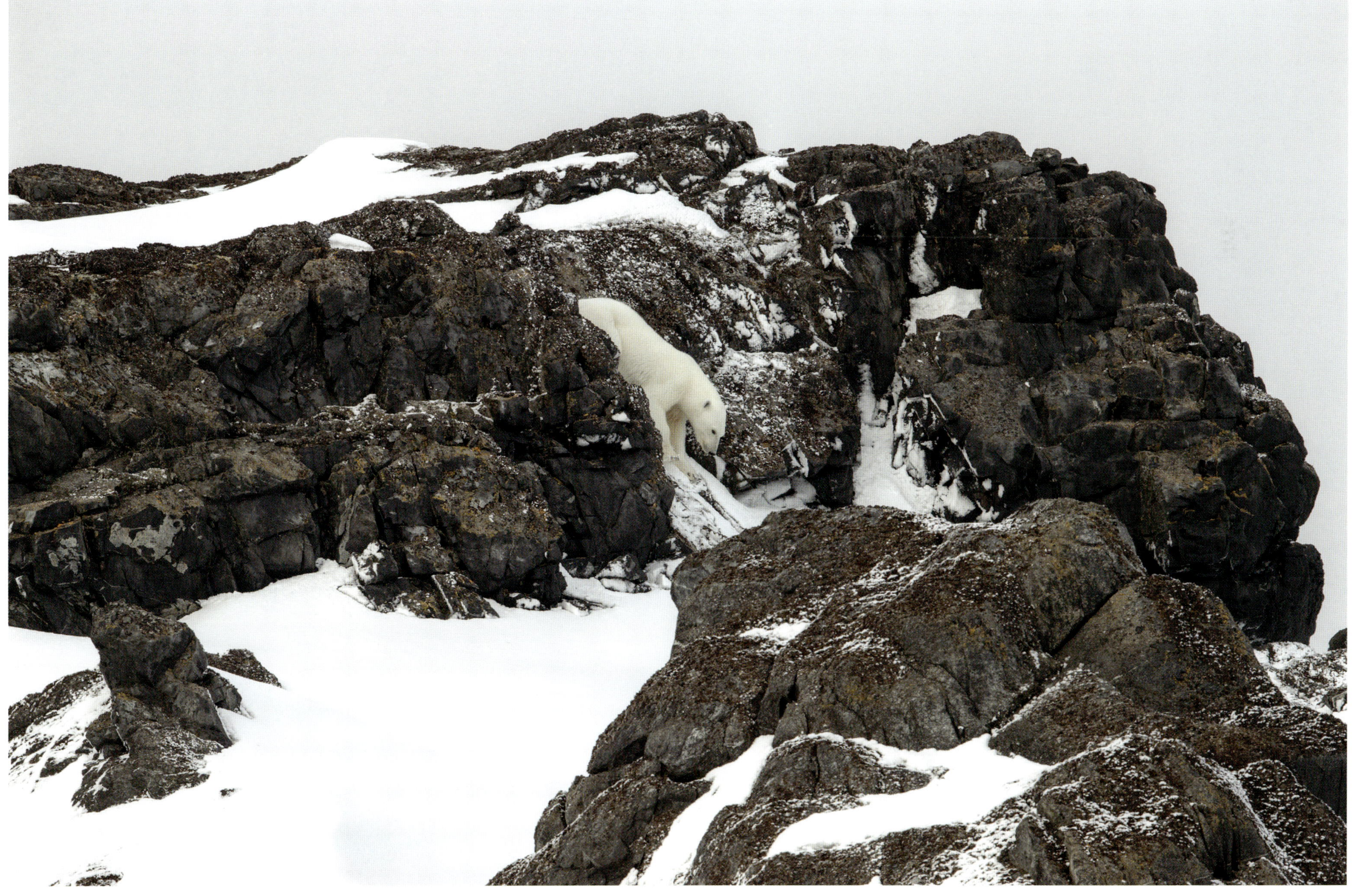

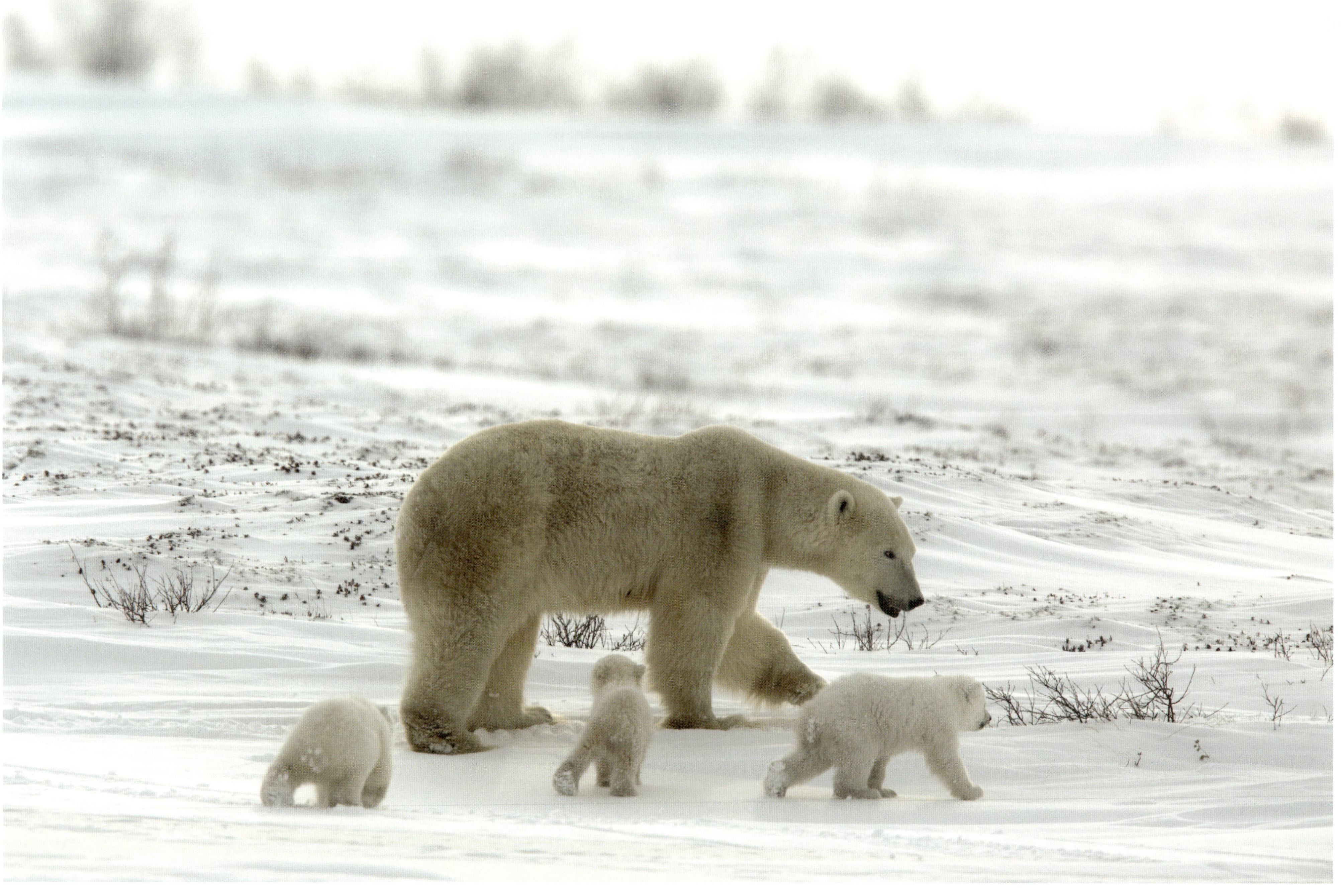

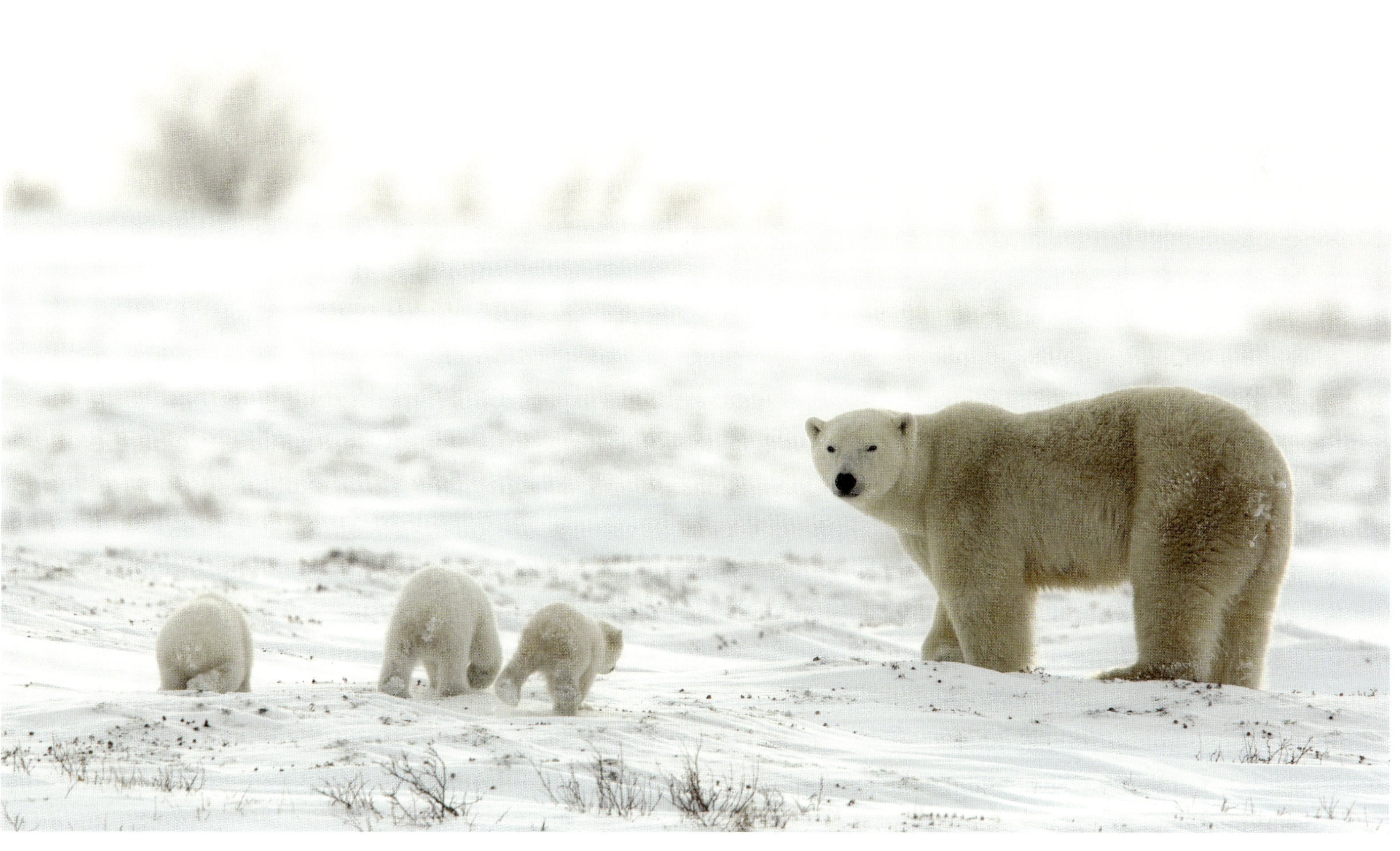

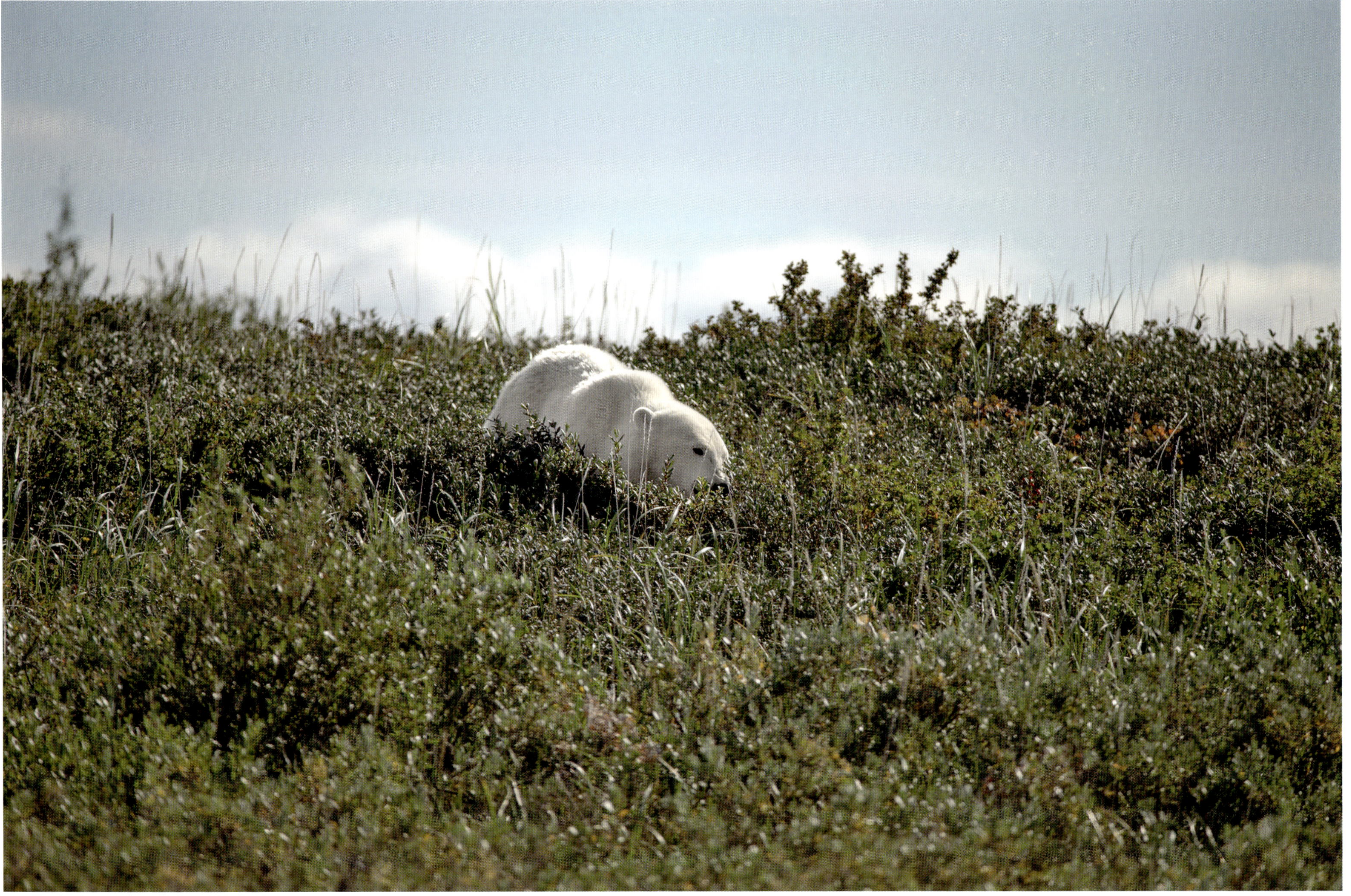

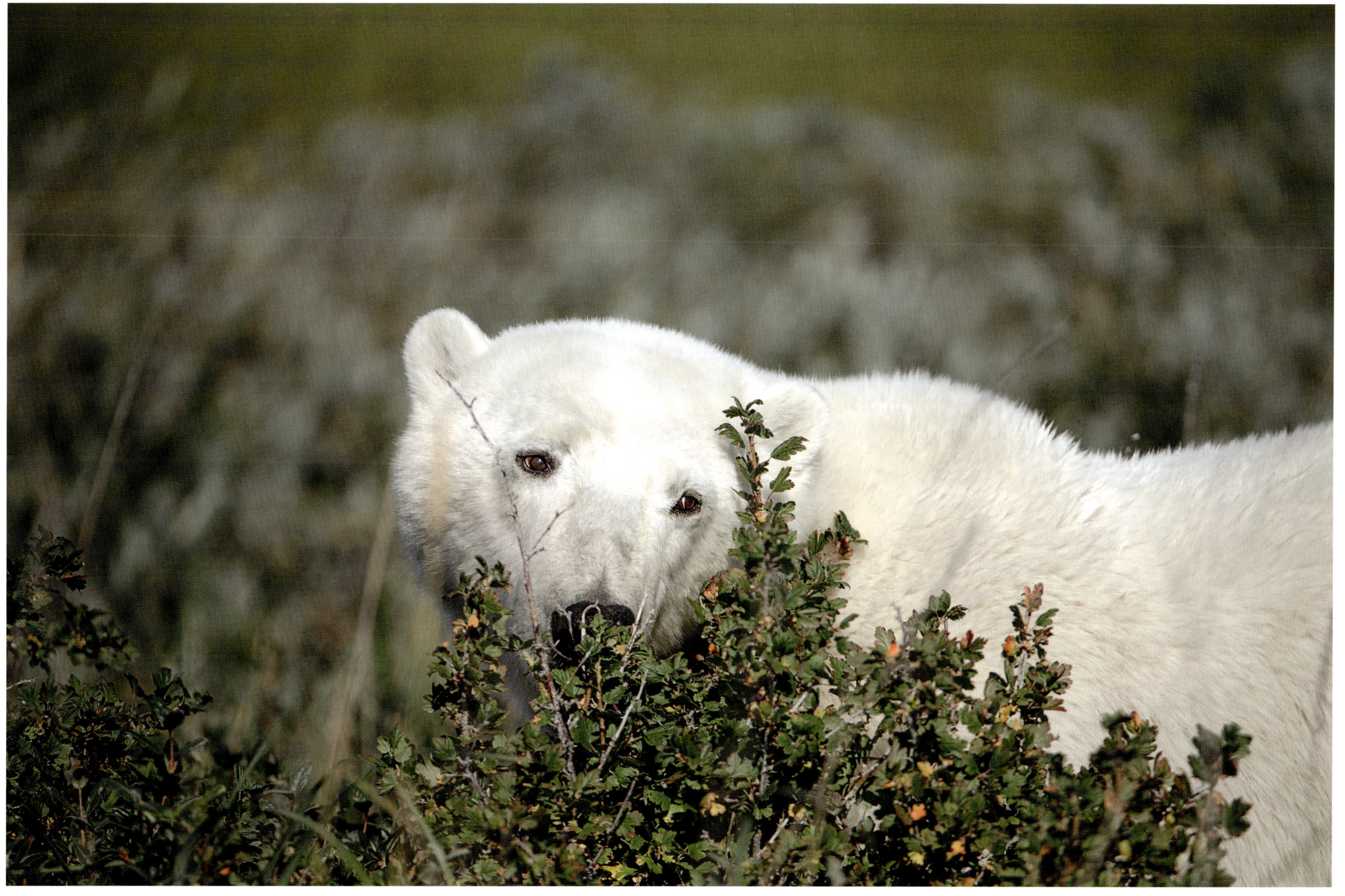

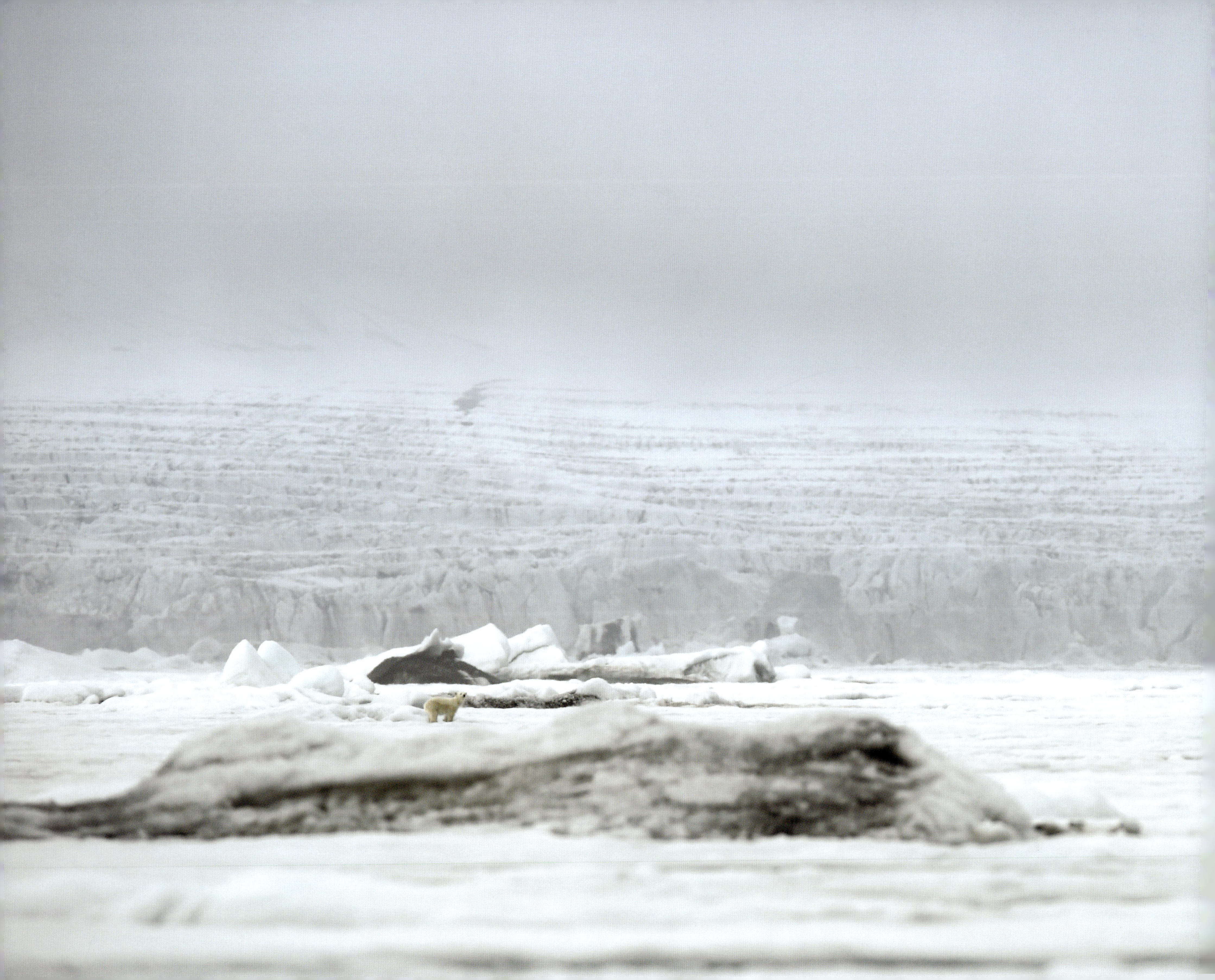

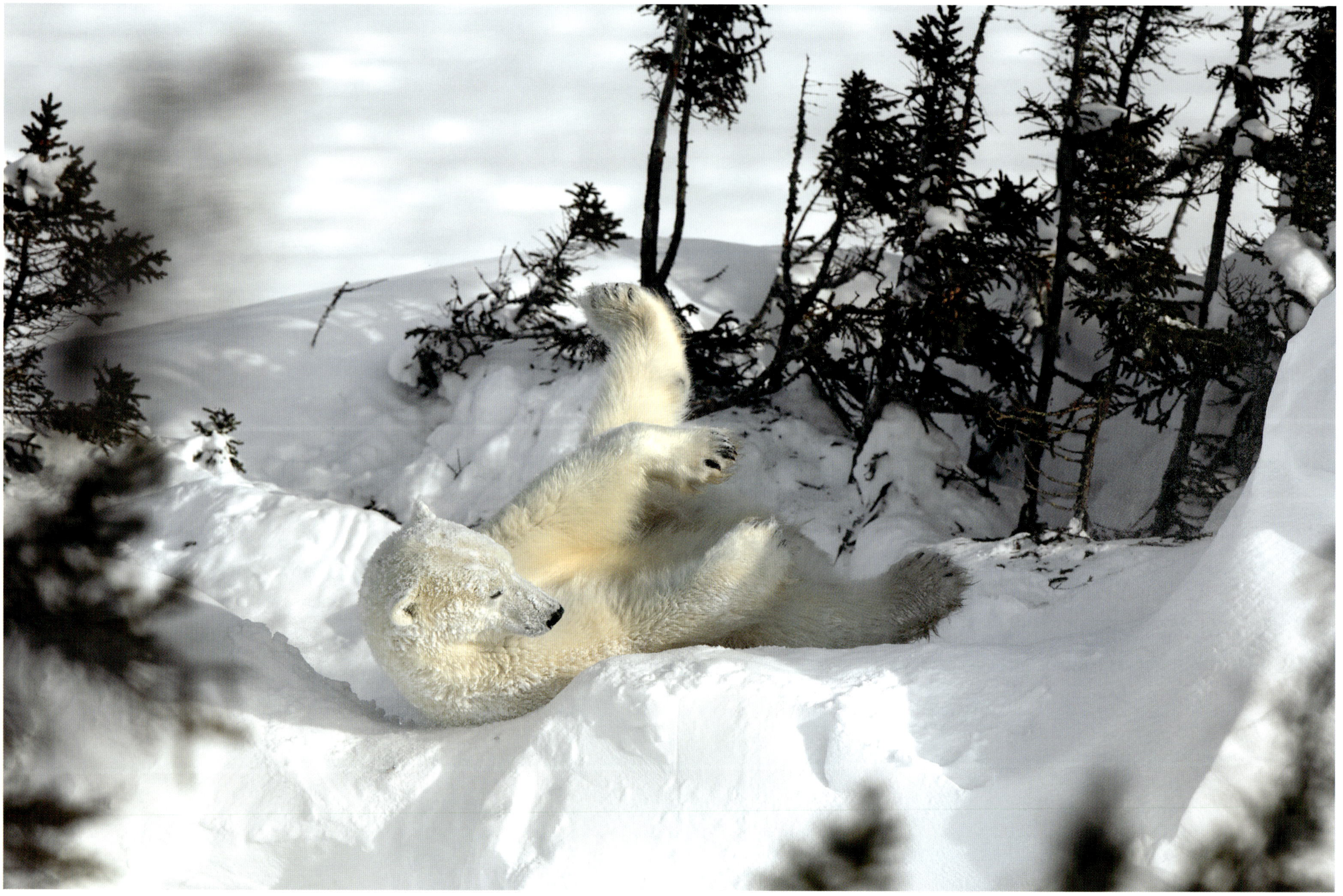

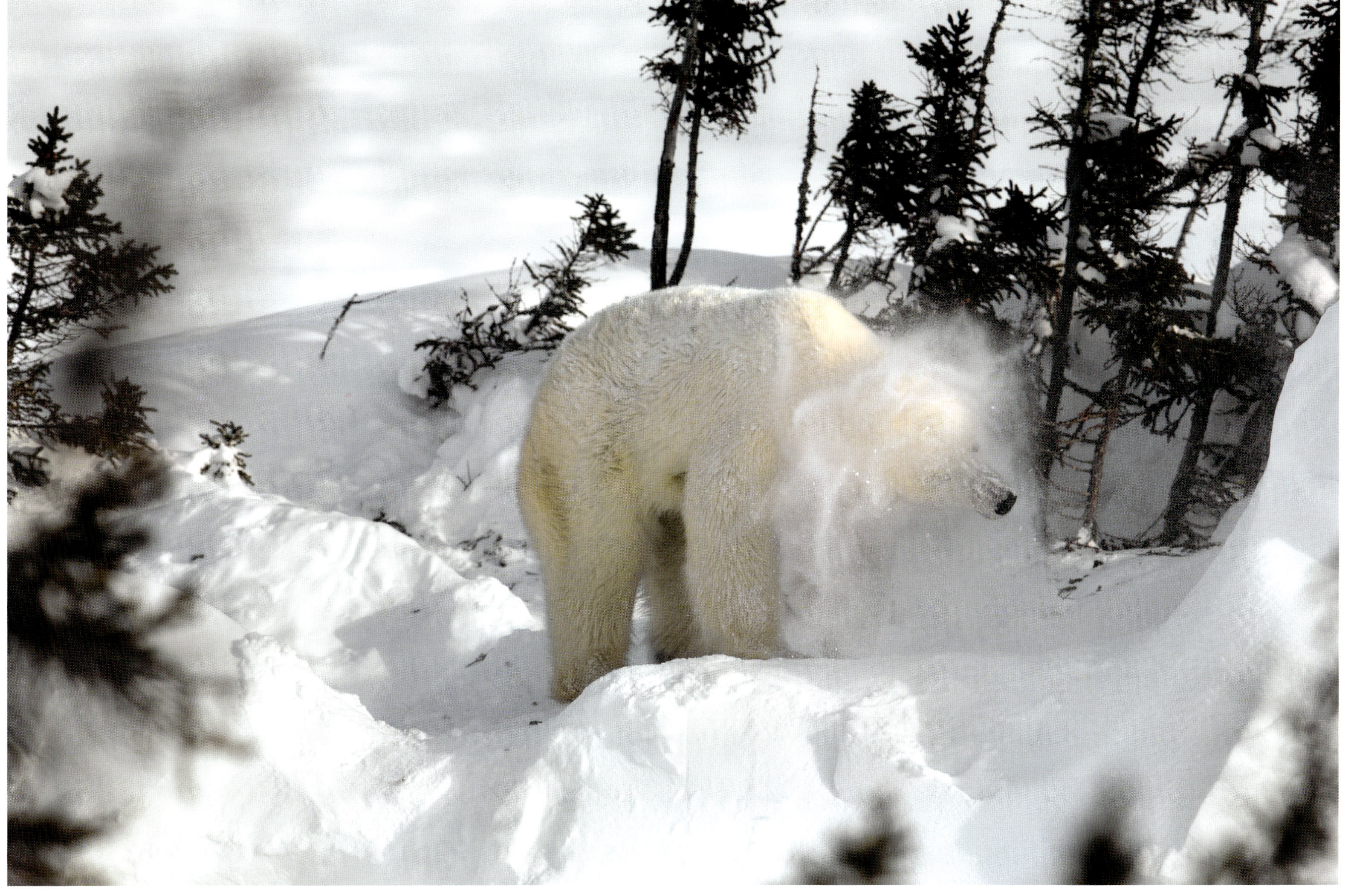

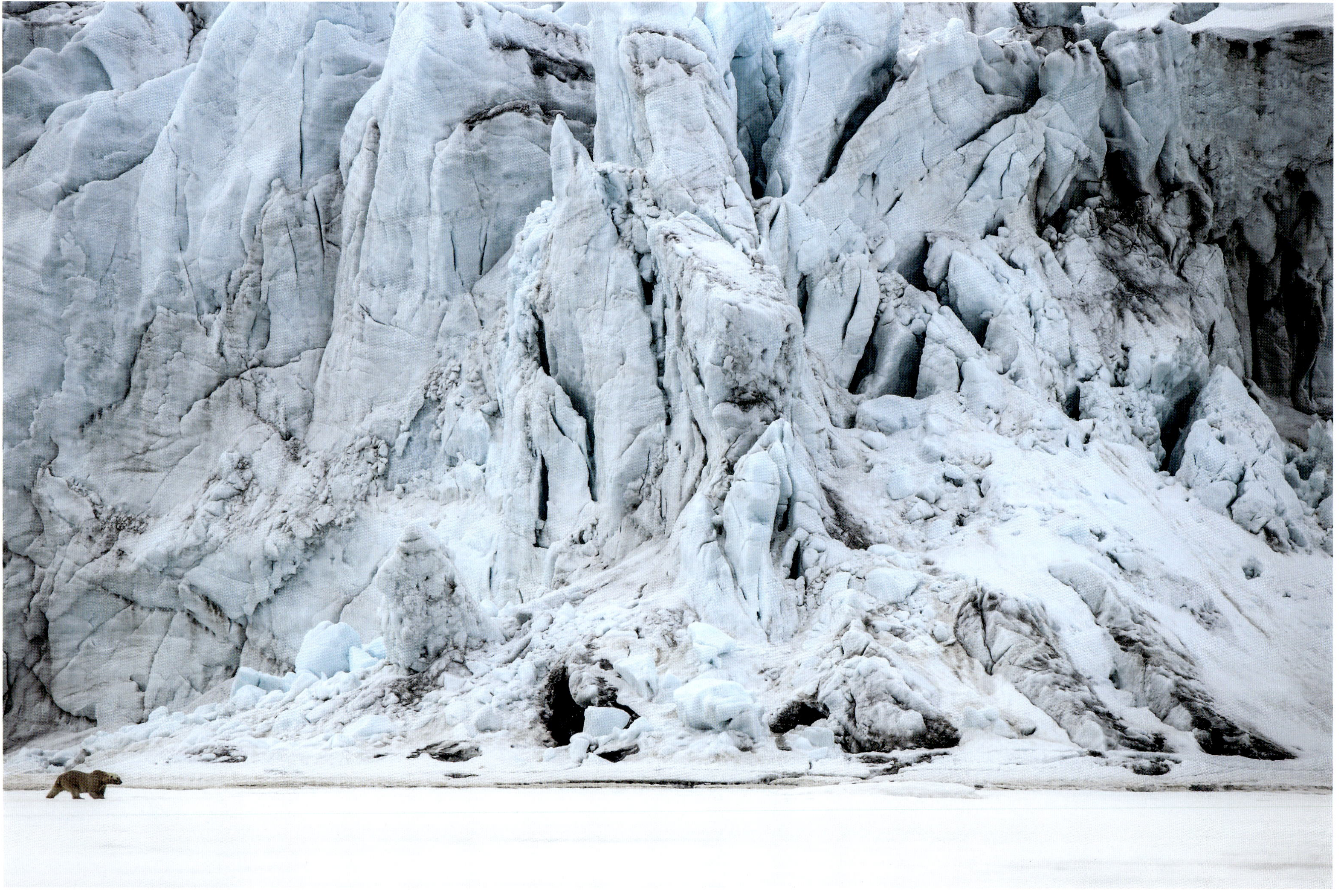

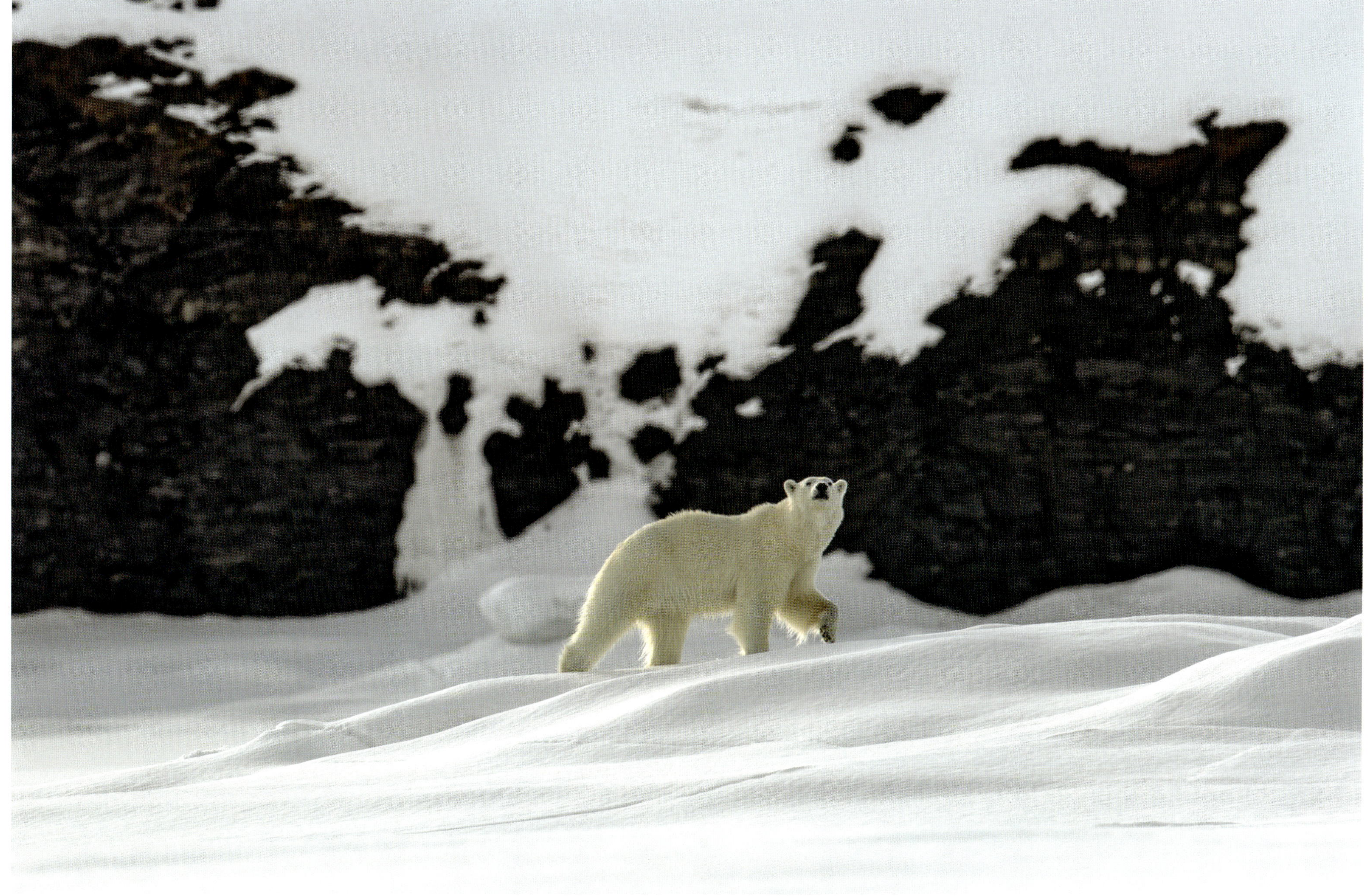

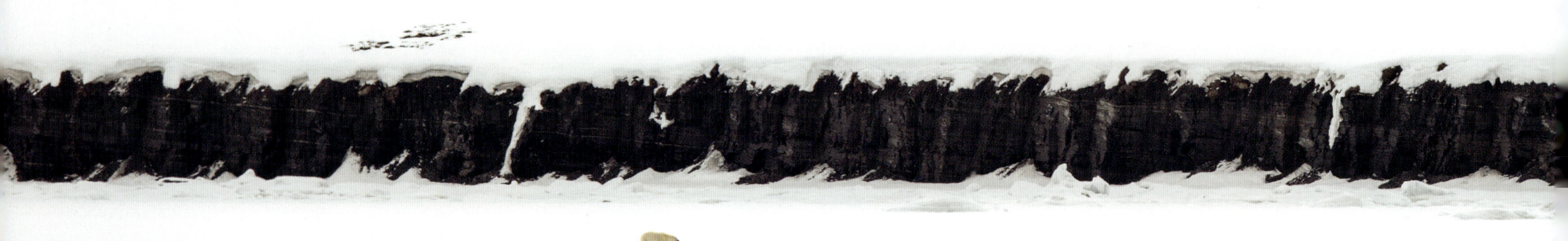

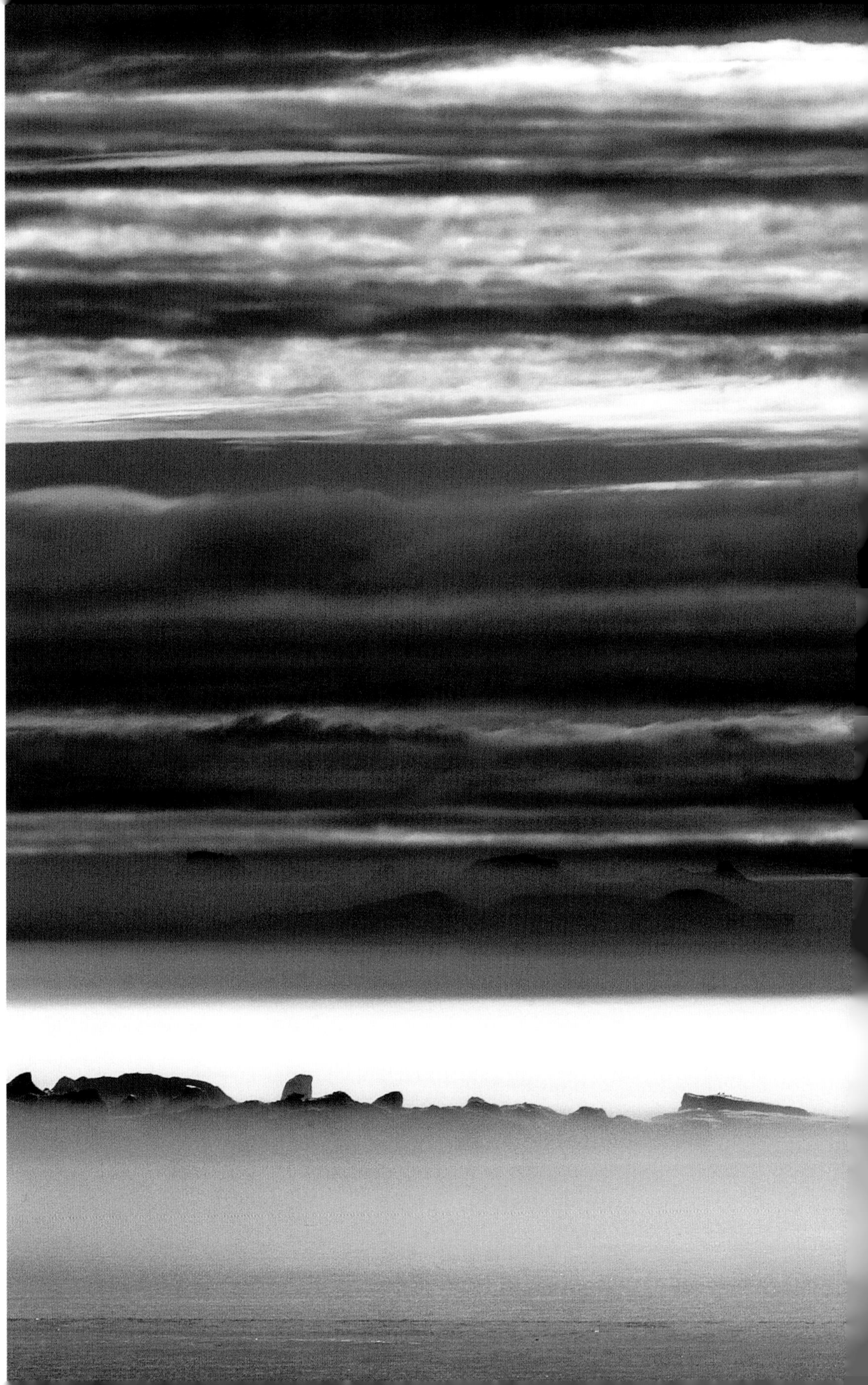

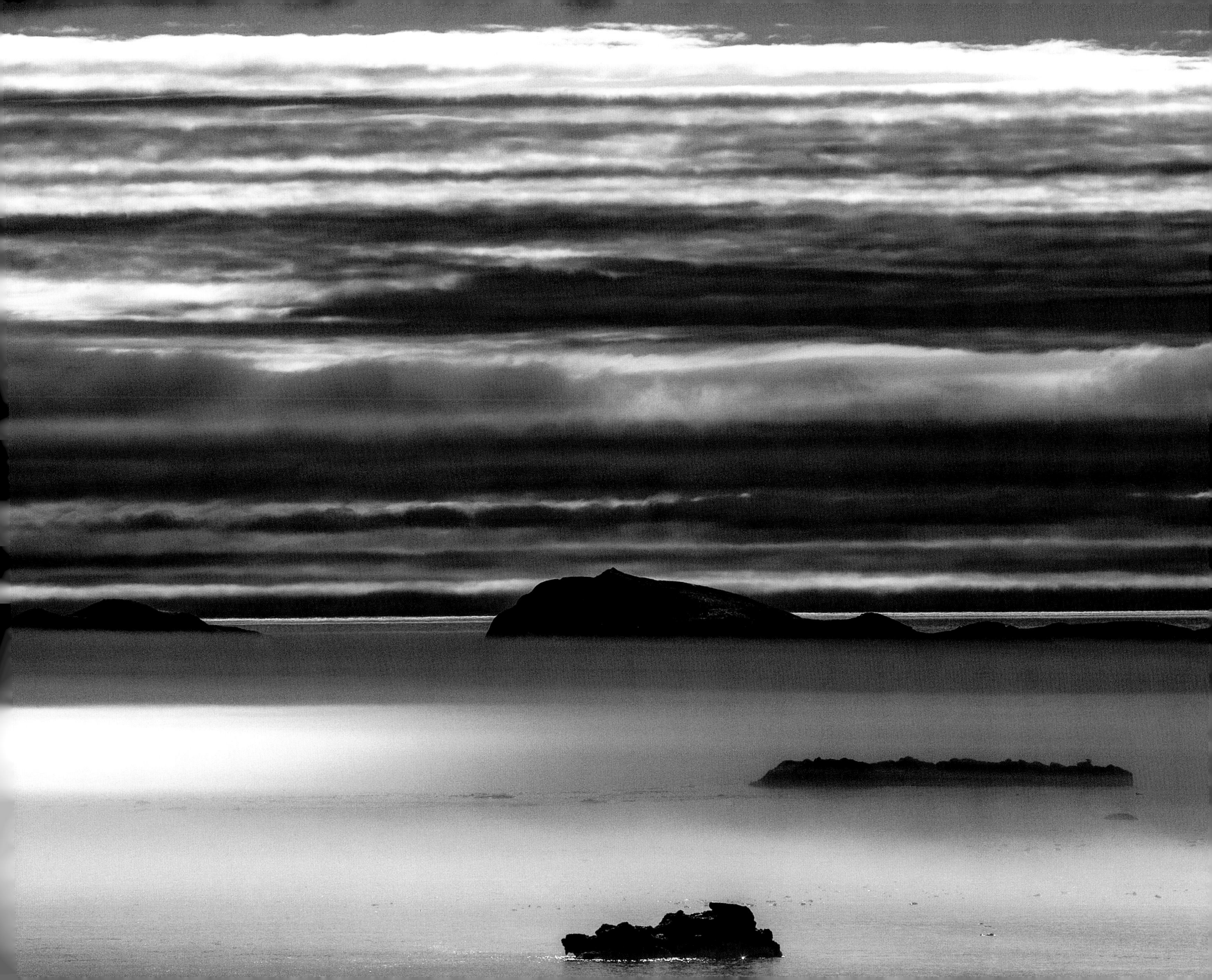

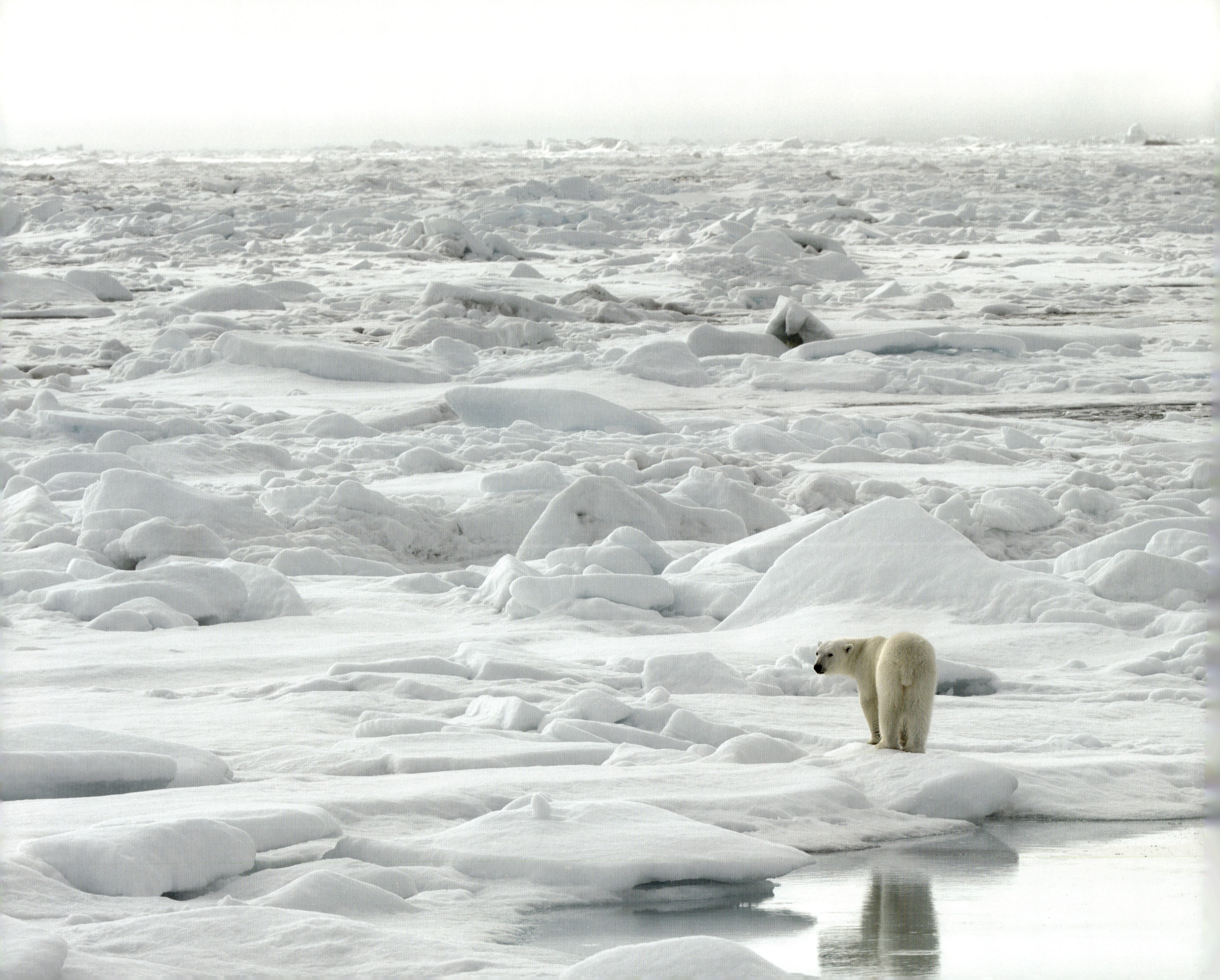

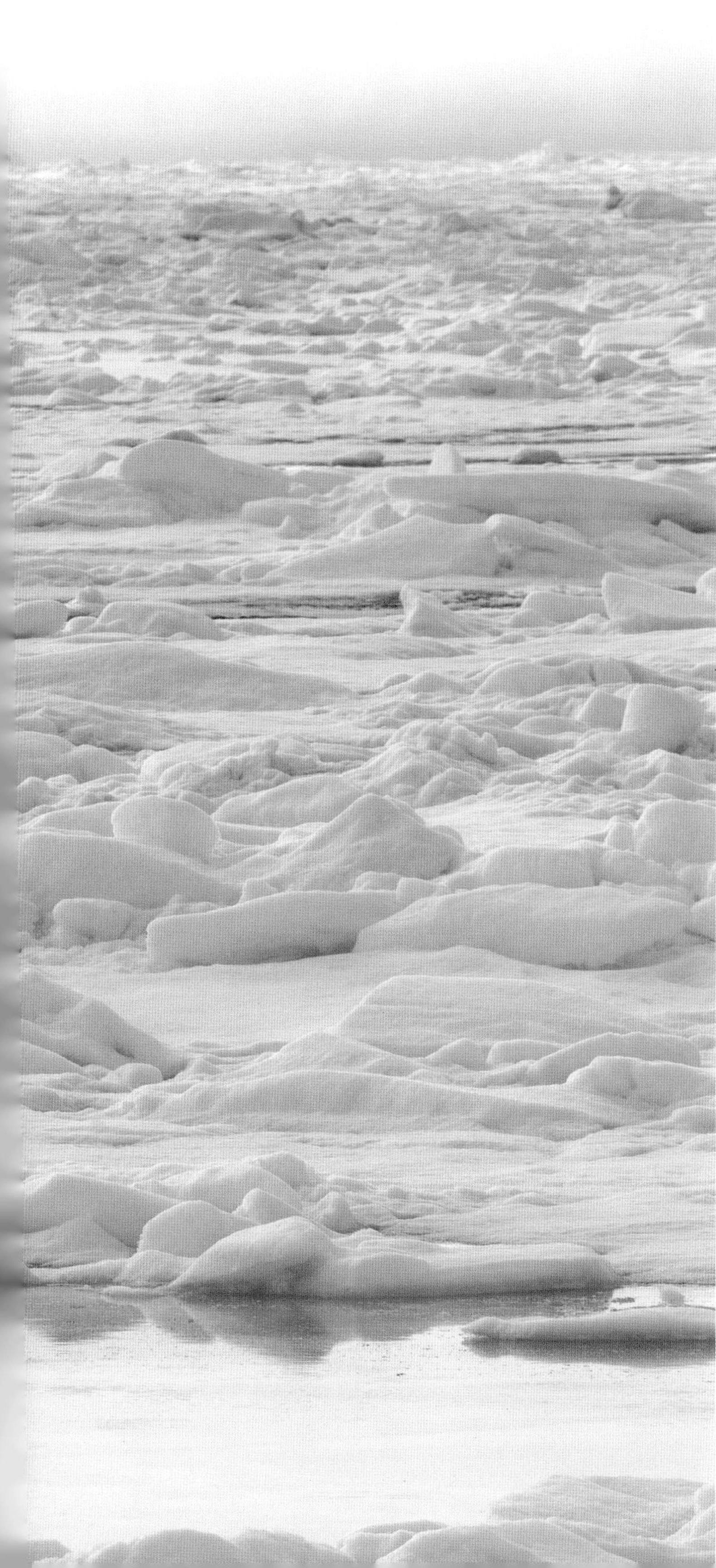

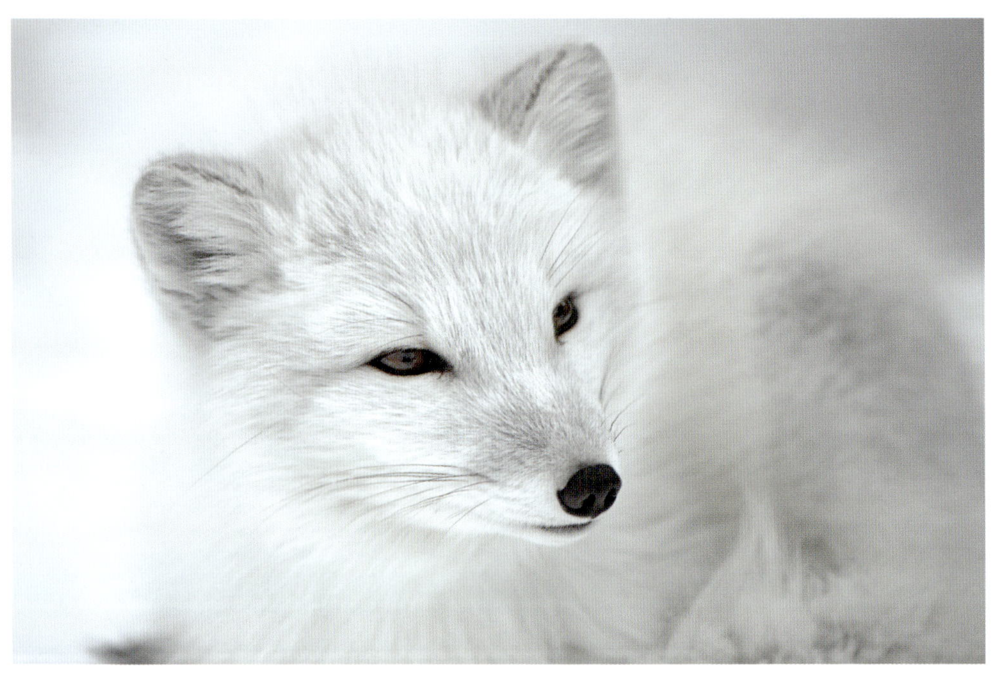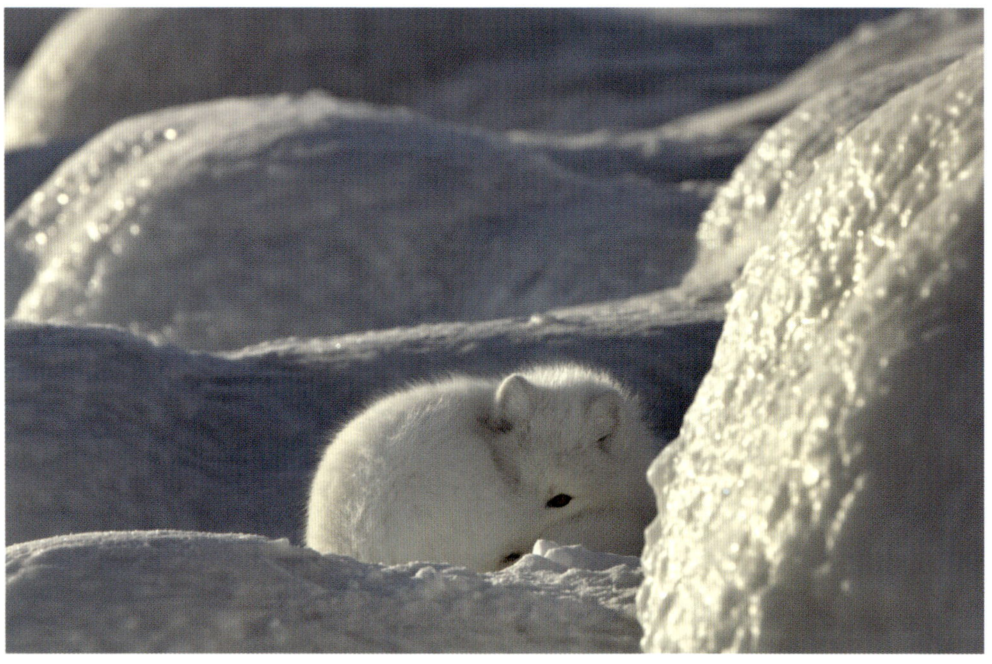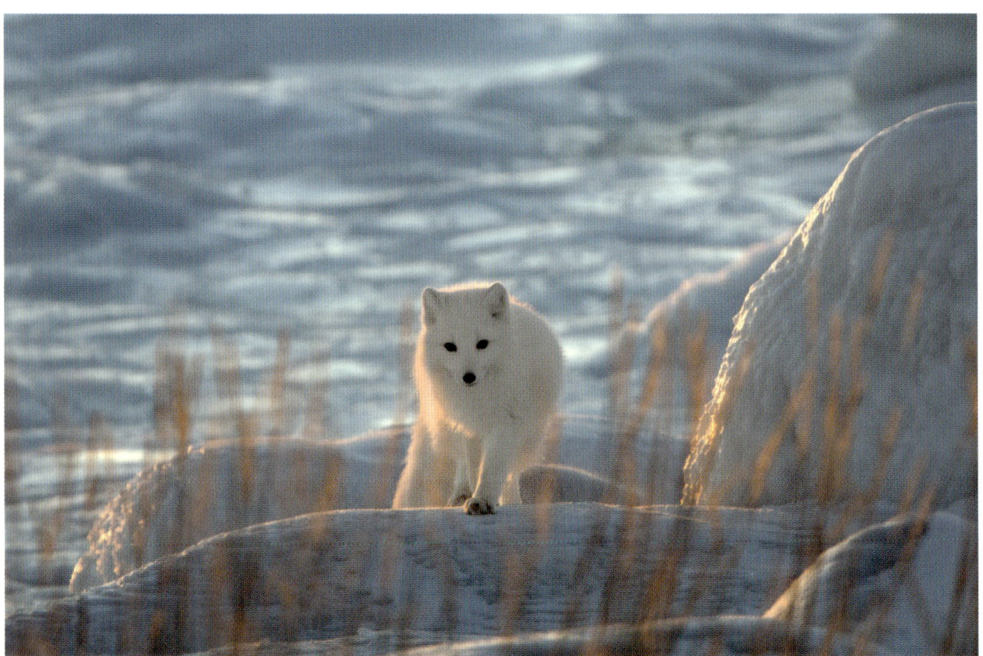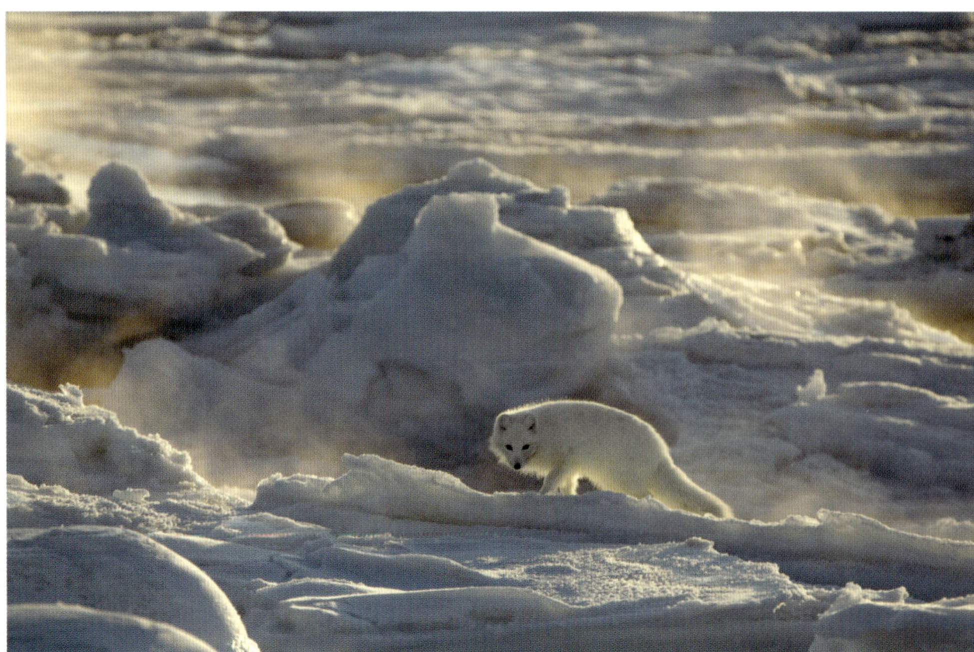

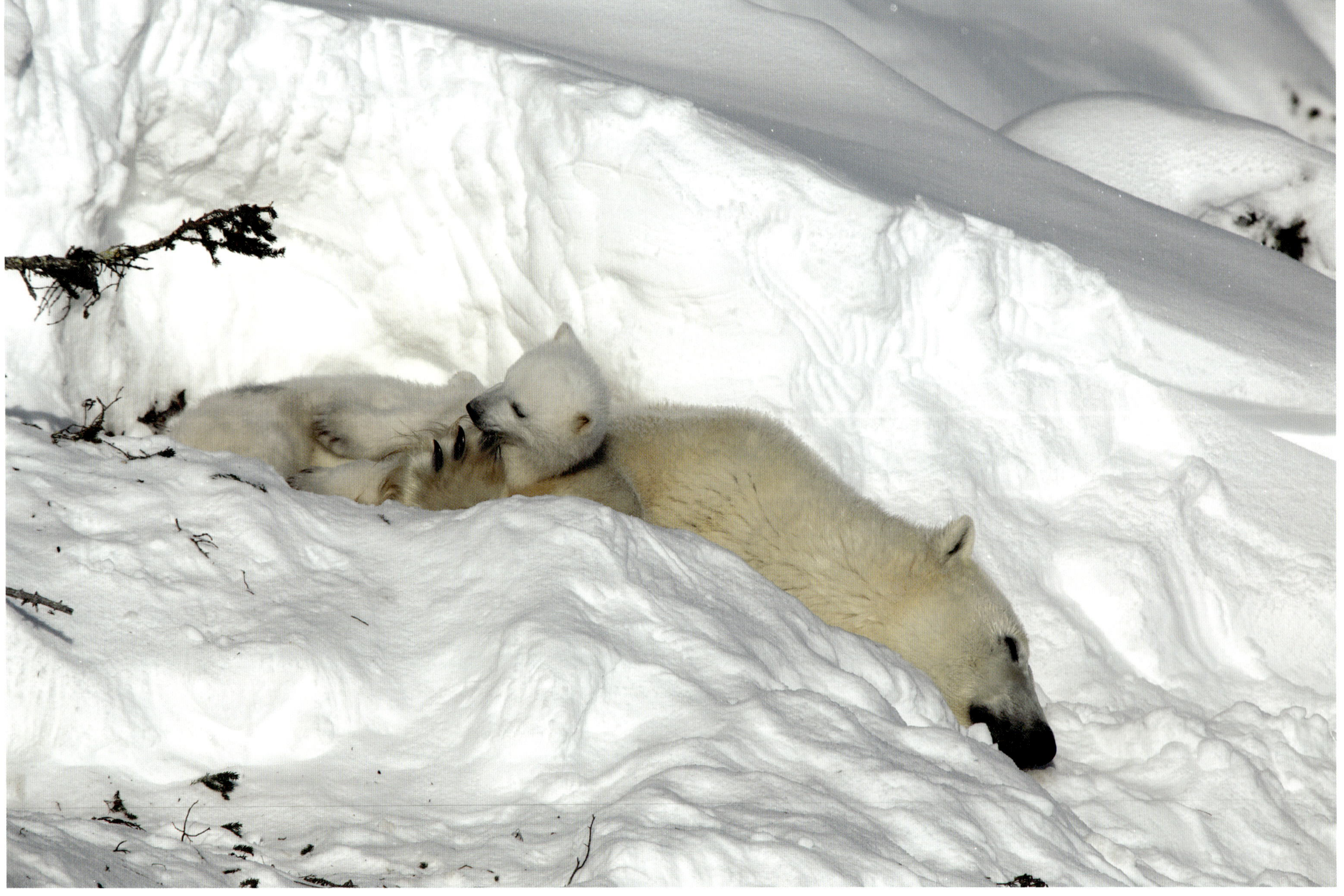

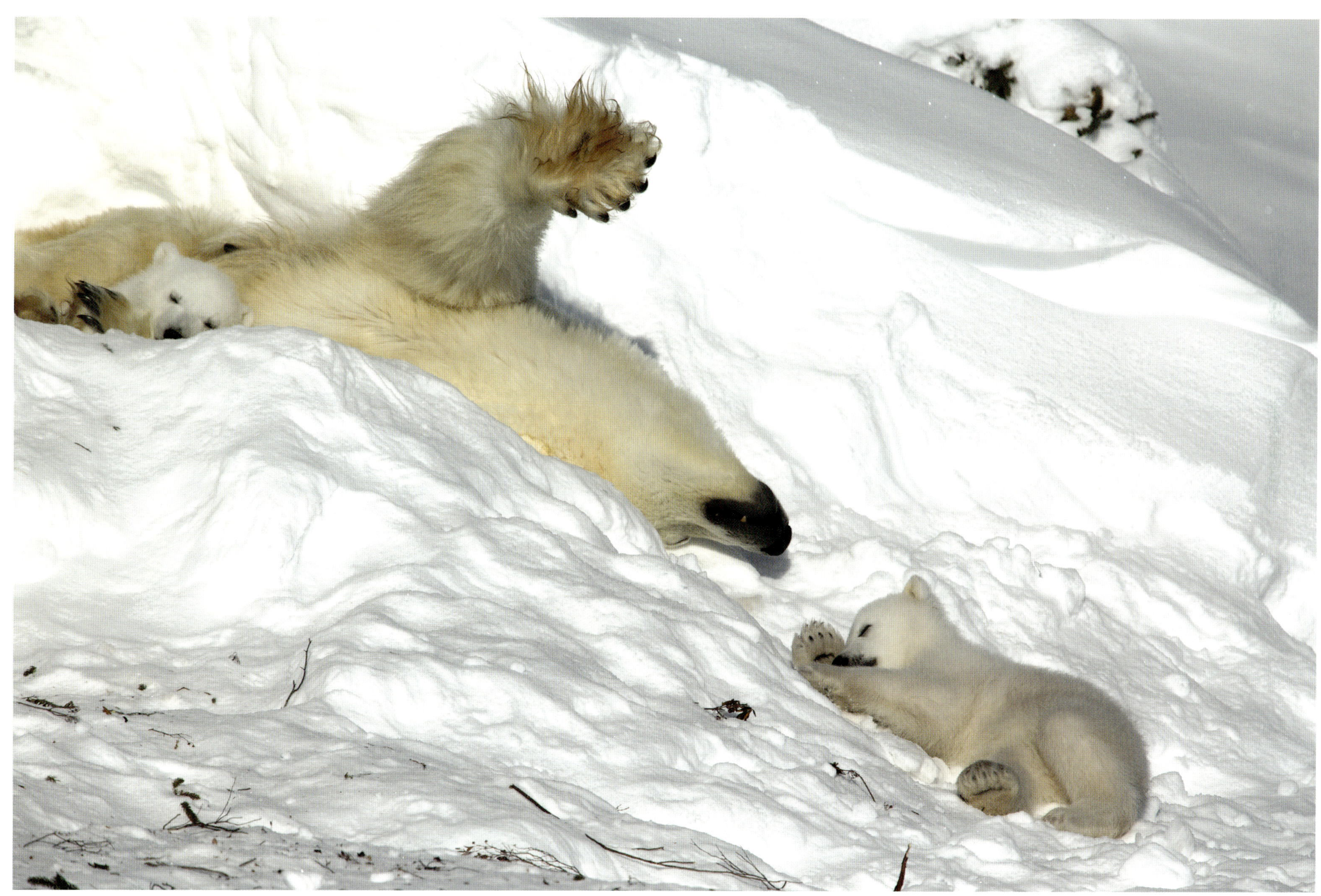

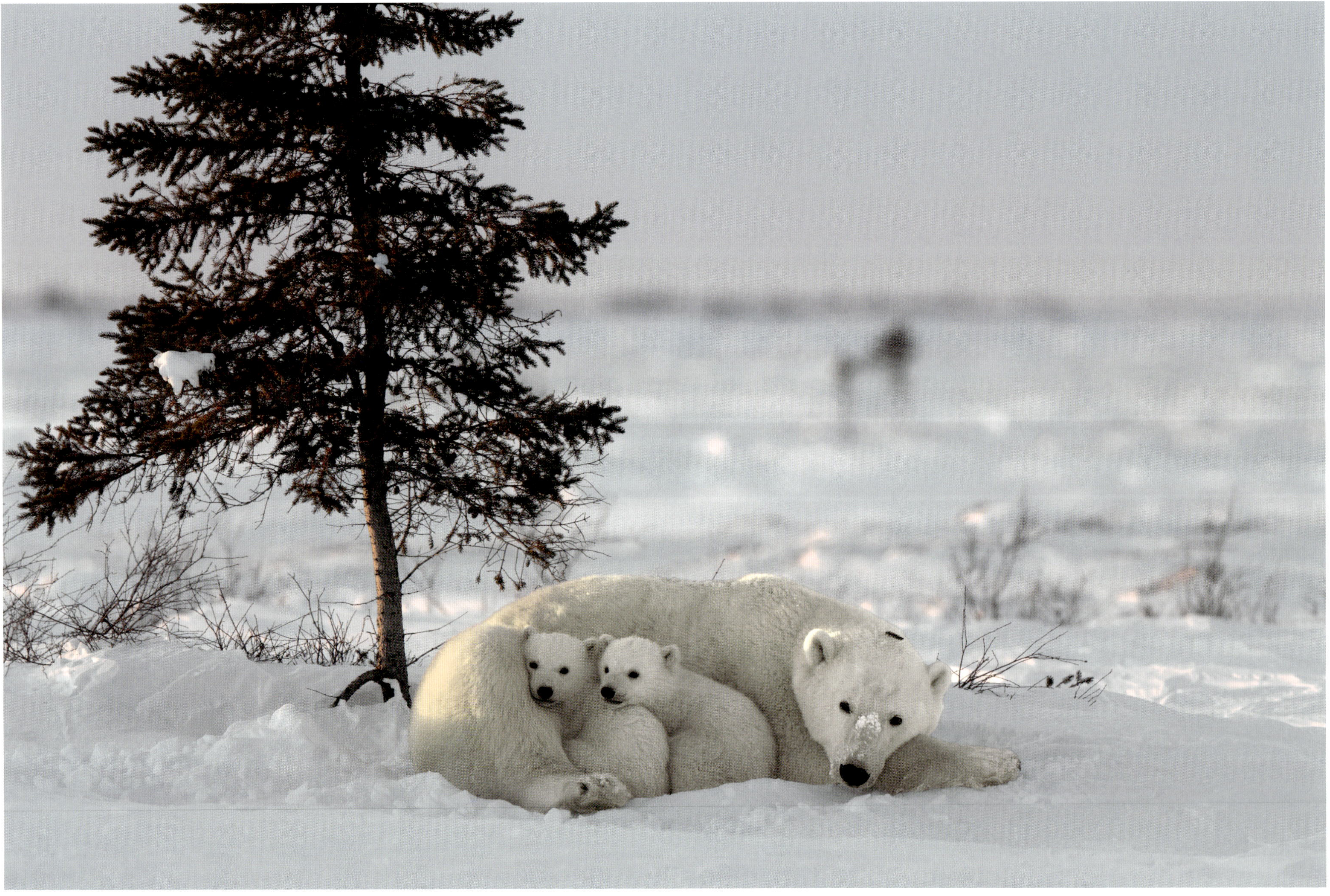

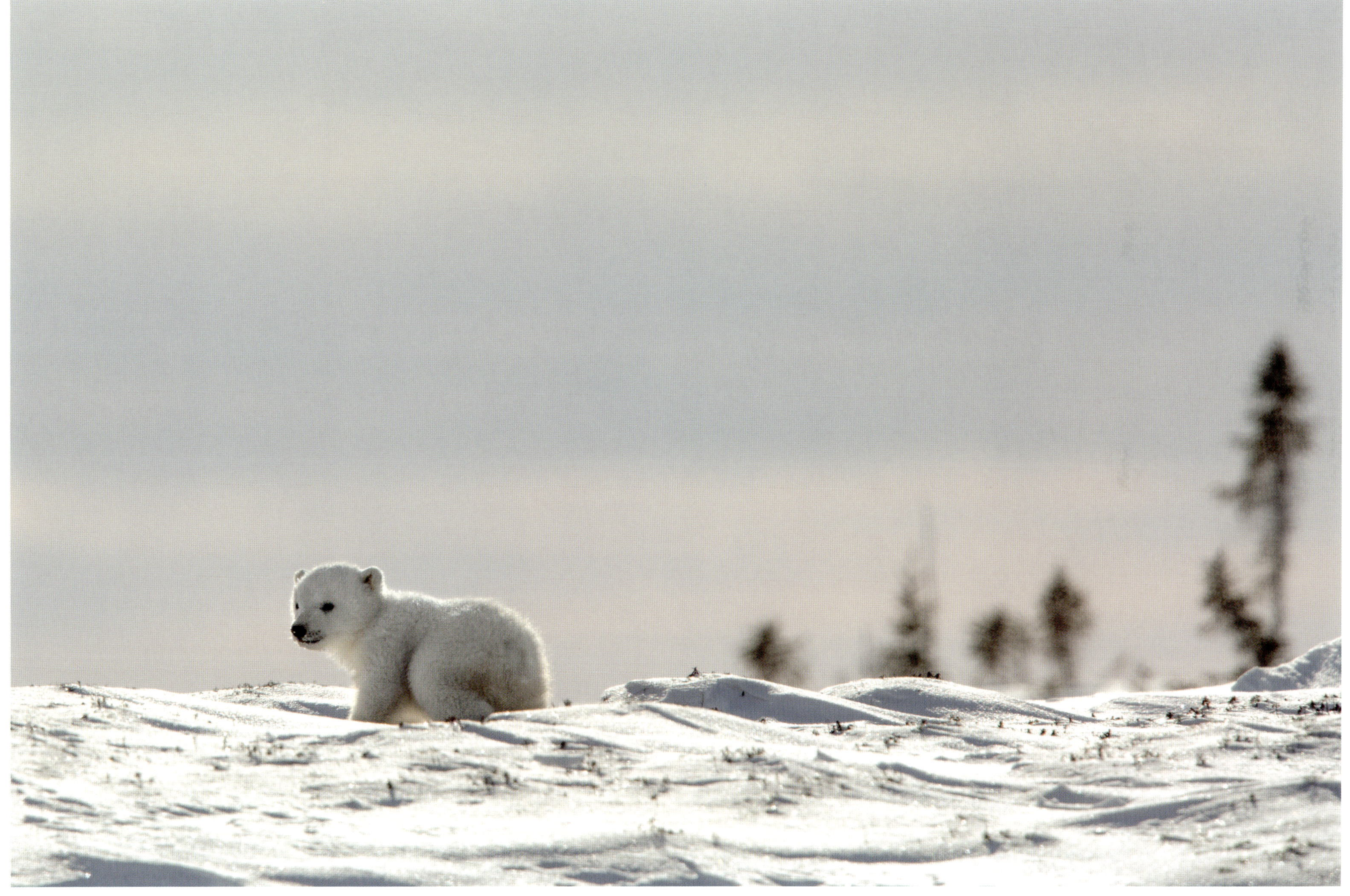

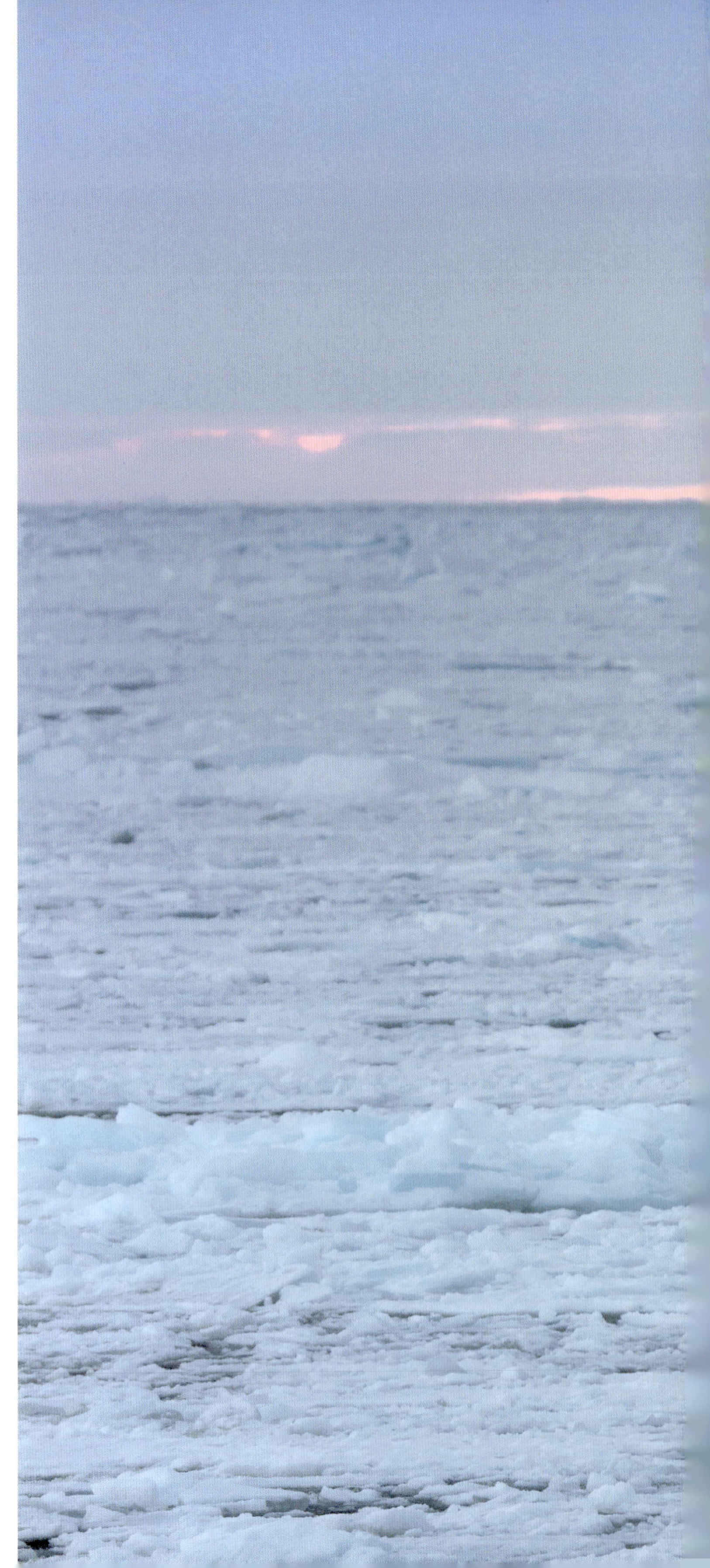

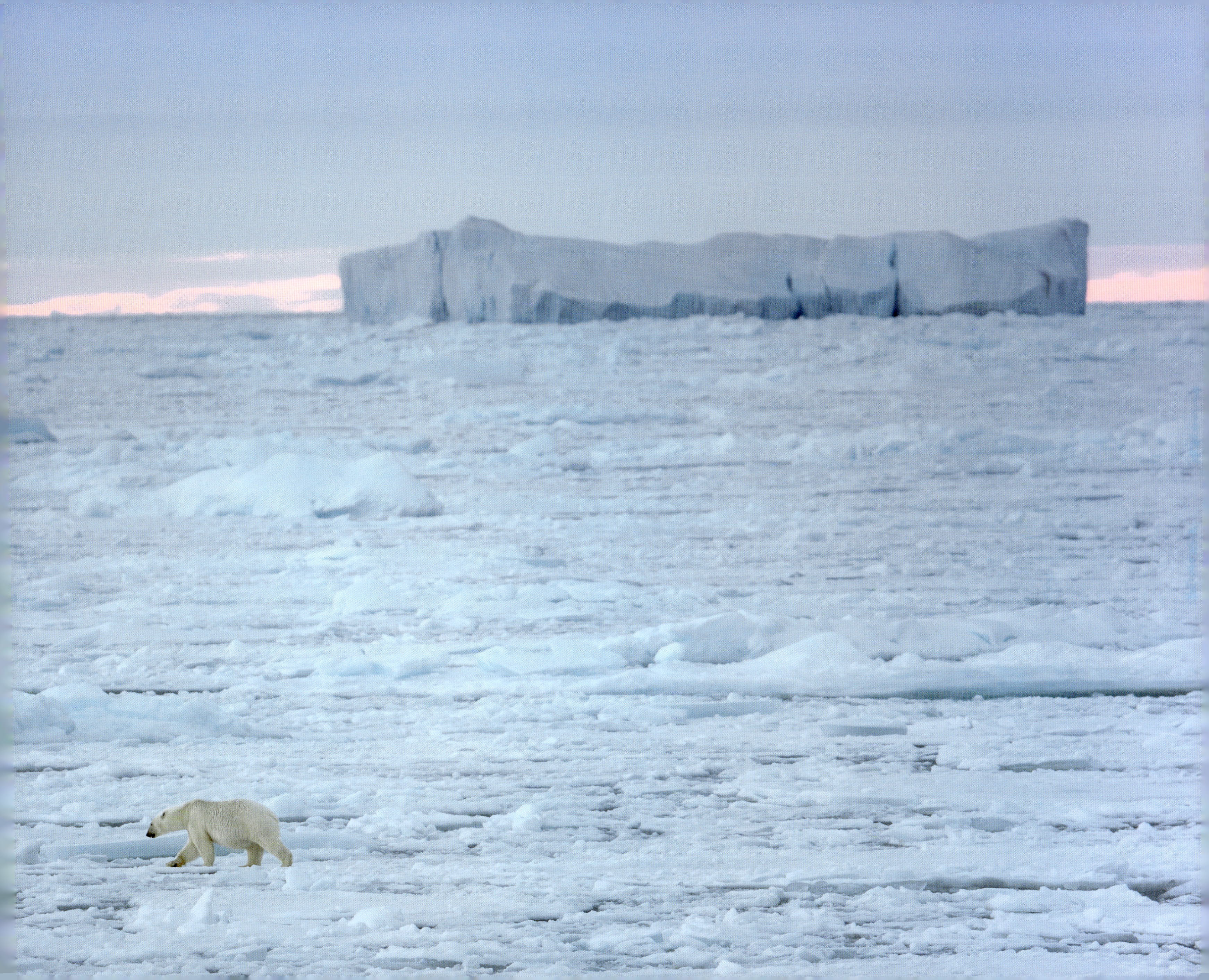

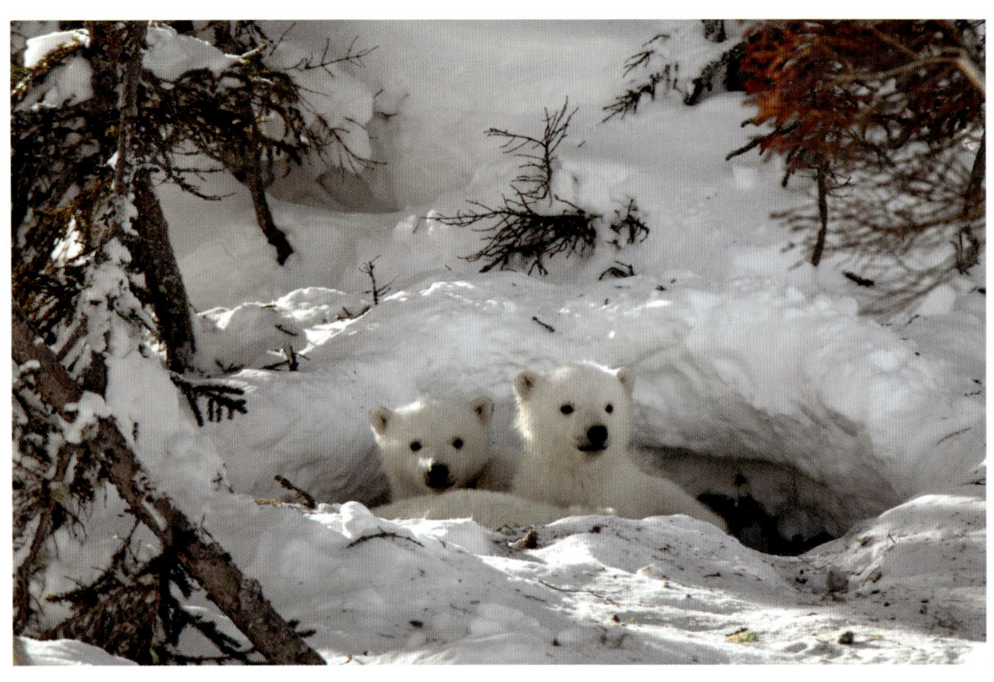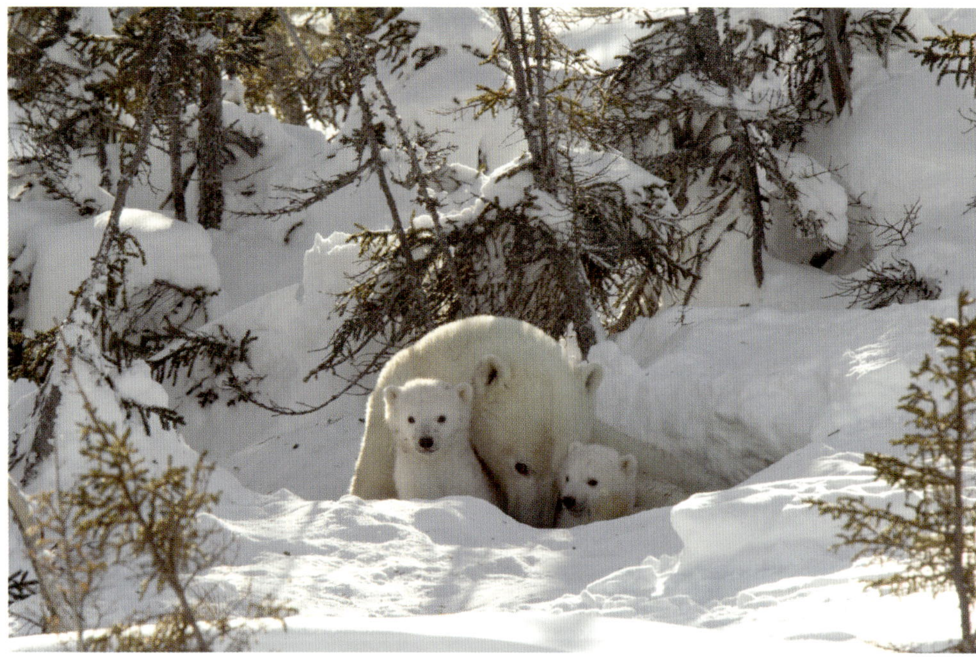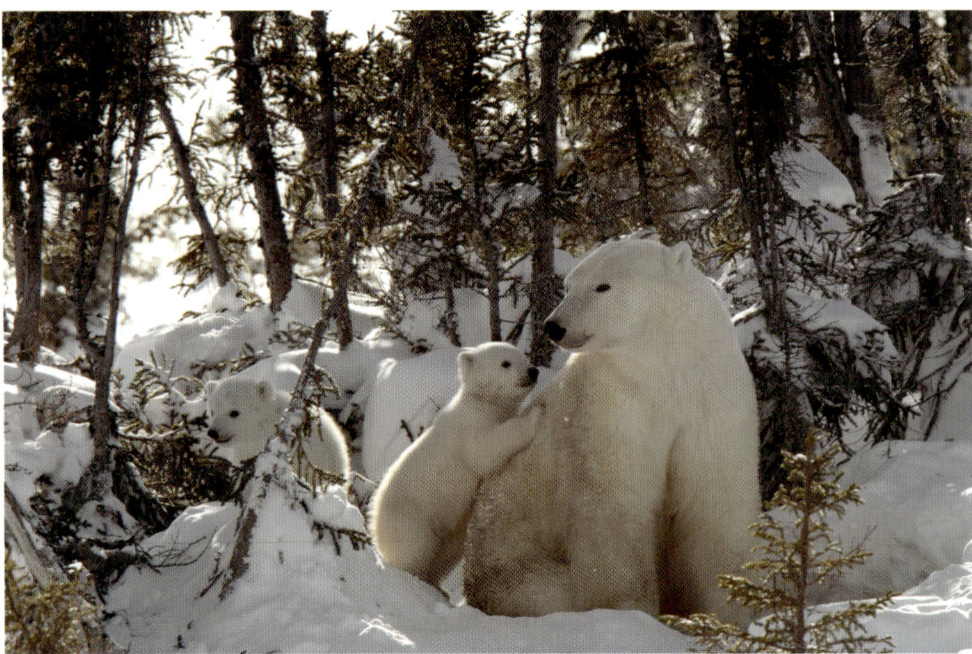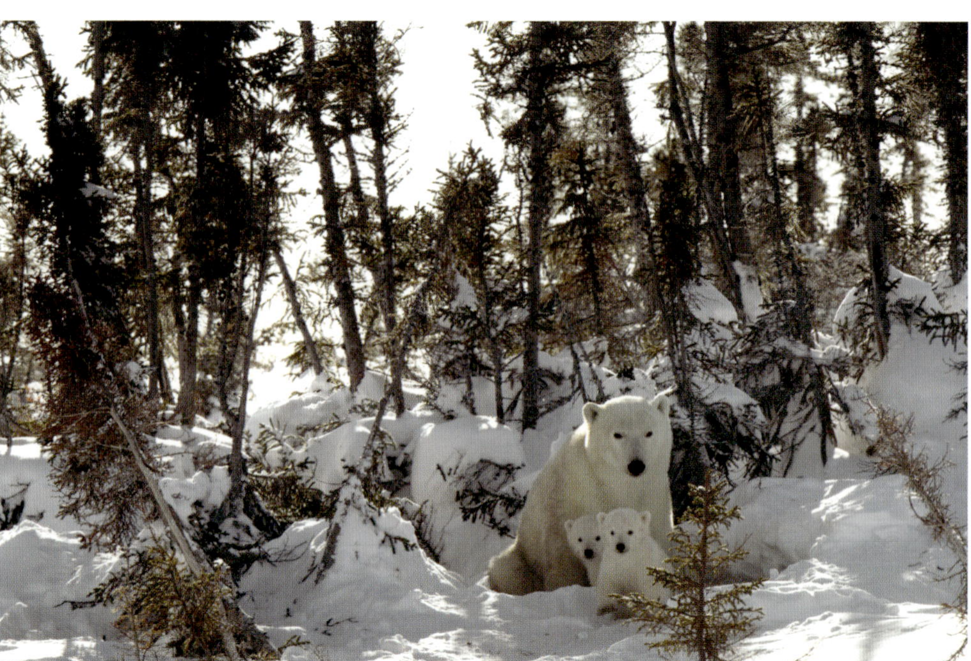

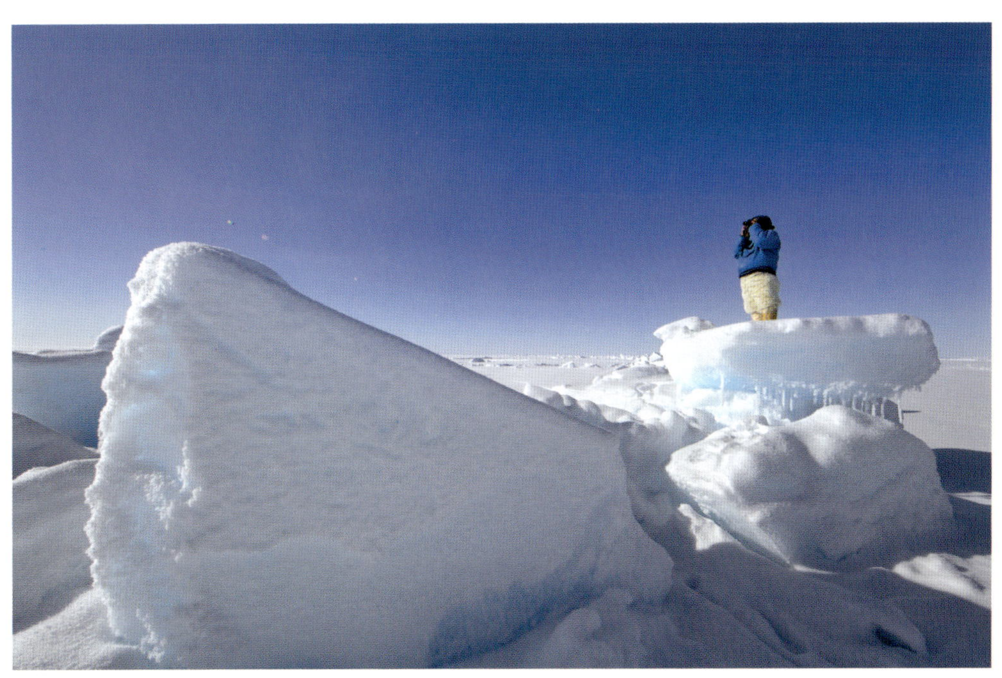
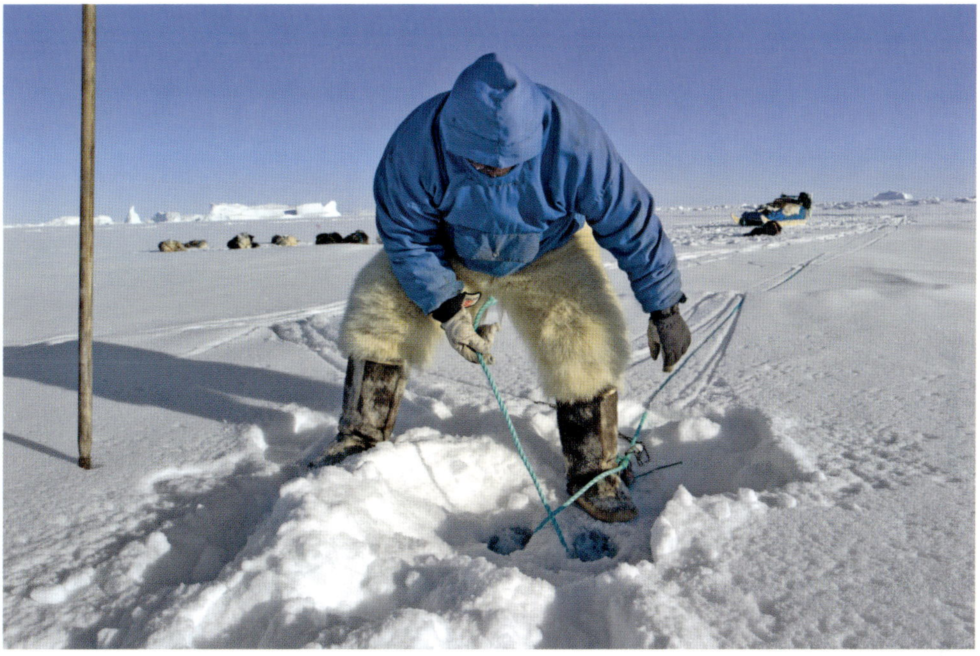
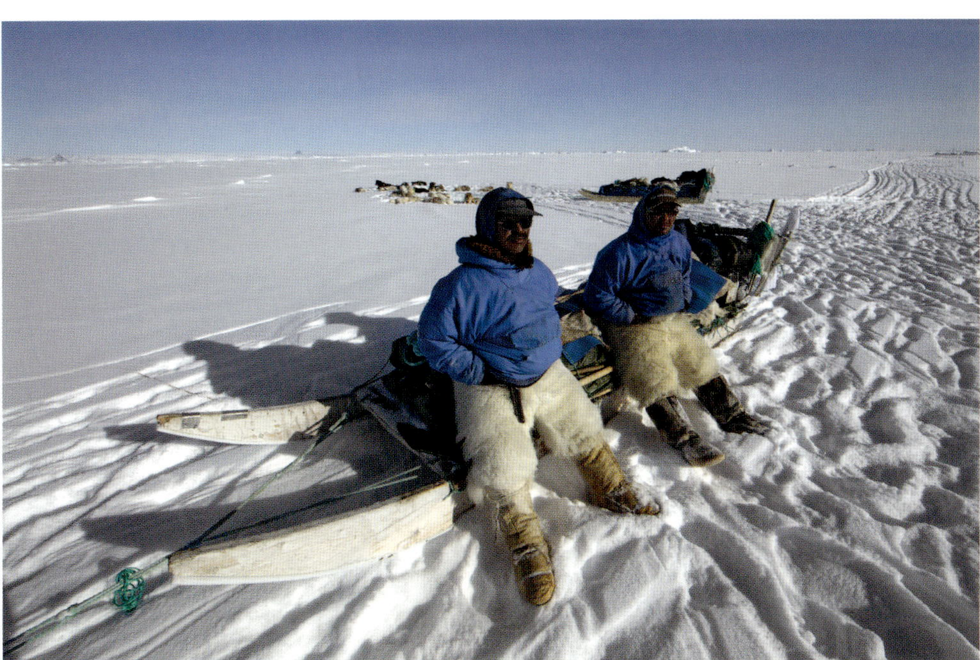
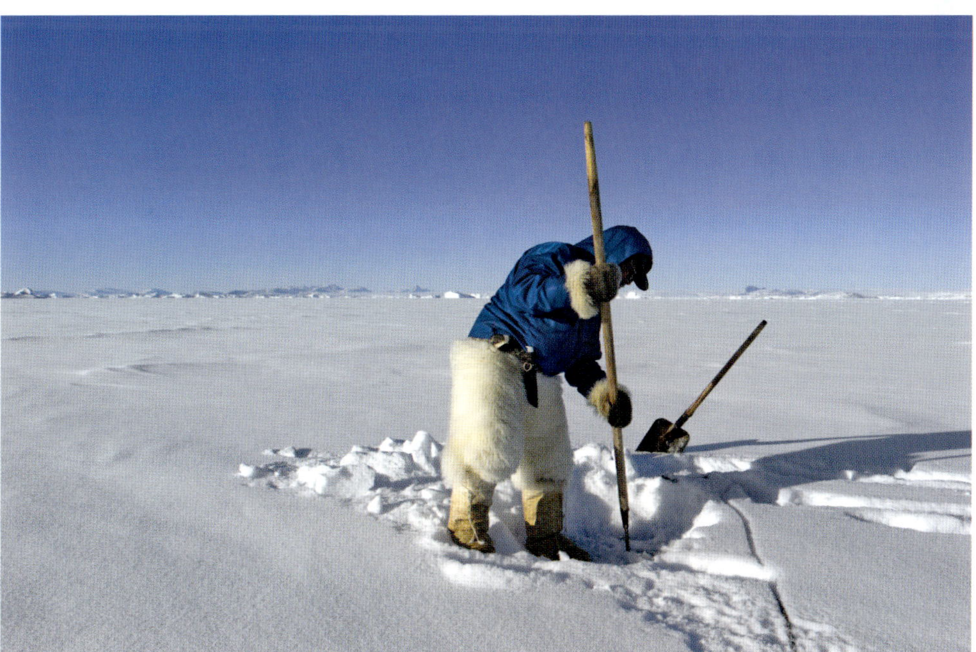

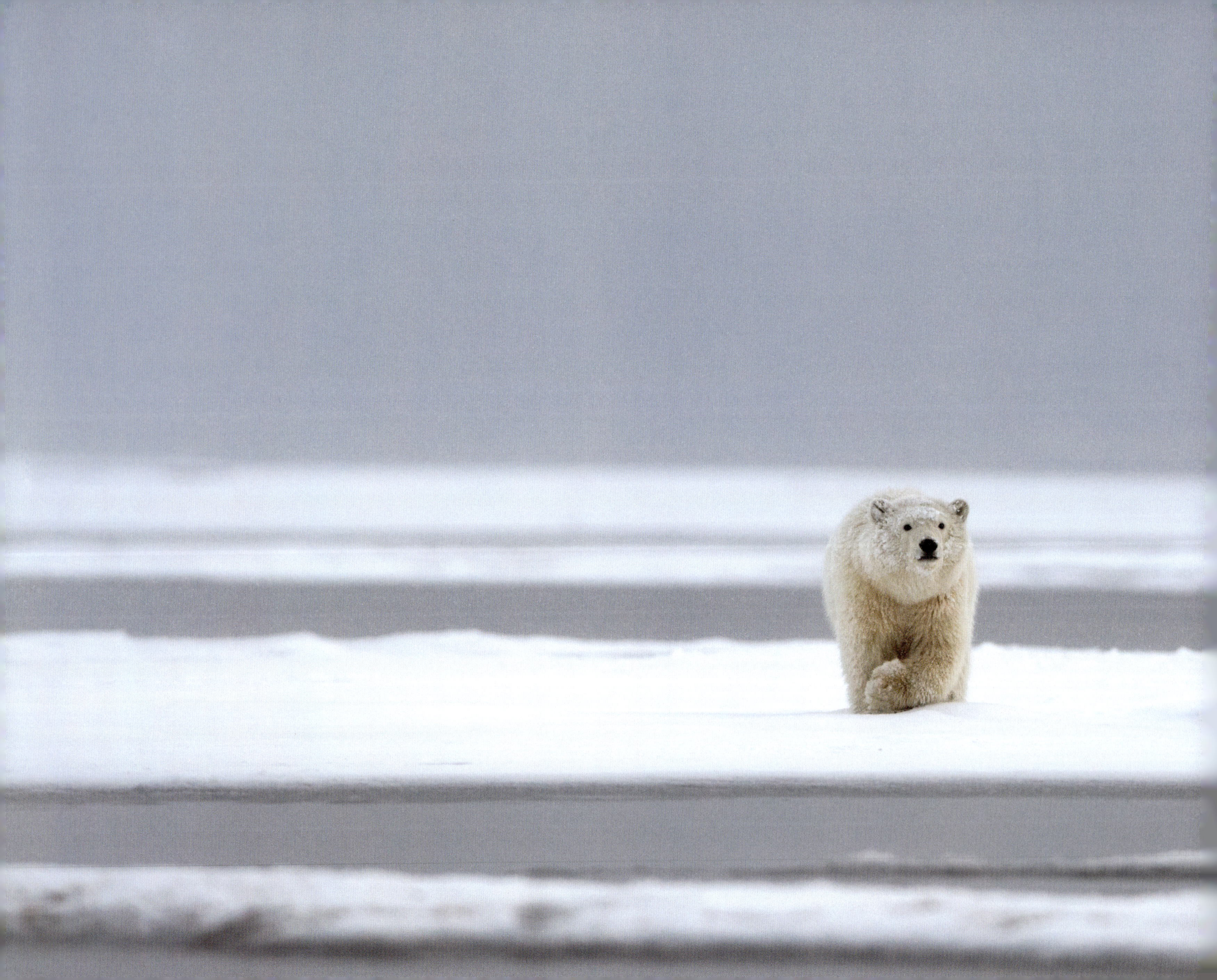

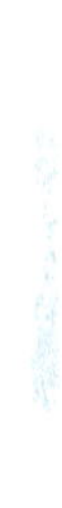

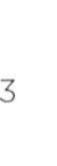

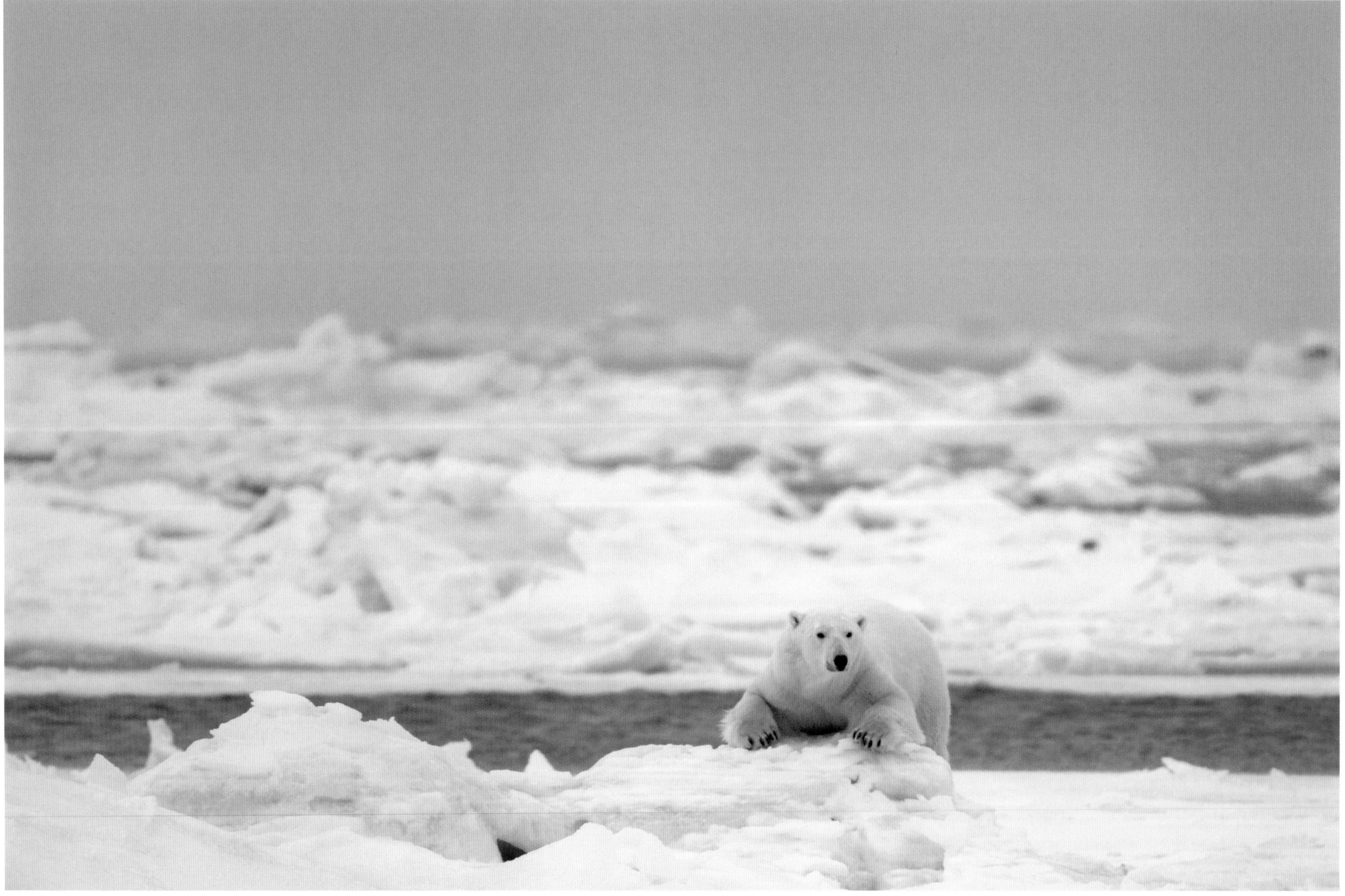

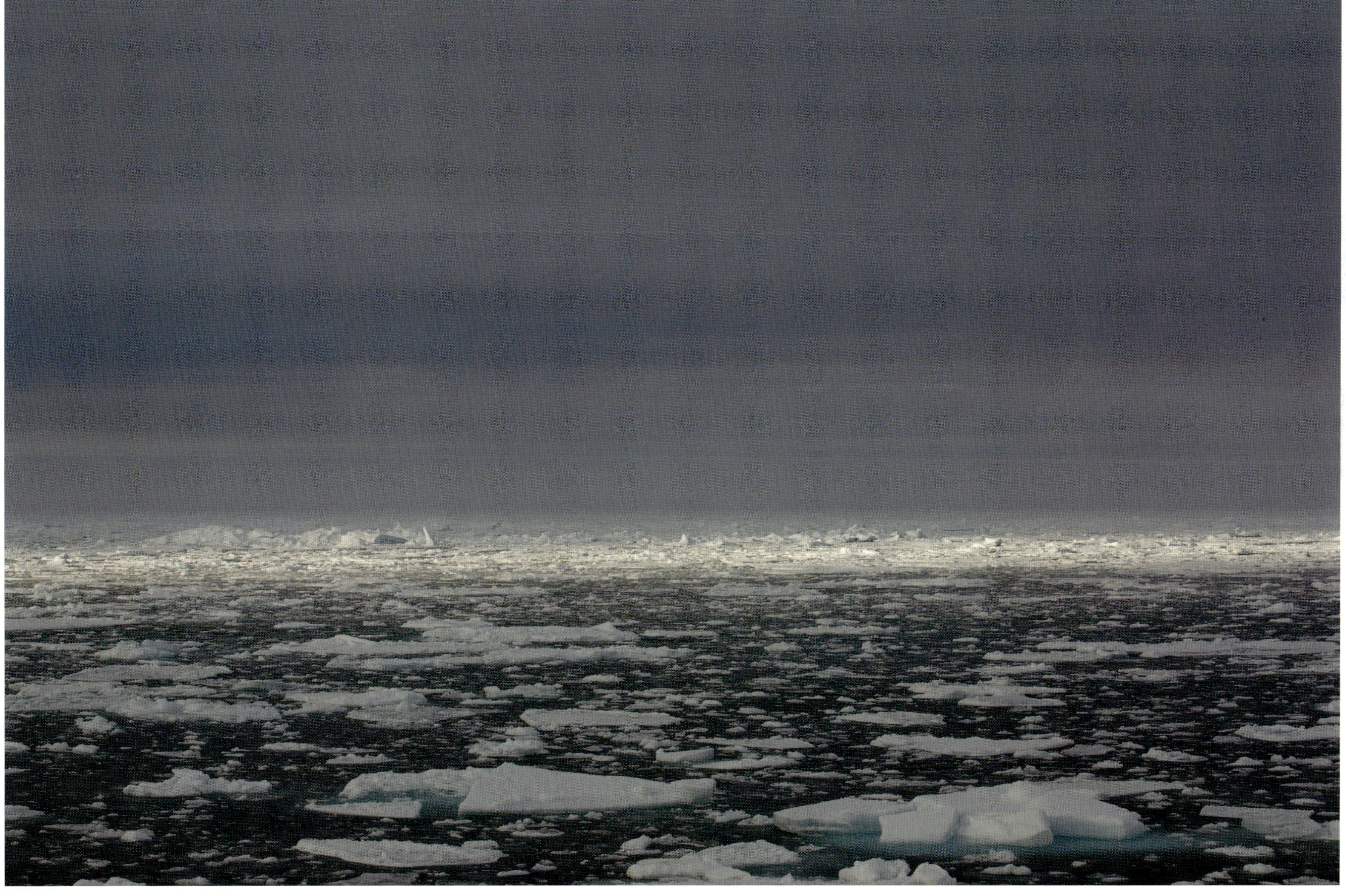

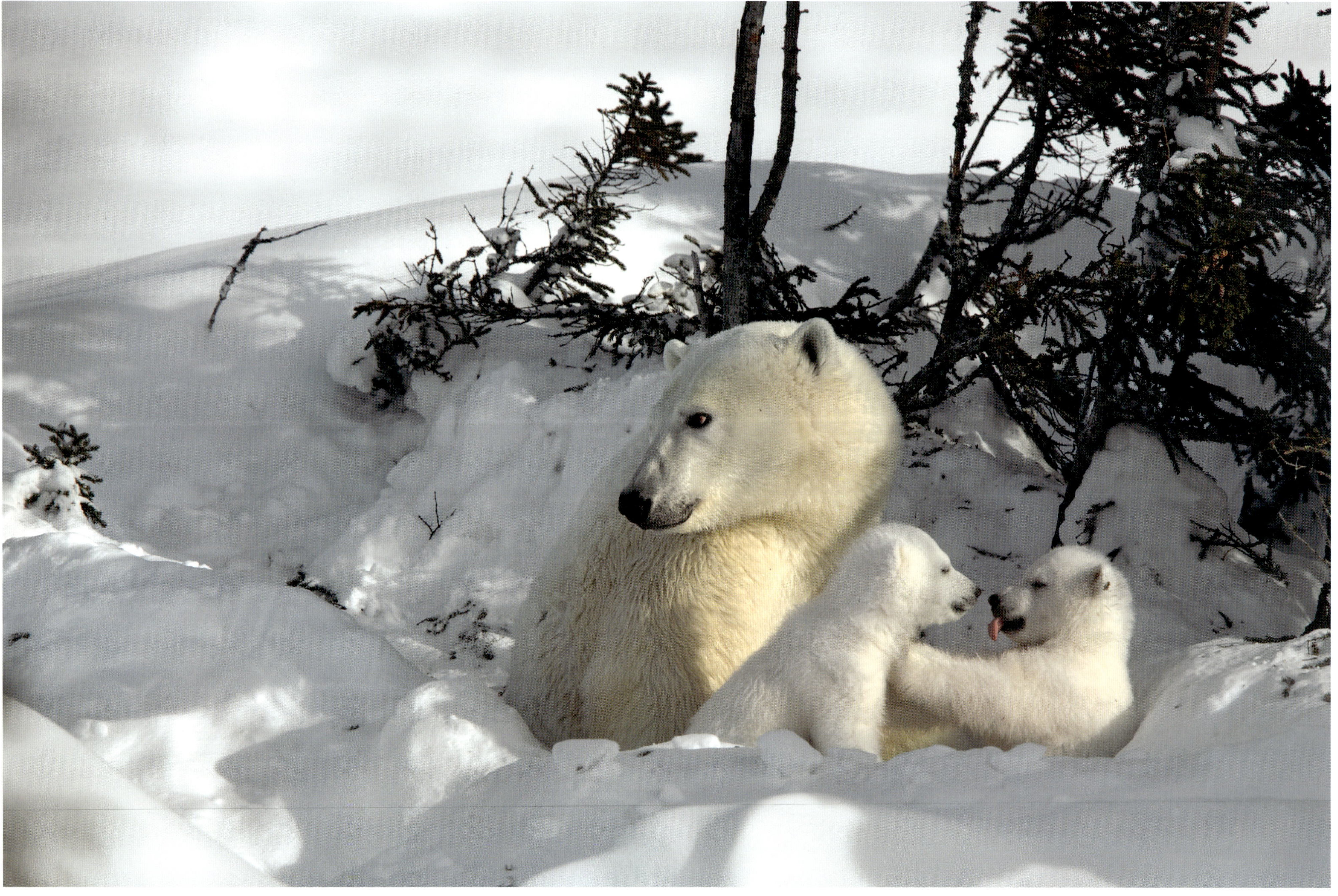

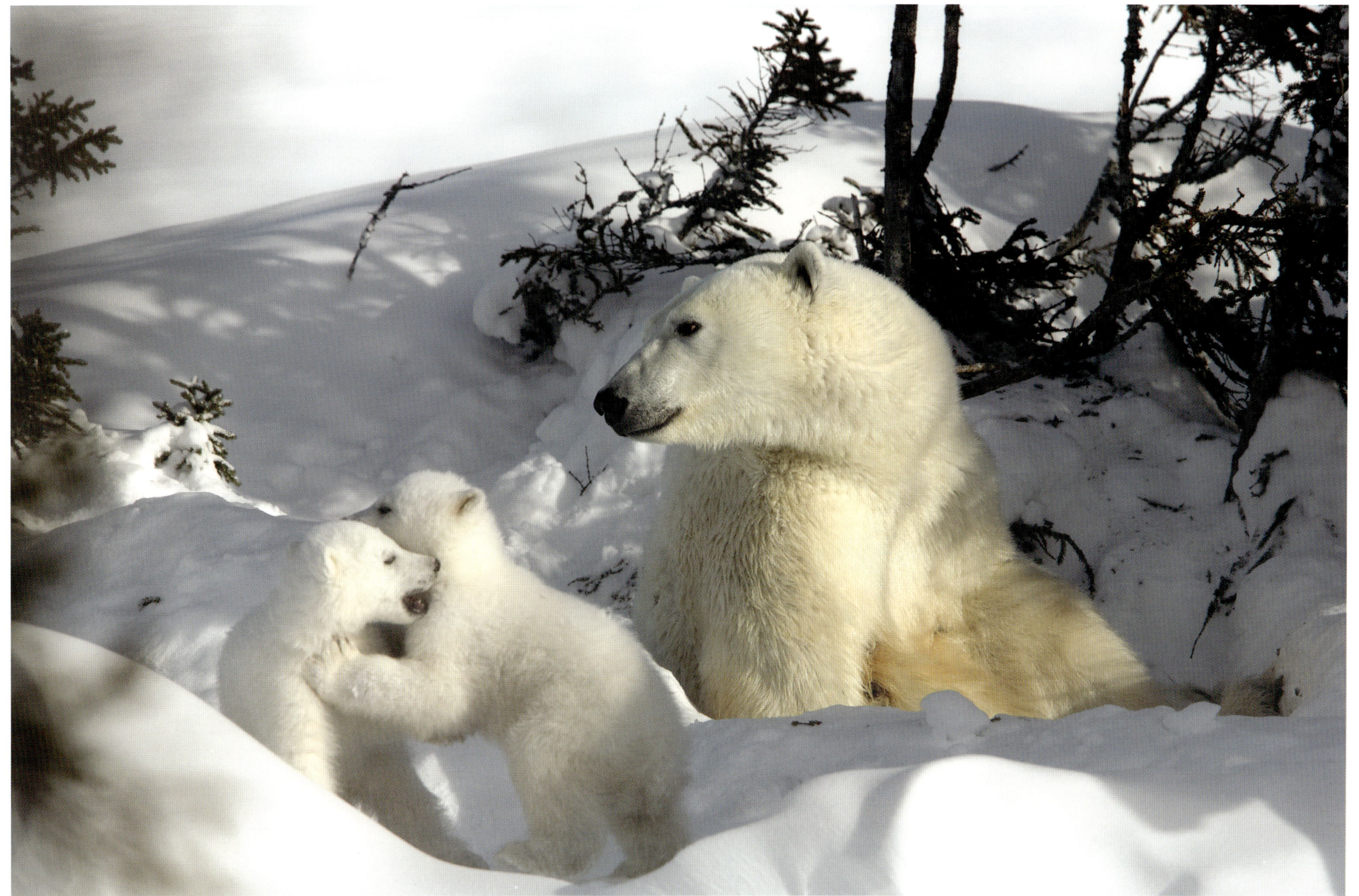

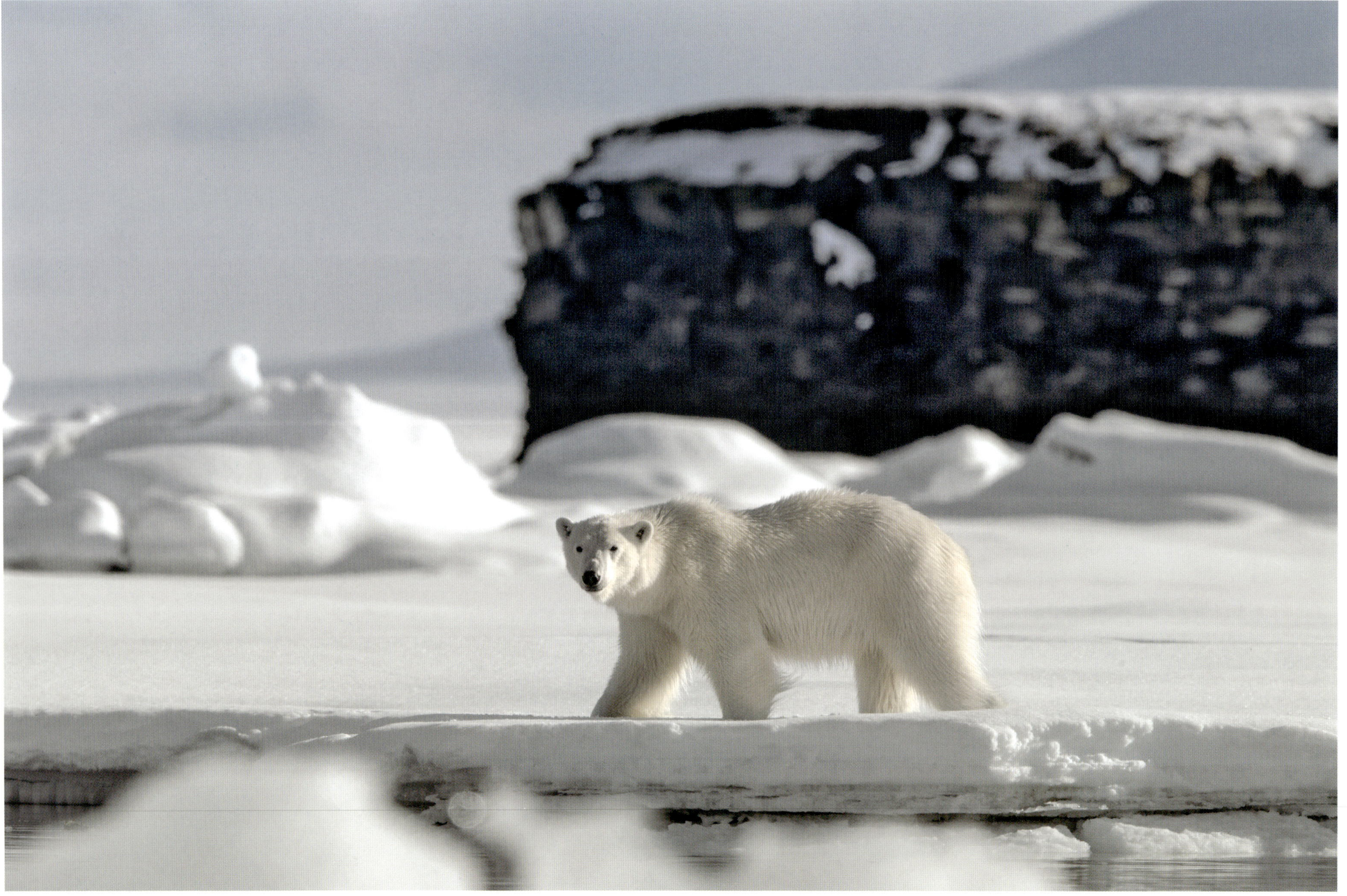

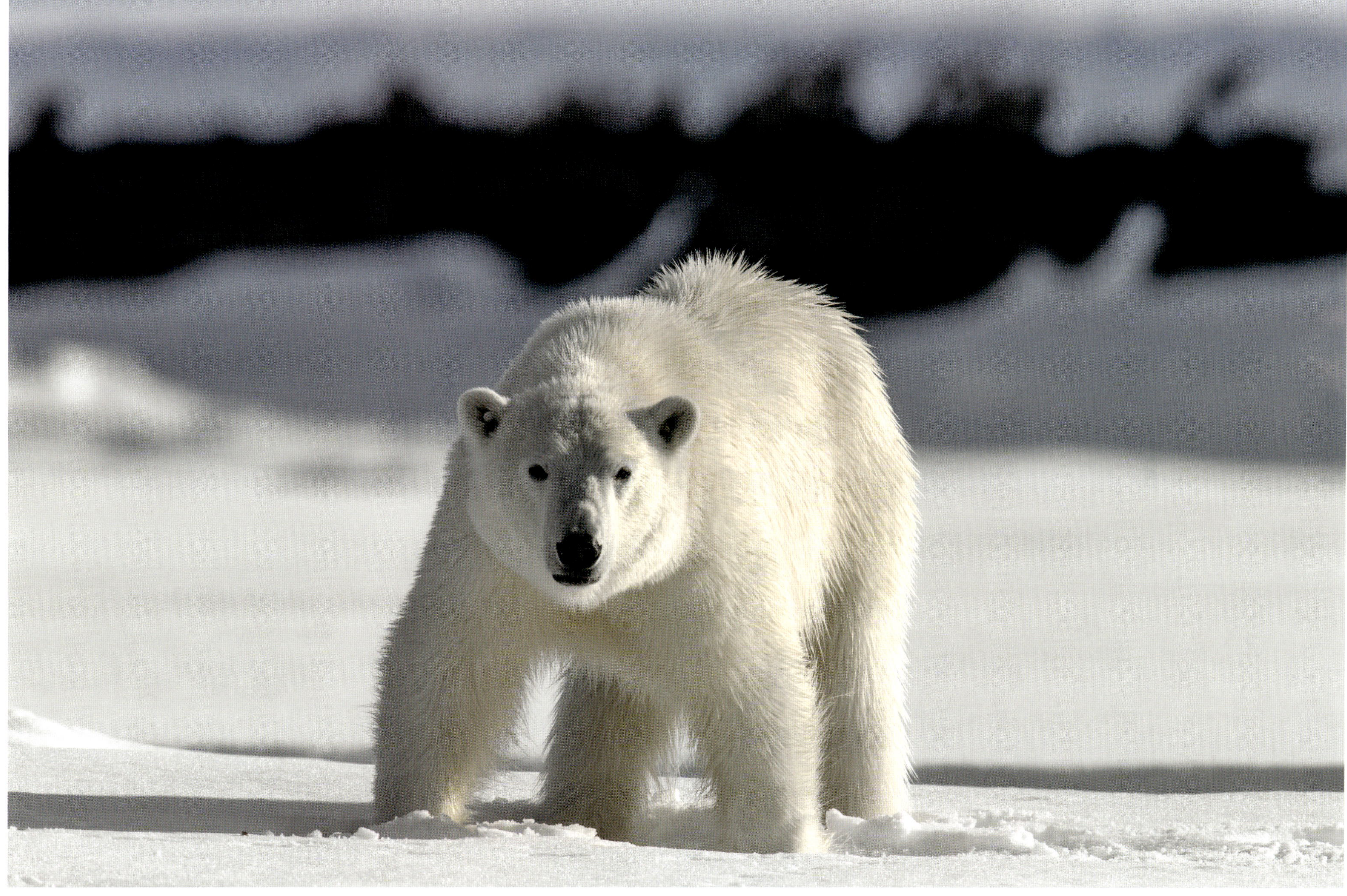

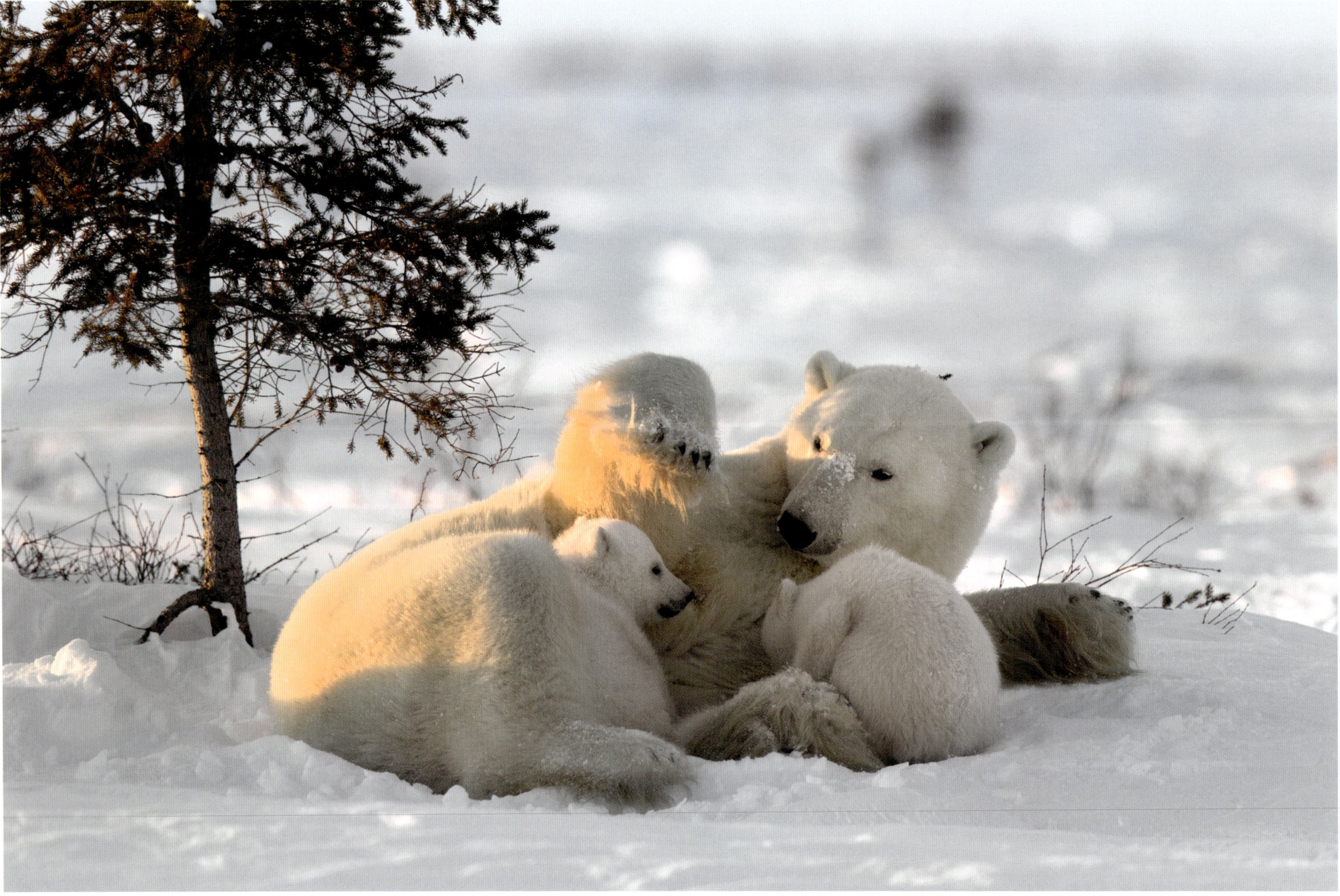

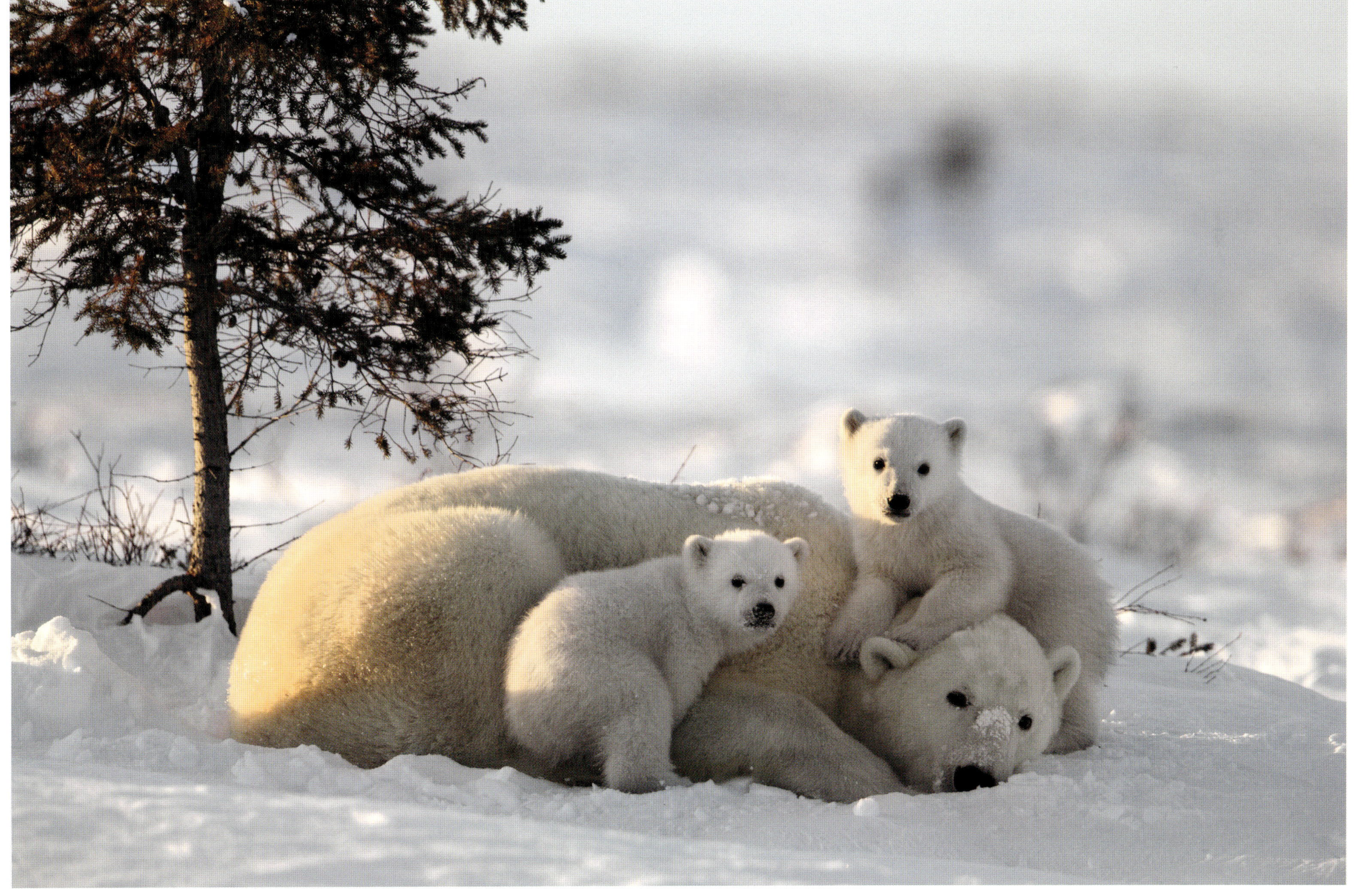

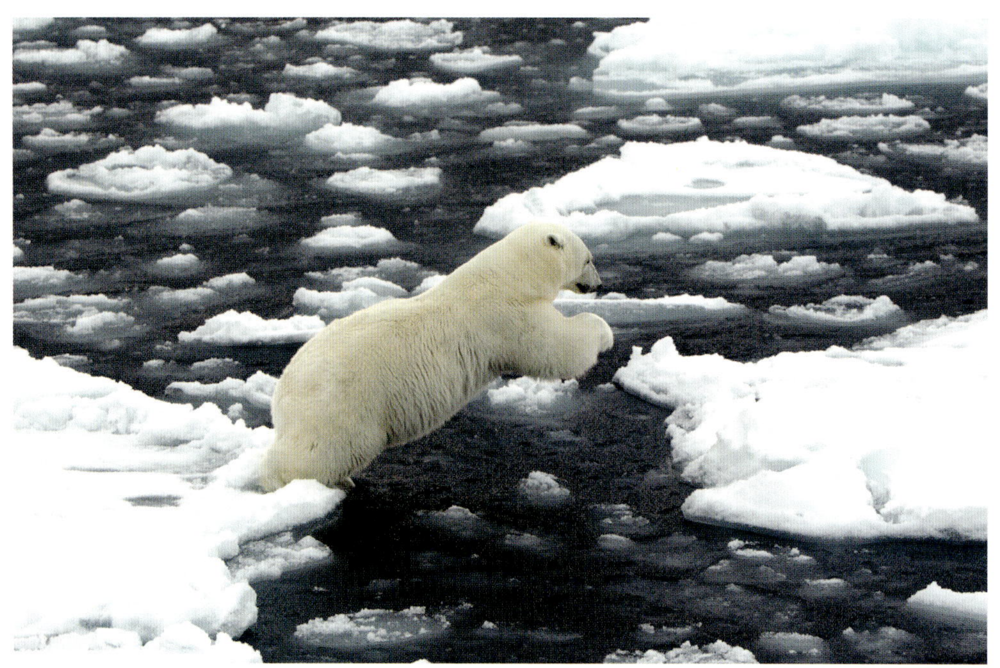
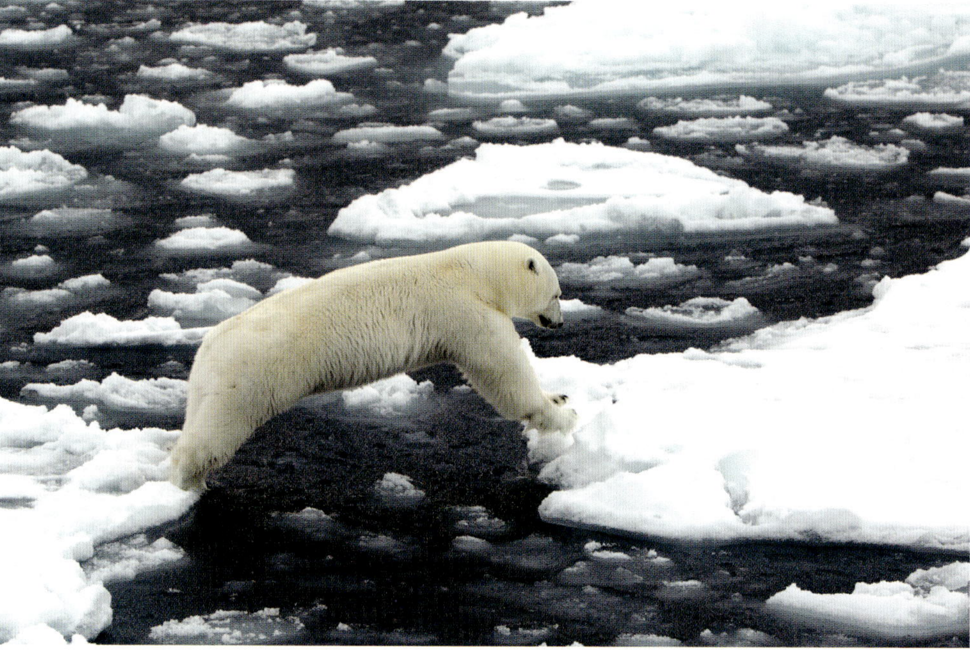
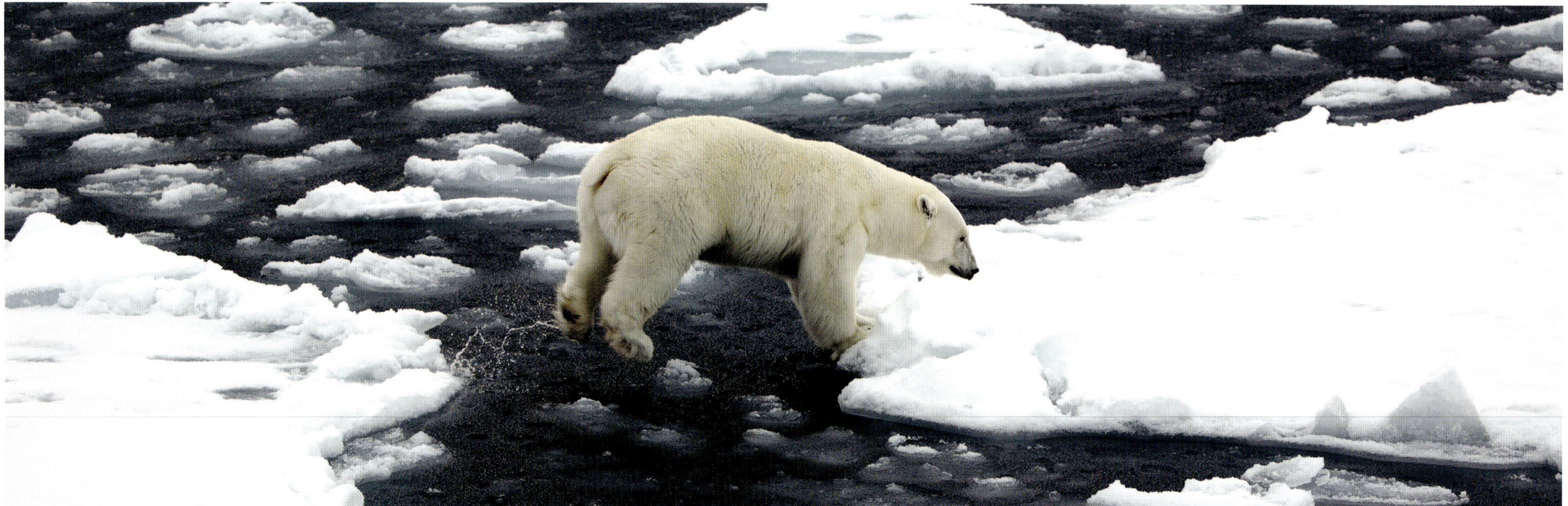

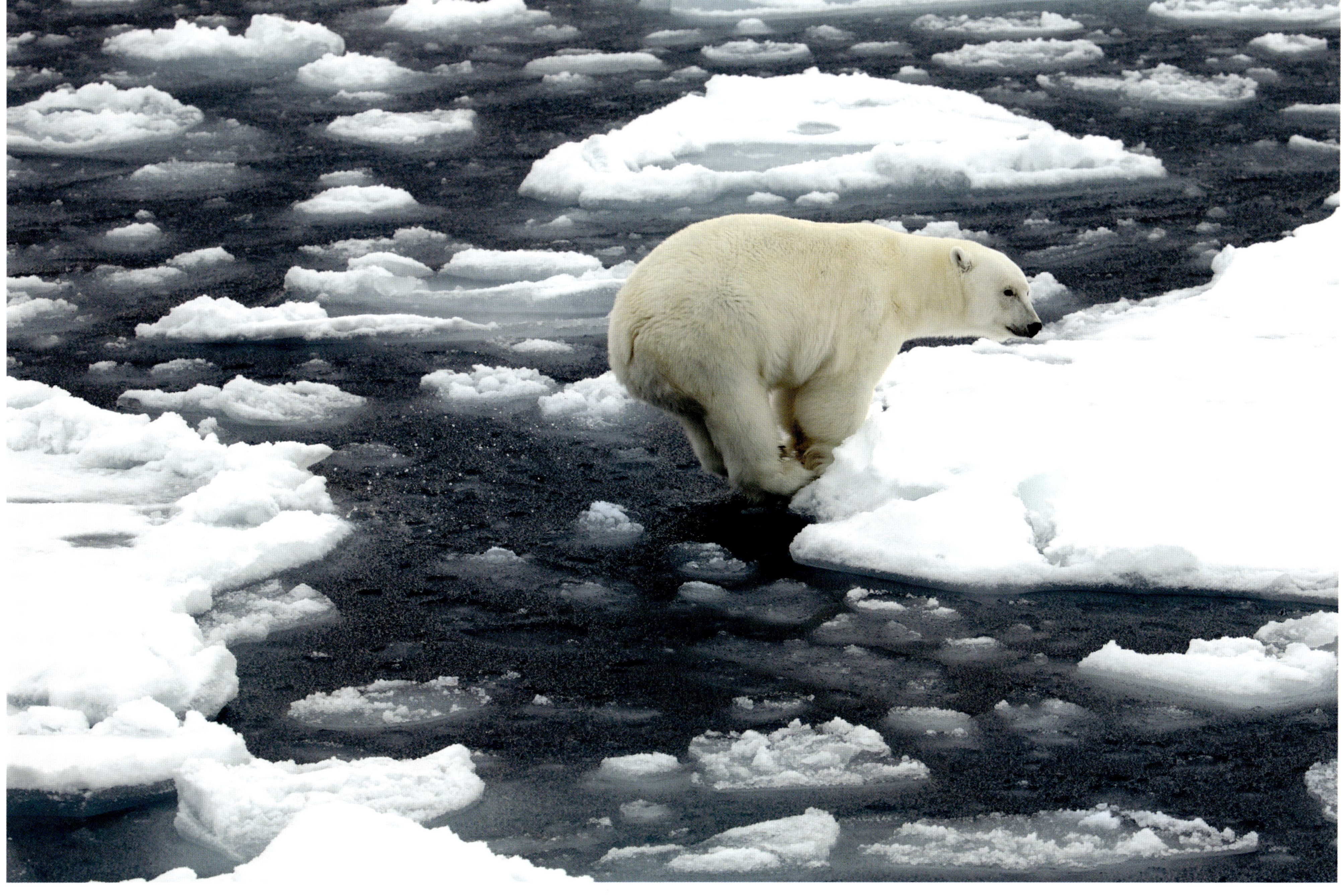

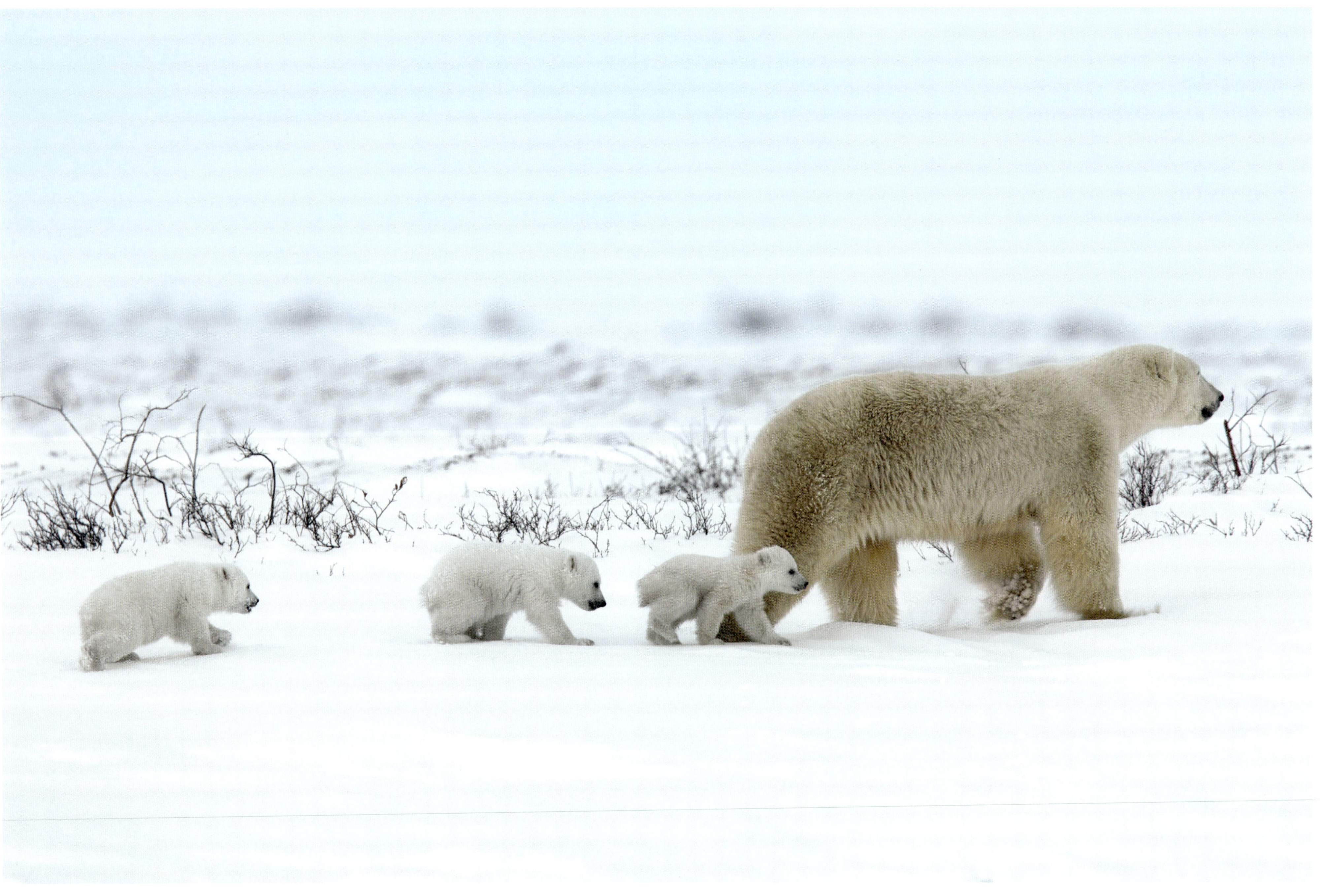

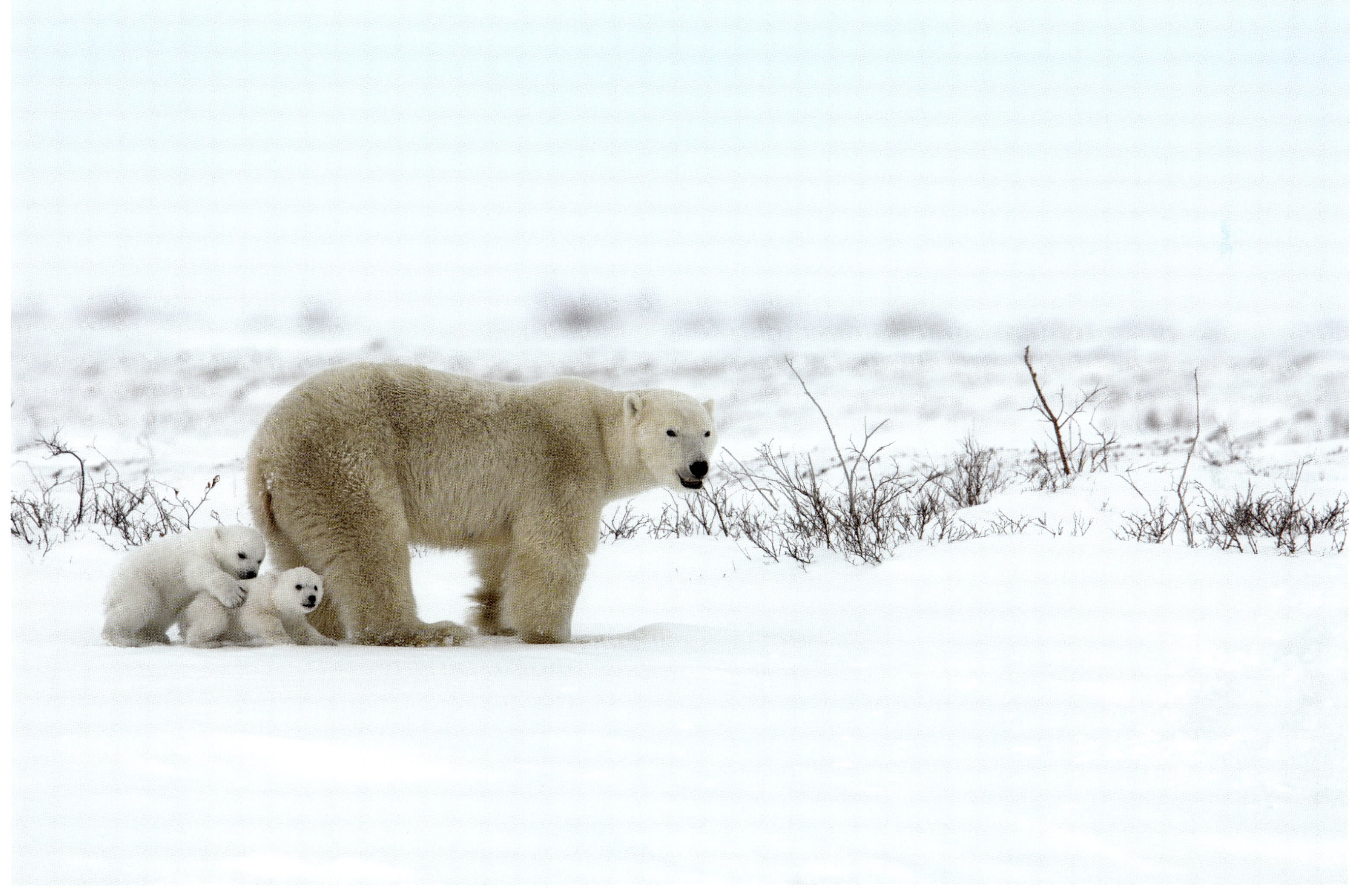

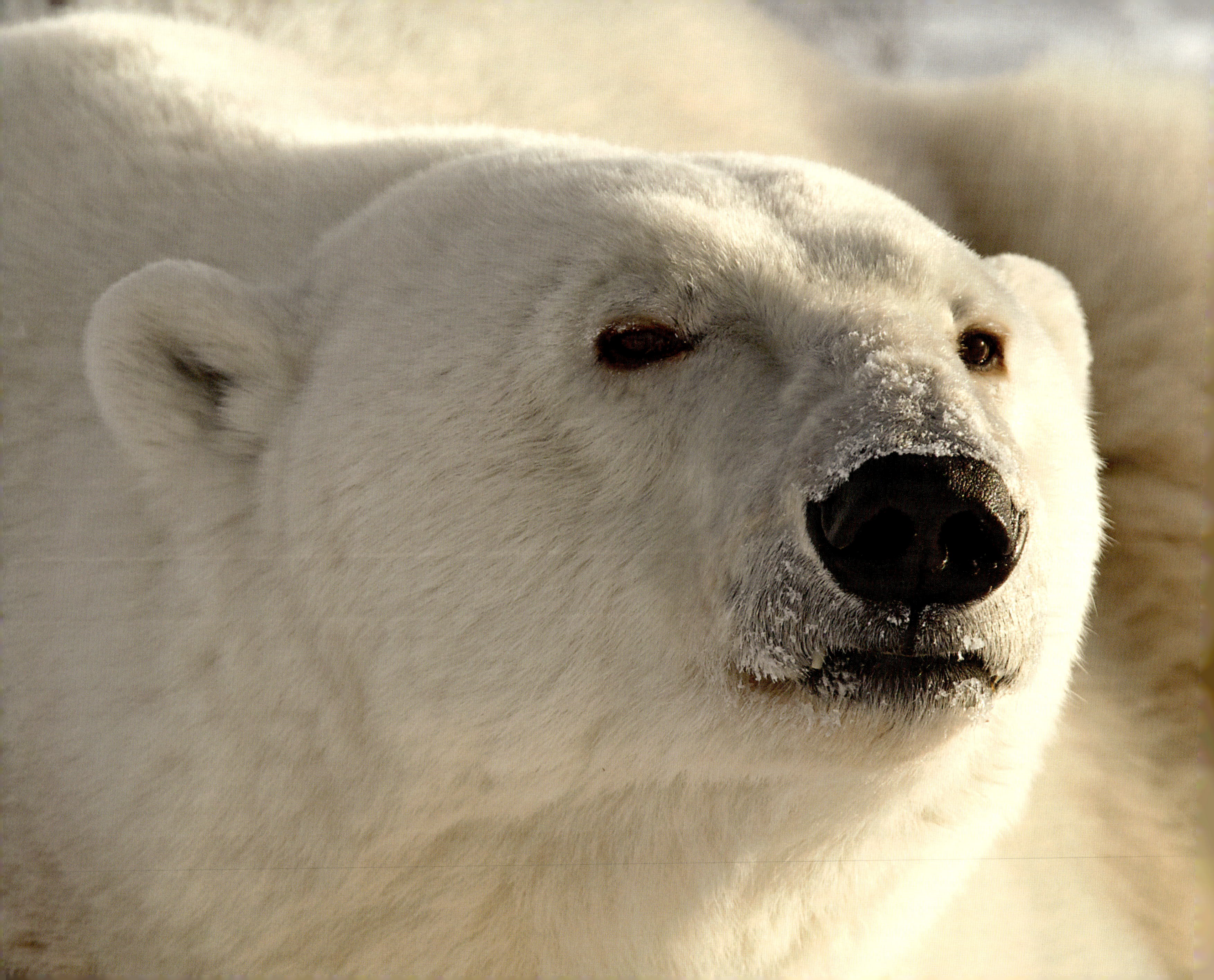

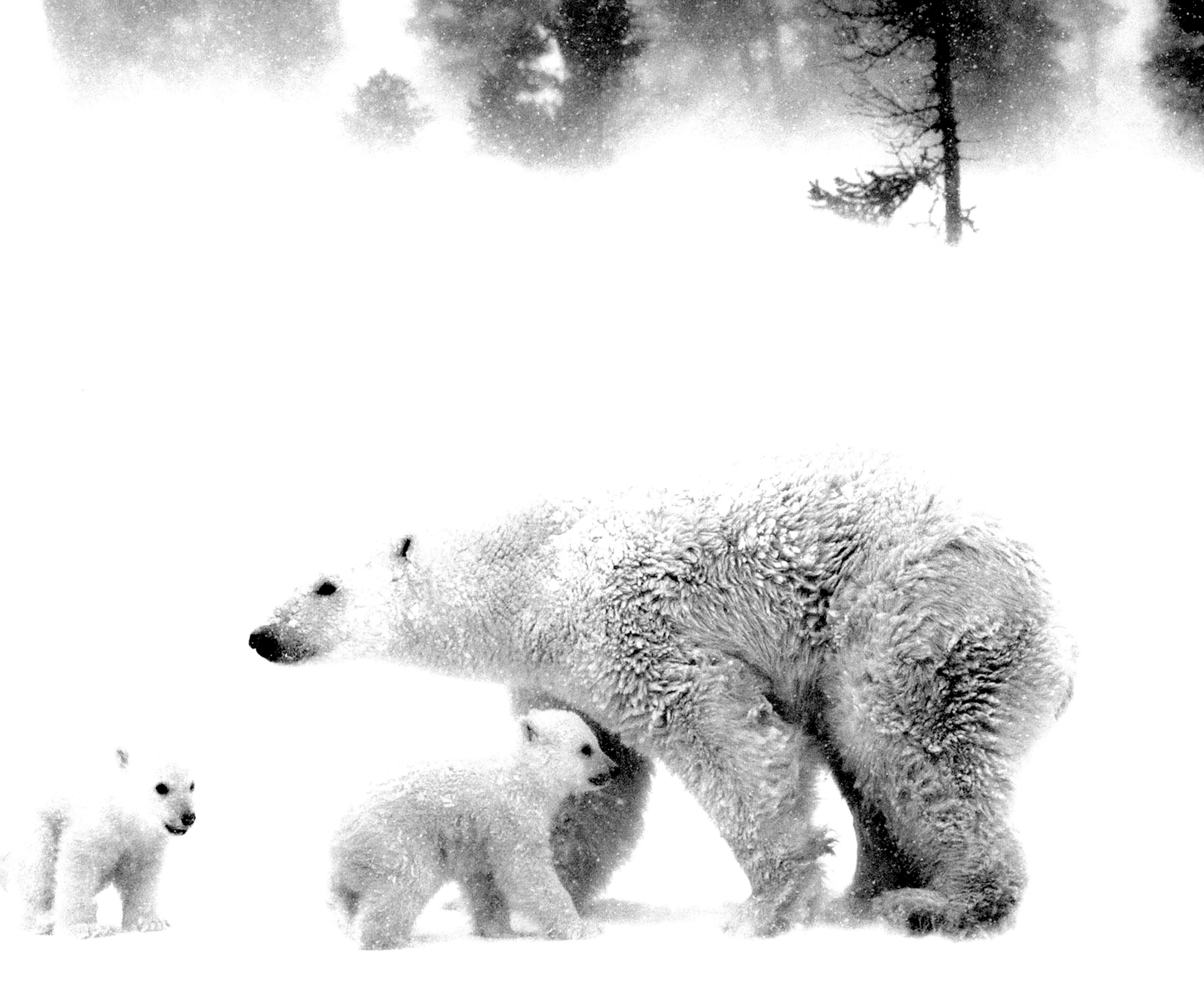

CAPTIONS

[The photographs date from 1992 onwards]

p. 16/17: Hudson Bay, Manitoba, Canada.

p. 18/19: Barter Island, Alaska, United States of America.

p. 20/21: Wapusk National Park, Manitoba, Canada.

p. 22/23: Bakanukta, Svalbard, Norway.

p.24: Seal River, Hudson Bay, Manitoba, Canada.

p. 25: Nelson River, Hudson Bay, Manitoba, Canada.

p. 26/27: Wapusk National Park, Manitoba, Canada.

p. 28/29: Bakanbukta, Svalbard, Norway.

p. 30/31: Rindersbukta, Svalbard, Norway.

p. 32/33: Kvitøya, Svalbard, Norway.

p. 34/35: Wapusk National Park, Manitoba, Canada.

p. 36/37: Seal River, Hudson Bay, Manitoba, Canada.

p. 38/39: Kaktovik, Barter Island, Alaska, United States of America.

p. 40/41: Wapusk National Park, Manitoba, Canada.

p. 42/43: Wapusk National Park, Manitoba, Canada.

p. 44/45: (polar bear and beluga whale) Wichebukta, Svalbard, Norway.

p. 46: Wapusk National Park, Manitoba, Canada.

p. 47: Barter Island, Alaska, United States of America.

p. 48: Nelson River, Hudson Bay, Manitoba, Canada.

p. 49: Seal River, Hudson Bay, Manitoba, Canada.

p. 50/51: Kaktovik, Barter Island, Alaska, United States of America.

p. 52/53: Seal River, Hudson Bay, Manitoba, Canada.

p. 54: Upernavik, Greenland, Denmark.

p. 55: Bakanbukta, Svalbard, Norway.

p. 56: Svalbard, Norway (upper left: walruses, Phippsøya/ lower left: walrus, Murchisonfjord/ upper right: common seals, Fuglejorden/lower right: bearded seal, King's Bay).

p. 57: (walrus), Murchisonfjord, Svalbard, Norway.

p. 58/59: Wapusk National Park, Manitoba, Canada.

p. 60/61: Kaktovik, Barter Island, Alaska, United States of America.

p. 62: Monacobreen, Svalbard, Norway.

p. 63: Kaktovik, Barter Island, Alaska, United States of America.

p. 64/65: Kaktovik, Barter Island, Alaska, United States of America.

p. 66/67: Churchill, Manitoba, Canada.

p. 68: Wat'chee, Canada.

p. 69: Kaktovik, Barter island, Alaska, United States of America.

p. 70/71: Wapusk National Park, Manitoba, Canada.

p. 72/73: Churchill, Manitoba, Canada.

p. 74: Kvitøya, Svalbard, Norway.

p. 75: Karl XII-øya, Svalbard, Norway.

p. 76/77: Kaktovik, Barter Island, Alaska, United States of America.

p. 78: Kongsfjord, Svalbard, Norway.

p. 79: Ekmanfjorden, Svalbard, Norway.

p. 80/81: Nelson River, Hudson Bay, Manitoba, Canada.

p. 82/83: Nelson River, Hudson Bay, Manitoba, Canada.

p. 84/85: Bakanbukta, Svalbard, Norway.

p. 86: Kaktovik, Barter Island, Alaska, United States of America.

p. 87: Kronebreen, Svalbard, Norway.

p. 88: Kaktovik, Barter Island, Alaska, United States of America.

p. 89: Wapusk National Park, Manitoba, Canada.

p. 90/91: Kaktovik, Barter Island, Alaska, Canada.

p. 92: Churchill, Manitoba, Canada.

p. 93: Wapusk National Park, Manitoba, Canada.

p. 94/95: Smeerenburgford, Svalbard, Norway (left). Rindersbukta, Svalbard, Norway, (right).

p. 96: Pond Inlet, Nunavut, Canada.

p. 97: Kaktovik, Barter Island, Alaska, United States of America.

p. 98/99: Kaktovik, Barter Island, Alaska, United States of America.

p. 100/101: Kaktovik, Barter Island, Alaska, United States of America.

p. 102/103: $82.37°N$, Arctic Ocean, Svalbad, Norway.

p. 104: Bakanbukta, Svalbard, Norway.

p. 105: Ekmanfjorden, Svalbard, Norway.

p. 106: Bear's lair, Churchill, Manitoba, Canada and Wapusk National Park.

p. 107: Seal River, Hudson Bay, Manitoba, Canada.

p. 108/109: Wapusk National Park, Manitoba, Canada.

p. 110/111: Kvitøya, Svalbard, Norway.

p. 112/113: Karl XII-øya, Svalbard, Norway.

p. 114/115: Churchill and Wapusk National Park, Manitoba, Canada.

p. 116: Churchill, Manitoba, Canada.

p. 117: Kongsfjord, Svalbard, Norway.

p.118/119: Churchill and Wapusk National Park, Manitoba, Canada.

p. 120/121: Kvitøya, Svalbard, Norway.

p. 122/123: Churchill and Wapusk National Park, Manitoba, Canada.

p. 124/125: Churchill and Wapusk National Park, Manitoba, Canada.

p. 126/127 and 128/129: Karl XII-øya, Svalbard, Norway.

p. 130/131: Bakanbukta, Svalbard, Norway.

p. 132/133: Churchill, Manitoba, Canada.

p. 134: Svalbard, Norway.

p. 135: Frozen Arctic Ocean.

p. 136/137: Churchill, Wapusk National Park, Manitoba, Canada.

p. 138/139: Ekmanfjorden, Svalbard, Norway.

p. 140/141: Seal River, Hudson Bay, Manitoba, Canada.

p. 142: Frozen Arctic Ocean, $82.2°N$, Svalbard, Norway.

p. 143: Kaktovik, Barter Island, Alaska, United States of America.

p. 144: Wapusk National Park, Churchill, Manitoba, Canada.

p. 145: Kaktovik, Barter Island, Alaska, United States of America.

p. 146/147: Churchill, Manitoba, Canada.

p. 148/149: The Bone Pile, Kaktovik, Barter Island, Alaska, United States of America.

p. 150/151: Kaktovik, Barter Island, Alaska, United States of America.

ANSWERS FOR IQ-PB TEST

1. C. Black. **2.** C. 40kmph. **3.** B. Up to 8.75 cm. **4.** D. Spring. **5.** C. Winter. **6.** D. Everything (mother's milk, seal, whale). **7.** B. 10 to 20%. **8.** B. From 900g to 1kg. **9.** D. 18 to 21 years. **10.** B. 450kg. **11.** C. 15 to 20%. **12.** A. It travels with the wind behind it. **13.** D. About 60%.

BIOGRAPHIES

Michel Rawicki

Michel Rawicki was born in Paris in 1950. At the age of ten, he discovered his two great passions in life: photography, thanks to his Kodak Starflash (with the flash on top); and ice, during a trip with his parents to Chamonix. He was an intern with Claude Lelouch at Films 13, then became a full-time professional photographer in a studio. In 1988 he founded the StockImage agency, soon to become one of France's leading independent image libraries; he was its director for 20 years. In 1993, Rawicki's discovery of Greenland and icebergs caused him to take a new path in his photographic career. After the world of ice, he turned naturally towards the human and animal inhabitants who lived there. This rugged world brought Michel back to basics and the struggle for survival. In these icy surroundings he first met the polar bear, the animal which still occupies his extensive travels.

He is a popular public speaker, as well as a member of the Société de Géographie and the Société des Explorateurs Français. He is the author of *L'Appel du Froid* (Wikki Planet, 2016).

Rémy Marion

Rémy Marion is a lecturer and film director; the author of 25 books and numerous articles about the polar regions. He is the co-director and co-author of *Métamorphoses de l'ours polaire*, and of *Fort comme un ours* (two documentary films, each 52 minutes long, made for ARTE).

He was born in Honfleur in 1961 and is now the director of Pôles d'images; he has been accompanying Polar travellers since 1988 and is a permanent consultant to the association Pôles Actions; he is a member of the Société de Géographie and of the Société des Explorateurs Français.

Hubert Reeves

Hubert Reeves was born in Montreal in 1932; he is an astrophysicist and teaches cosmology in Montreal and Paris. He is a great populariser, and has published many very well-received books. He is honorary president of Humanité et Biodiversité and of the Agence française pour la biodiversité.

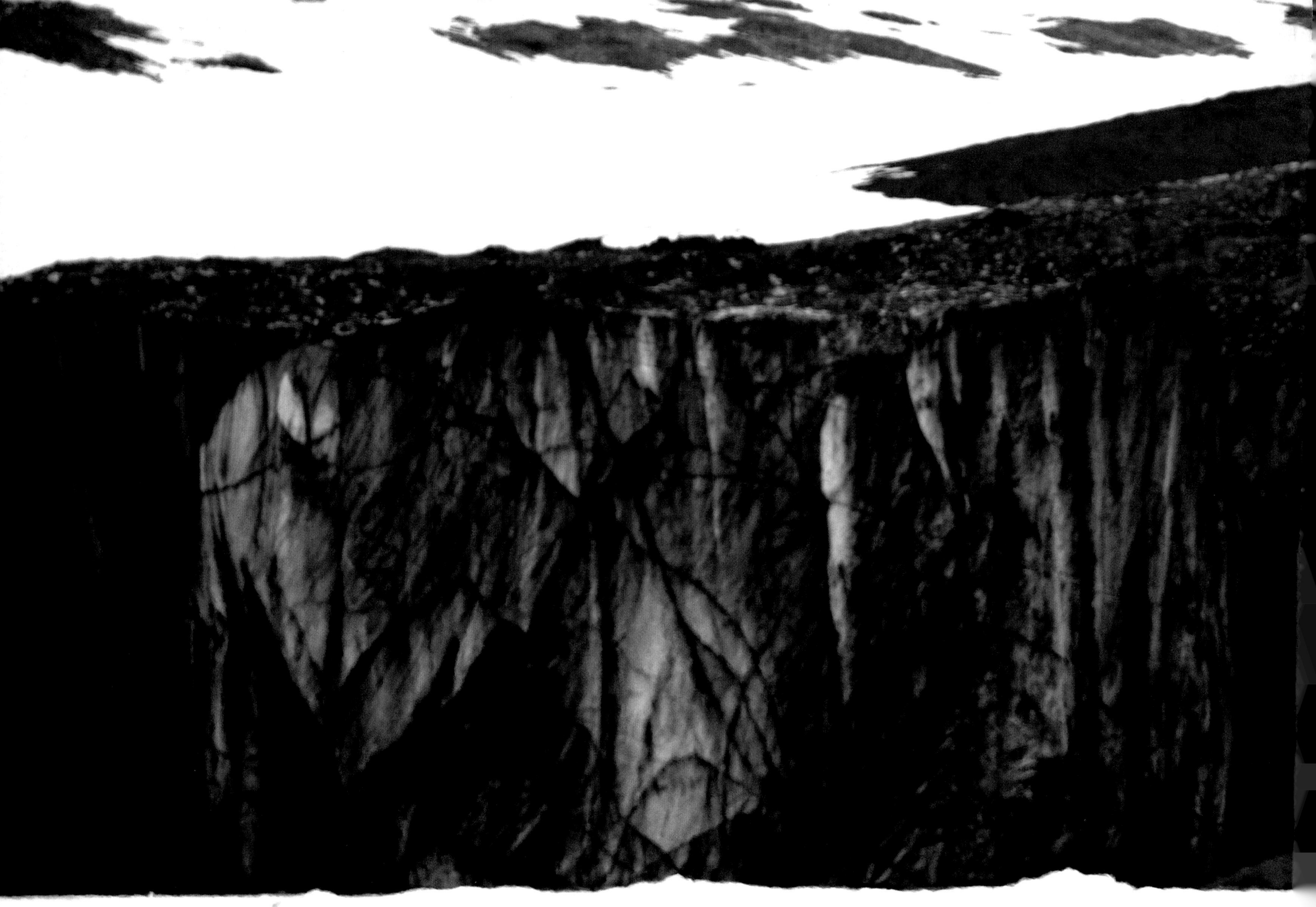